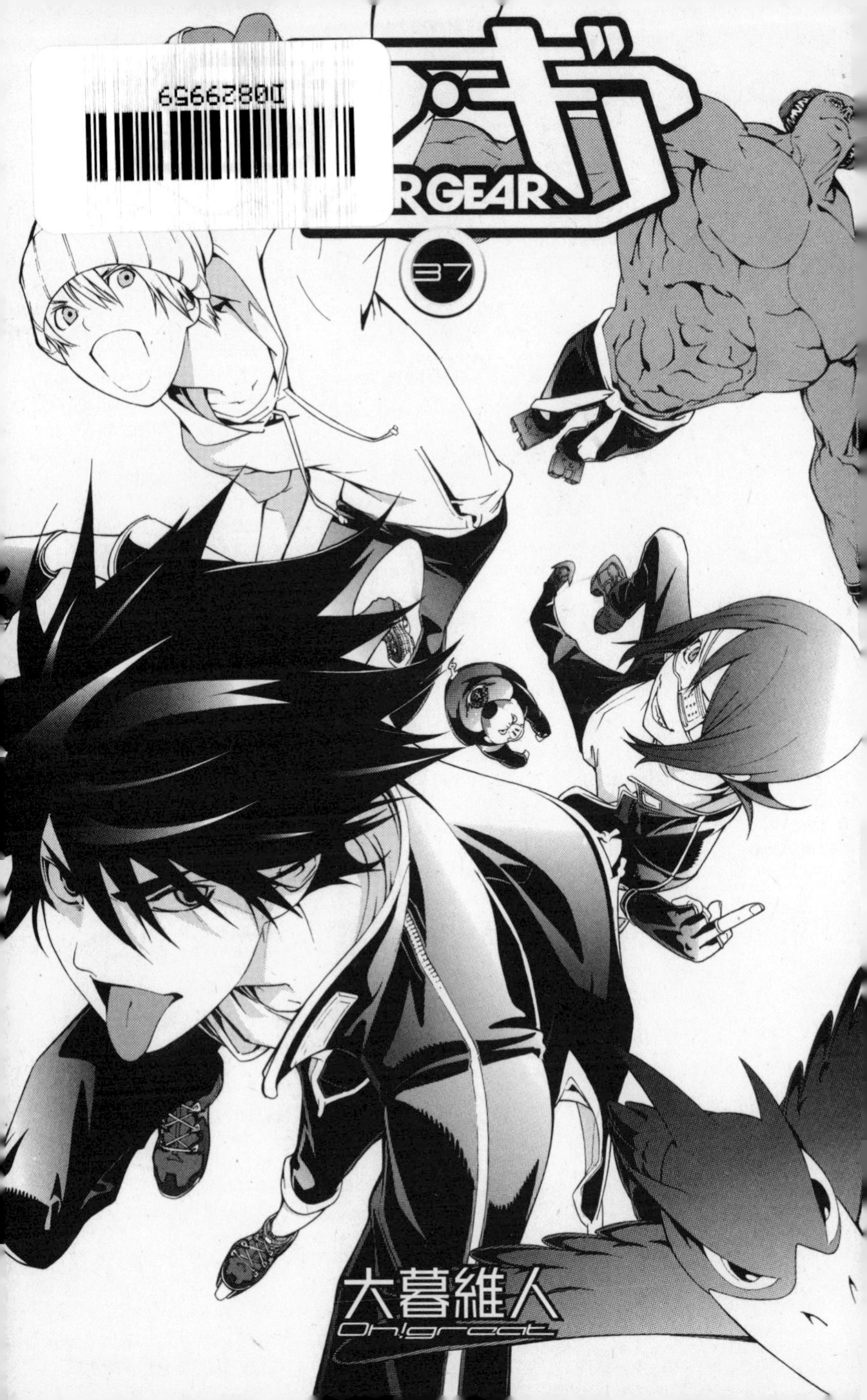
ギ
R GEAR
37
大暮維人
Oh!great

The Story Thus Far... & Principal Characters

It's reaching the climax of the Gram Scale Tournament, the event that determines the ruler of the Air Treck world!! In an attempt to tilt the scales to their favor, Genesis takes Rika prisoner and tries to coerce

> Then none of it had any value... not me, not you, not this world!!

> Let it fall to ruin.

Sleeping Forest to leave their home turf in the Factory and come to Earth. Ikki and company rush to Rika's rescue on the aircraft carrier. Team Kogarasumaru narrowly wins each of its fights, one after the other--but they fail to rescue Rika, leaving them nearly at empty. To overcome this challenge, Ikki heads toward Kururu at the core of the carrier to create the

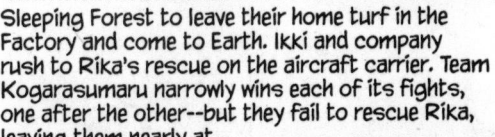

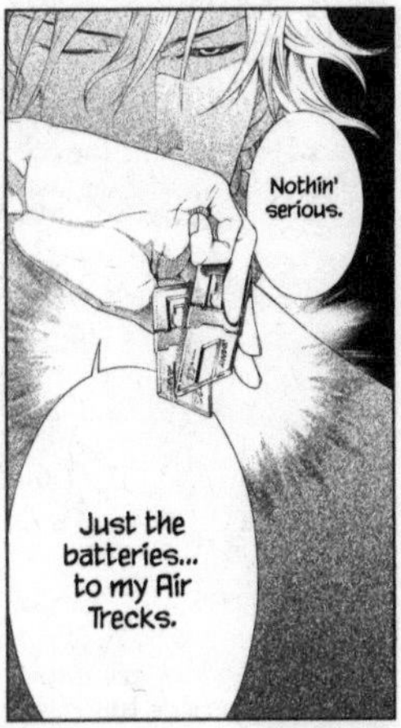

> Nothin' serious.

> Just the batteries... to my Air Trecks.

Storm Regalia, but Kururu was unable to tune it. So in her place, Ikki delegates Ringo to be his Link Tuner and craft the Storm Regalia. In order to stop Sora Takeuchi's cruel ambitions, Ikki and Ringo travel to the Tower of Trophaeum for the final battle! Here are the rules: all attacks are legal. It's a two-on-two

match: Sora & Rika vs. Ikki & Ringo. Sora and Ikki's Regalias are at full strength, and whichever team gets to ground level from the 35,000-meter tower first wins.

Who will the future smile upon?!

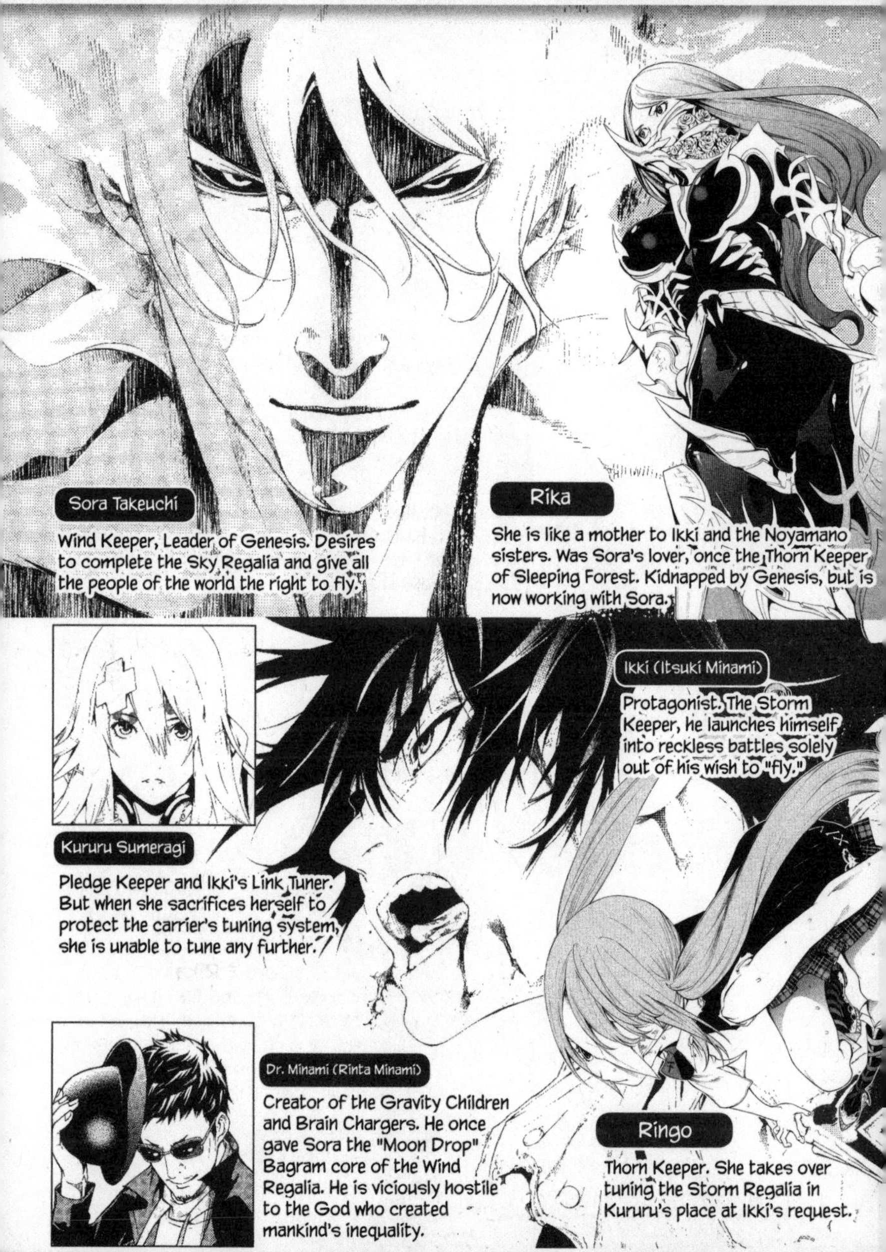
Sora Takeuchi
Wind Keeper, Leader of Genesis. Desires to complete the Sky Regalia and give all the people of the world the right to fly.
Rika
She is like a mother to Ikki and the Noyamano sisters. Was Sora's lover, once the Thorn Keeper of Sleeping Forest. Kidnapped by Genesis, but is now working with Sora.
Kururu Sumeragi
Pledge Keeper and Ikki's Link Tuner. But when she sacrifices herself to protect the carrier's tuning system, she is unable to tune any further.
Ikki (Itsuki Minami)
Protagonist. The Storm Keeper, he launches himself into reckless battles solely out of his wish to "fly."
Dr. Minami (Rinta Minami)
Creator of the Gravity Children and Brain Chargers. He once gave Sora the "Moon Drop" Bagram core of the Wind Regalia. He is viciously hostile to the God who created mankind's inequality.
Ringo
Thorn Keeper. She takes over tuning the Storm Regalia in Kururu's place at Ikki's request.

Emblem Design: Kei Machida
*Text in logo: Punk kid

CONTENTS

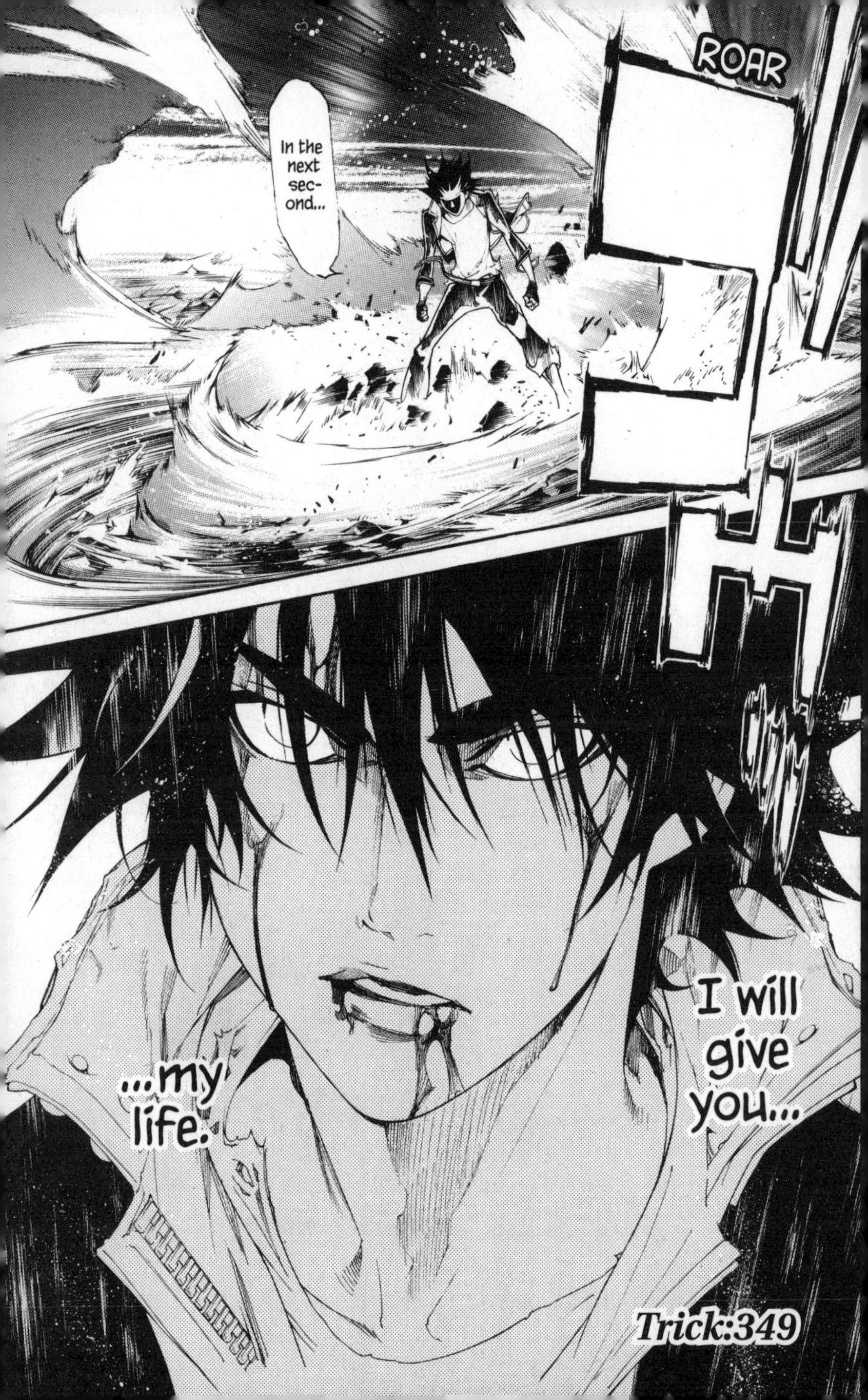
ROAR
In the next sec- ond...
I will give you...
...my life.
Trick:349

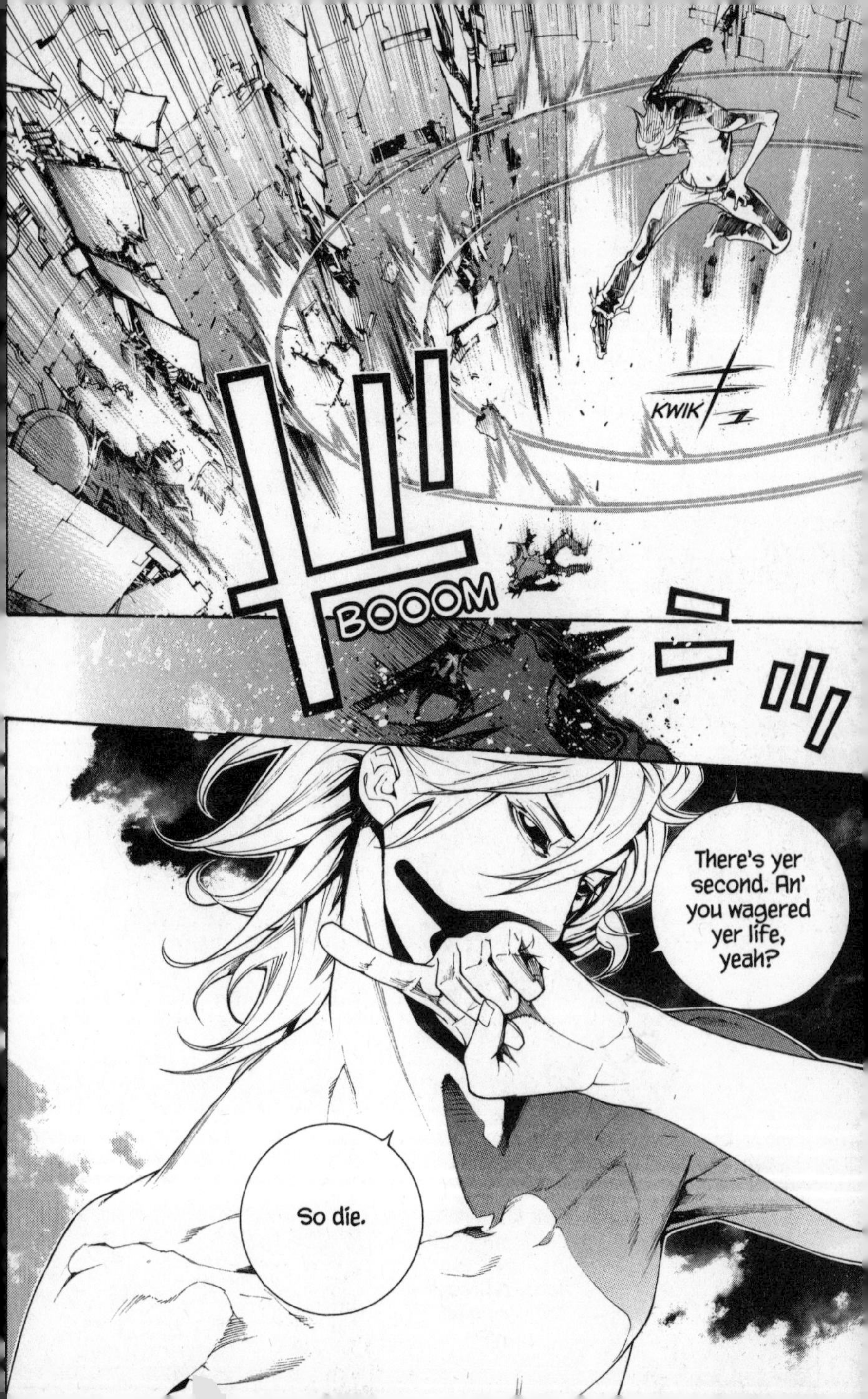
KWIK
BOOOM
There's yer second. An' you wagered yer life, yeah?
So die.

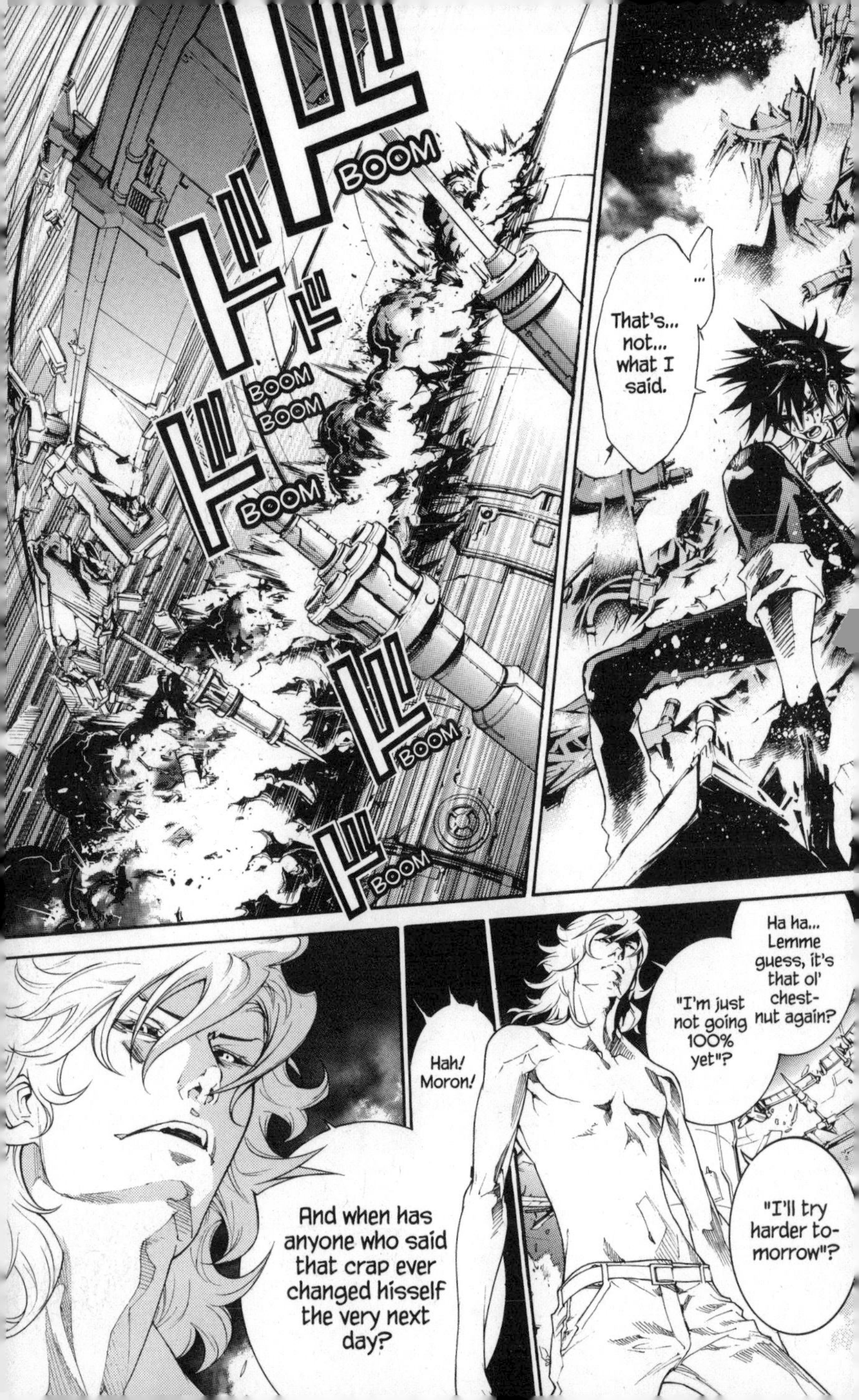
...
That's... not... what I said.
BOOM
BOOM
BOOM
BOOM
BOOM
BOOM
Ha ha... Lemme guess, it's that ol' chest-nut again?
"I'm just not going 100% yet"?
"I'll try harder to-morrow"?
Hah! Moron!
And when has anyone who said that crap ever changed hisself the very next day?

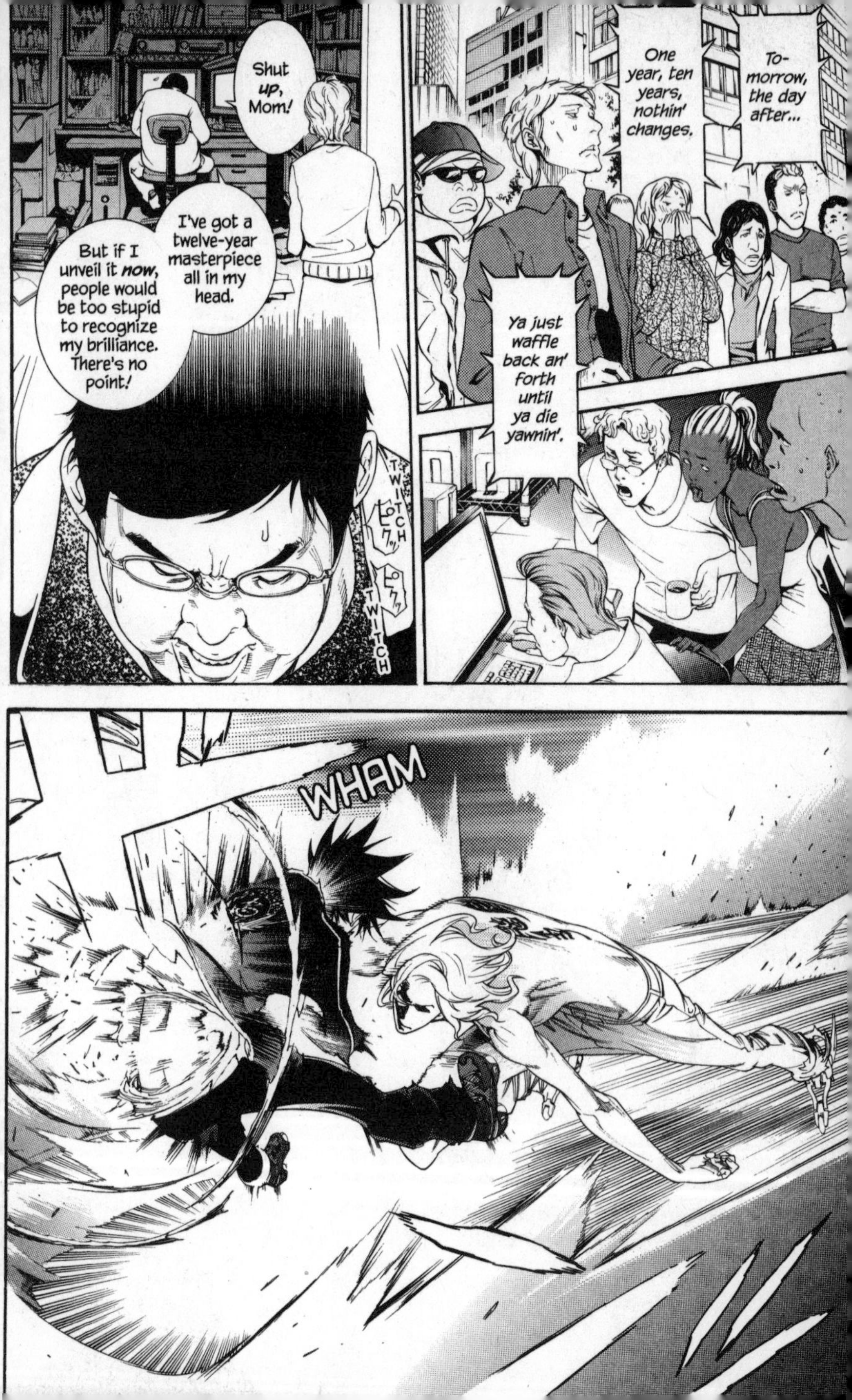
To-morrow, the day after...
One year, ten years, nothin' changes.
Ya just waffle back an' forth until ya die yawnin'.
Shut up, Mom!
I've got a twelve-year masterpiece all in my head.
But if I unveil it *now*, people would be too stupid to recognize my brilliance. There's no point!
TWITCH TWITCH
WHAM

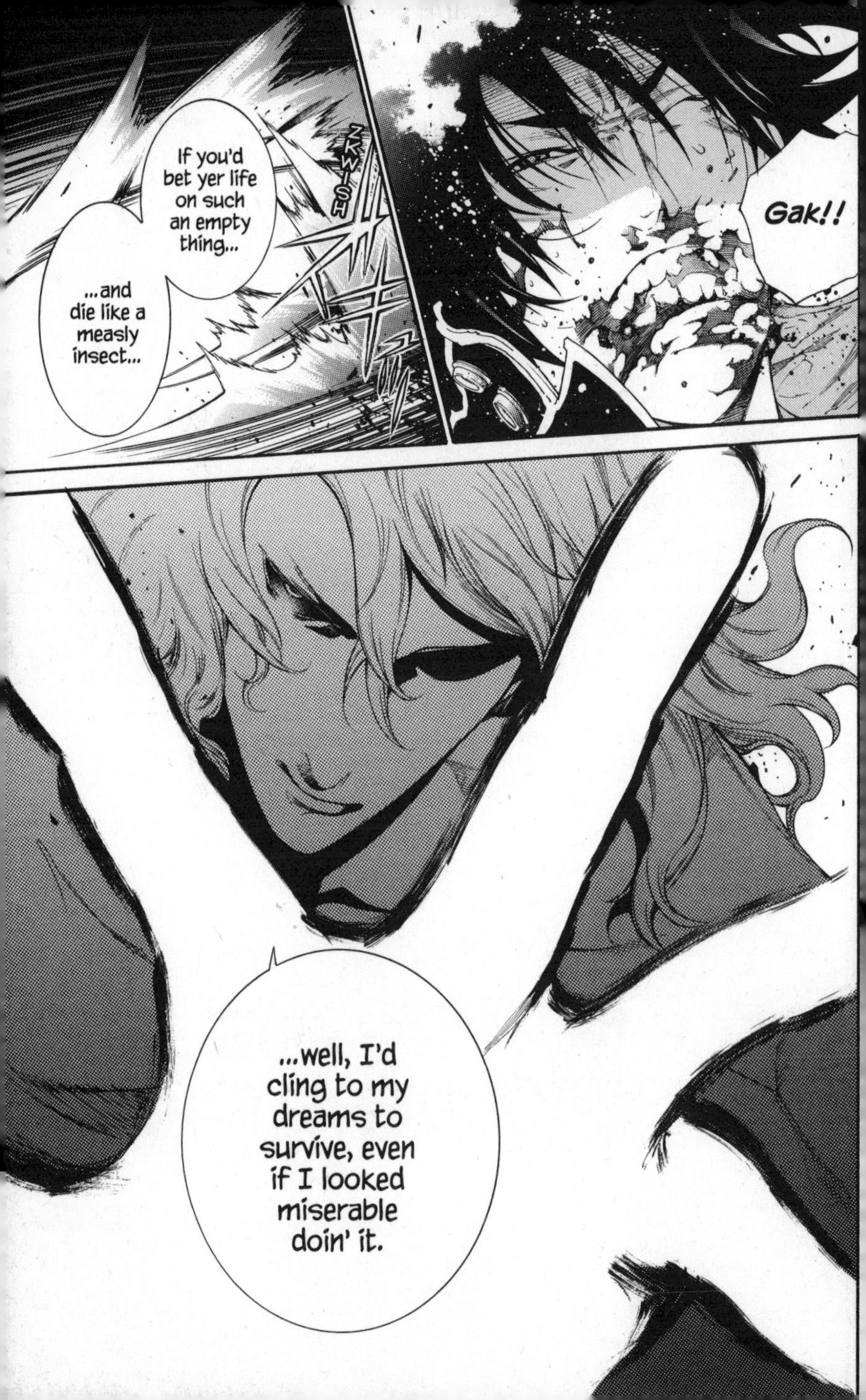
Gak!!
If you'd bet yer life on such an empty thing...
ZKWISH
...and die like a measly insect...
...well, I'd cling to my dreams to survive, even if I looked miserable doin' it.

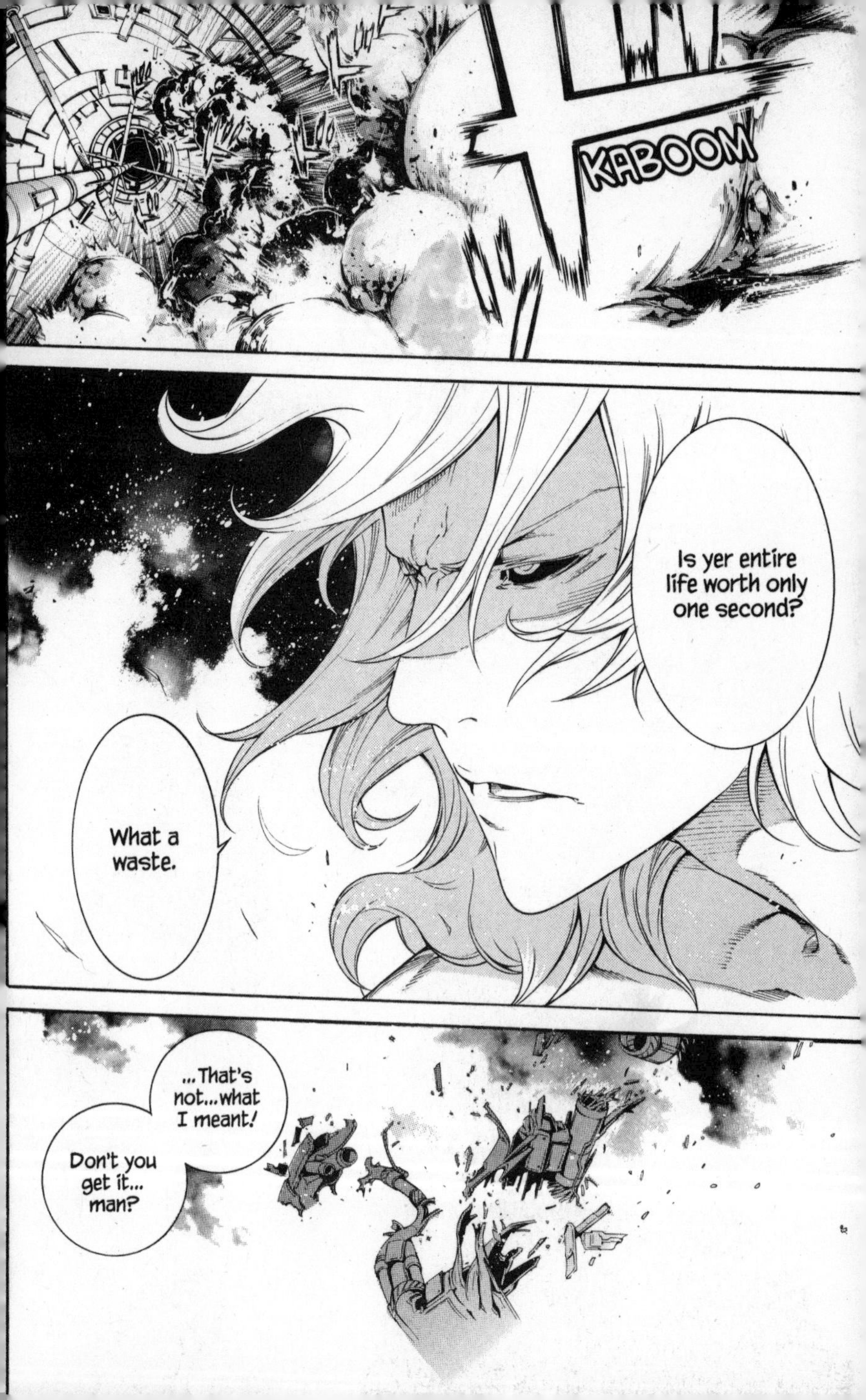
KABOOM
Is yer entire life worth only one second?
What a waste.
...That's not...what I meant!
Don't you get it... man?

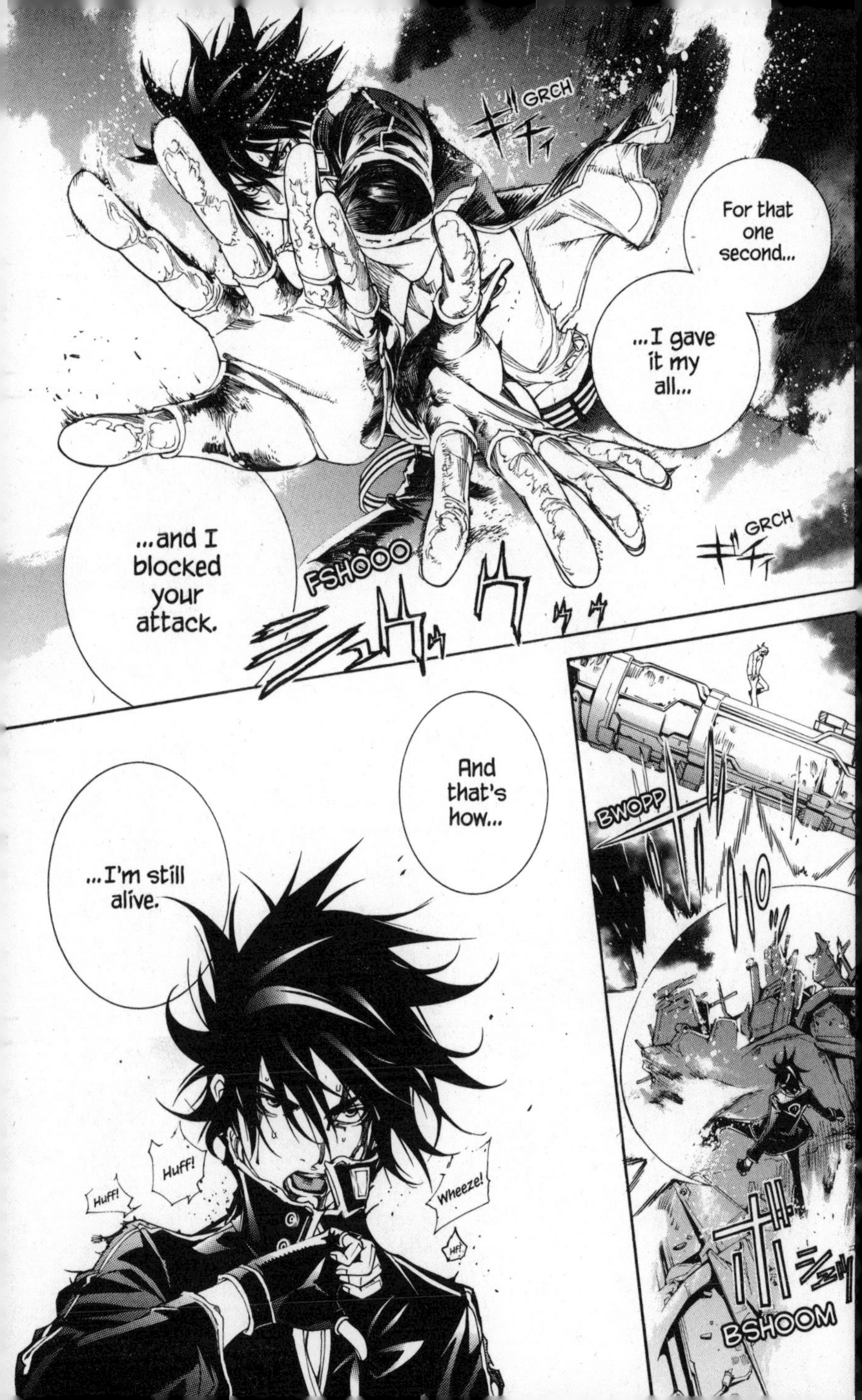
GRCH
For that one second...
...I gave it my all...
GRCH
FSHOOO
...and I blocked your attack.
BWOPP
BSHOOM
And that's how...
...I'm still alive.
Huff!
Huff!
Wheeze!
Hf!

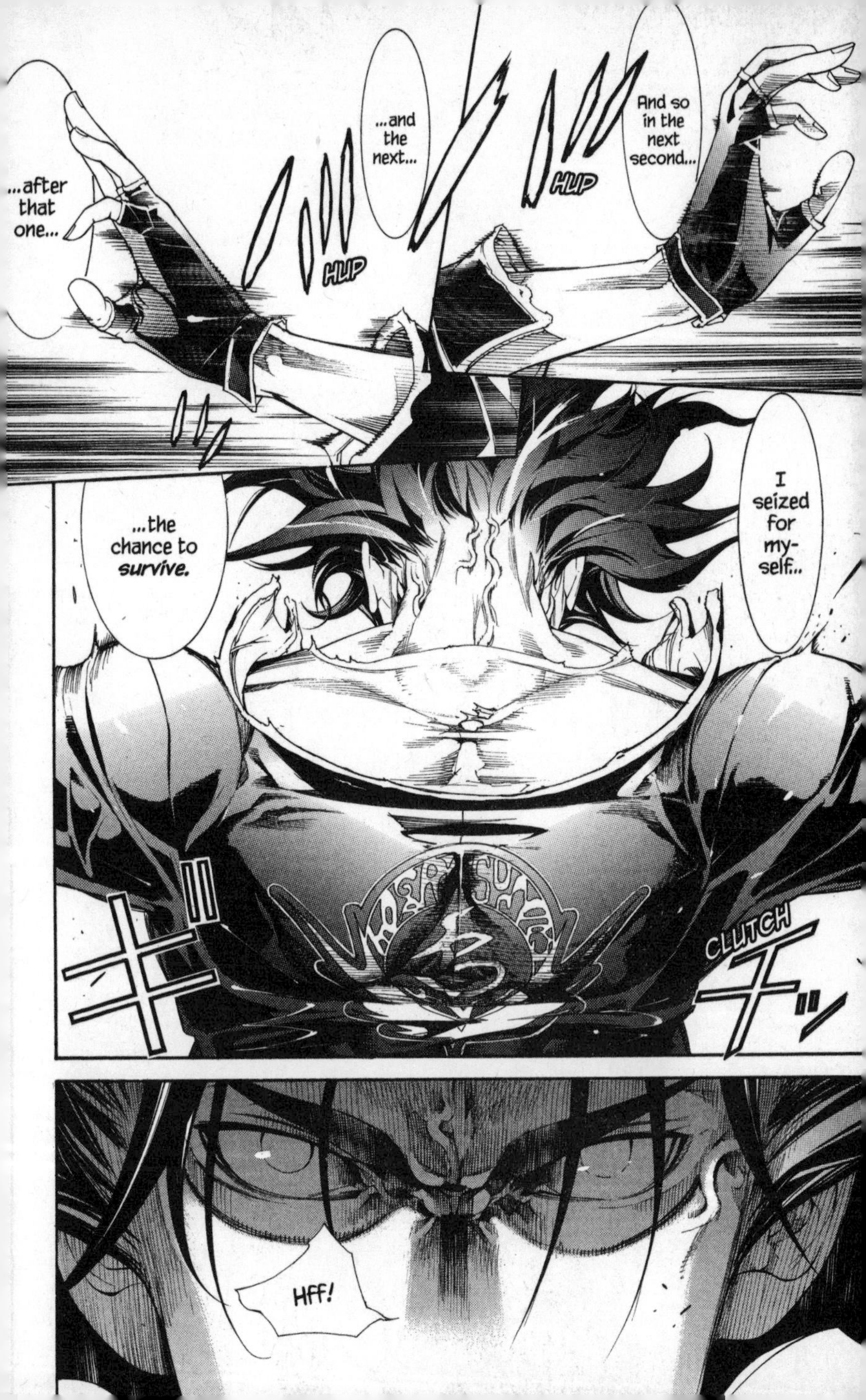
And so in the next second...
HUP
...and the next...
HUP
...after that one...
I seized for my-self...
...the chance to *survive.*
CLUTCH
HFF!

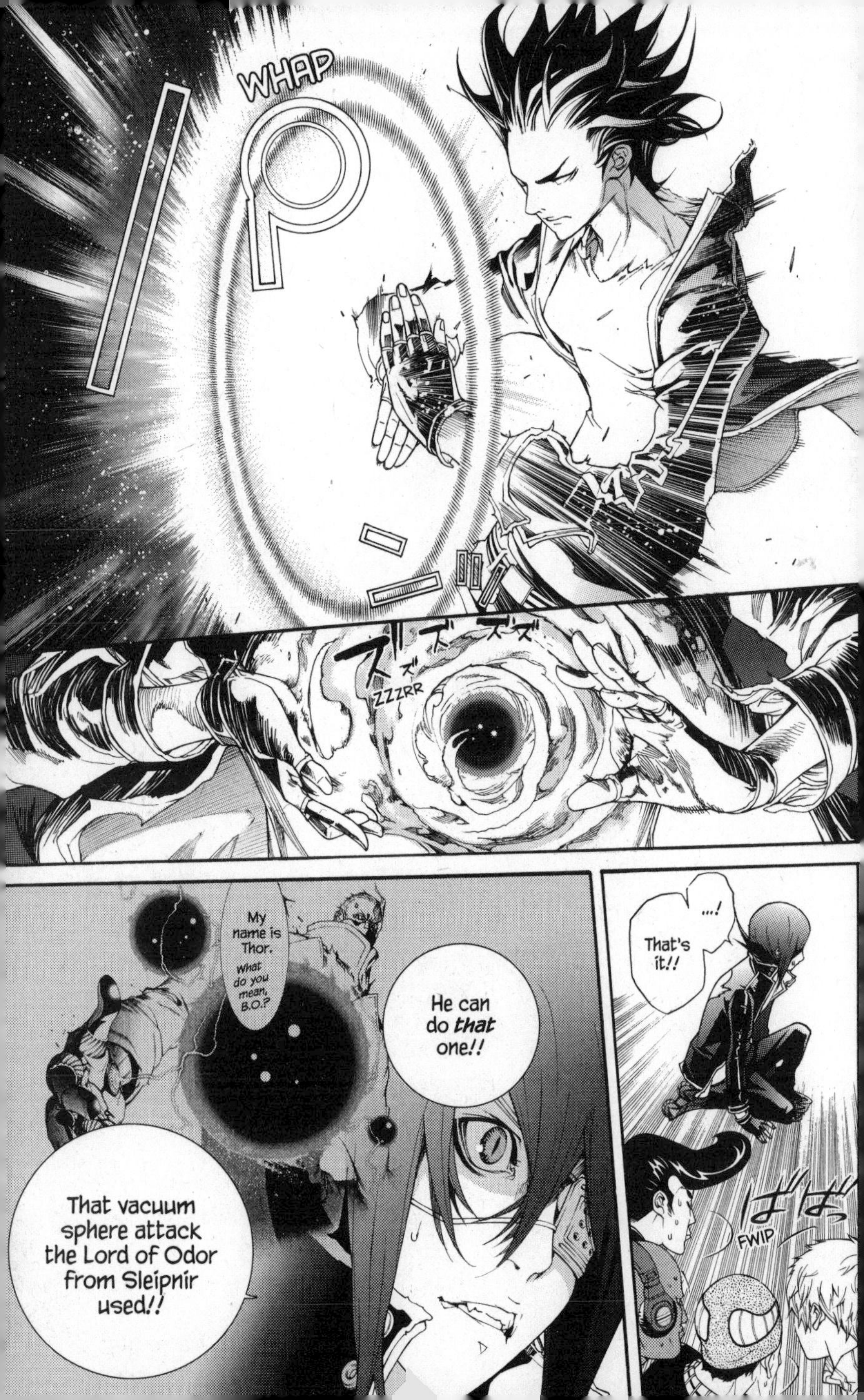
WHAP
ZZZRR
...!
That's it!!
FWIP
That vacuum sphere attack the Lord of Odor from Sleipnir used!!
He can do *that* one!!
My name is Thor. What do you mean, B.O.?

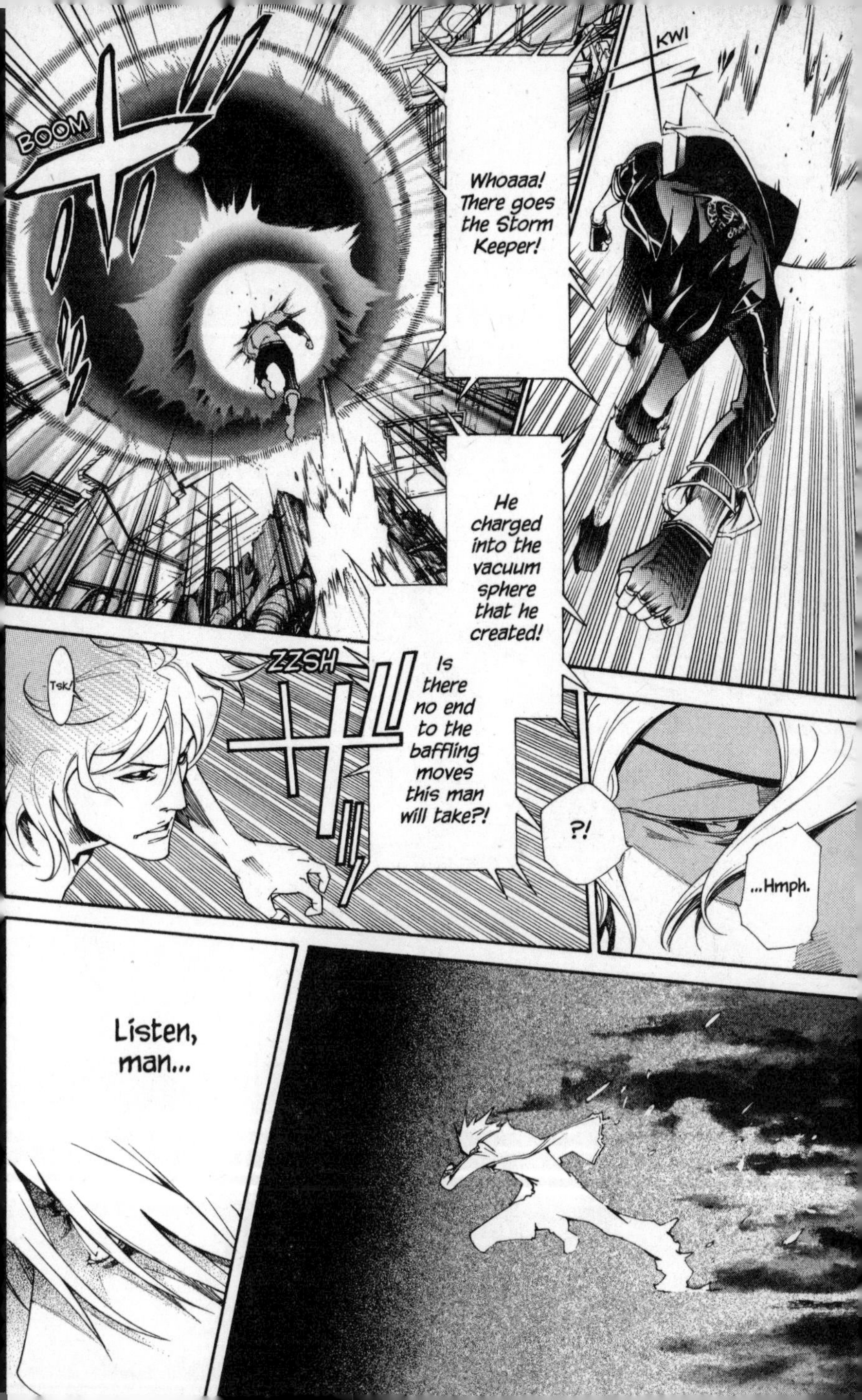
KWI
Whoaaa! There goes the Storm Keeper!
BOOM
He charged into the vacuum sphere that he created!
?!
...Hmph.
Is there no end to the baffling moves this man will take?!
ZZSH
Tsk!
Listen, man...

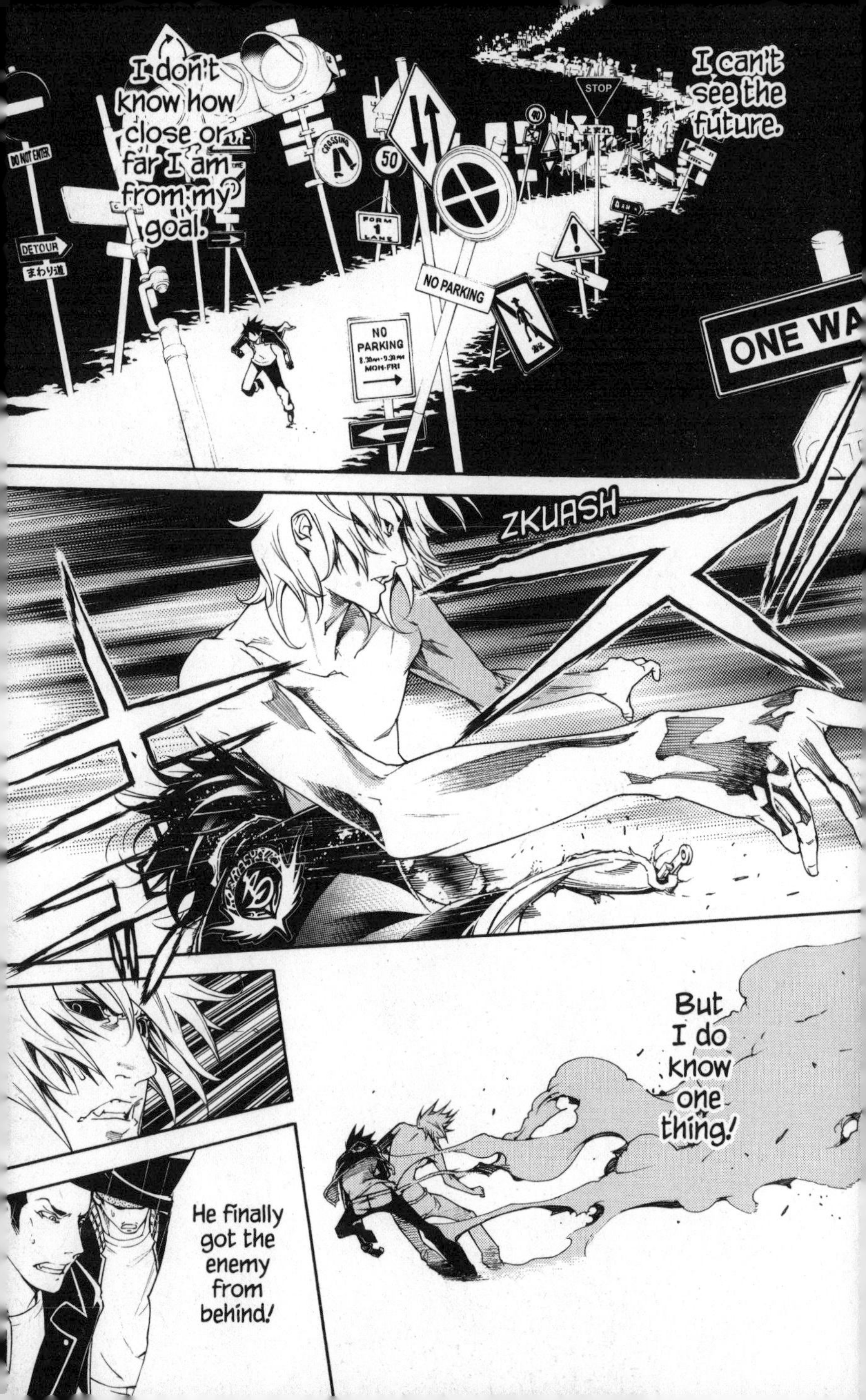
I can't see the future.
STOP
ONE WA
NO PARKING
NO PARKING 8:30am-9:30pm MON-FRI
50
CROSSING
FORM 1 LANE
I don't know how close or far I am from my goal.
DO NOT ENTER
DETOUR
まわり道
ZKUASH
But I do know one thing!
He finally got the enemy from behind!

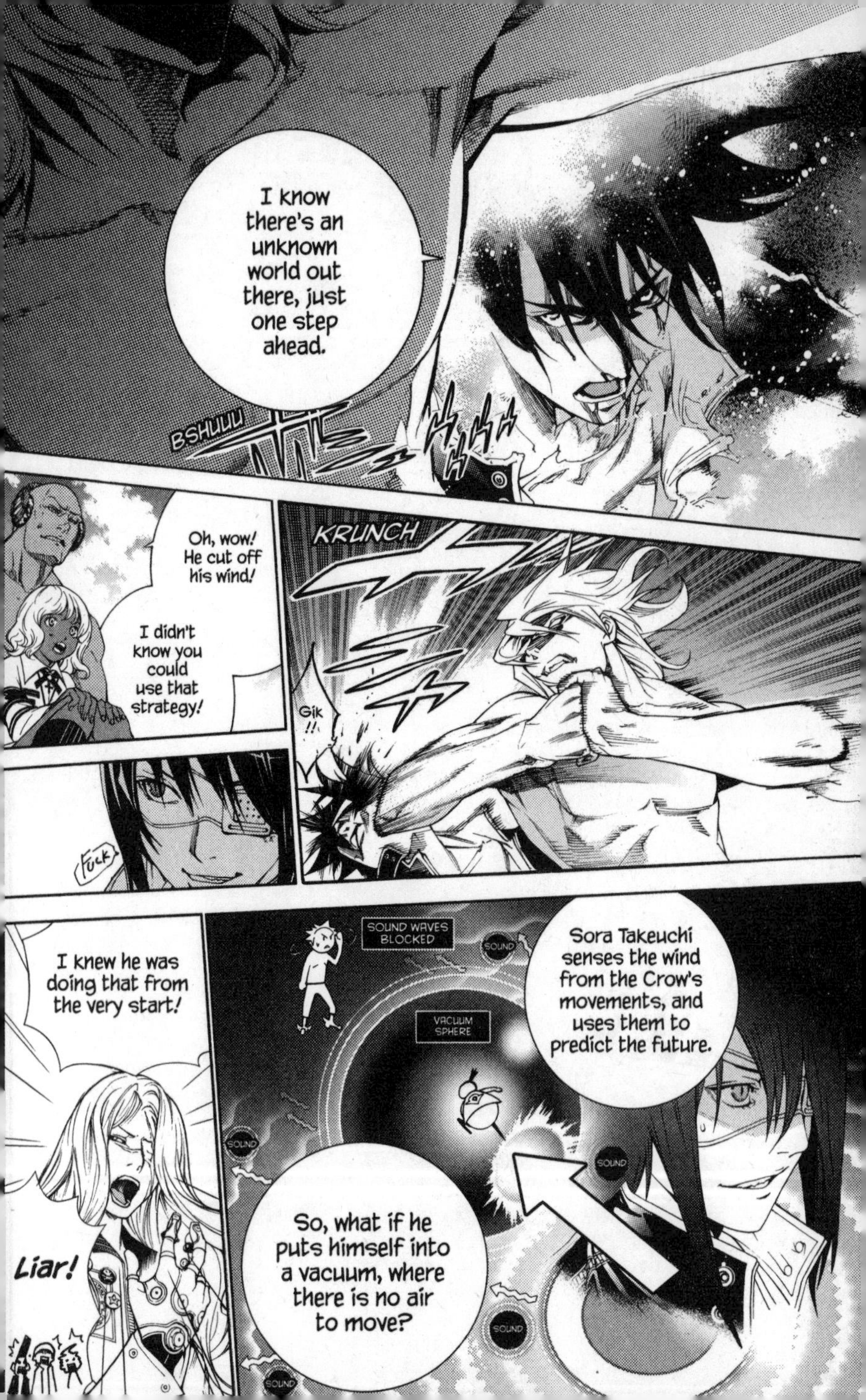
I know there's an unknown world out there, just one step ahead.
BSHUUU
KRUNCH
Gik !!
Oh, wow! He cut off his wind!
I didn't know you could use that strategy!
Fuck
Sora Takeuchi senses the wind from the Crow's movements, and uses them to predict the future.
SOUND WAVES BLOCKED
VACUUM SPHERE
SOUND
So, what if he puts himself into a vacuum, where there is no air to move?
I knew he was doing that from the very start!
Liar!

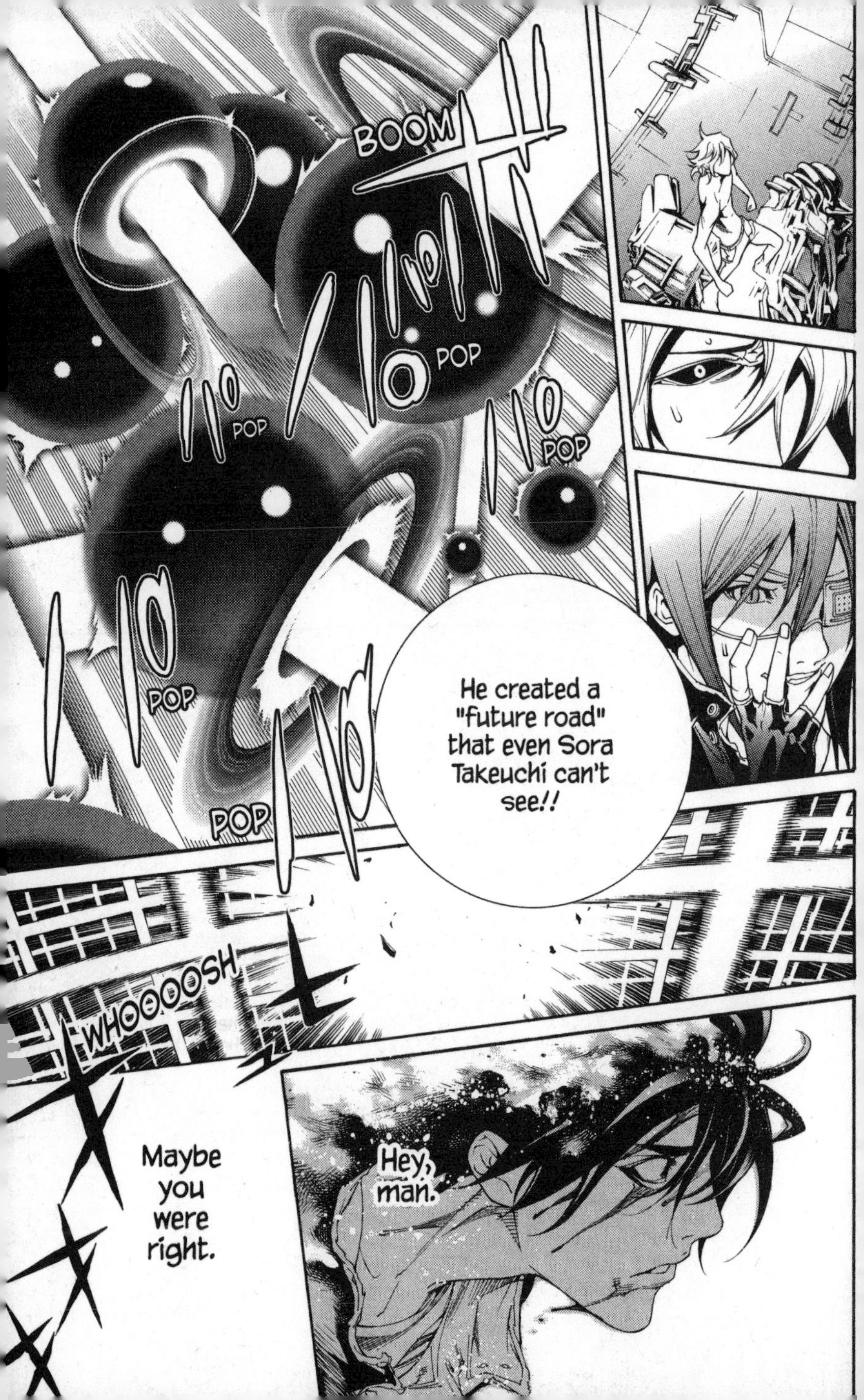
BOOM
POP
POP
POP
POP
POP
He created a "future road" that even Sora Takeuchi can't see!!
WHOOOOSH
Hey, man.
Maybe you were right.

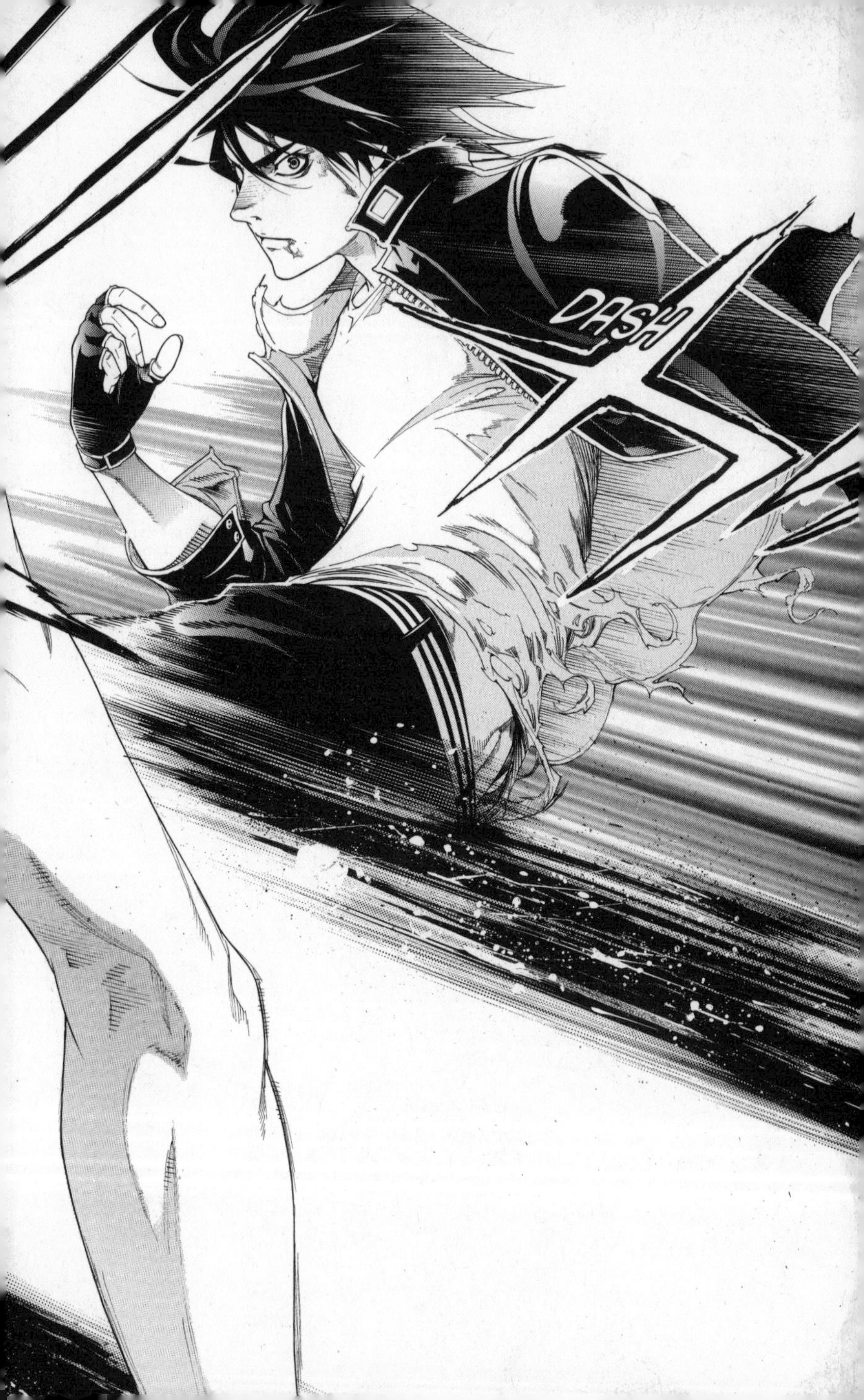
DASH

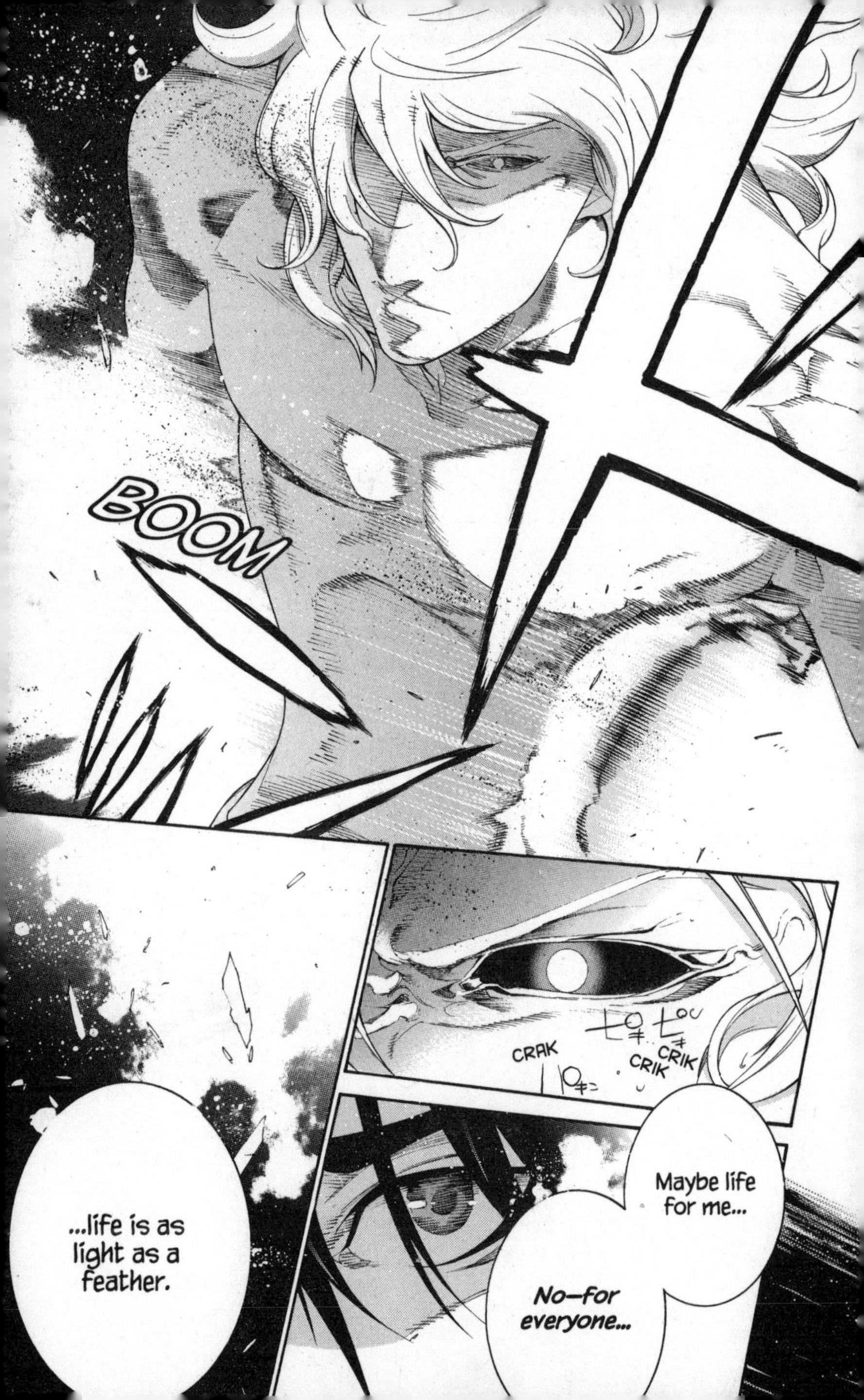
BOOM
CRIK
CRIK
CRAK
Maybe life for me...
No—for everyone...
...life is as light as a feather.

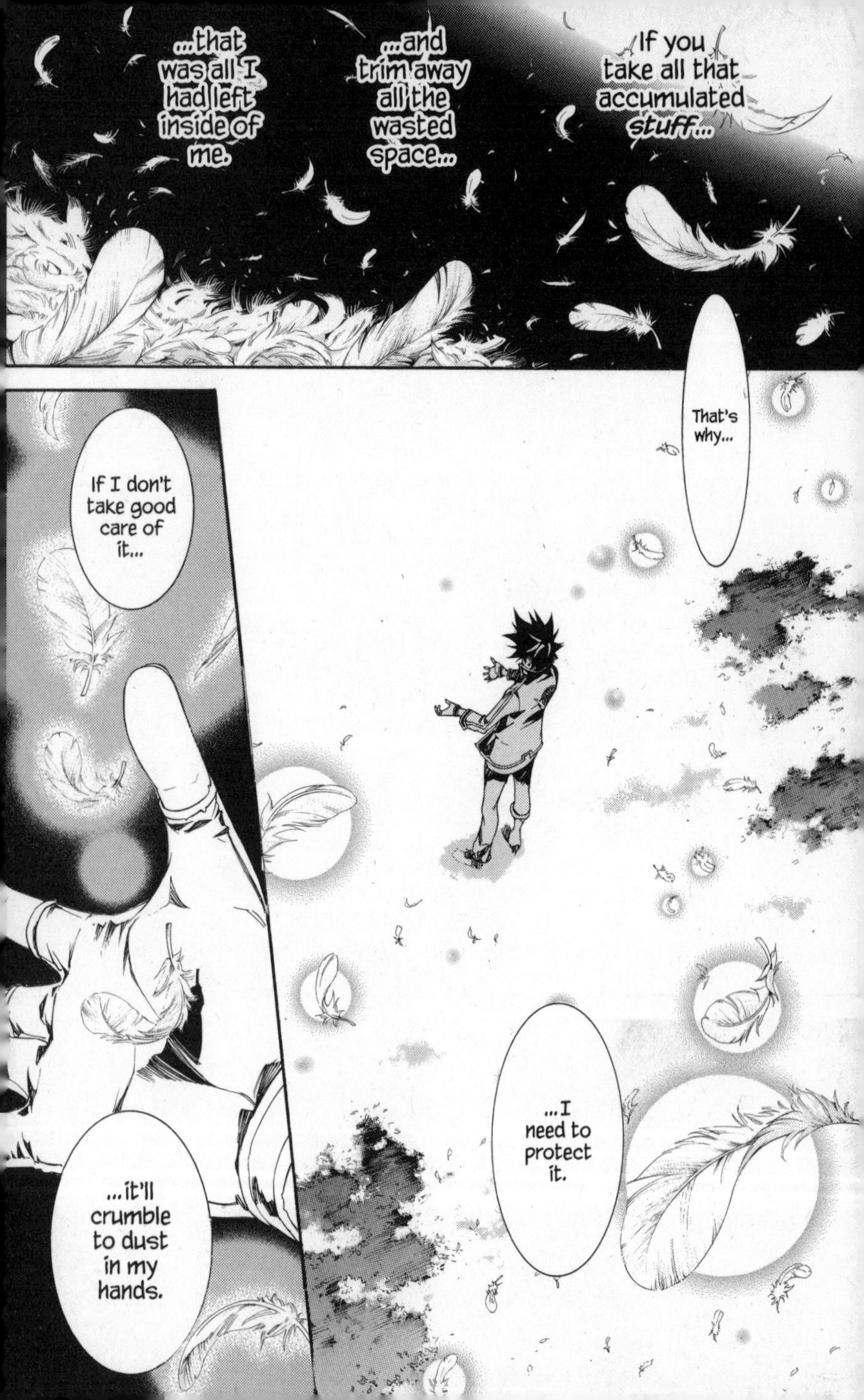
If you take all that accumulated stuff...
...and trim away all the wasted space...
...that was all I had left inside of me.
That's why...
...I need to protect it.
If I don't take good care of it...
...it'll crumble to dust in my hands.

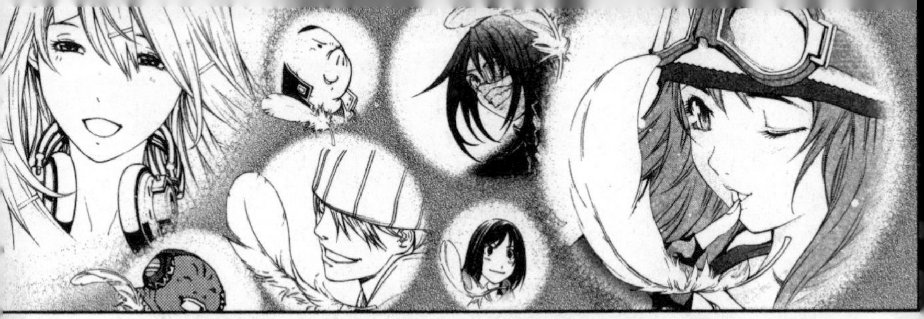

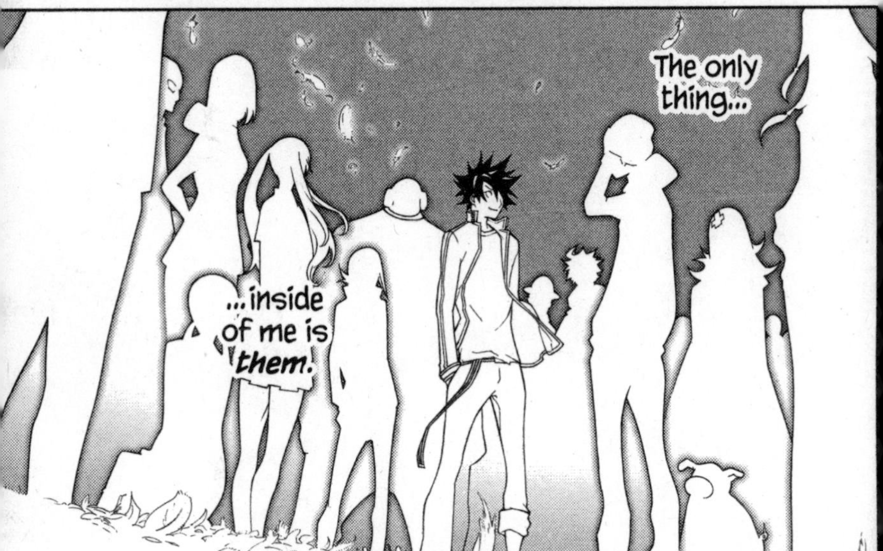
The only thing...
...inside of me is *them*.

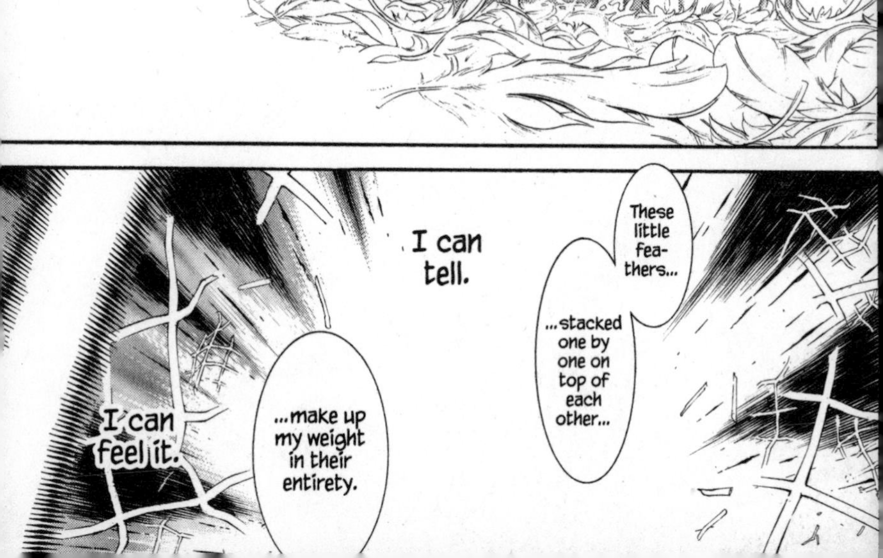
These little fea-thers...
...stacked one by one on top of each other...
I can tell.
...make up my weight in their entirety.
I can feel it.

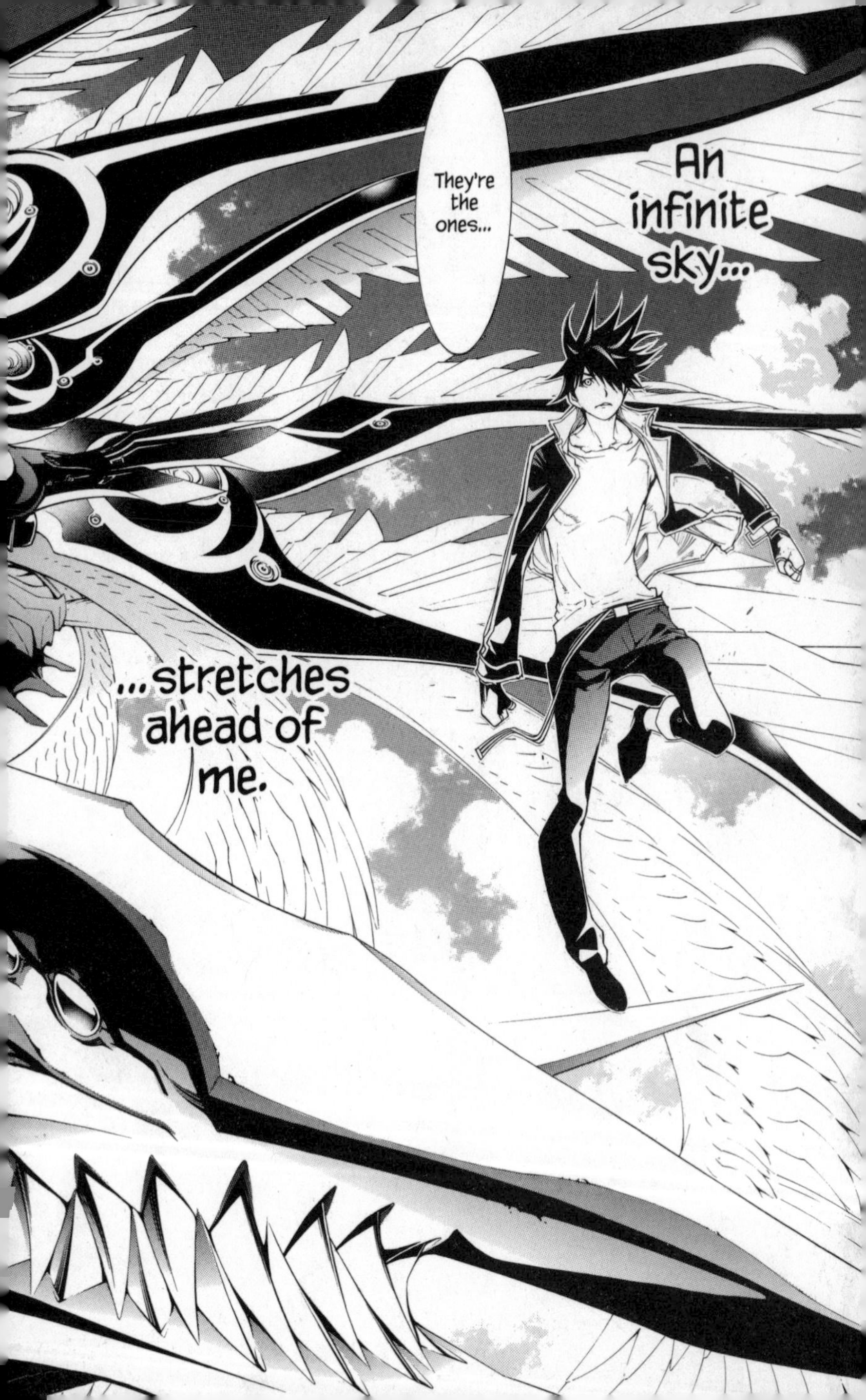
An infinite sky...
They're the ones...
...stretches ahead of me.

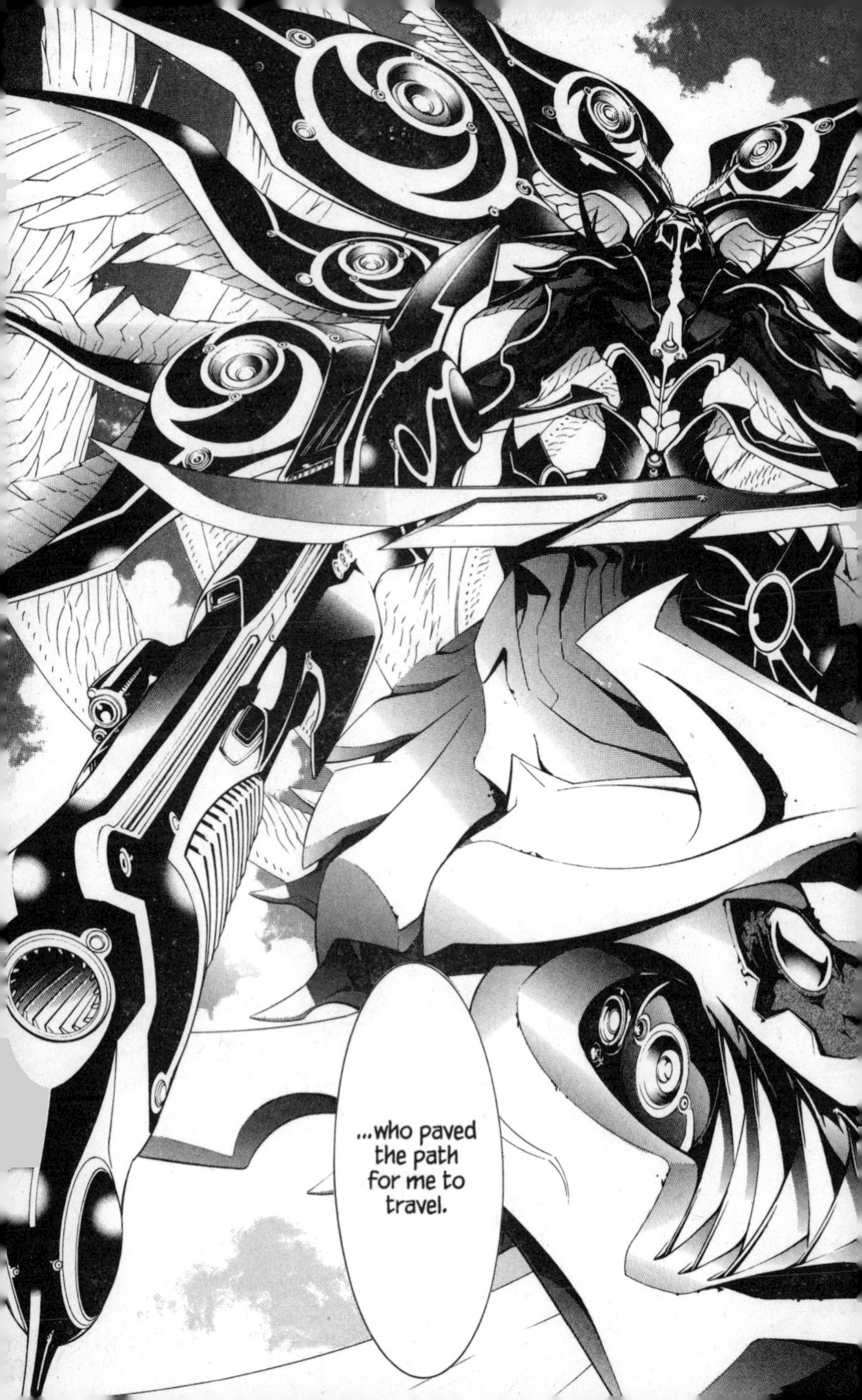
...who paved the path for me to travel.

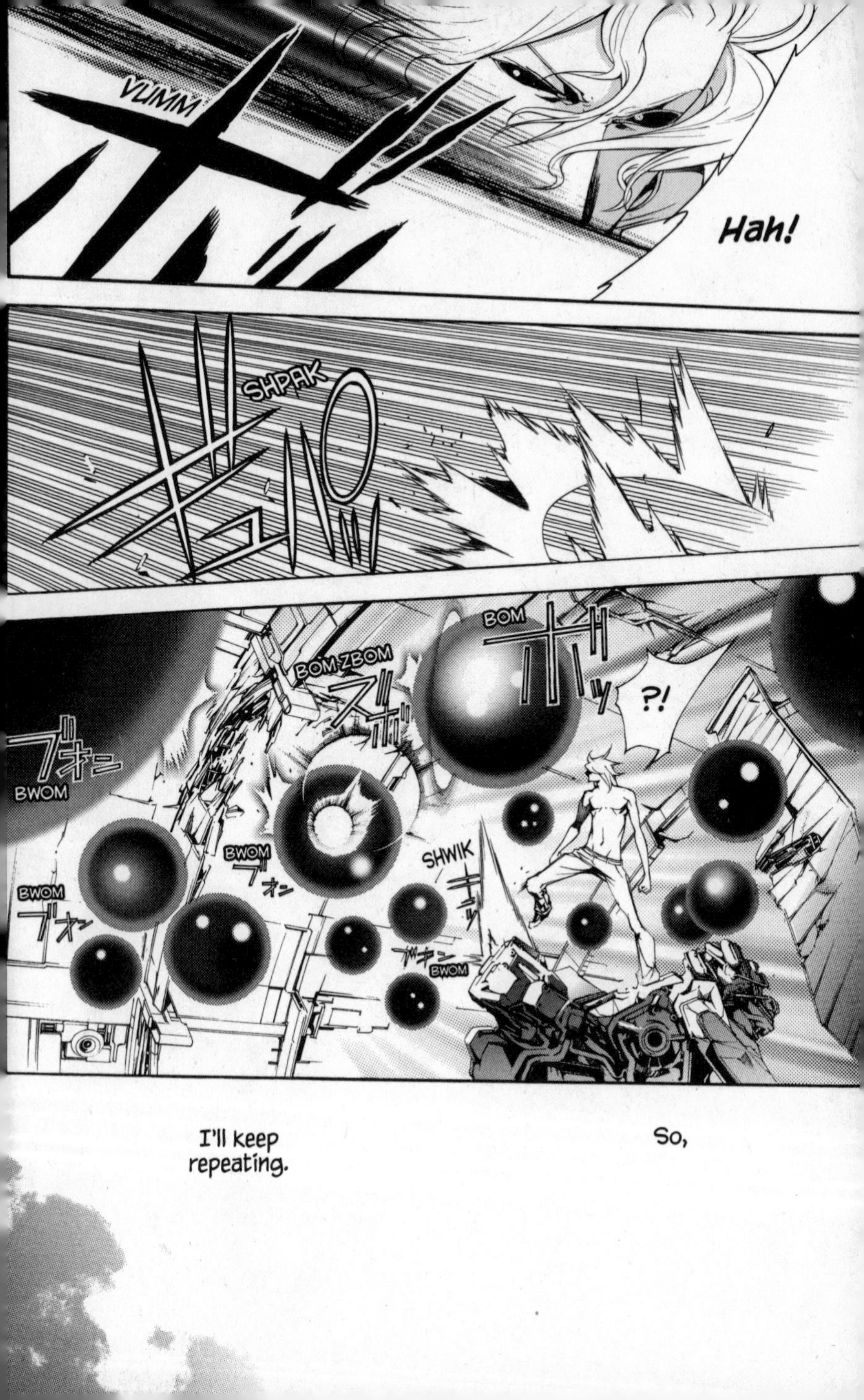
Hah!
VUMM
SHPAK
BOM
?!
BOM ZBOM
BWOM
SHWIK
BWOM
BWOM
BWOM
So,
I'll keep repeating.

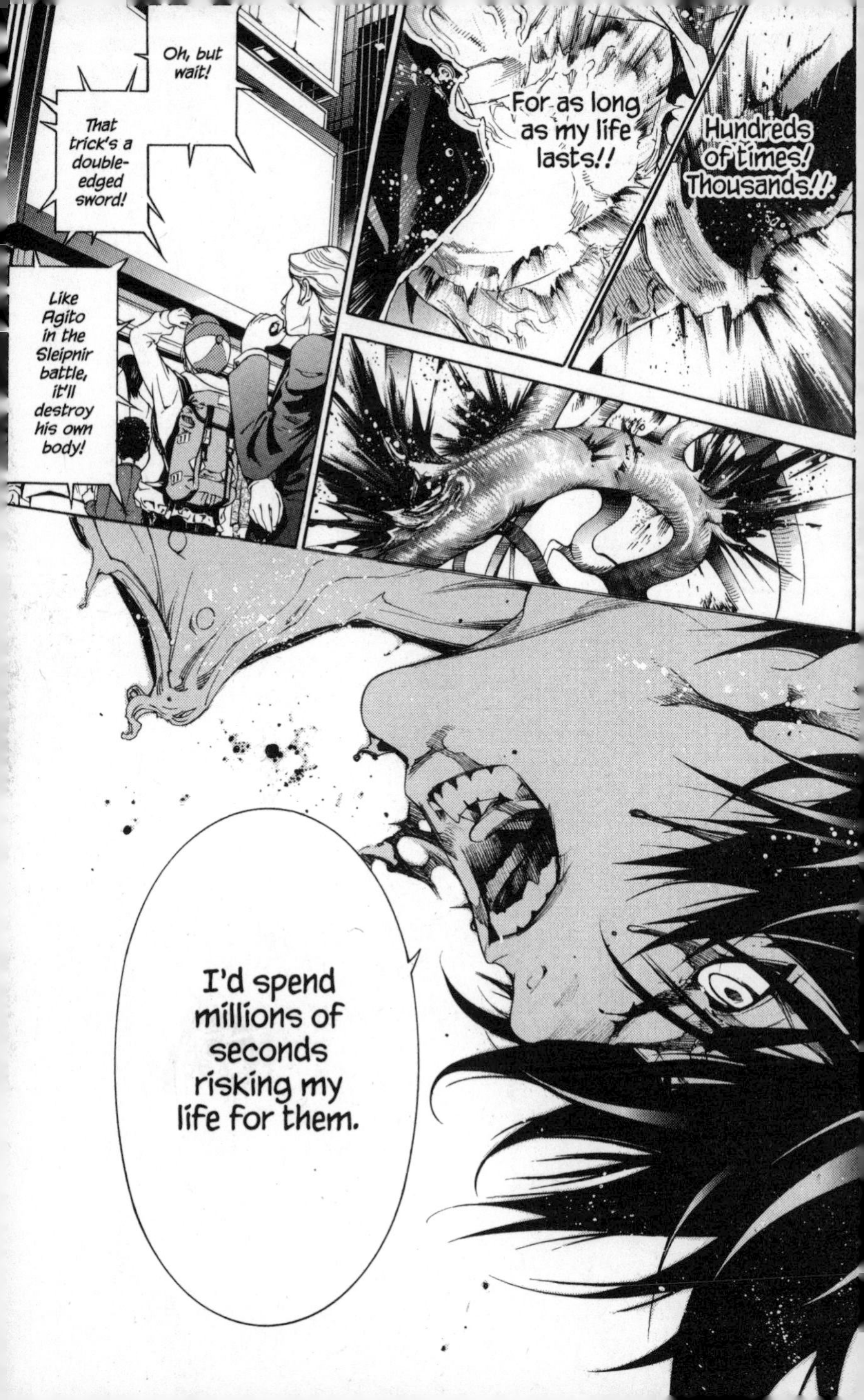
Hundreds of times! Thousands!!
For as long as my life lasts!!
Oh, but wait!
That trick's a double-edged sword!
Like Agito in the Sleipnir battle, it'll destroy his own body!
I'd spend millions of seconds risking my life for them.

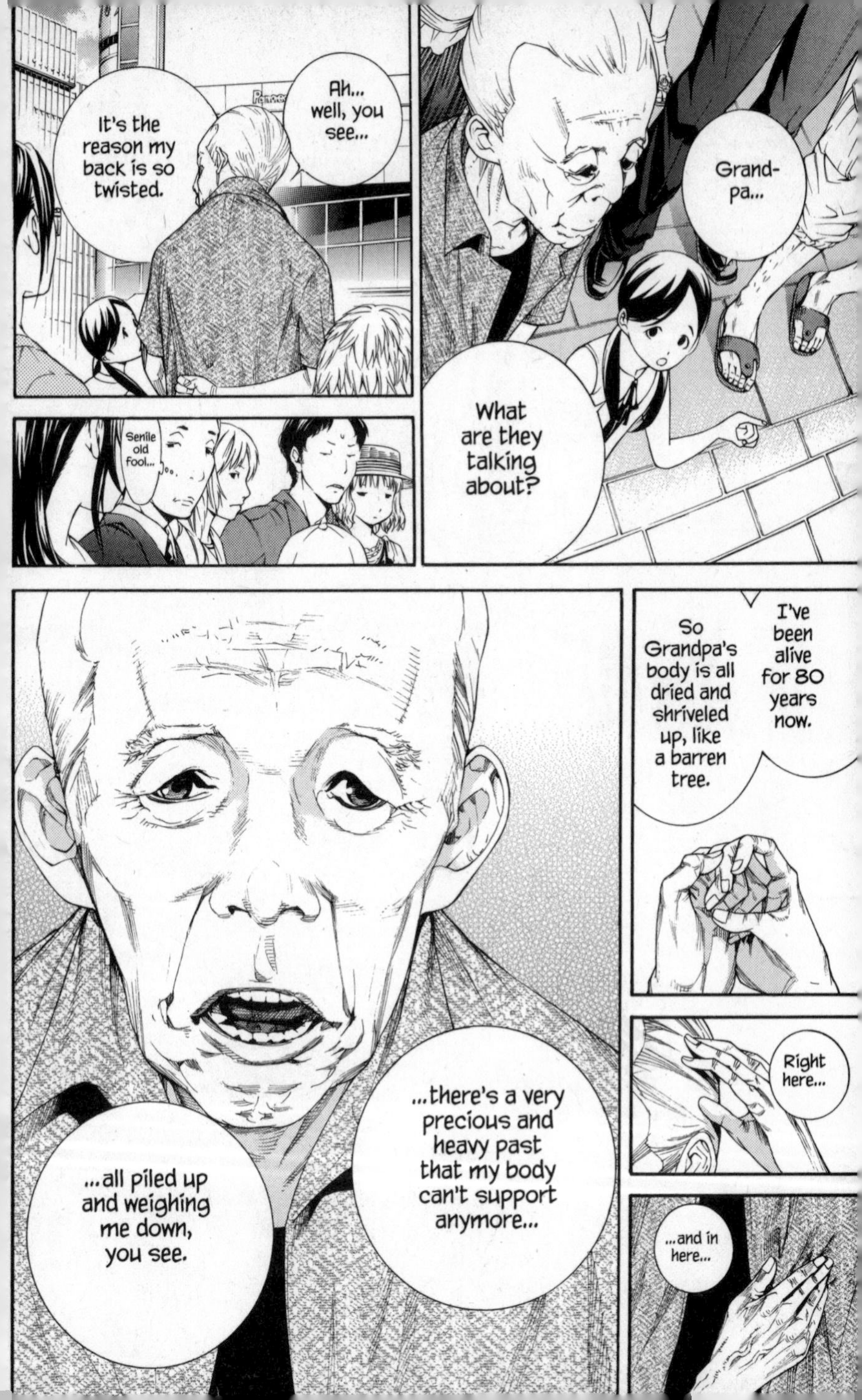
Grand-pa...
What are they talking about?
Ah... well, you see...
It's the reason my back is so twisted.
Senile old fool...
I've been alive for 80 years now.
So Grandpa's body is all dried and shriveled up, like a barren tree.
Right here...
...and in here...
...there's a very precious and heavy past that my body can't support anymore...
...all piled up and weighing me down, you see.

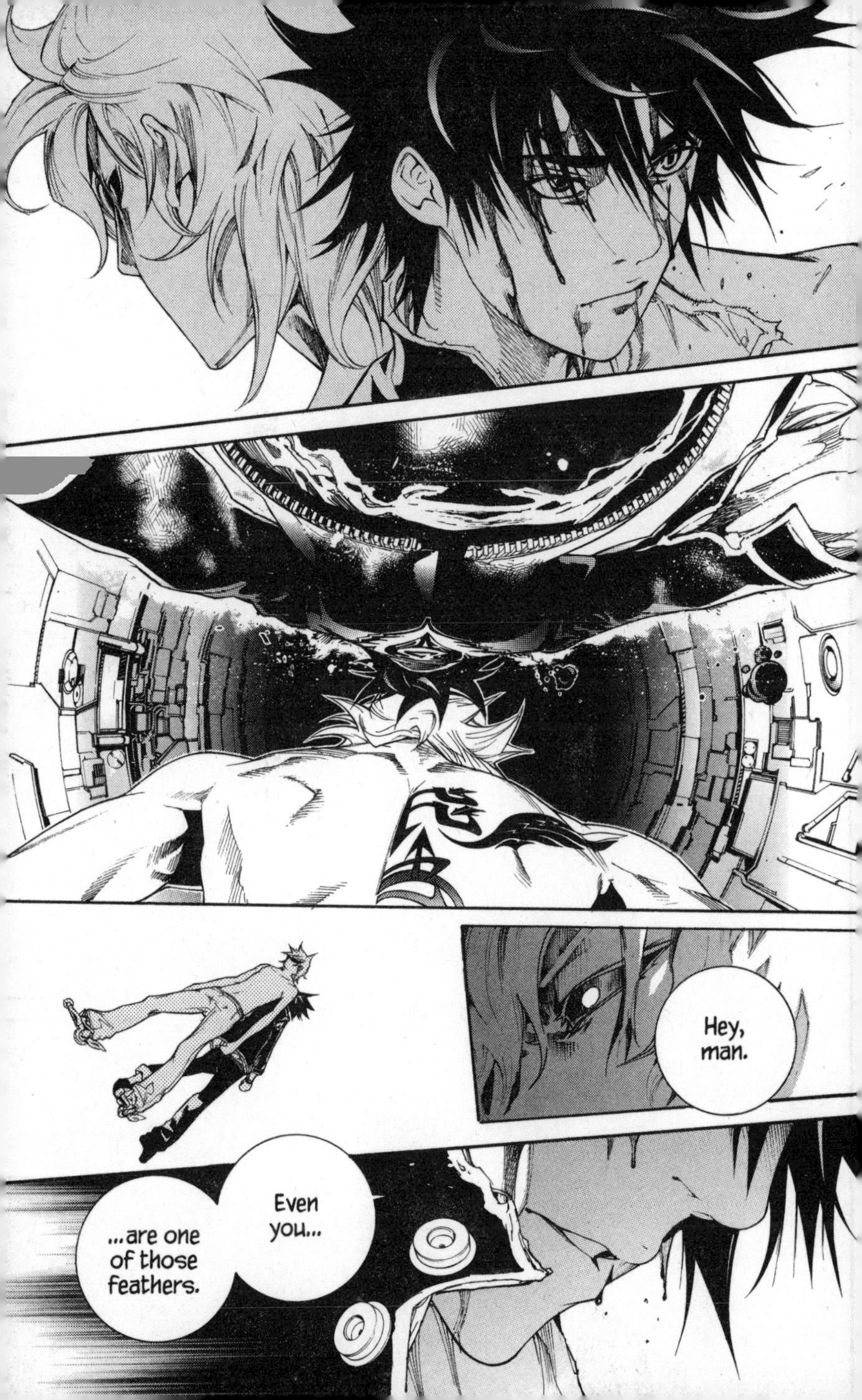
Hey, man.
Even you...
...are one of those feathers.

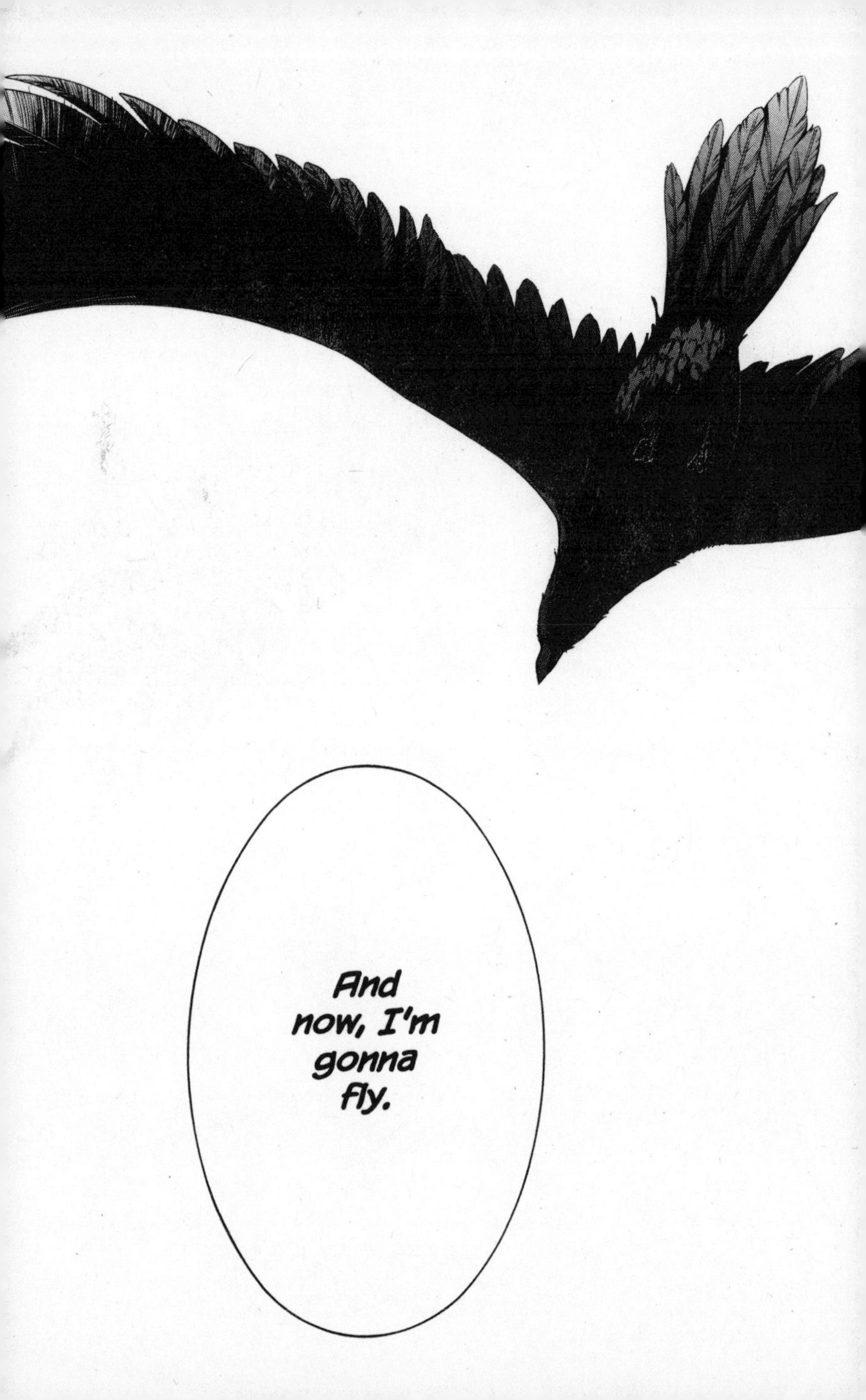
And now, I'm gonna fly.

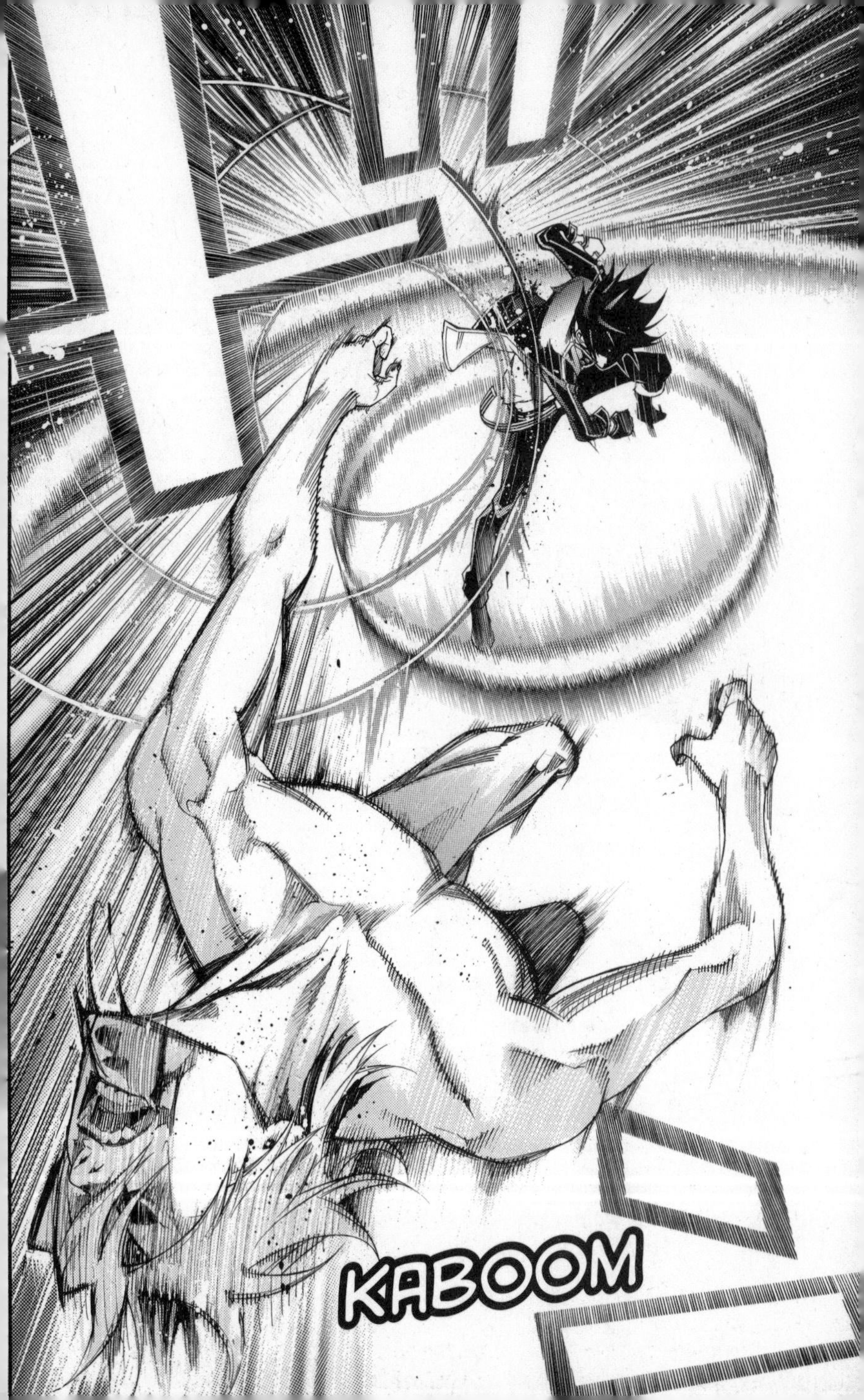
KABOOM

Trick:350

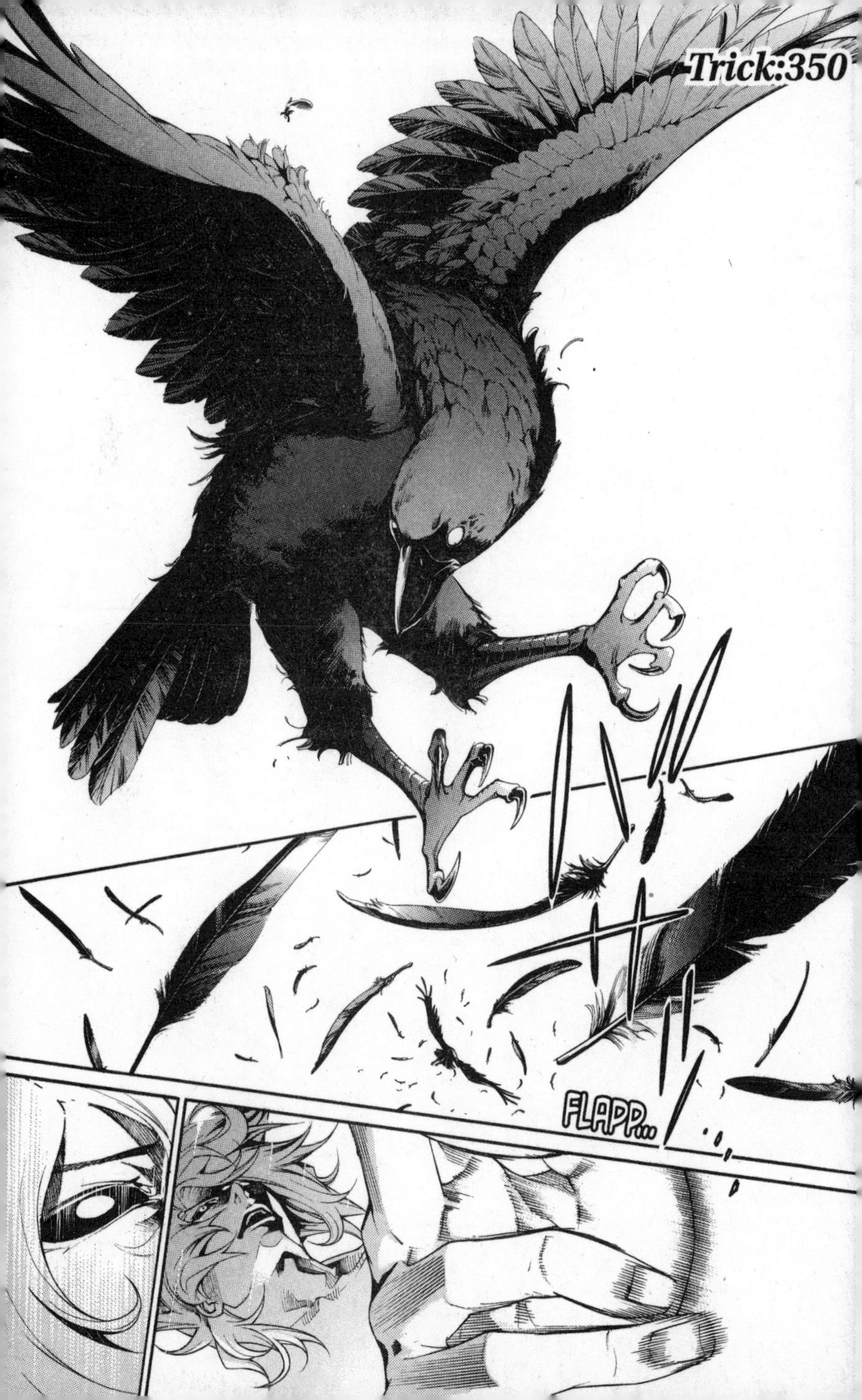
FLAPP...

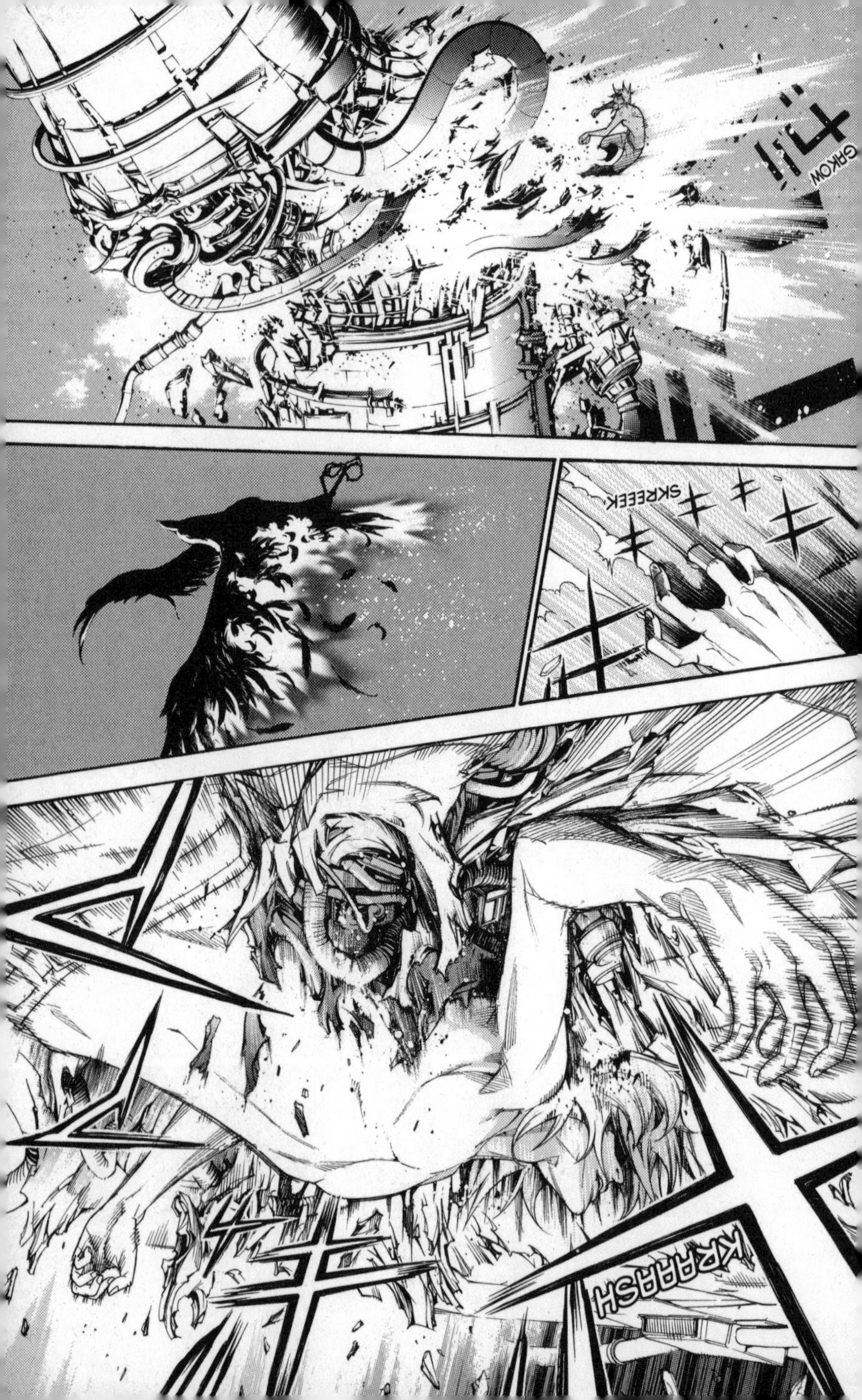
GRAKOW
SKREEEK
KRAAASH

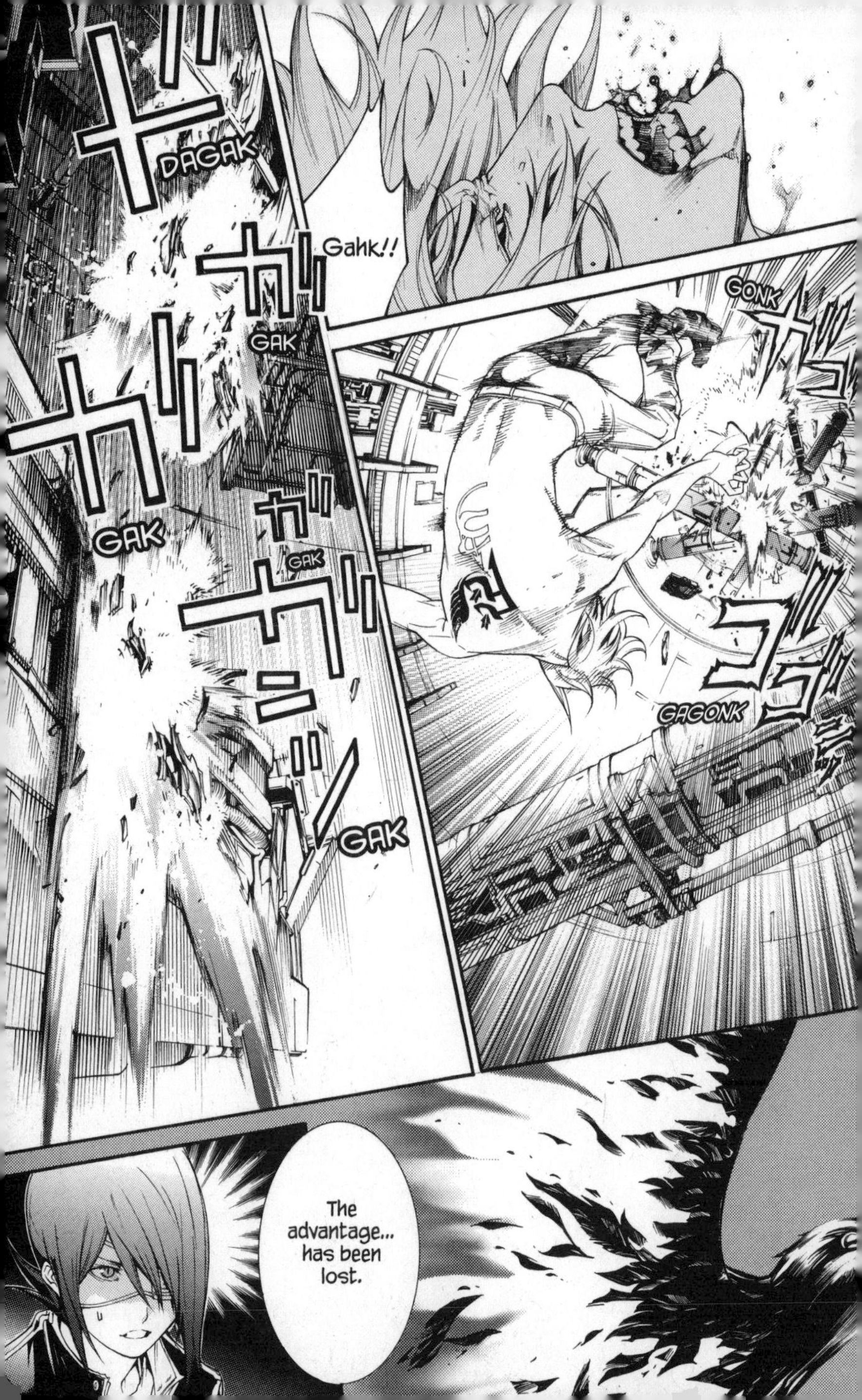
Gahk!!
GONK
GAGONK
DAGAK
GAK
GAK
GAK
GAK
The advantage... has been lost.

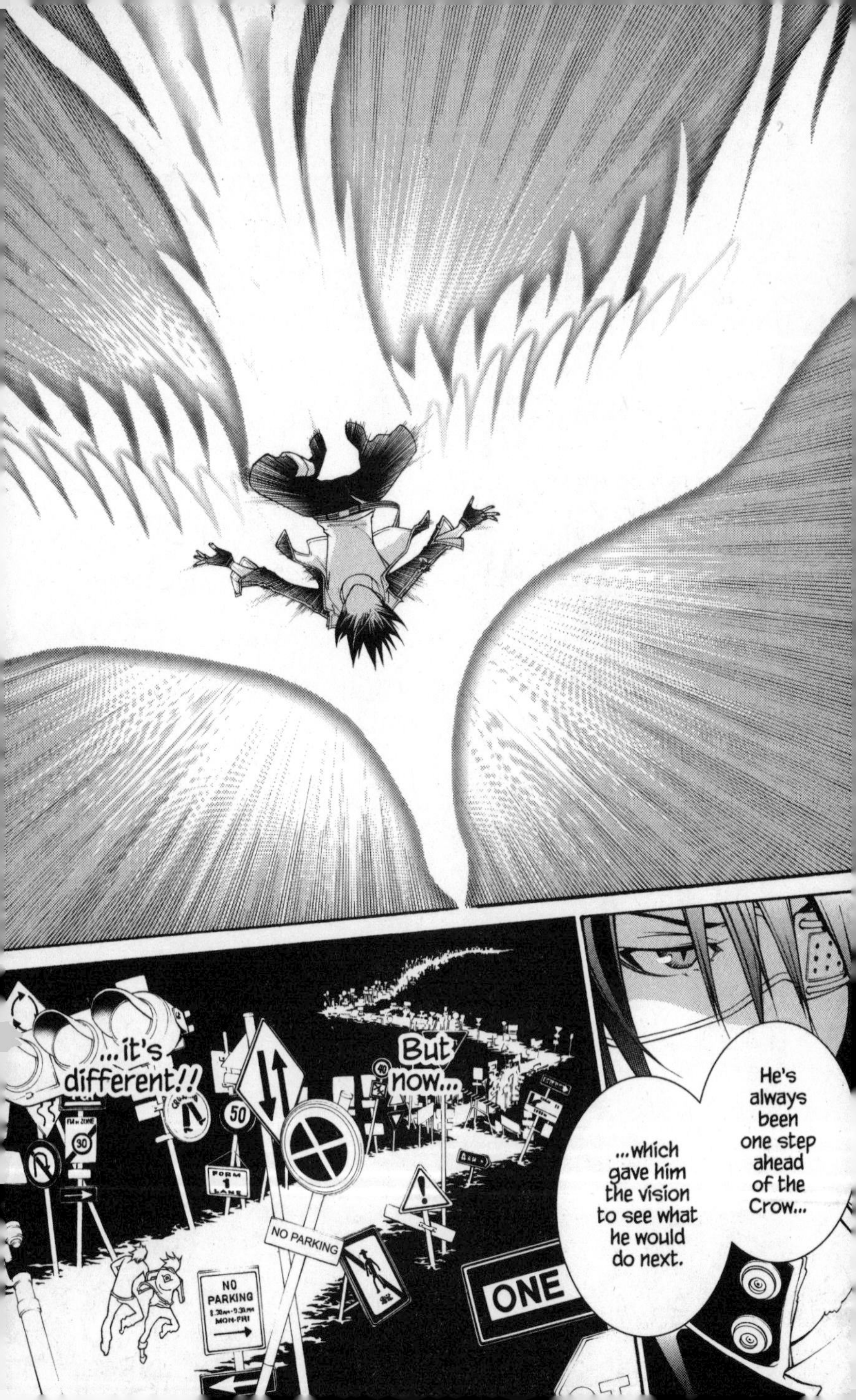
He's always been one step ahead of the Crow...
...which gave him the vision to see what he would do next.
ONE
But now...
...it's different!!
NO PARKING
NO PARKING
MON-FRI
FORM 1 LANE
50

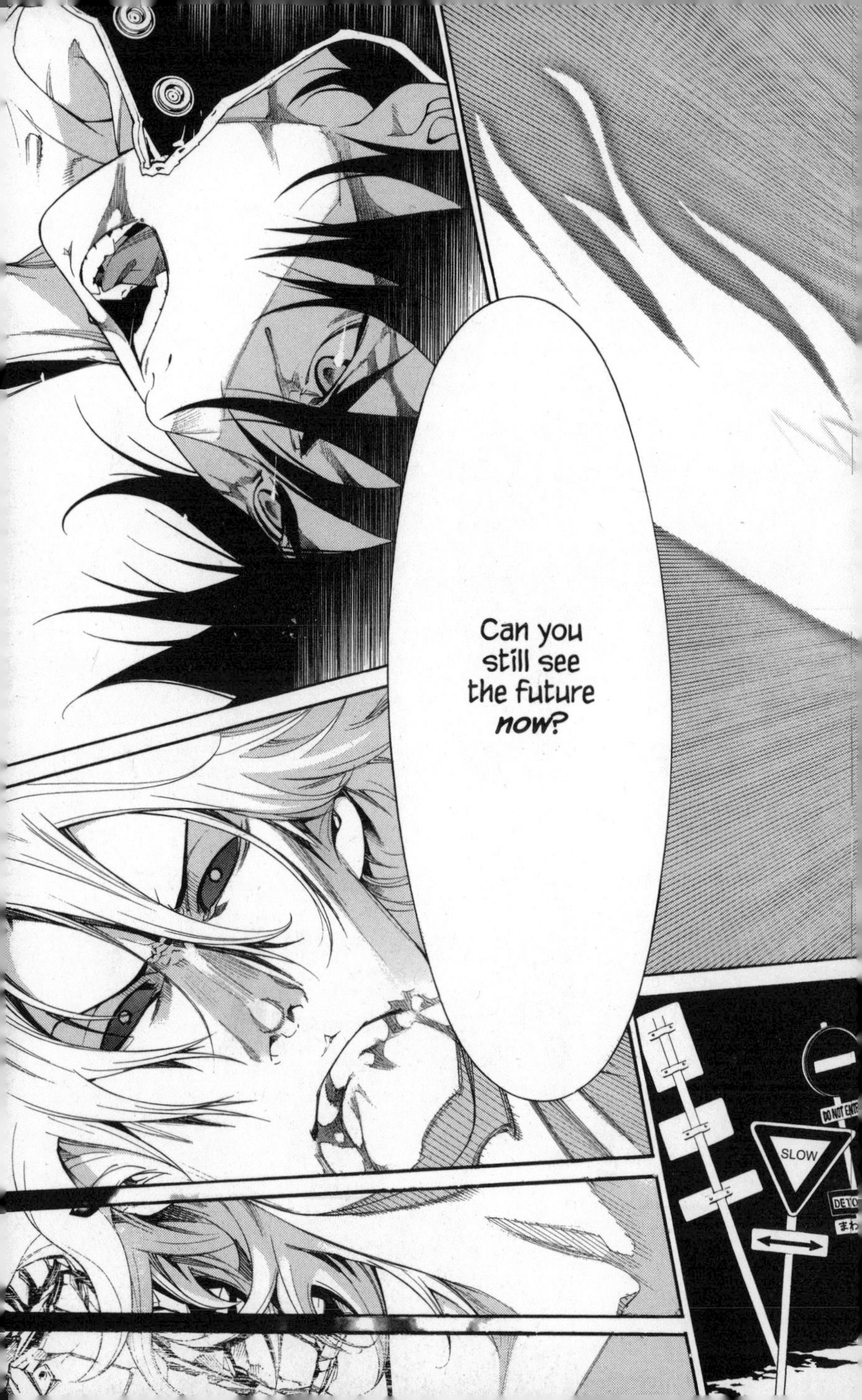
Can you still see the future *now*?
SLOW

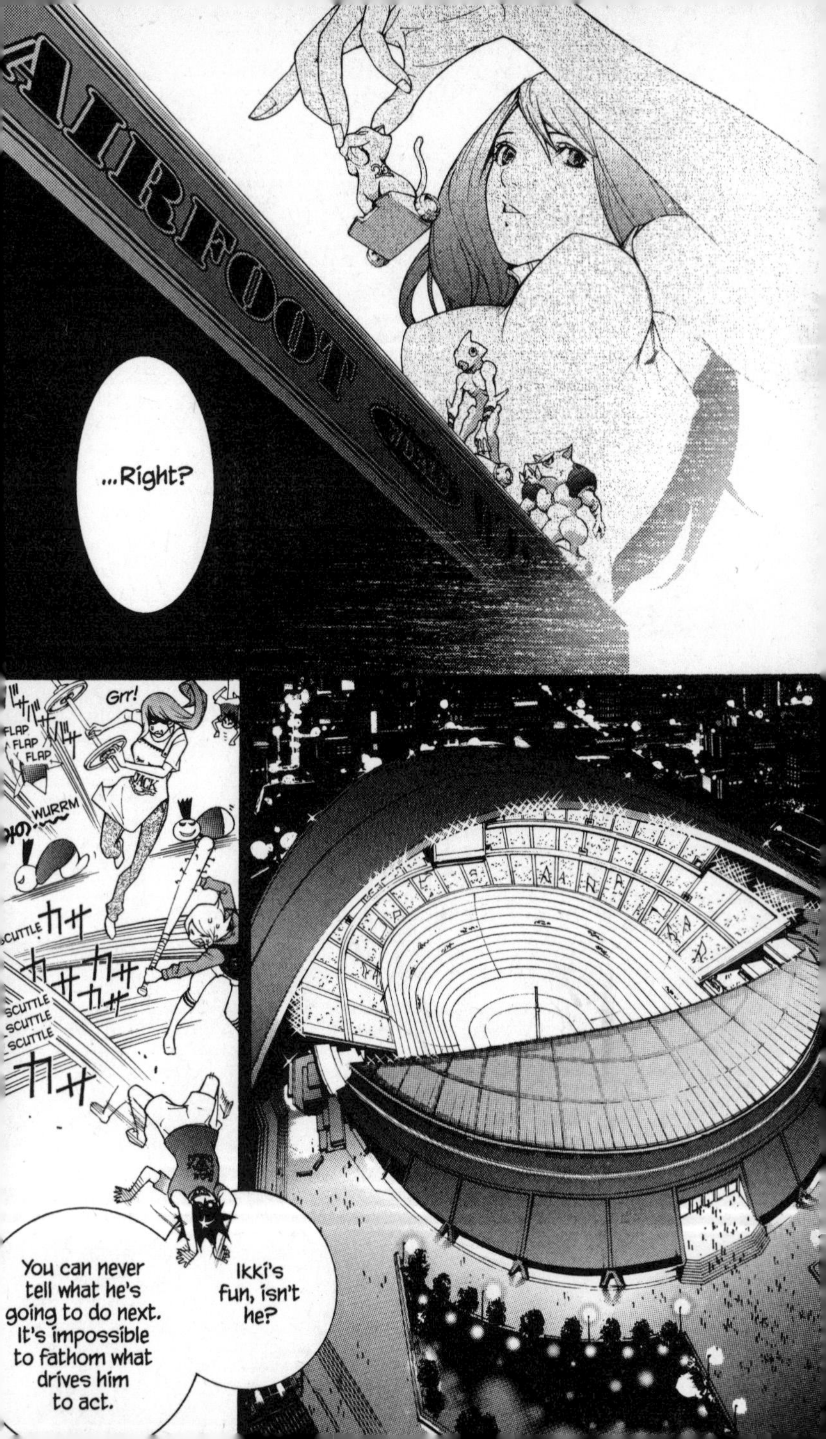
AIRFOOT
...Right?
Grr!
FLAP FLAP FLAP
WURRM
SCUTTLE
SCUTTLE SCUTTLE SCUTTLE
Ikki's fun, isn't he?
You can never tell what he's going to do next. It's impossible to fathom what drives him to act.

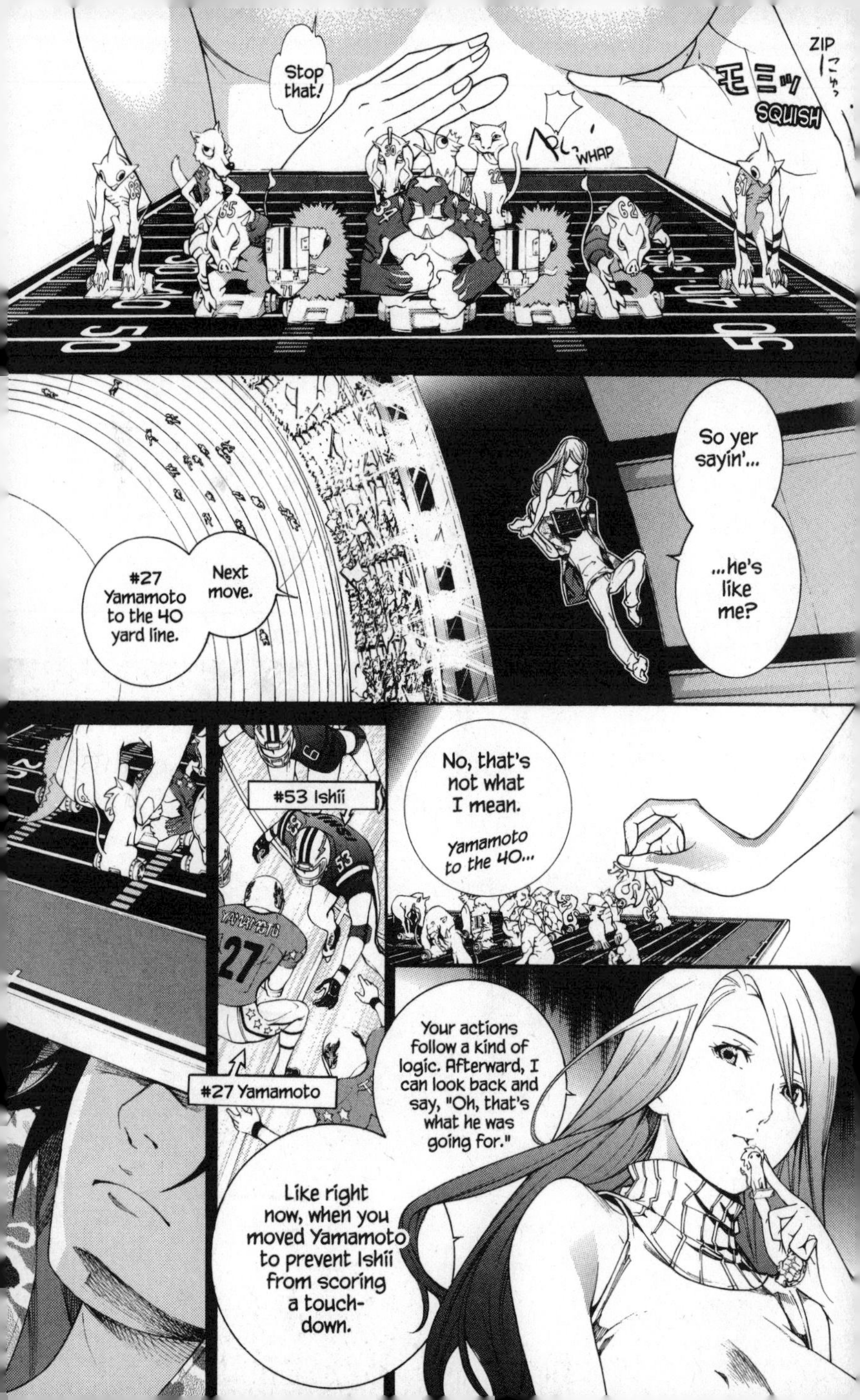
ZIP
SQUISH
Stop that!
WHAP
So yer sayin'...
...he's like me?
Next move.
#27 Yamamoto to the 40 yard line.
No, that's not what I mean.
Yamamoto to the 40...
#53 Ishii
#27 Yamamoto
Your actions follow a kind of logic. Afterward, I can look back and say, "Oh, that's what he was going for."
Like right now, when you moved Yamamoto to prevent Ishii from scoring a touch-down.

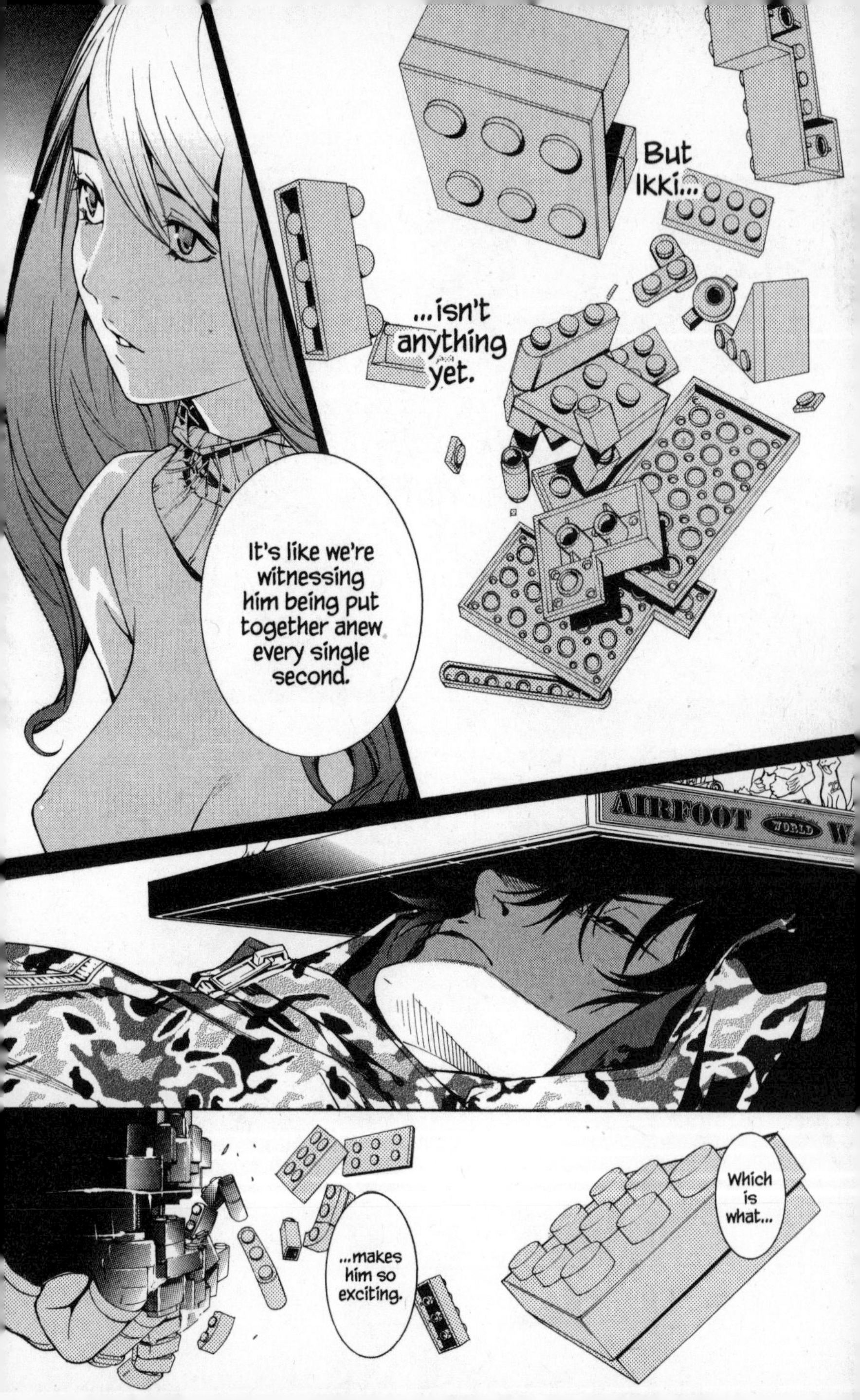
But Ikki...
...isn't anything yet.
It's like we're witnessing him being put together anew every single second.
AIRFOOT WORLD W
Which is what...
...makes him so exciting.

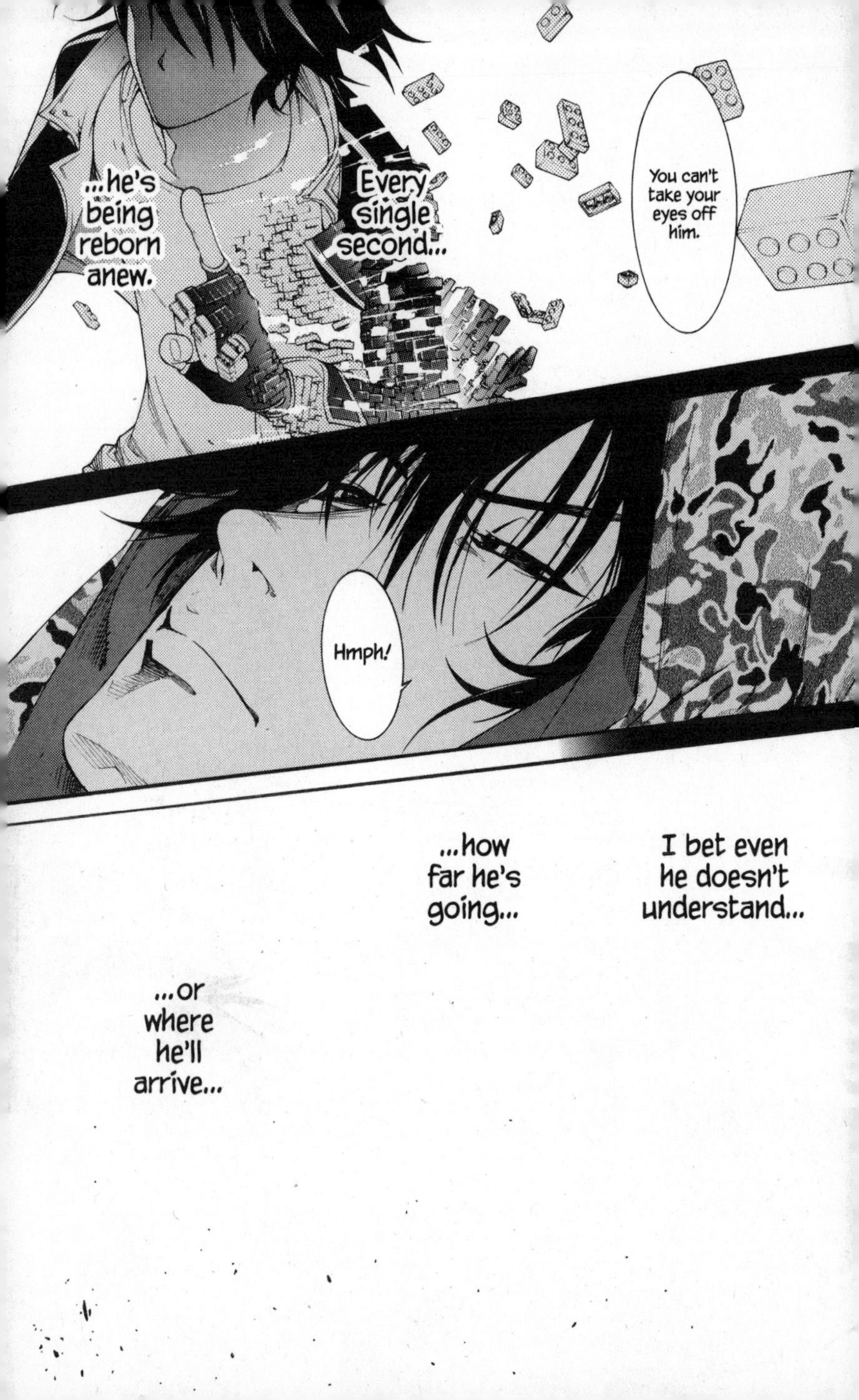

You can't take your eyes off him.
Every single second...
...he's being reborn anew.
Hmph!
I bet even he doesn't understand...
...how far he's going...
...or where he'll arrive...

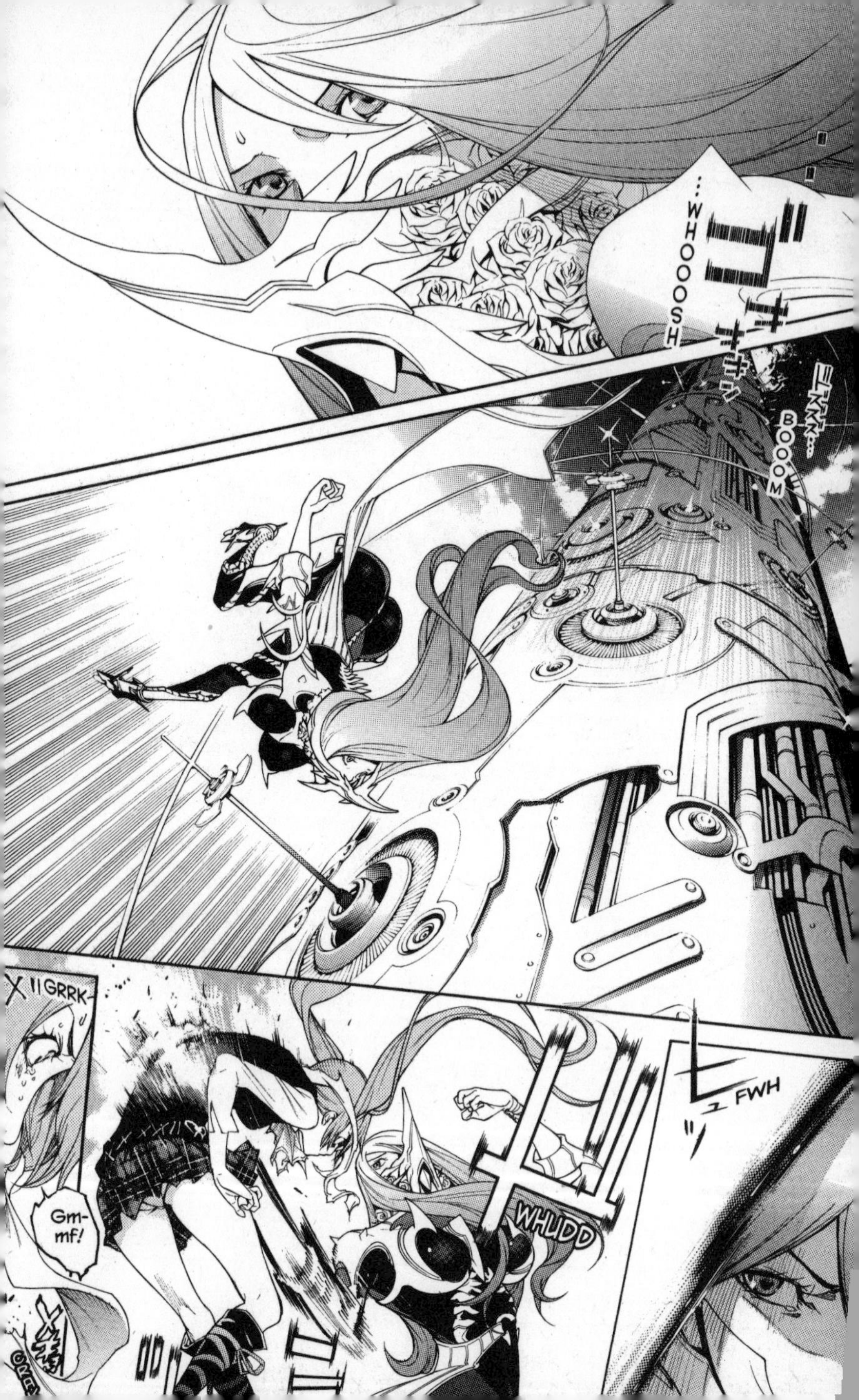

WHOOOSH...
BOOOM
FWH
WHUDD
GRRK
Gm-mf!

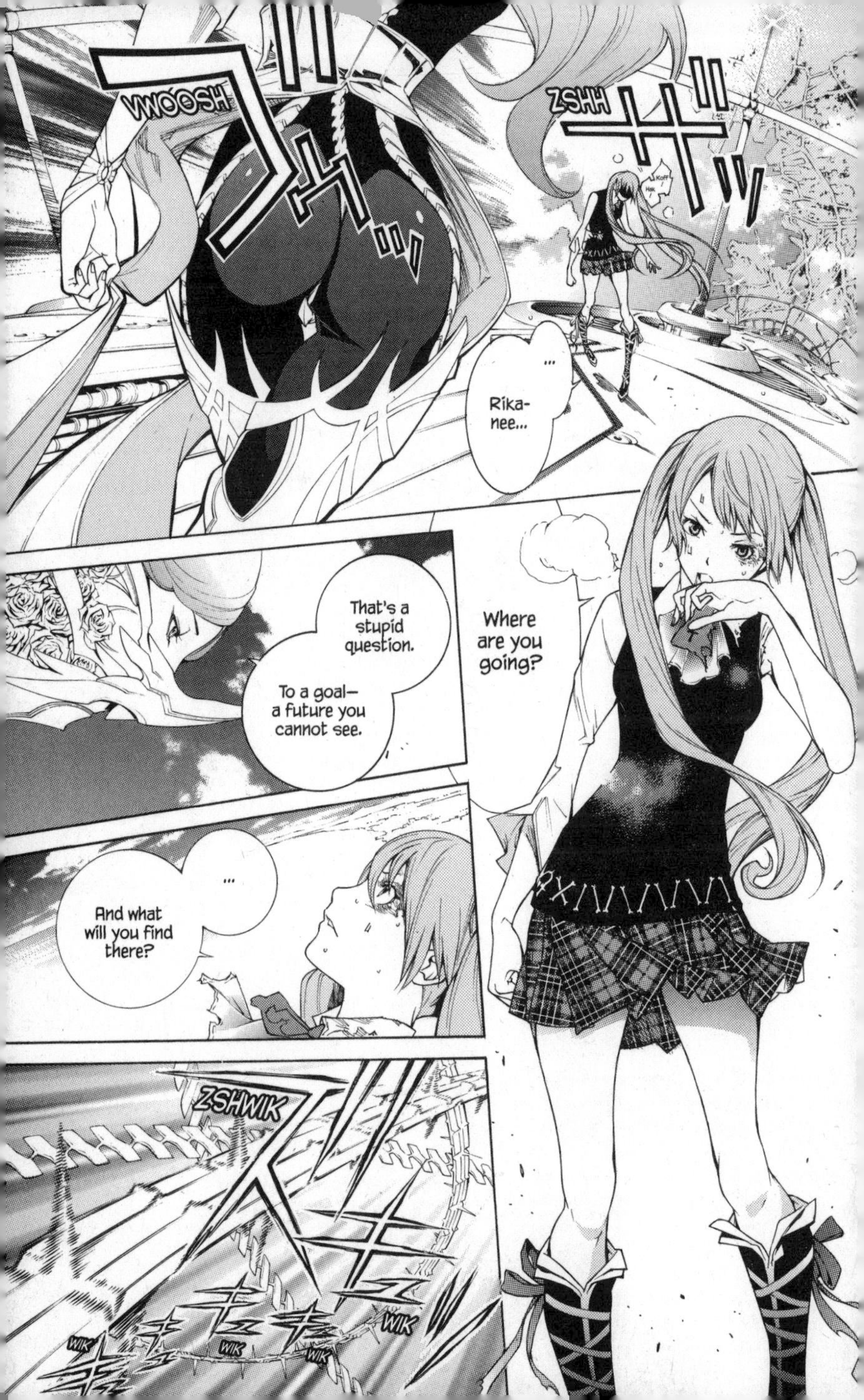
ZSHH
Koff
Hak
...
Rika-nee...
VWOOSH
Where are you going?
That's a stupid question.
To a goal— a future you cannot see.
...
And what will you find there?
ZSHWIK
WIK
WIK
WIK
WIK

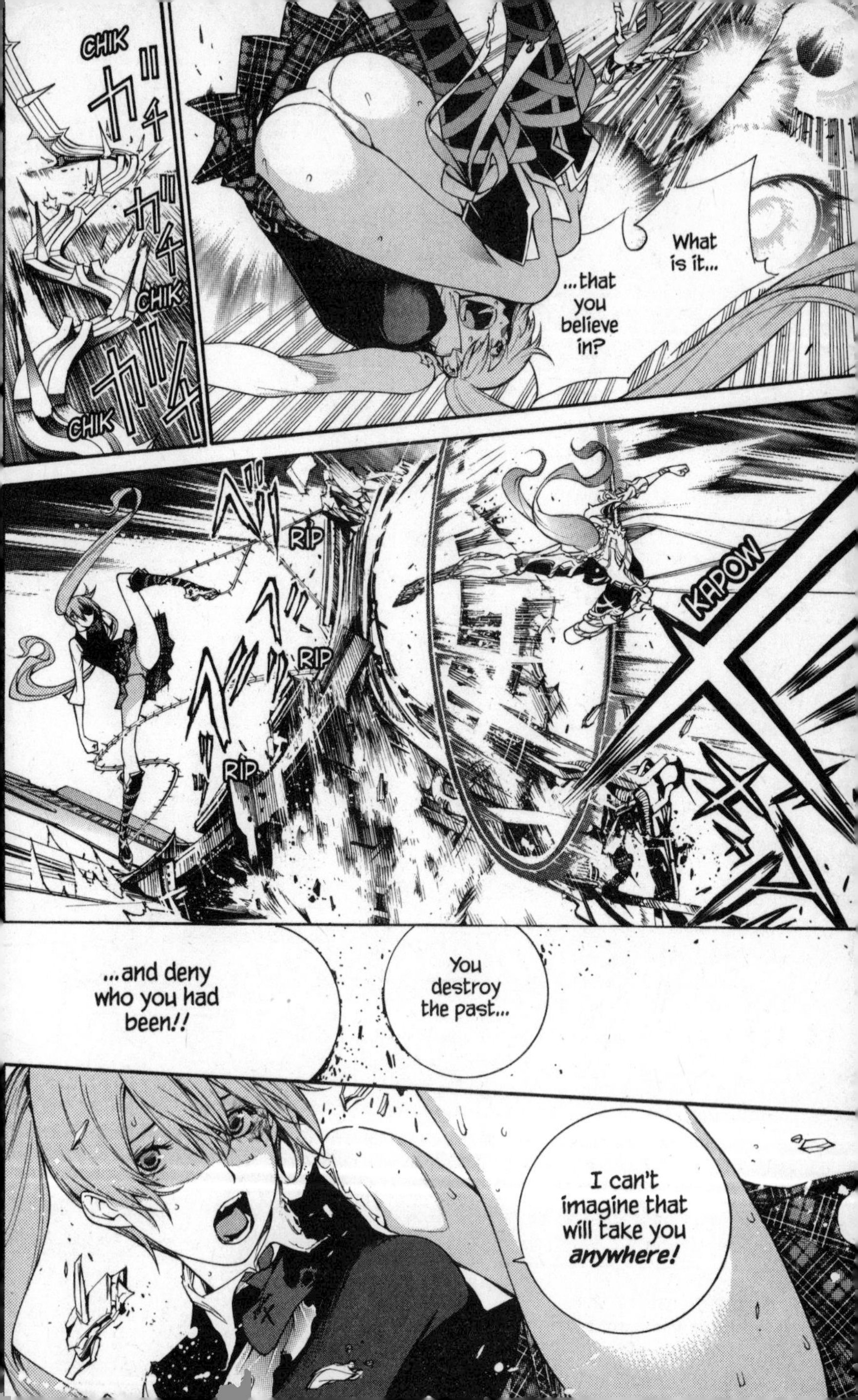
What is it...
...that you believe in?
CHIK
CHIK
CHIK
KAPOW
RIP
RIP
RIP
You destroy the past...
...and deny who you had been!!
I can't imagine that will take you *anywhere!*

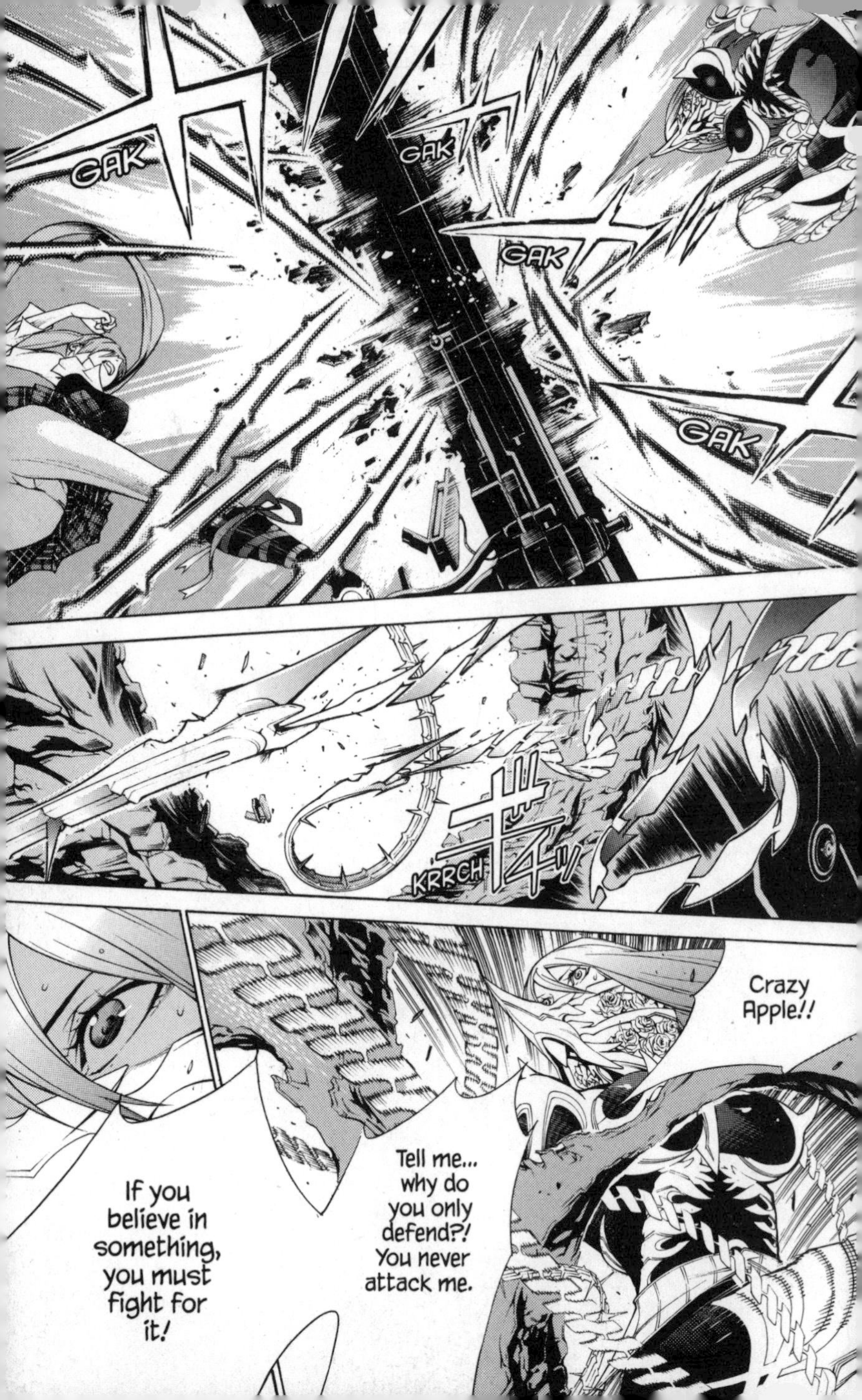
GAK
GAK
GAK
GAK
KRRCH
Crazy Apple!!
Tell me... why do you only defend?! You never attack me.
If you believe in something, you must fight for it!

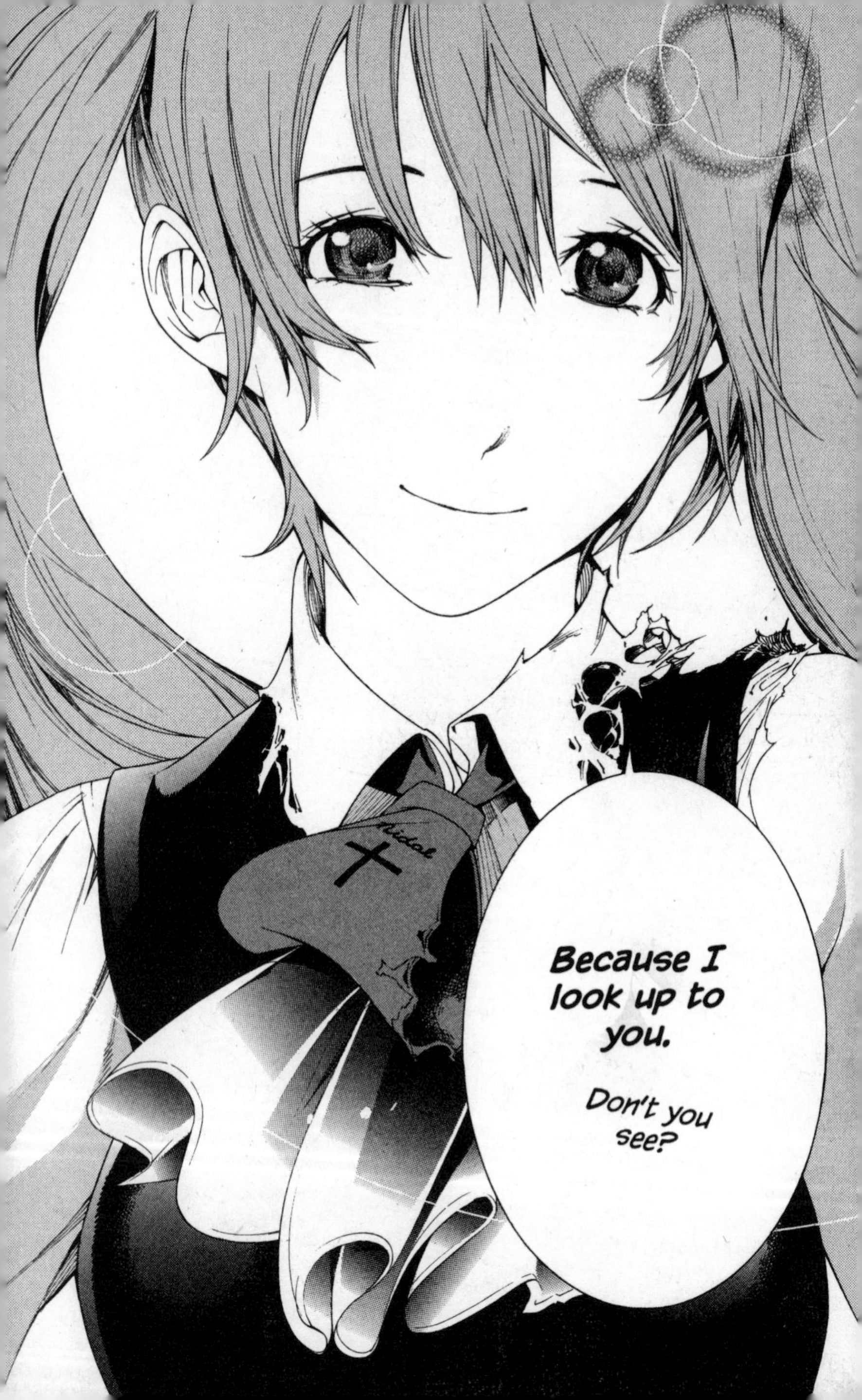
Because I look up to you.
Don't you see?

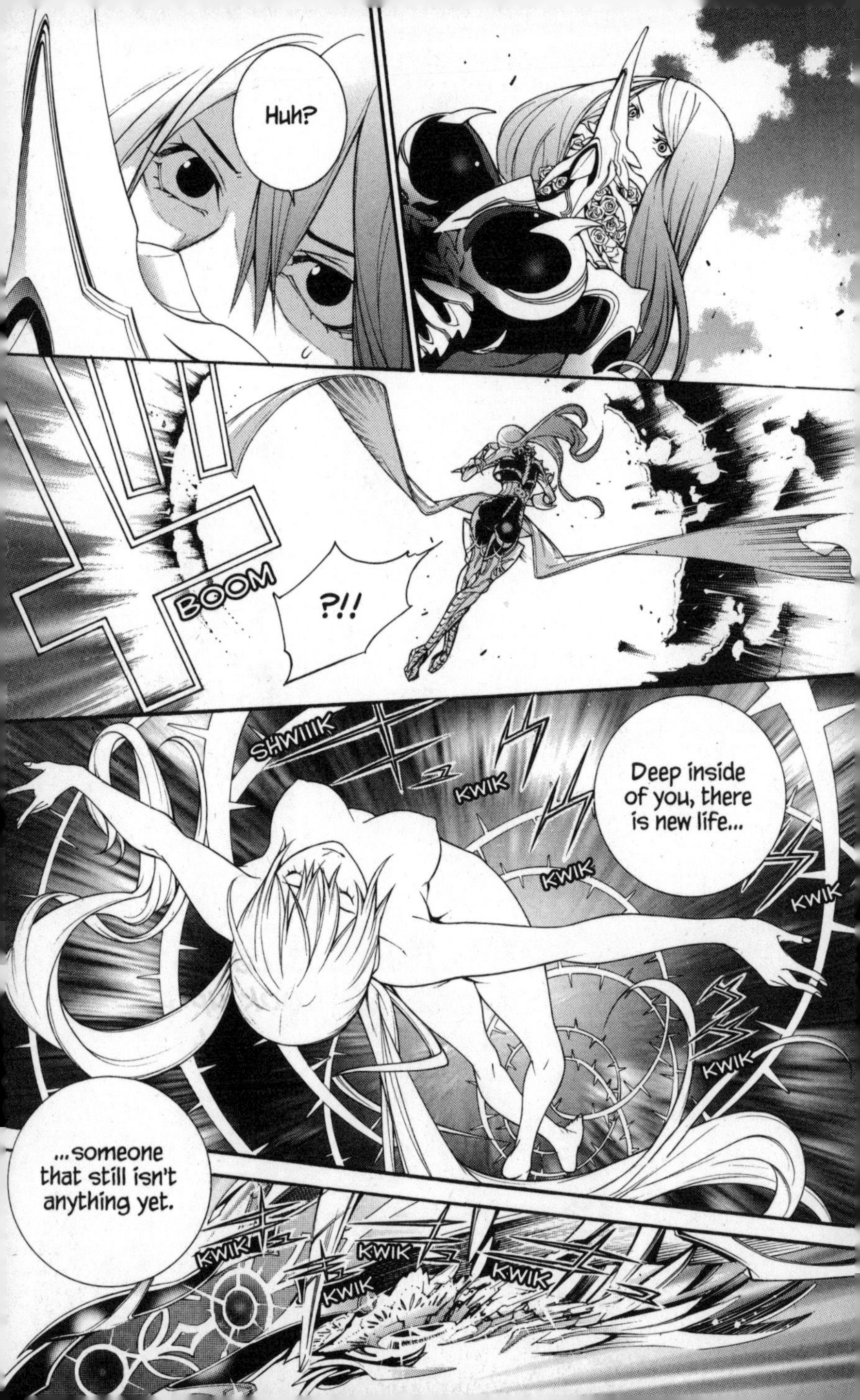
Huh?
BOOM
?!!
Deep inside of you, there is new life...
SHWIIIK
KWIK
KWIK
KWIK
KWIK
...someone that still isn't anything yet.
KWIK
KWIK
KWIK
KWIK

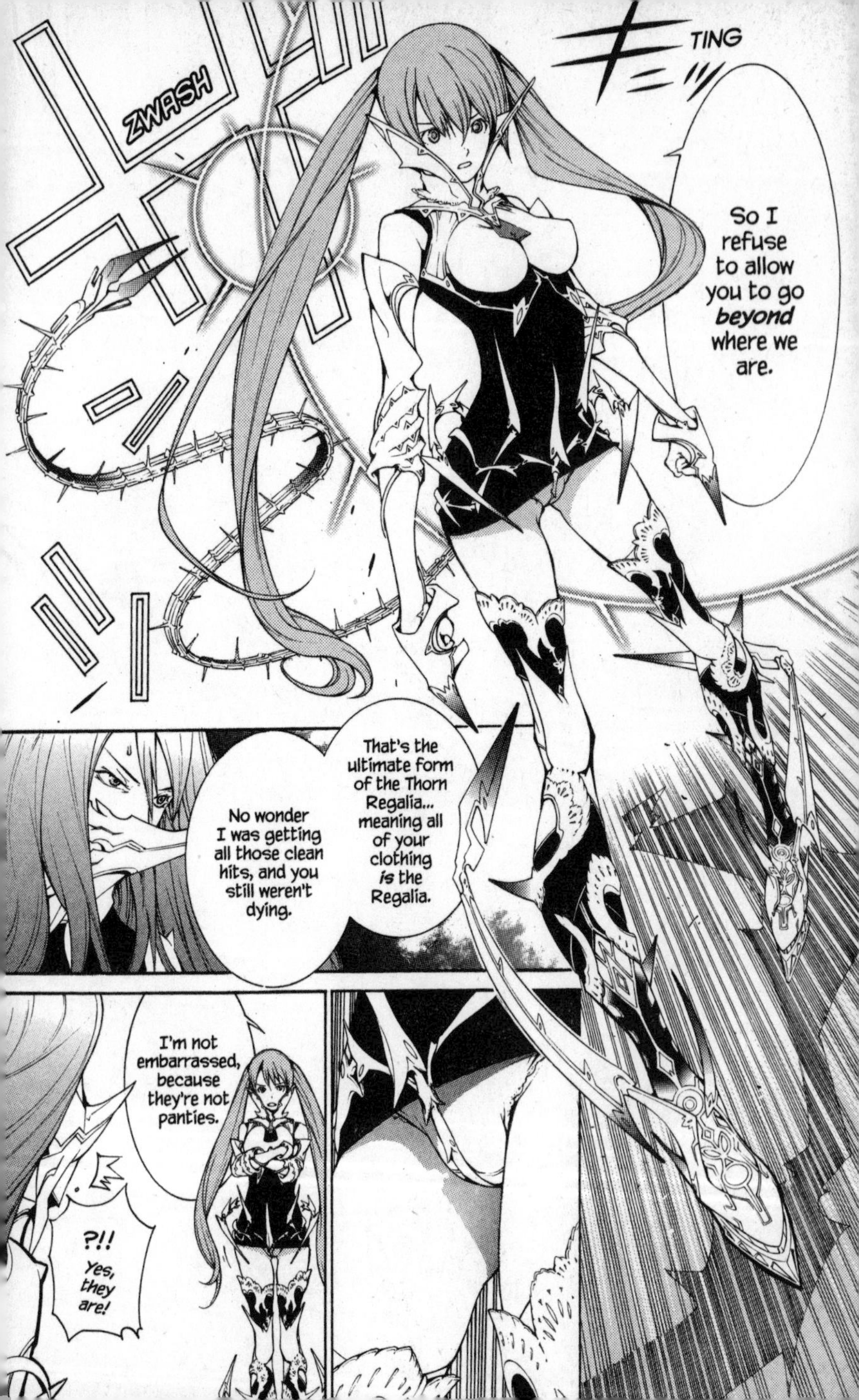
TING
So I refuse to allow you to go ***beyond*** where we are.
ZWASH
That's the ultimate form of the Thorn Regalia... meaning all of your clothing *is* the Regalia.
No wonder I was getting all those clean hits, and you still weren't dying.
I'm not embarrassed, because they're not panties.
?!! *Yes, they are!*

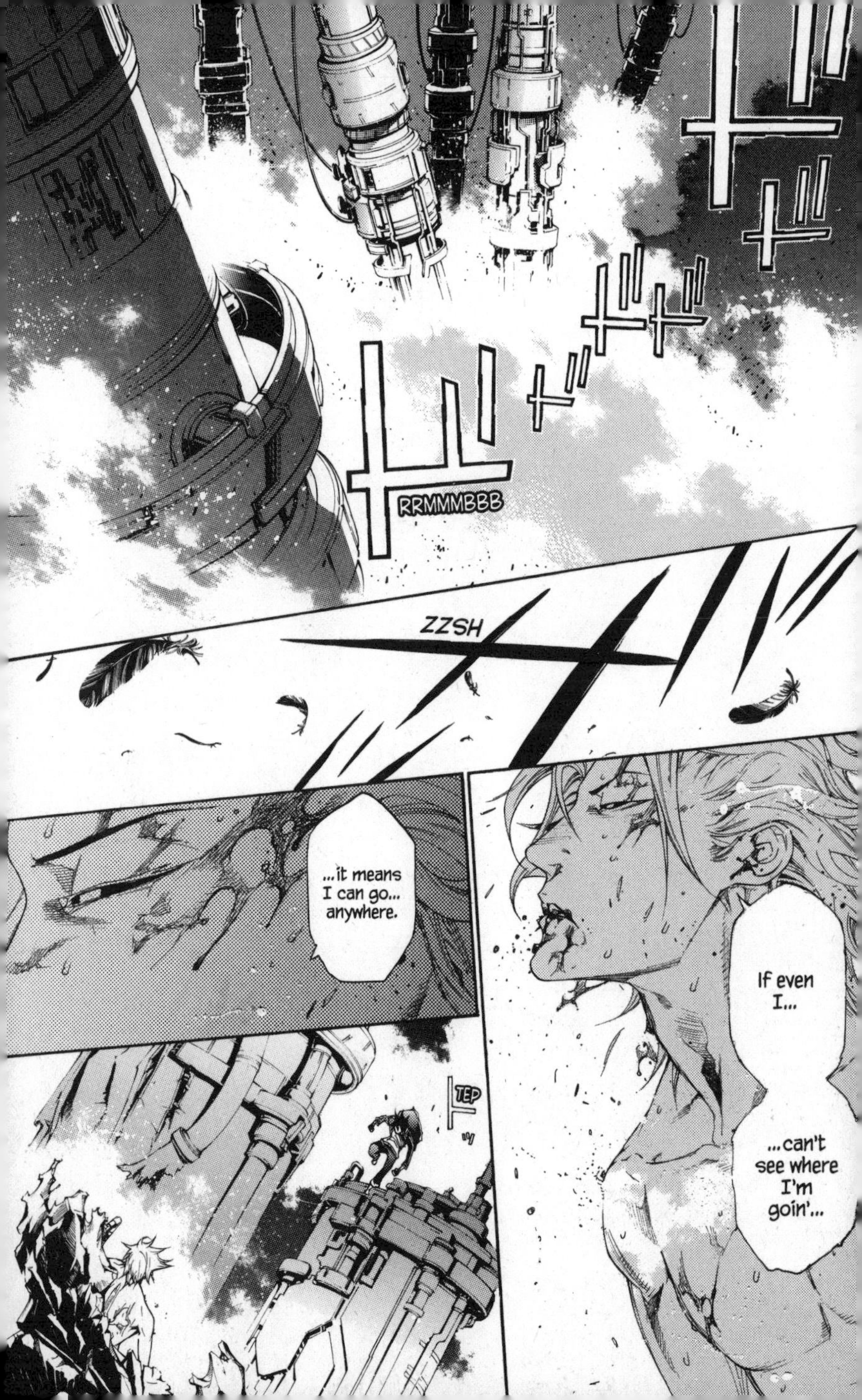
RRMMMBBB
ZZSH
If even I...
...can't see where I'm goin'...
...it means I can go... anywhere.
TEP

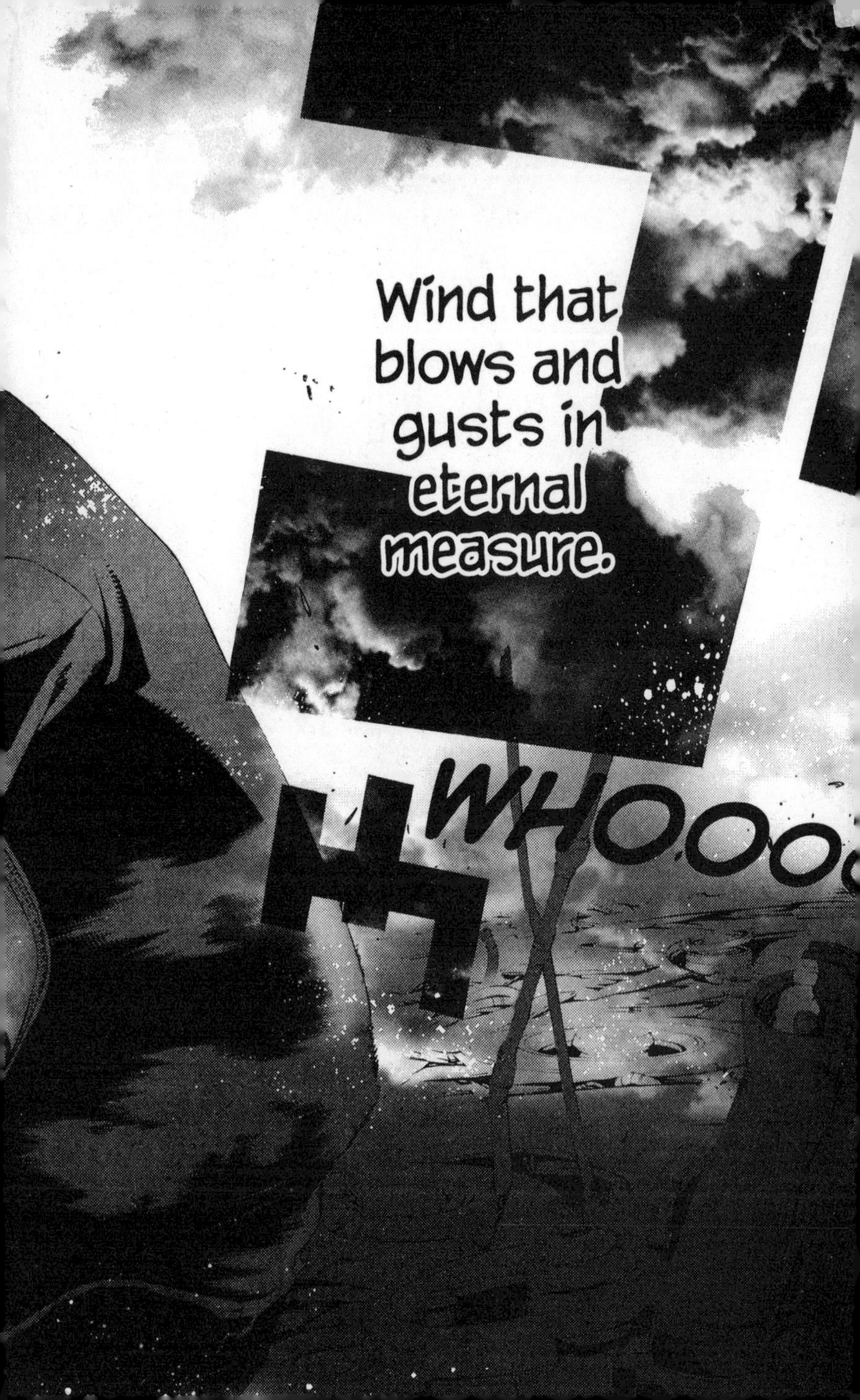
Wind that blows and gusts in eternal measure.
WHOOOO

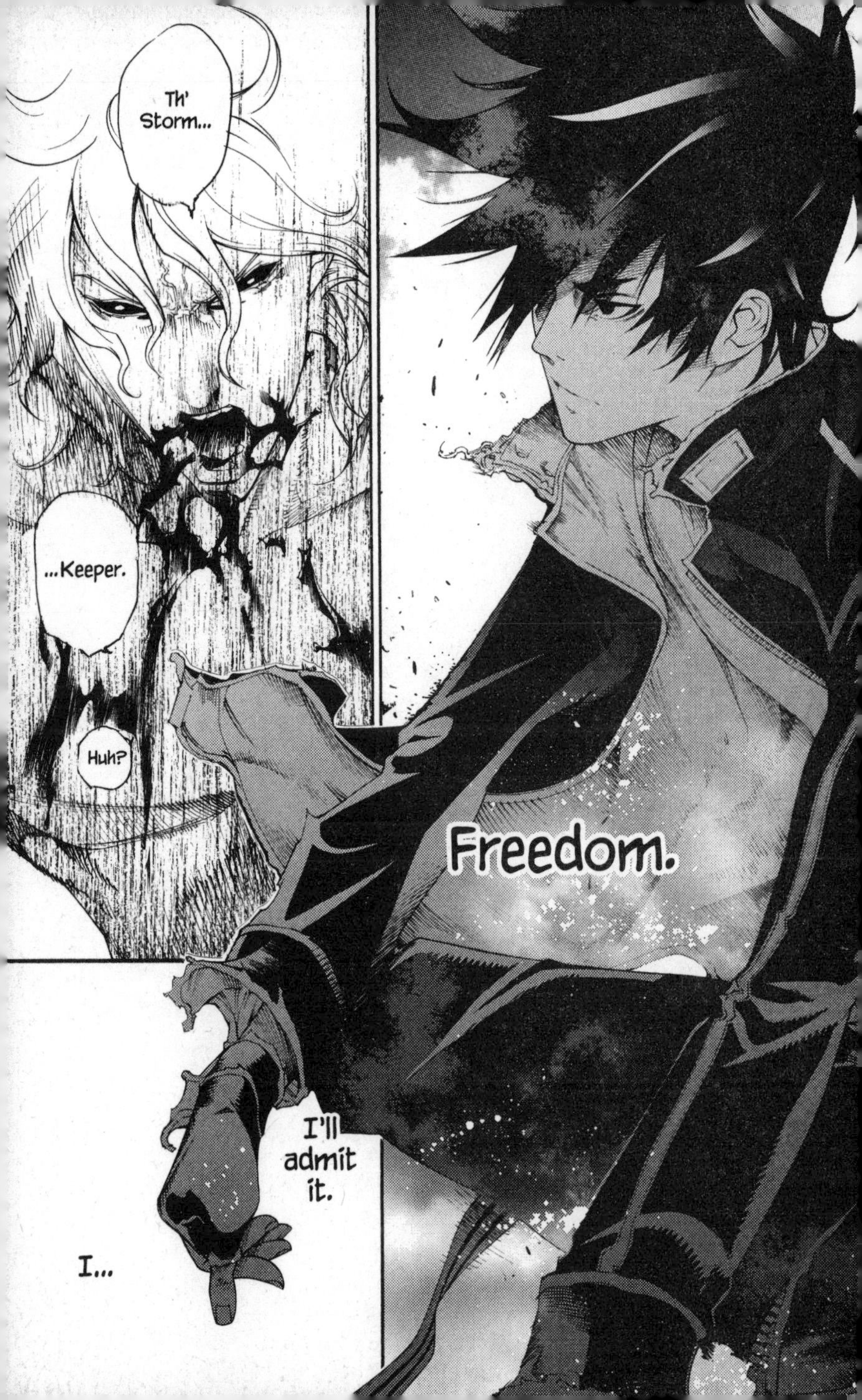
Freedom.
Th' Storm...
...Keeper.
Huh?
I'll admit it.
I...

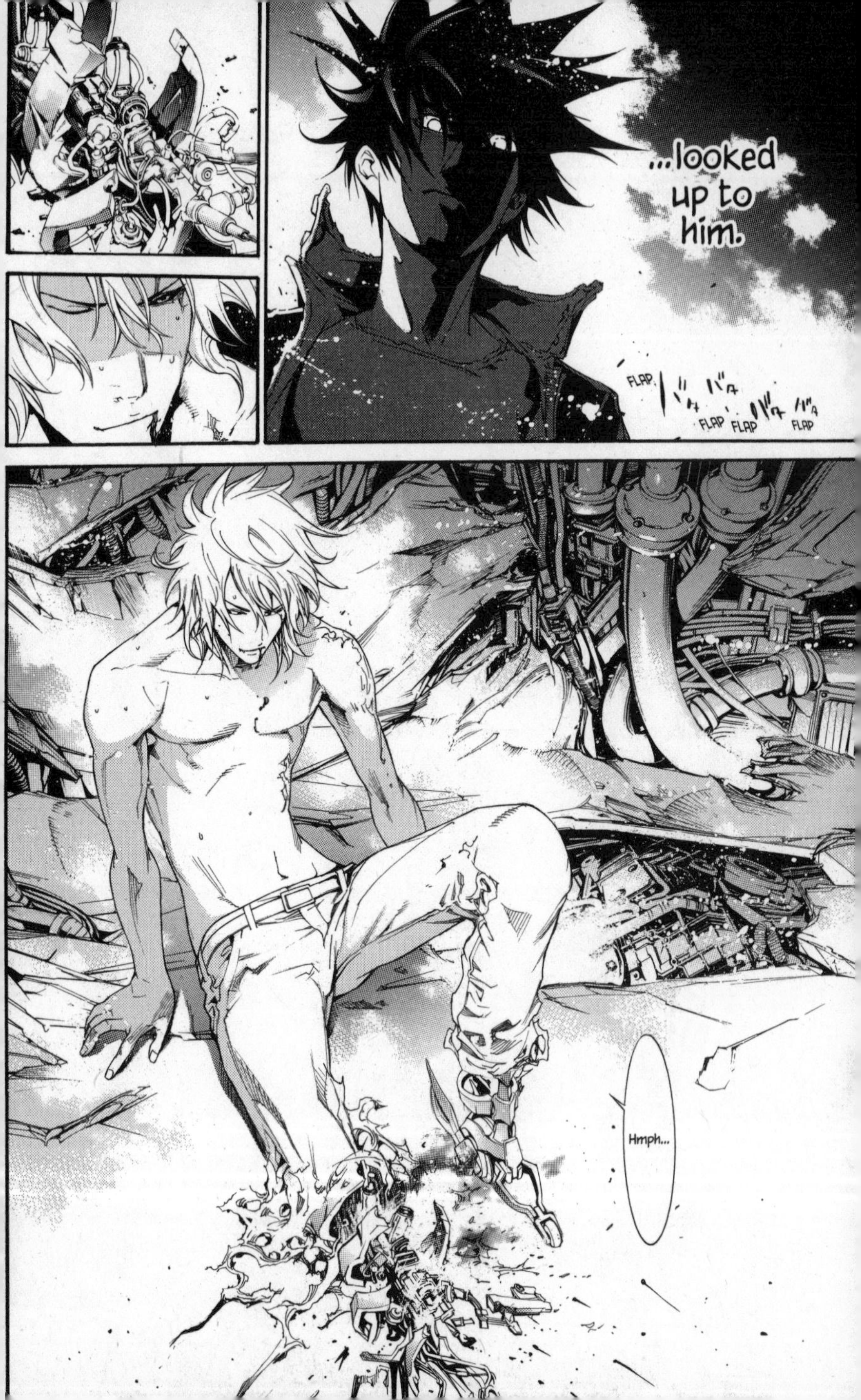
...looked up to him.
FLAP FLAP FLAP FLAP
バッ バァ バッ バァ
Hmph...

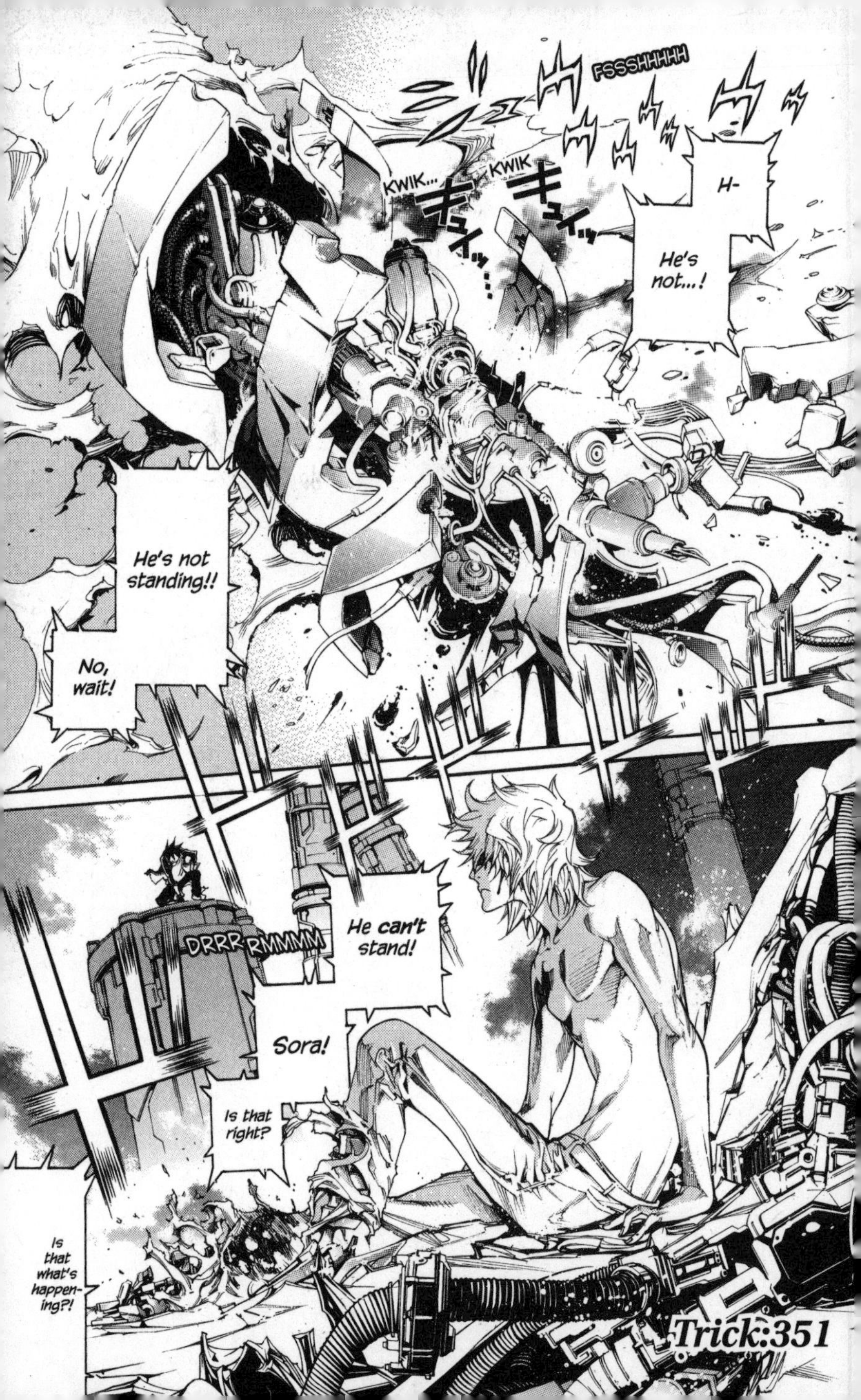
FSSSHHHHH
H-
He's not...!
KWIK... KWIK
He's not standing!!
No, wait!
He can't stand!
DRRR RMMMM
Sora!
Is that right?
Is that what's happening?!
Trick:351

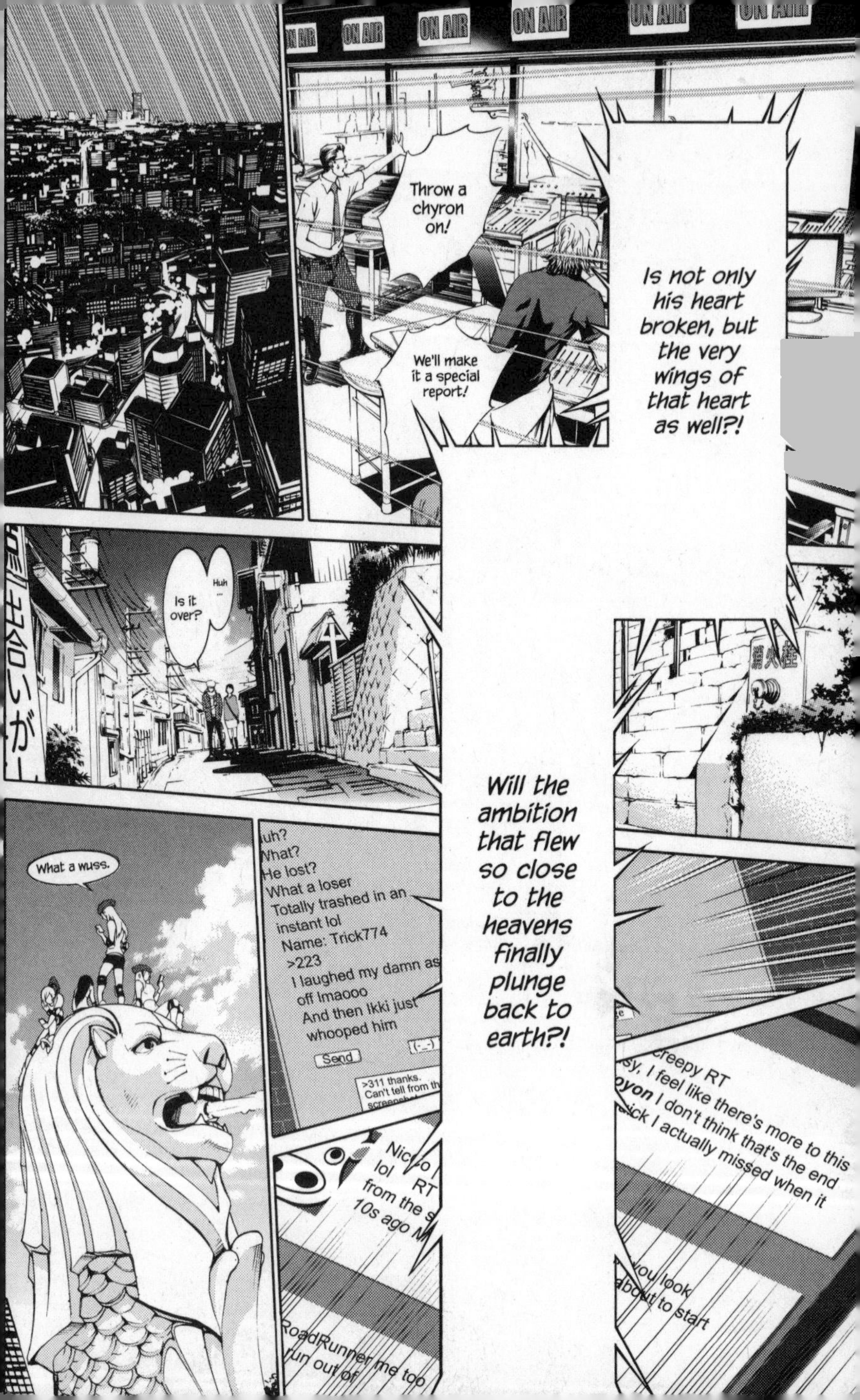
Throw a chyron on!
We'll make it a special report!
Is not only his heart broken, but the very wings of that heart as well?!
Huh...
Is it over?
Will the ambition that flew so close to the heavens finally plunge back to earth?!
creepy RT
sy, I feel like there's more to this
oyon I don't think that's the end
ck I actually missed when it
you look
about to start
Huh?
What?
He lost?
What a loser
Totally trashed in an instant lol
Name: Trick774
>223
I laughed my damn as
off lmaooo
And then Ikki just whooped him
Send
(-_-)
>311 thanks.
Can't tell from th
lol RT
from the s
10s ago
RoadRunner me too
run out of
What a wuss.

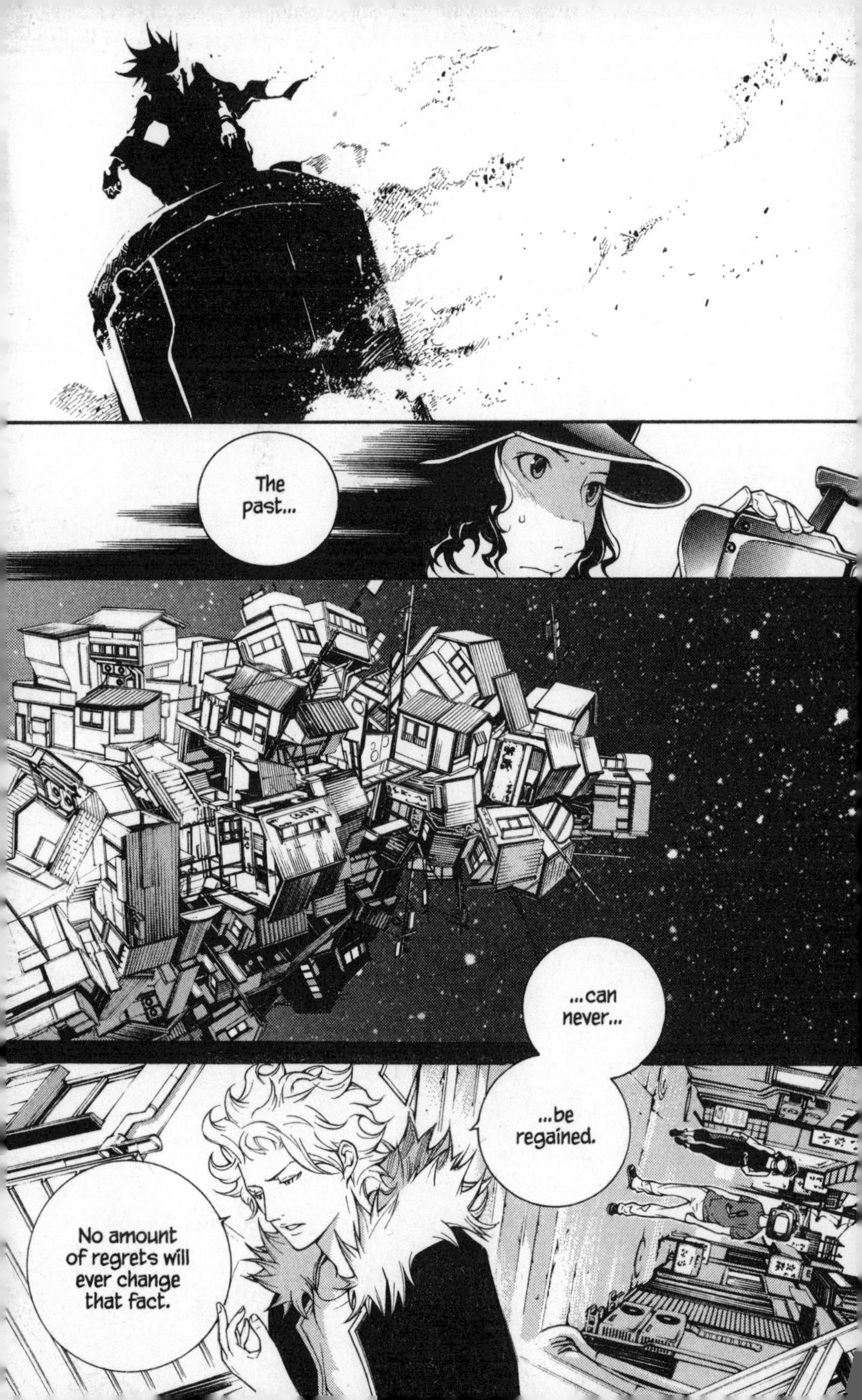
The past...
...can never...
...be regained.
No amount of regrets will ever change that fact.

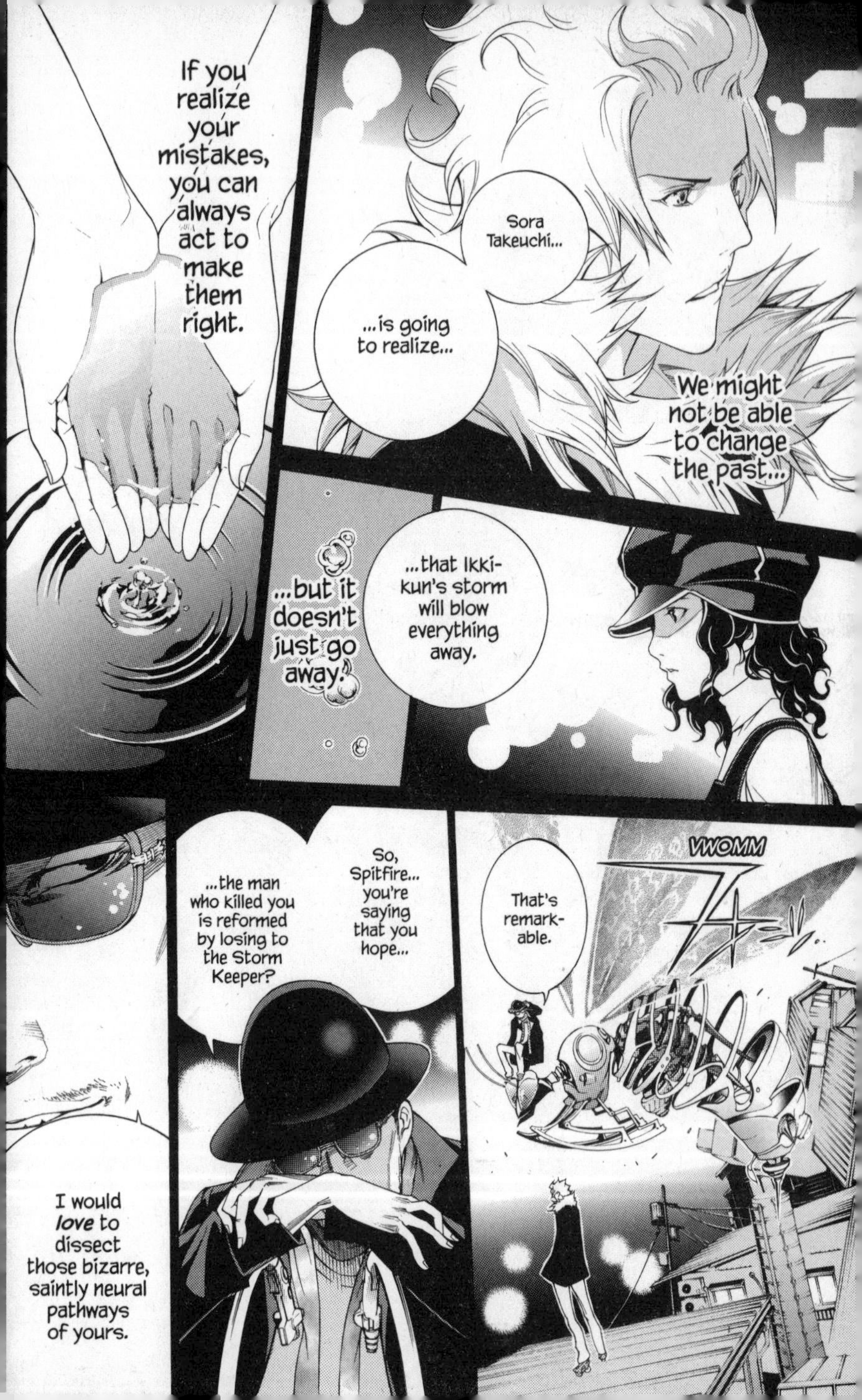
Sora Takeuchi...
...is going to realize...
...that Ikki-kun's storm will blow everything away.
We might not be able to change the past...
...but it doesn't just go away.
If you realize your mistakes, you can always act to make them right.
VWOMM
That's remark-able.
So, Spitfire... you're saying that you hope...
...the man who killed you is reformed by losing to the Storm Keeper?
I would *love* to dissect those bizarre, saintly neural pathways of yours.

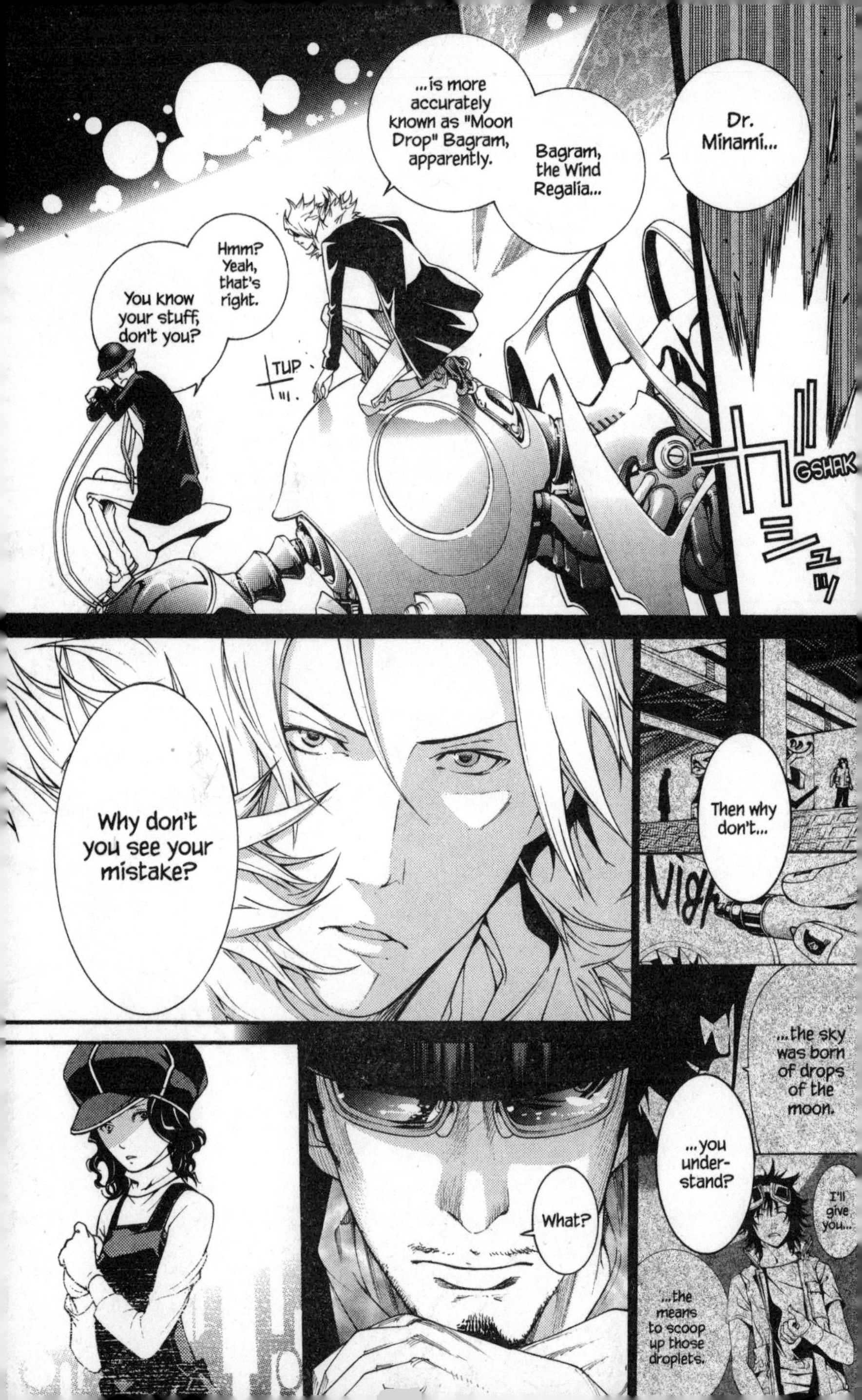
Dr. Minami...
Bagram, the Wind Regalia...
...is more accurately known as "Moon Drop" Bagram, apparently.
Hmm? Yeah, that's right.
You know your stuff, don't you?
TUP
GSHAK
Then why don't...
Why don't you see your mistake?
...the sky was born of drops of the moon.
...you under-stand?
I'll give you...
...the means to scoop up those droplets.
What?

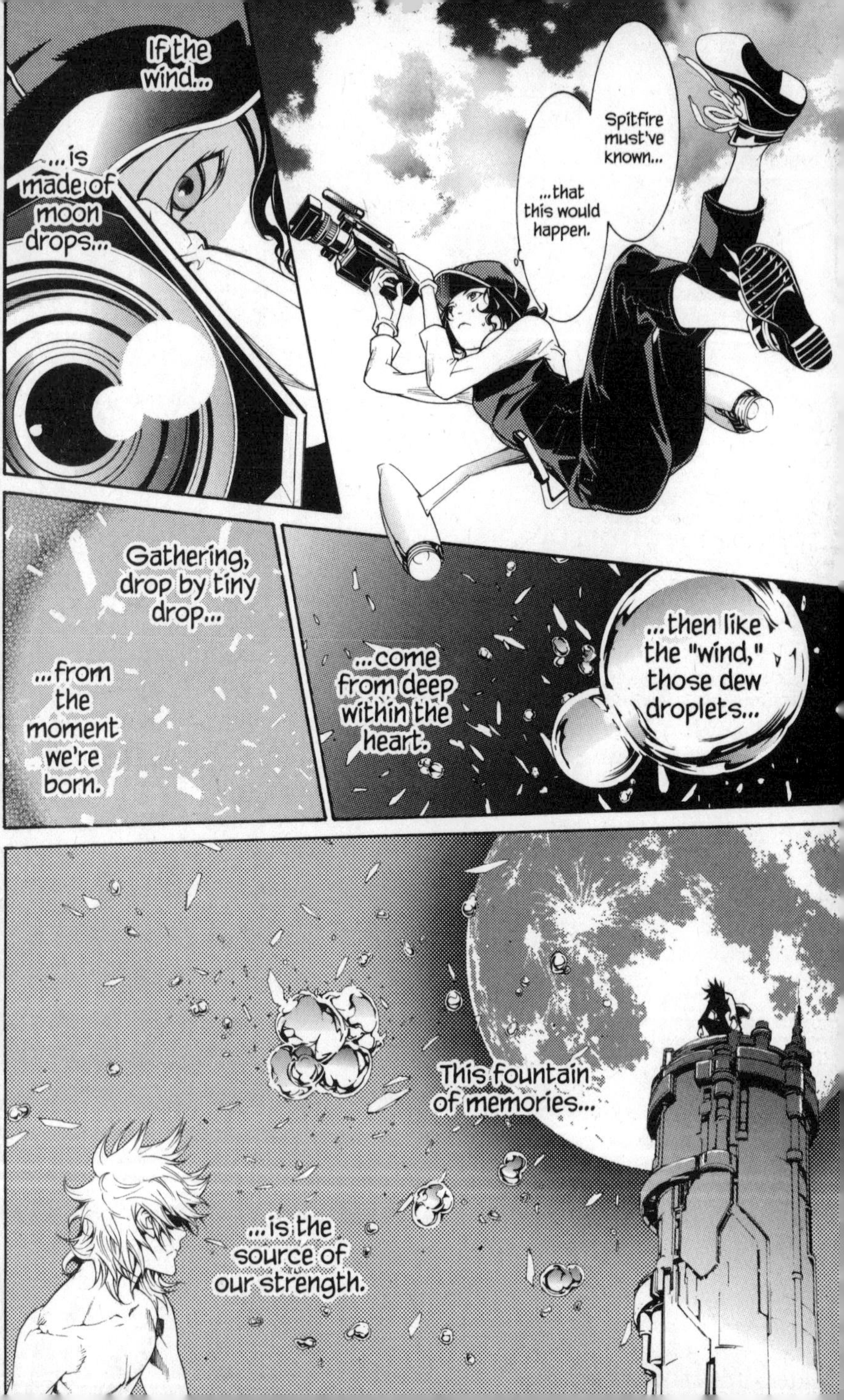
Spitfire must've known...
...that this would happen.
If the wind...
...is made of moon drops...
...then like the "wind," those dew droplets...
...come from deep within the heart.
Gathering, drop by tiny drop...
...from the moment we're born.
This fountain of memories...
...is the source of our strength.

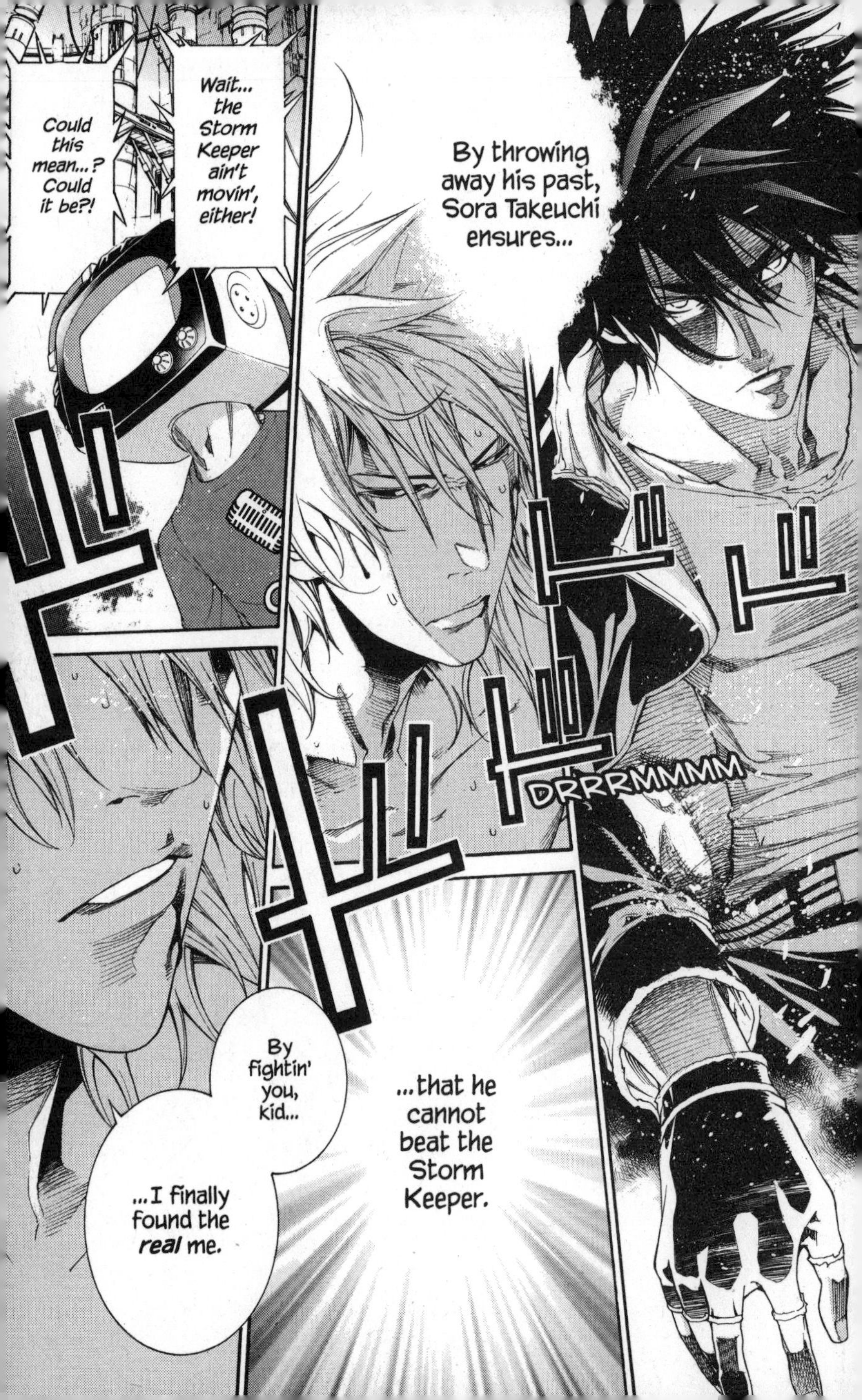
By throwing away his past, Sora Takeuchi ensures...
DRRRMMMM
...that he cannot beat the Storm Keeper.
Wait... the Storm Keeper ain't movin', either!
Could this mean...? Could it be?!
By fightin' you, kid...
...I finally found the *real* me.

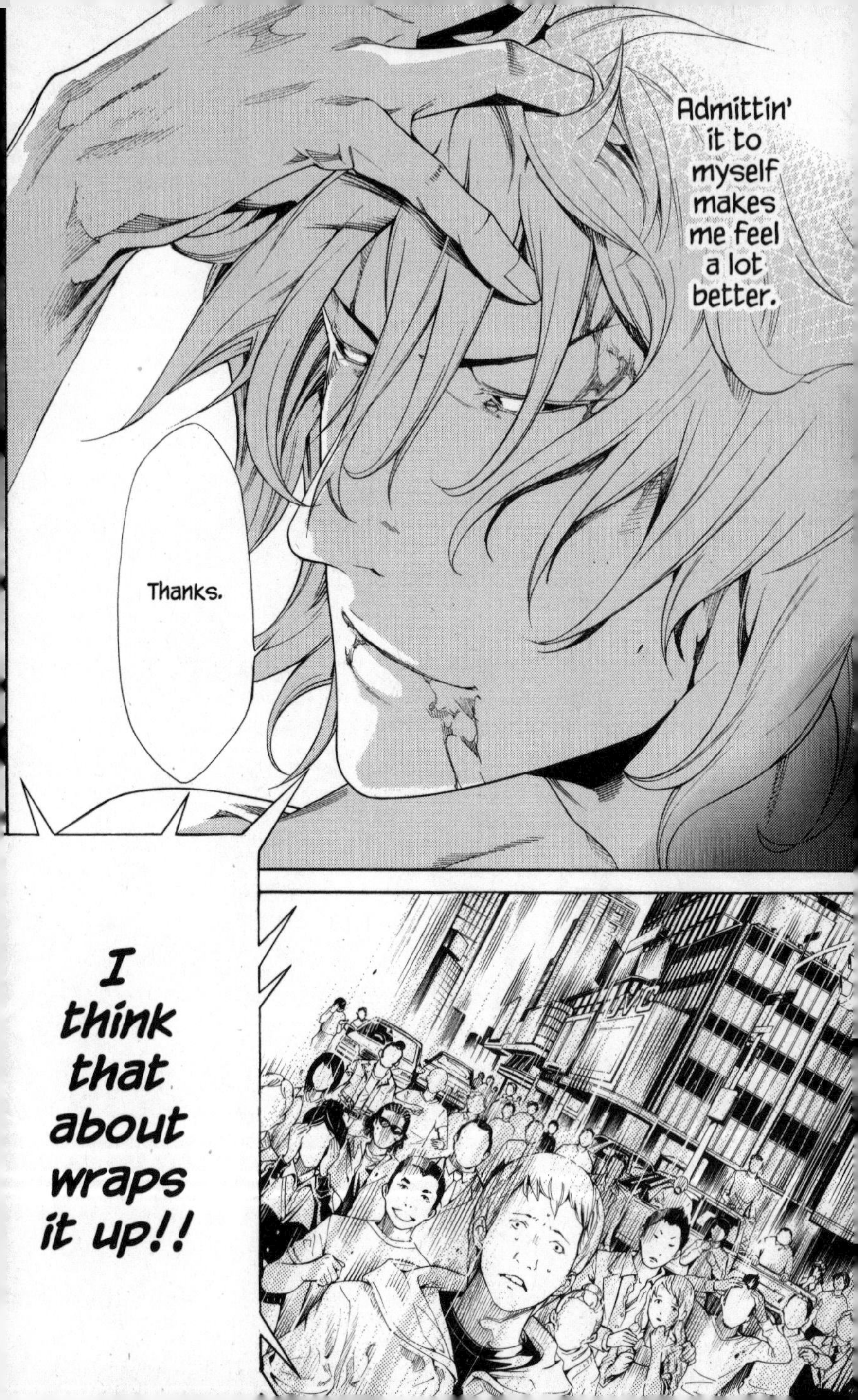
Admittin' it to myself makes me feel a lot better.
Thanks.
I think that about wraps it up!!

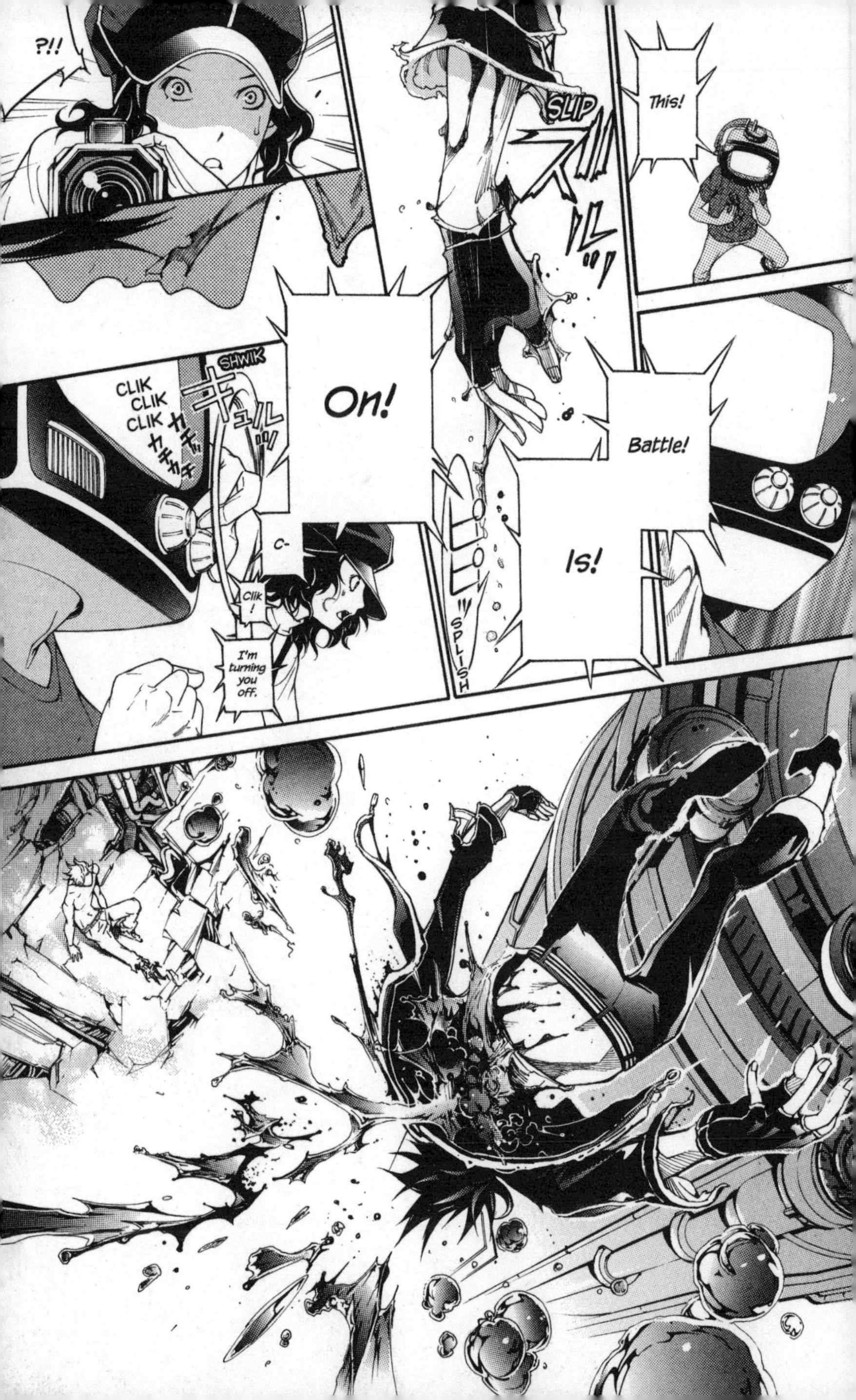
This!
SLIP
?!!
Battle!
Is!
SPLISH
On!
SHWIK
CLIK CLIK CLIK
C-
Clik!
I'm turning you off.

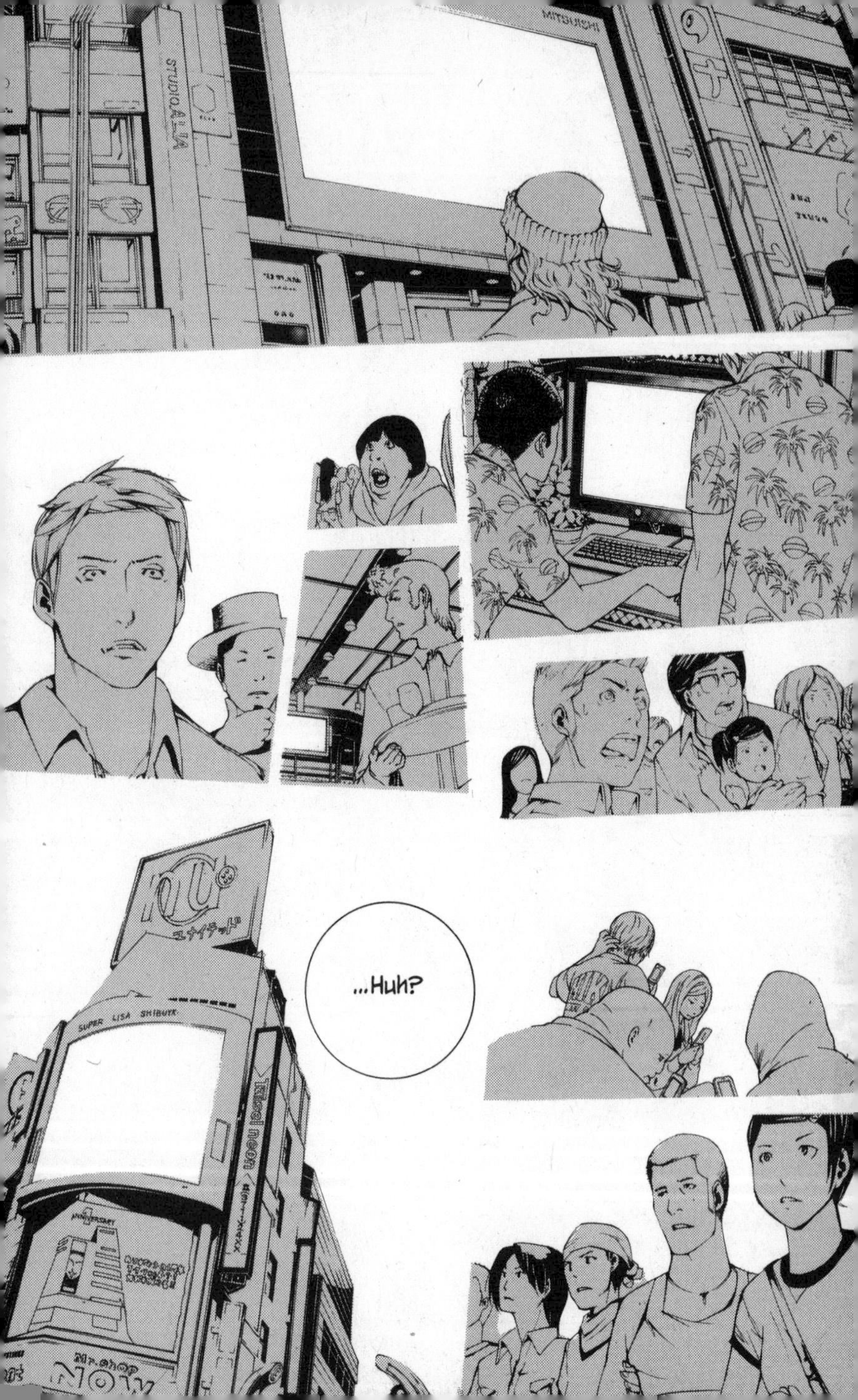
STUDIO ALTA
MITSUISHI
...Huh?
SUPER LISA SHIBUYA
Mr.shop

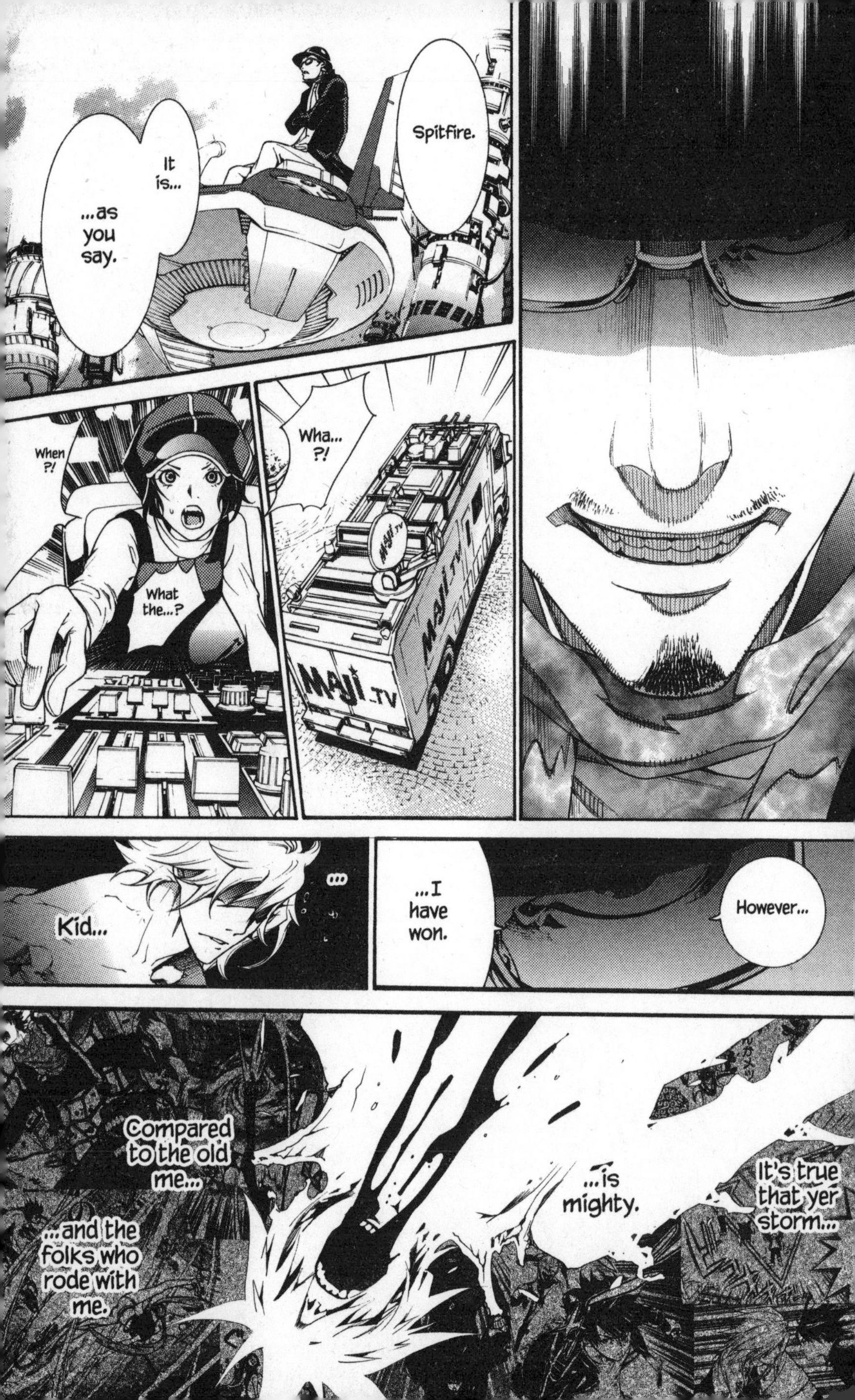
Spitfire.
It is...
...as you say.
Wha...?!
When?!
What the...?
However...
...I have won.
...
Kid...
It's true that yer storm...
...is mighty.
Compared to the old me...
...and the folks who rode with me.

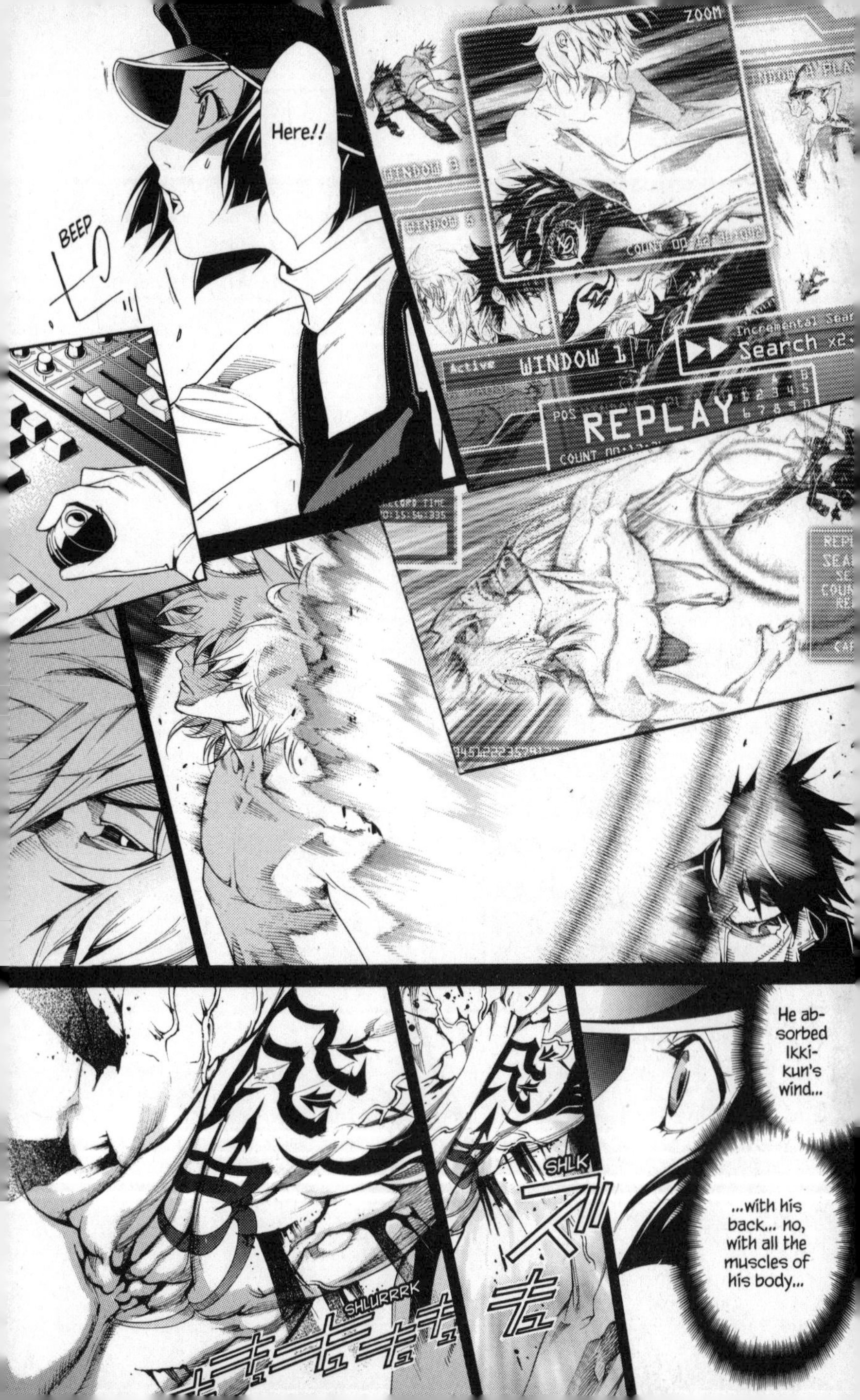
ZOOM
WINDOW 1
Active
Search x2
Incremental Search
REPLAY
POS
COUNT
RECORD TIME
00:15:56:335
BEEP
Here!!
He absorbed Ikki-kun's wind...
SHLK
...with his back... no, with all the muscles of his body...
SHLURRRK

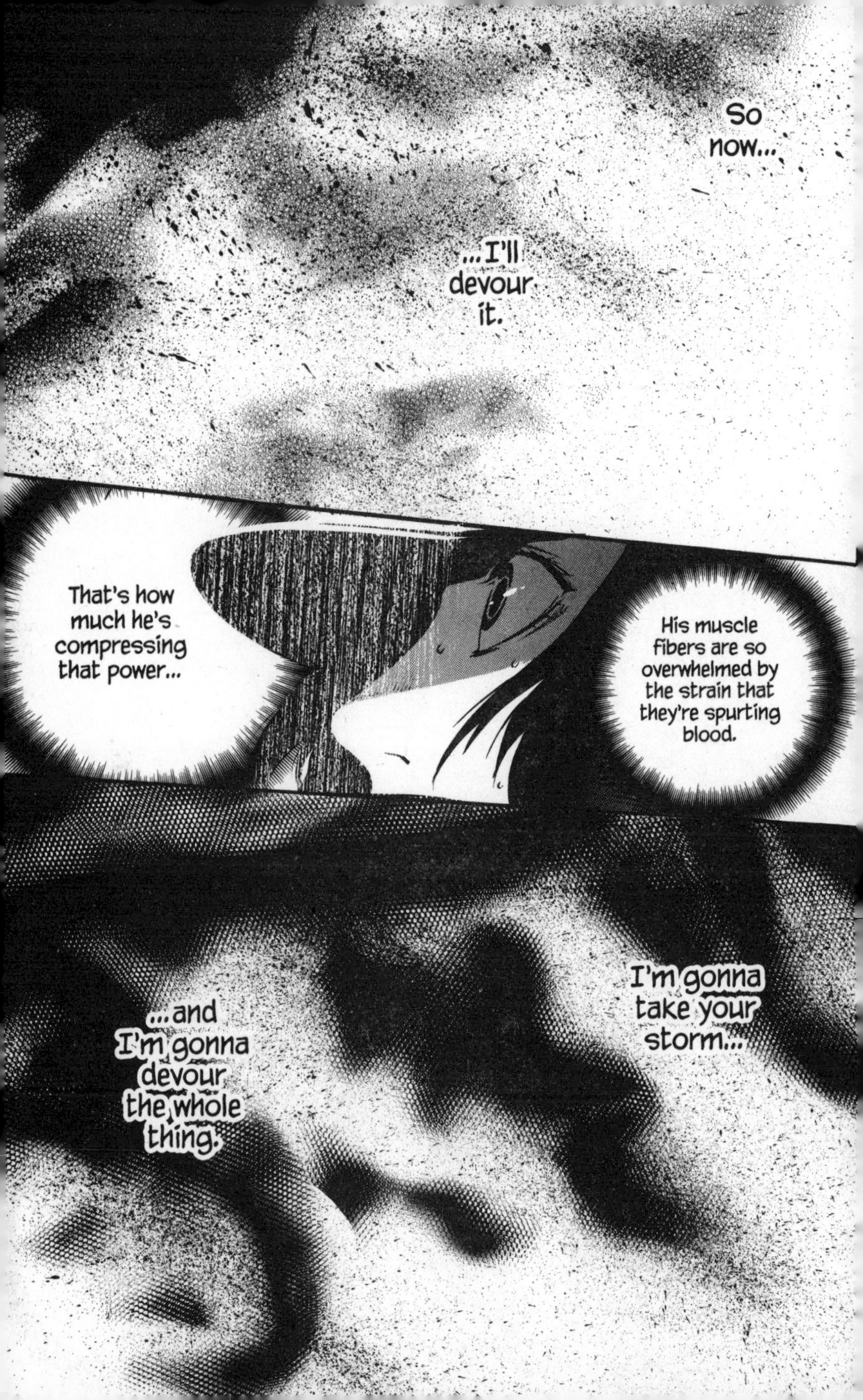
So now...
...I'll devour it.
His muscle fibers are so overwhelmed by the strain that they're spurting blood.
That's how much he's compressing that power...
I'm gonna take your storm...
...and I'm gonna devour the whole thing.

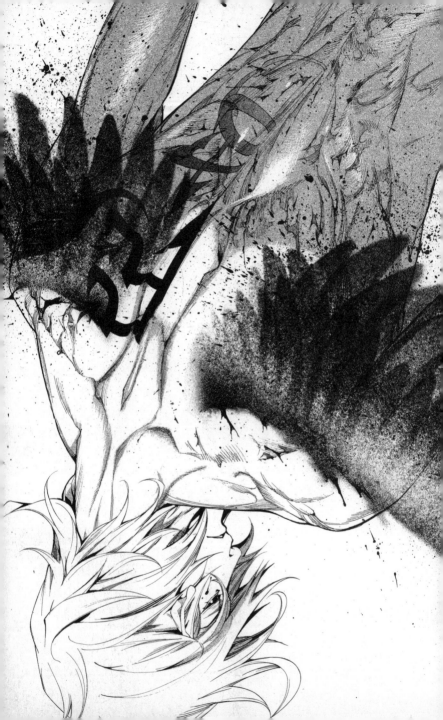

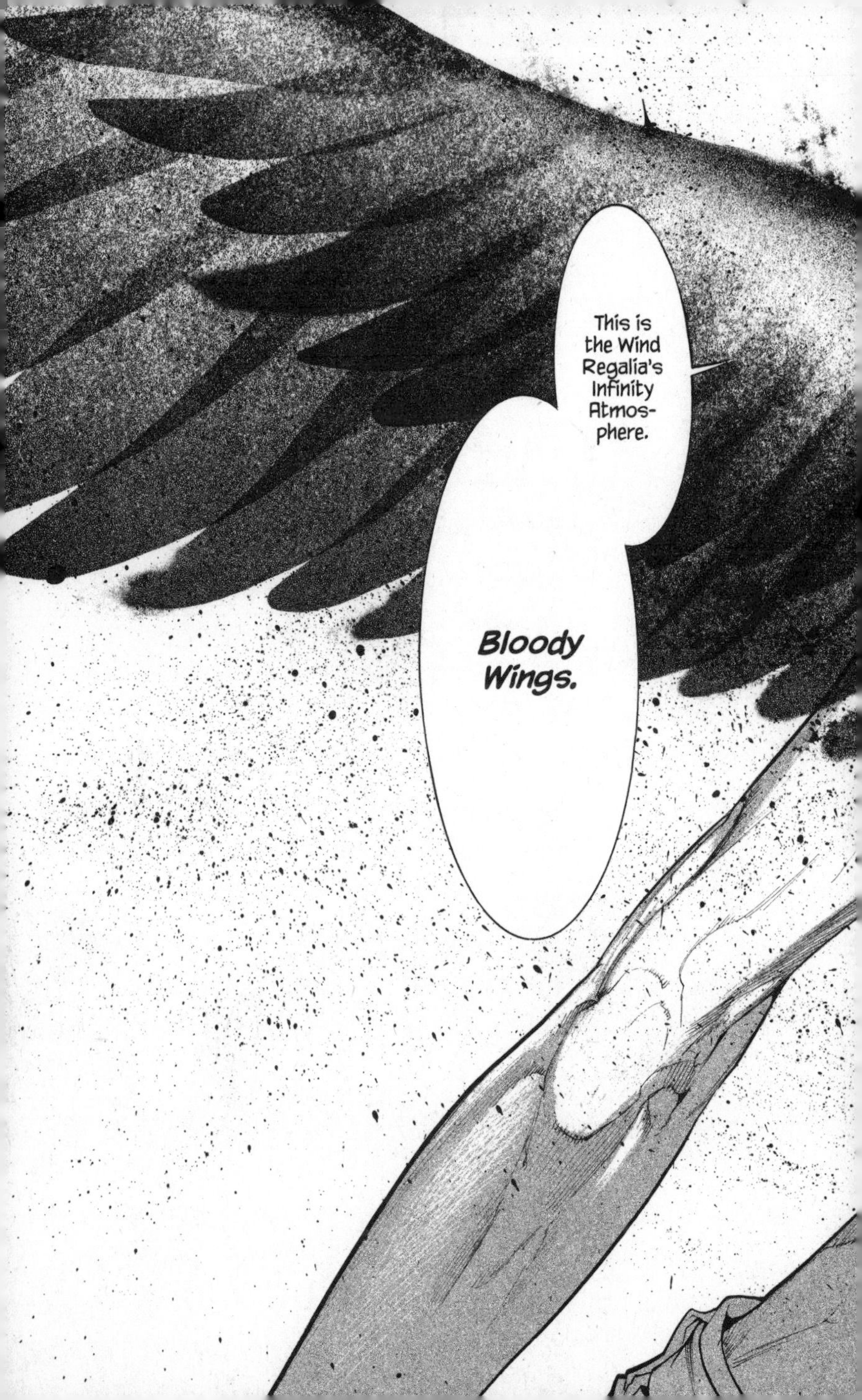
This is the Wind Regalia's Infinity Atmos- phere.
Bloody Wings.

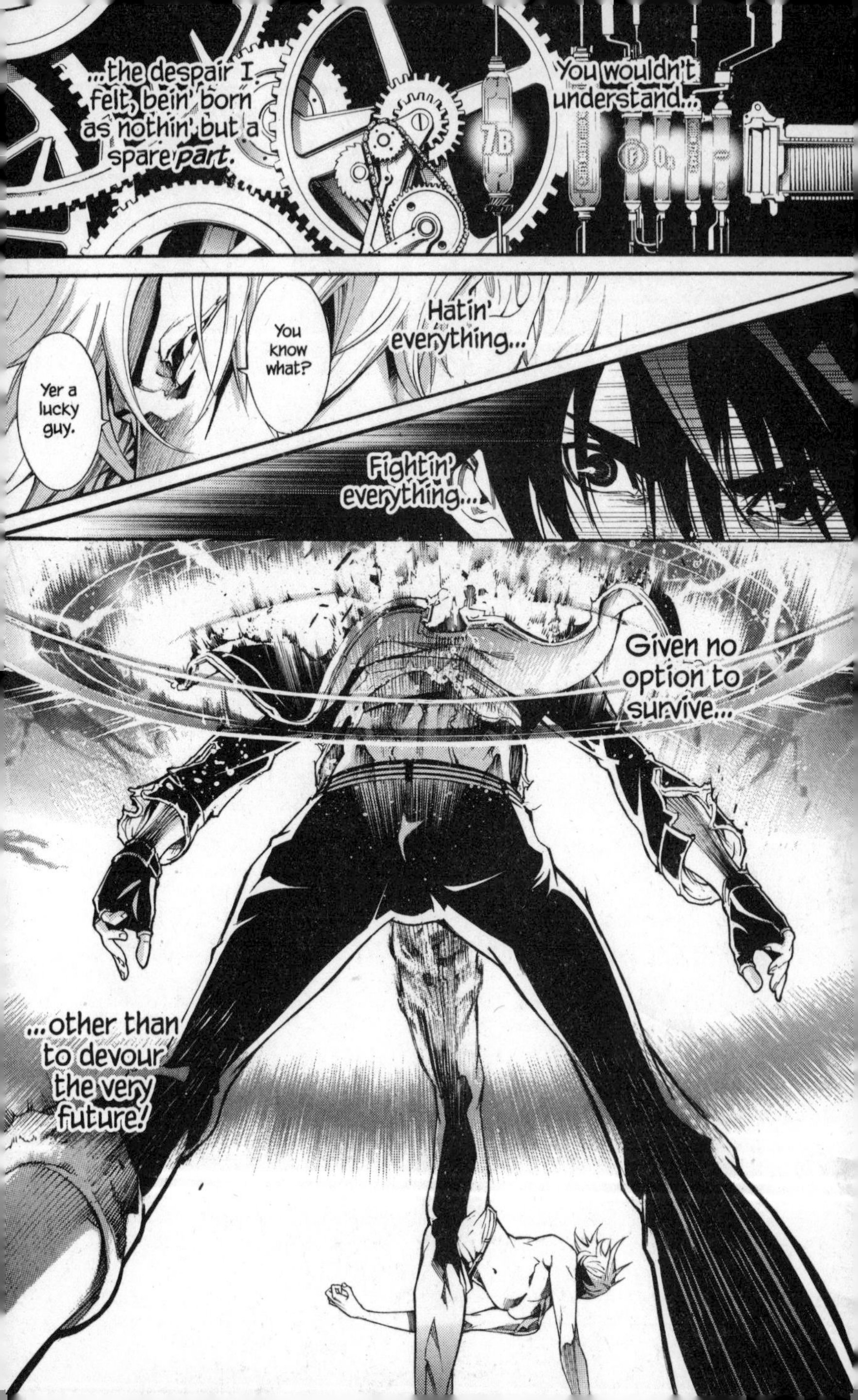

You wouldn't understand...
...the despair I felt, bein' born as nothin' but a spare part.
Hatin' everything...
You know what?
Yer a lucky guy.
Fightin' everything...
Given no option to survive...
...other than to devour the very future!

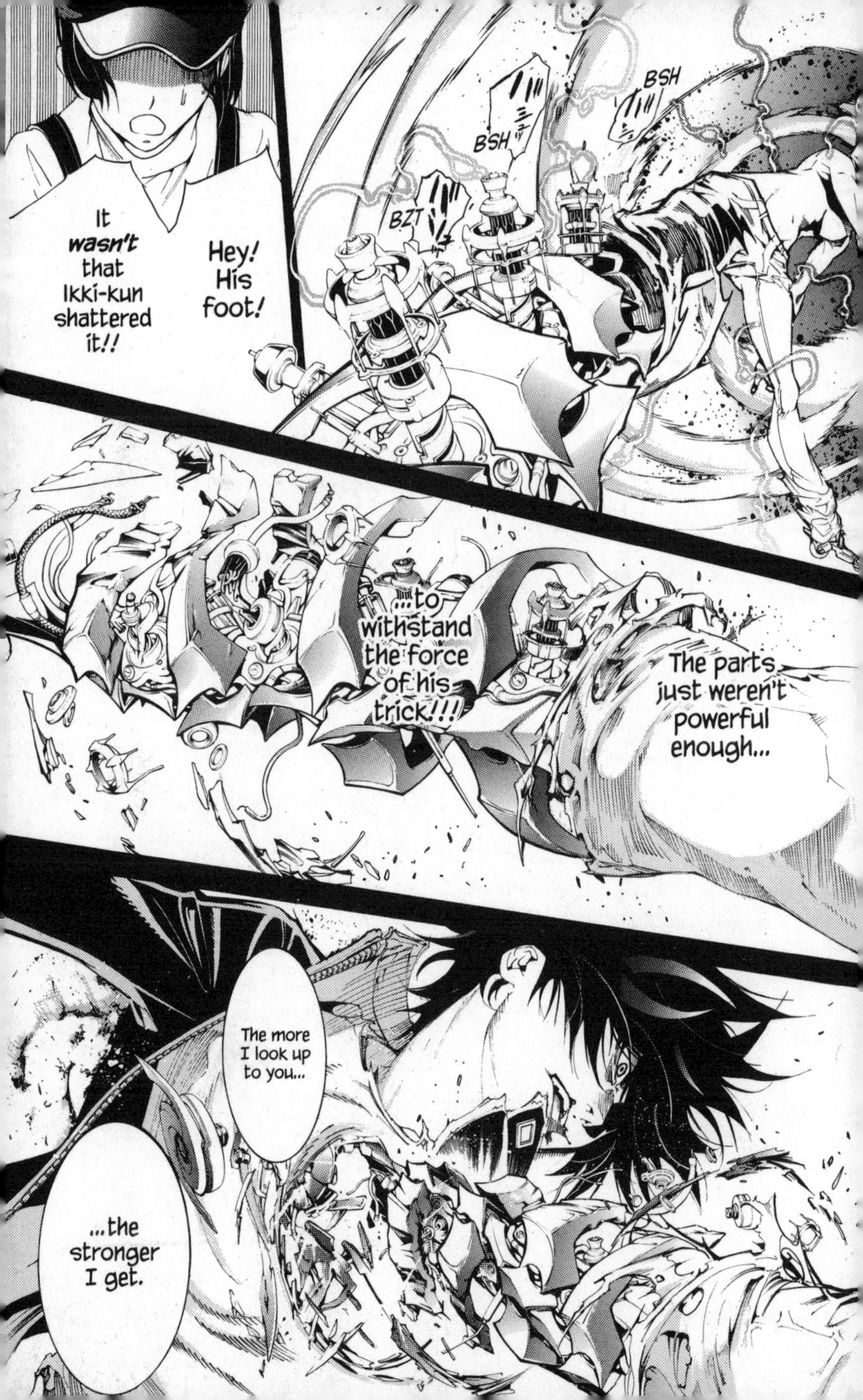
BSH
BSH
BZT
Hey! His foot!
It wasn't that Ikki-kun shattered it!!
The parts just weren't powerful enough...
...to withstand the force of his trick!!!
The more I look up to you...
...the stronger I get.

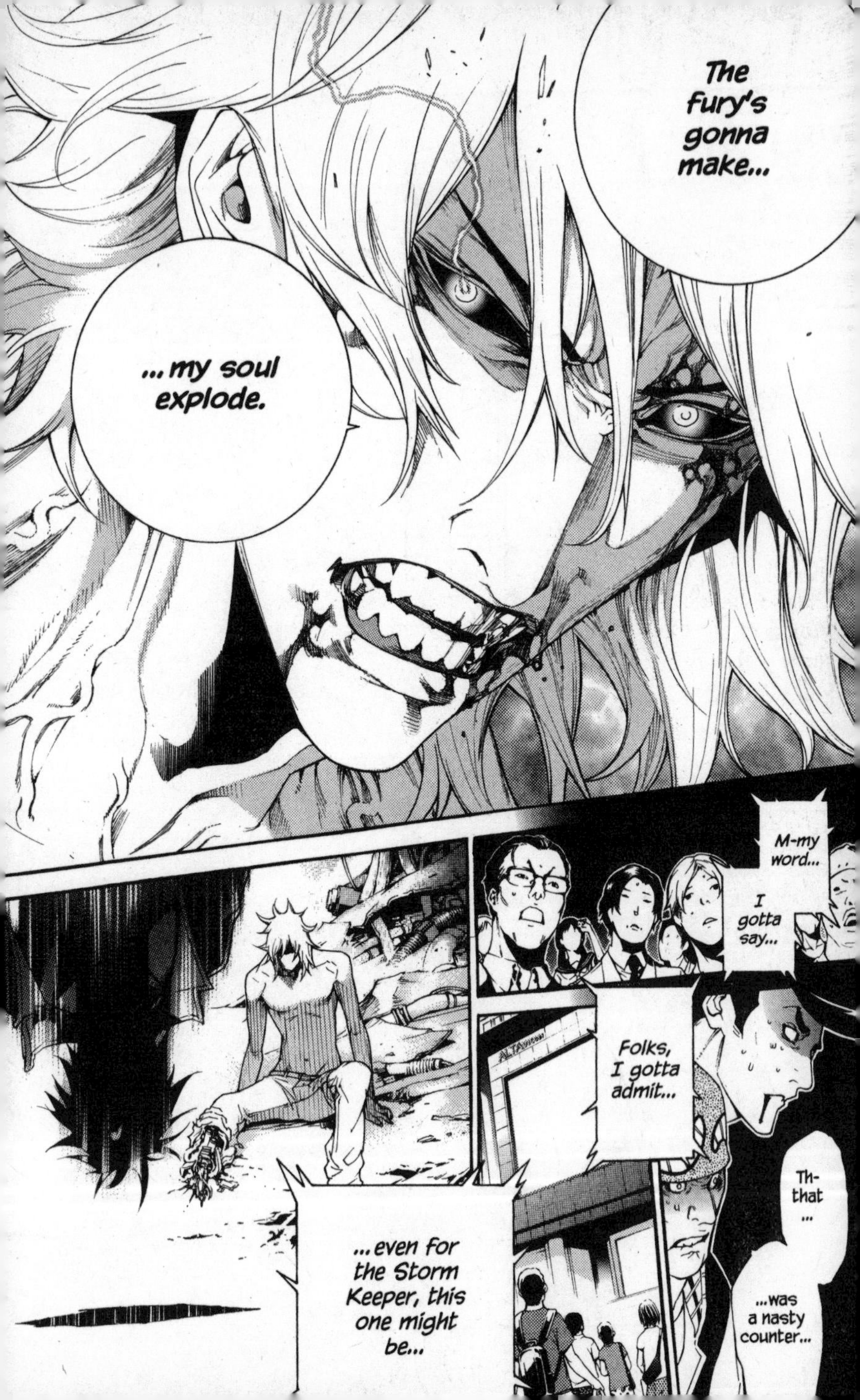
The fury's gonna make...
...my soul explode.
M-my word...
I gotta say...
Th-that ...
...was a nasty counter...
Folks, I gotta admit...
...even for the Storm Keeper, this one might be...

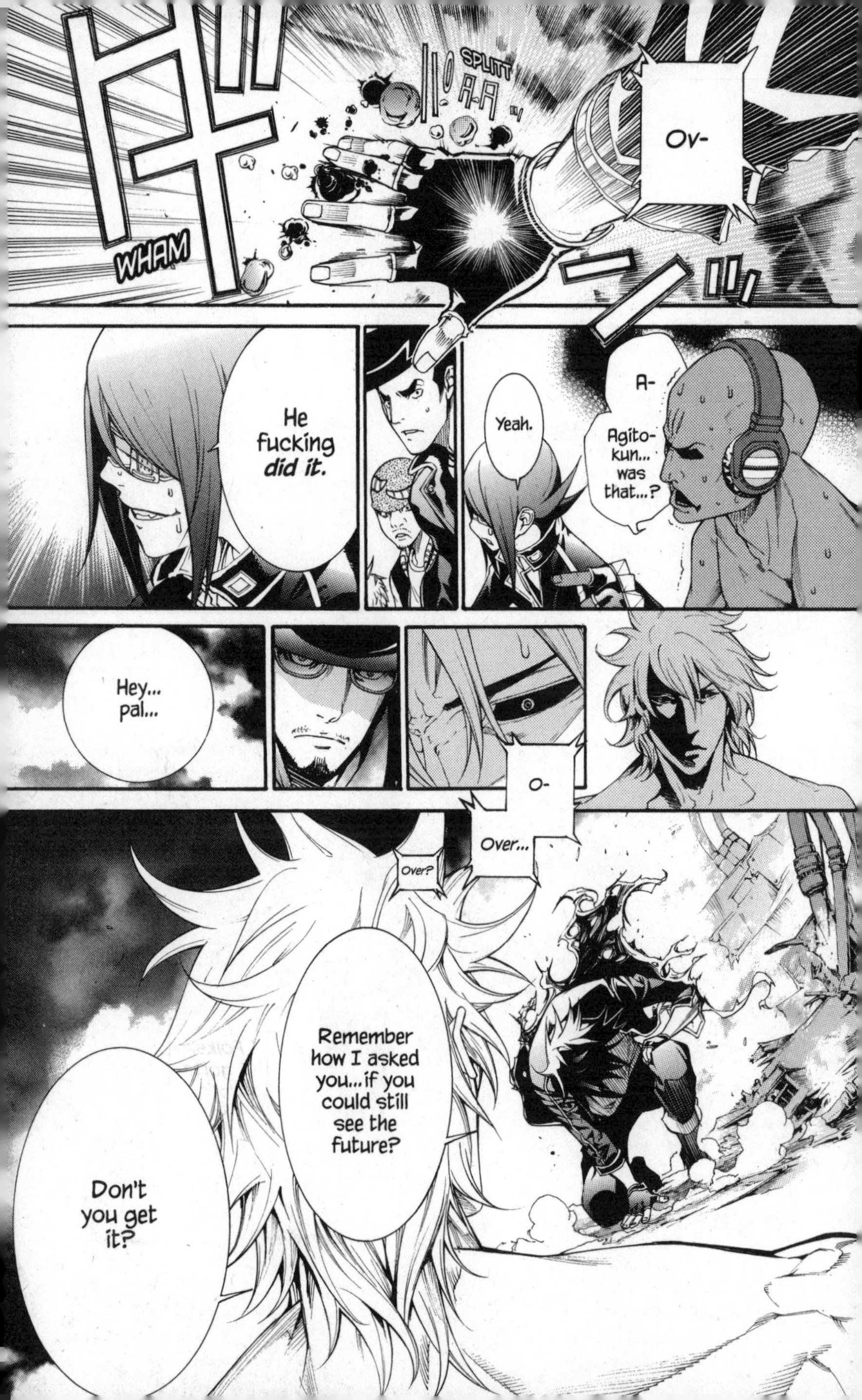
Ov-
SPLITT
WHAM
A- Agito-kun... was that...?
Yeah.
He fucking did it.
O-
Hey... pal...
Over...
Over?
Remember how I asked you...if you could still see the future?
Don't you get it?

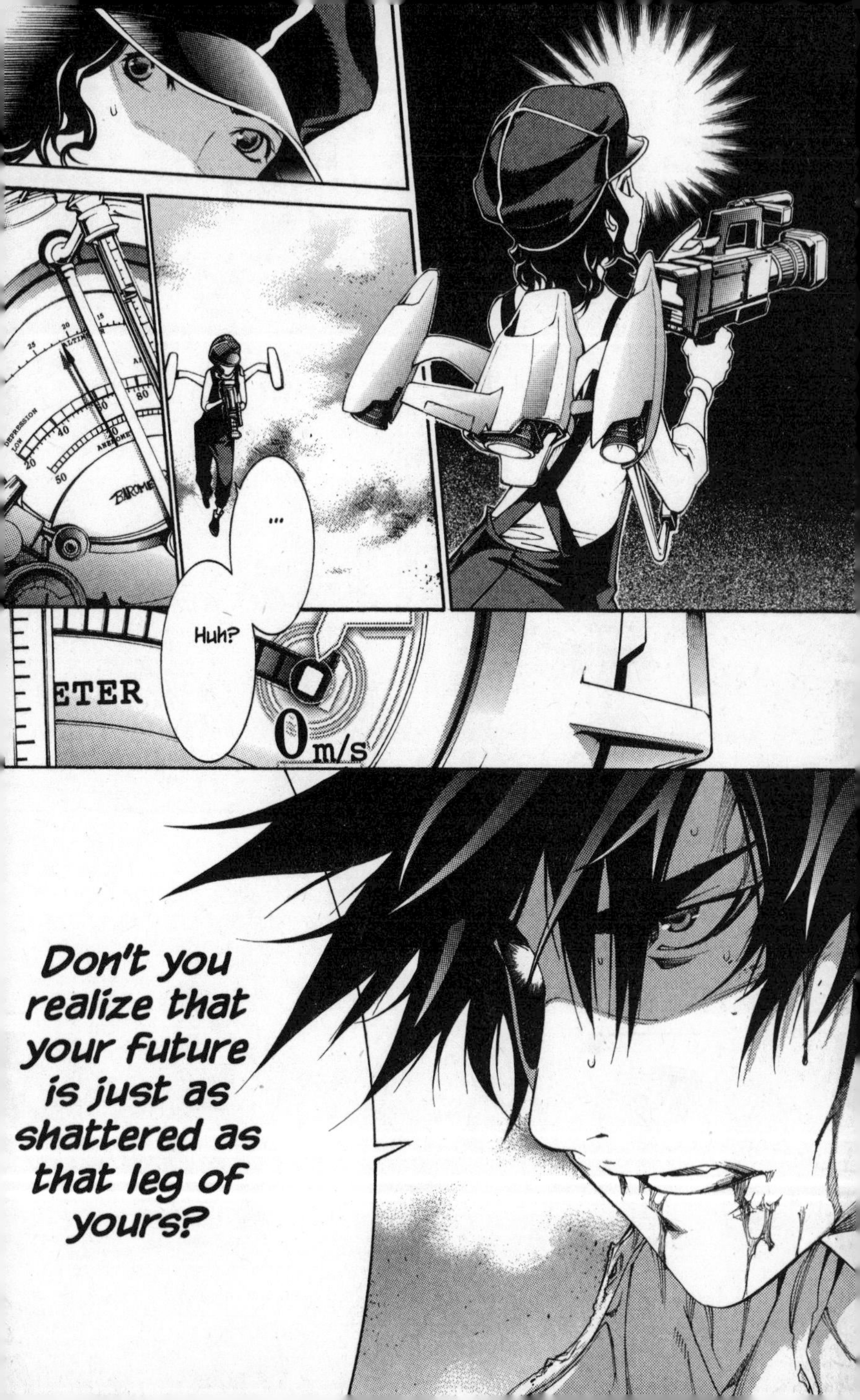
...
Huh?
ETER
0m/s
Don't you realize that your future is just as shattered as that leg of yours?

Trick:352

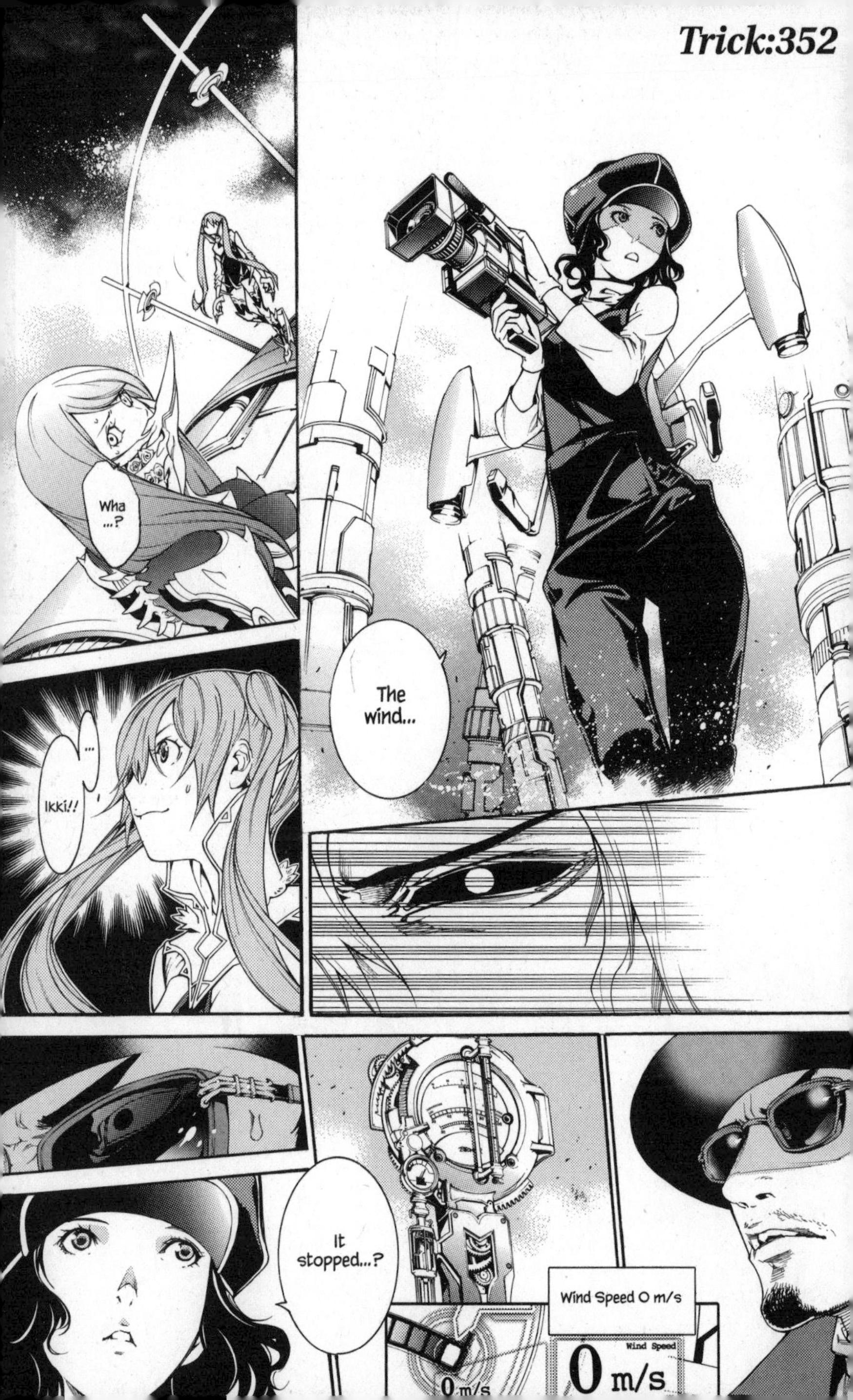

The wind...
Wha ...?
...
Ikki!!
Wind Speed 0 m/s
Wind Speed
0 m/s
0 m/s
It stopped...?

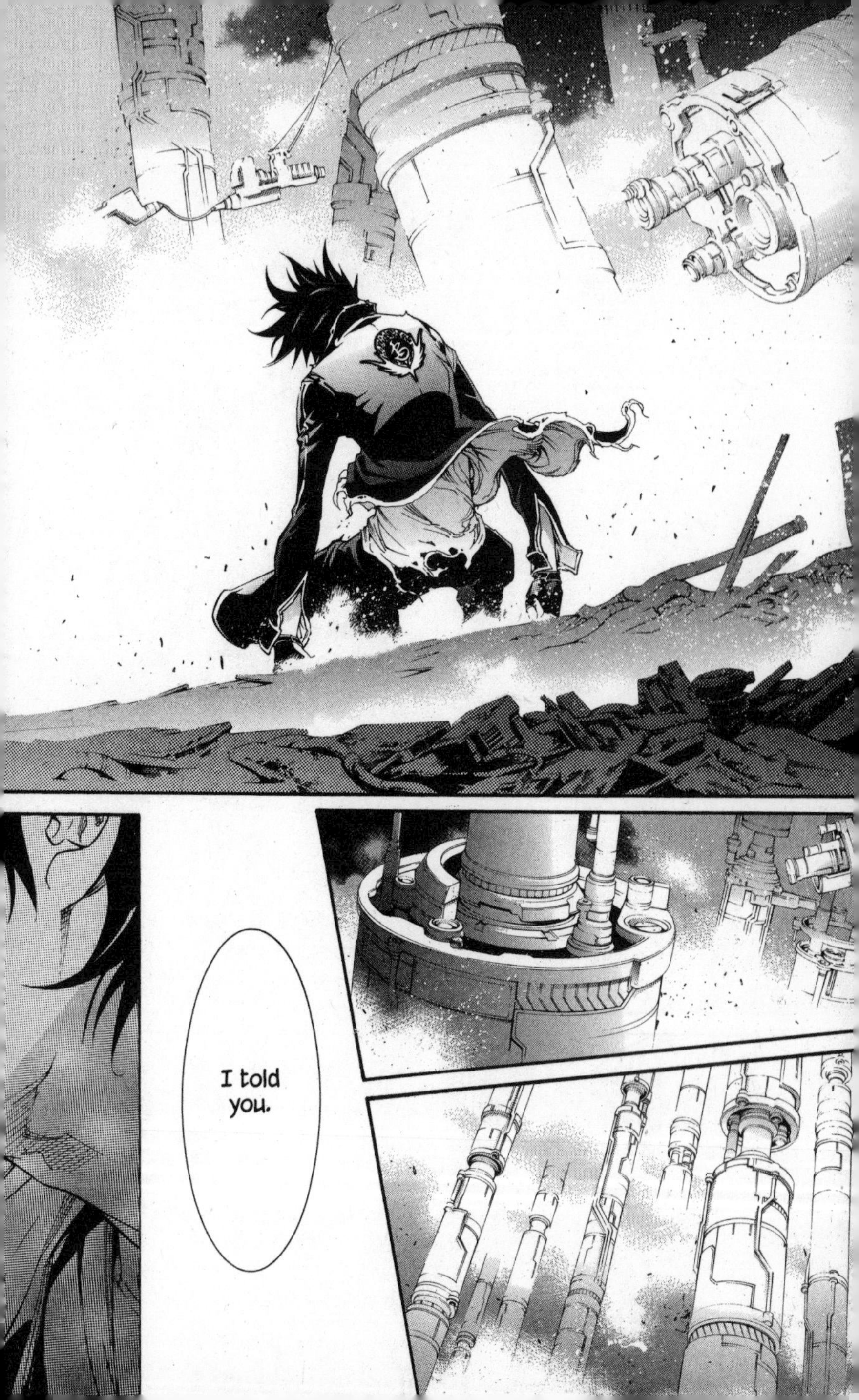
I told you.

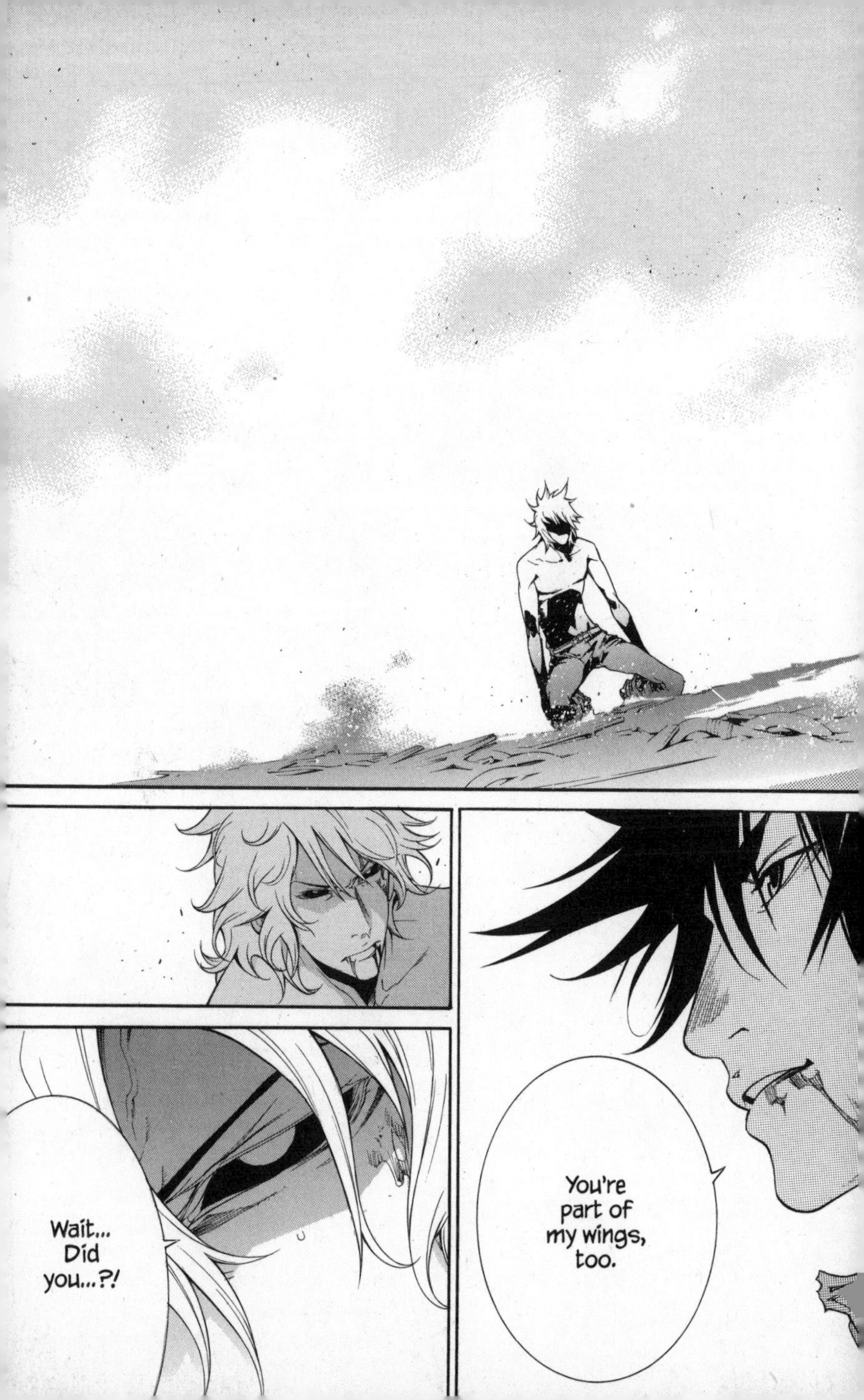
You're part of my wings, too.
Wait... Did you...?!

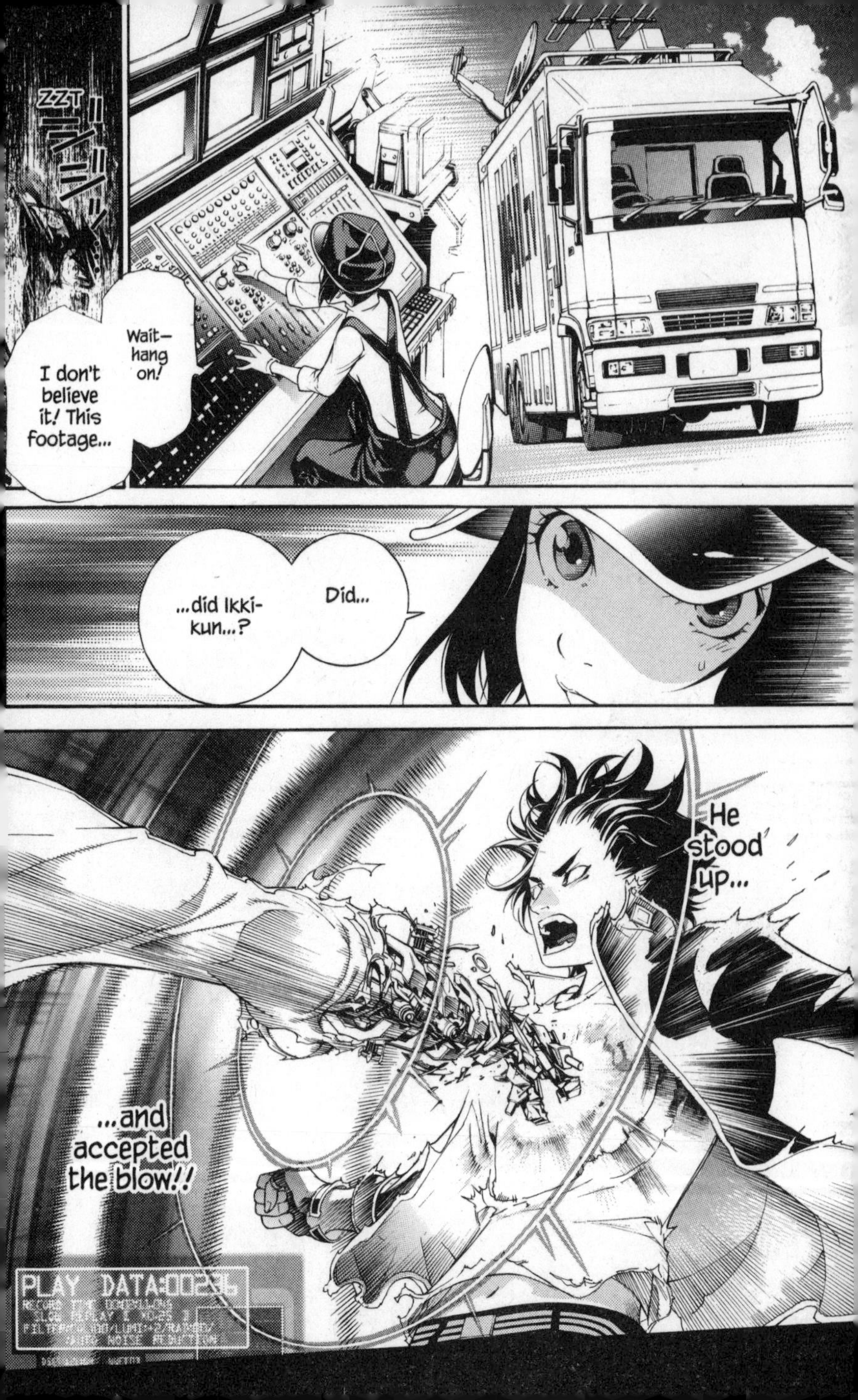
Wait—hang on!
I don't believe it! This footage...
ZZT
Did...
...did Ikki-kun...?
He stood up...
...and accepted the blow!!
PLAY DATA:00236

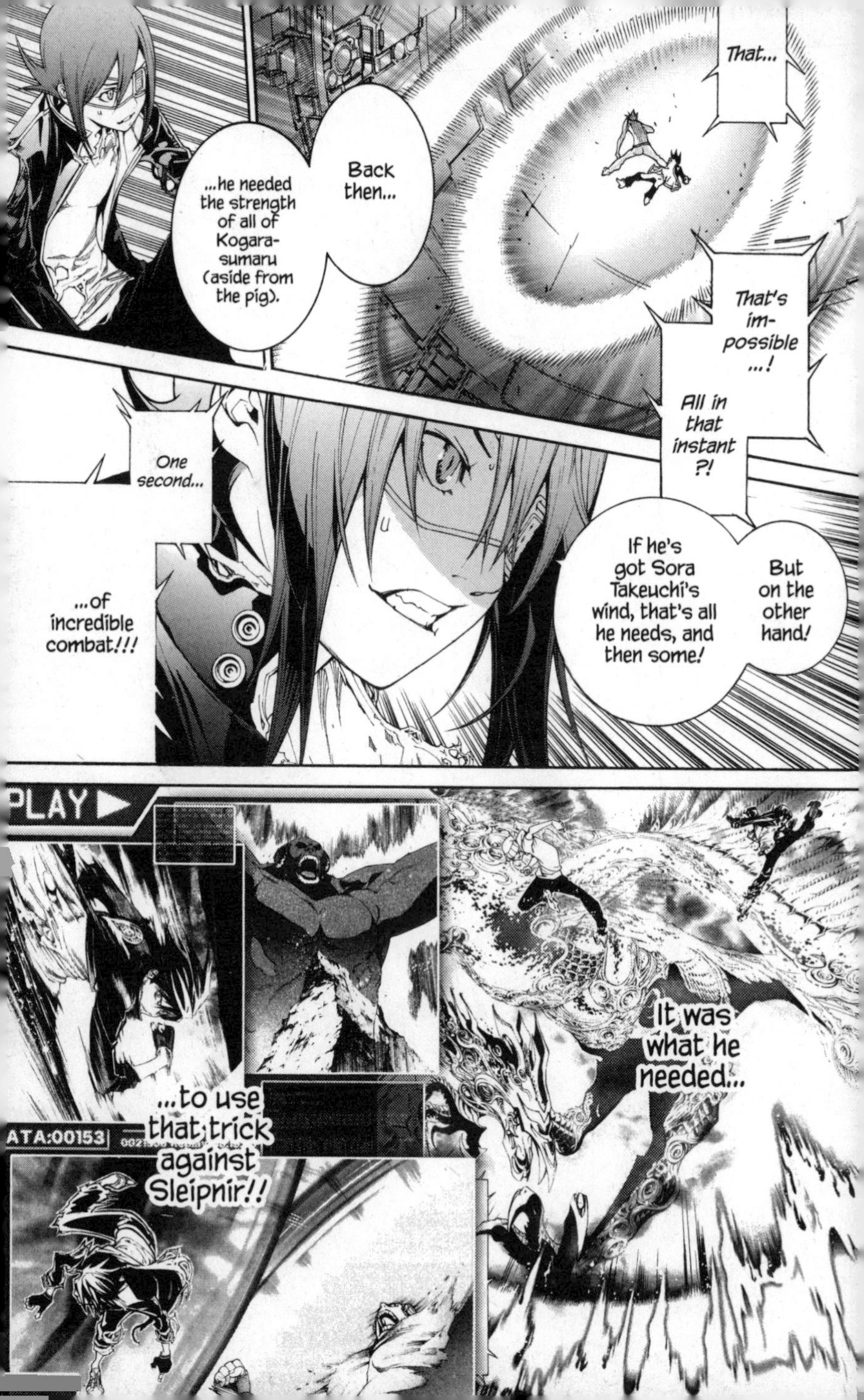
That...
Back then...
...he needed the strength of all of Kogara-sumaru (aside from the pig).
That's im-possible ...!
All in that instant ?!
But on the other hand!
If he's got Sora Takeuchi's wind, that's all he needs, and then some!
One second...
...of incredible combat!!!
It was what he needed...
PLAY ▶
ATA:00153
...to use that trick against Sleipnir!!

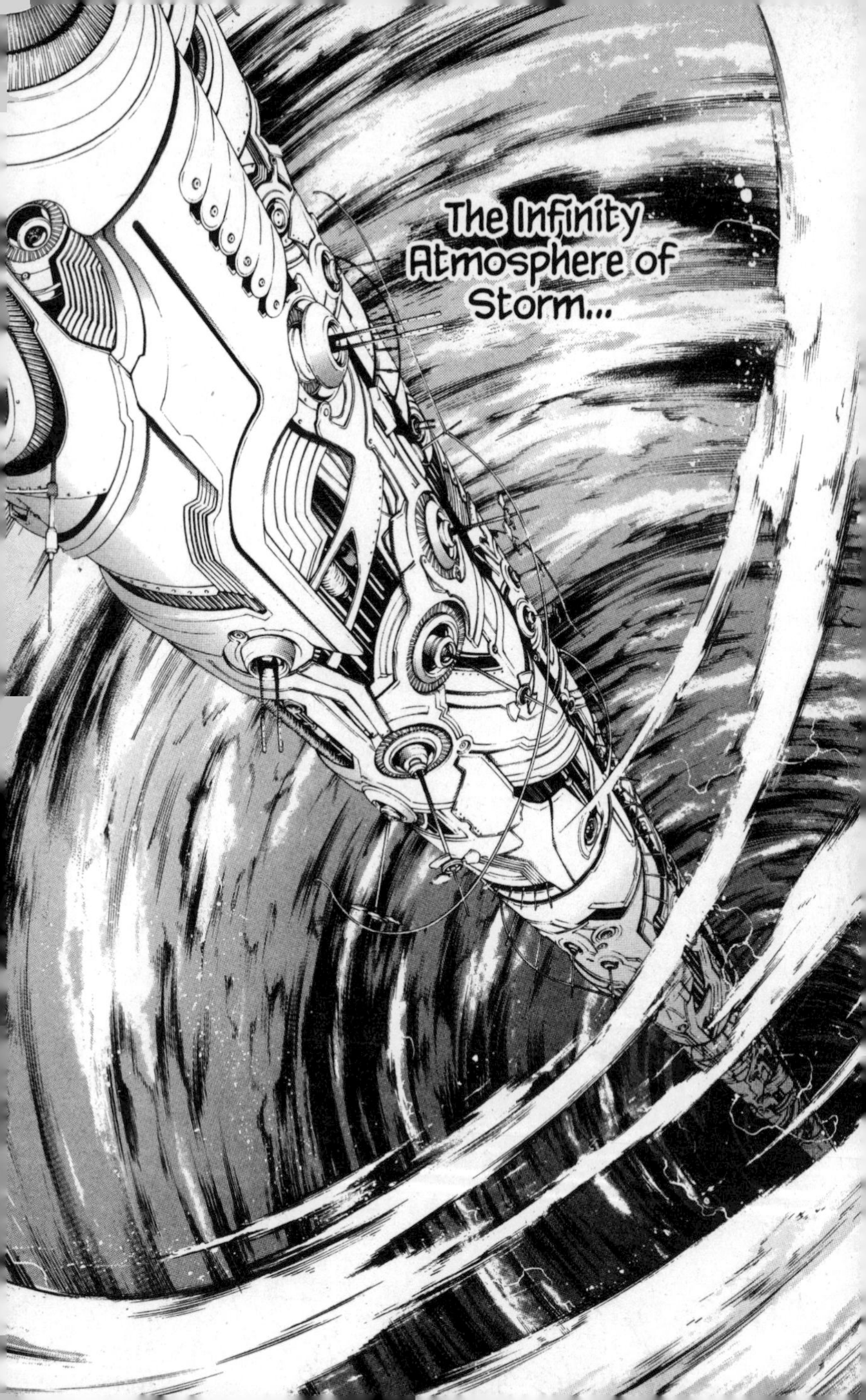
The Infinity Atmosphere of Storm...

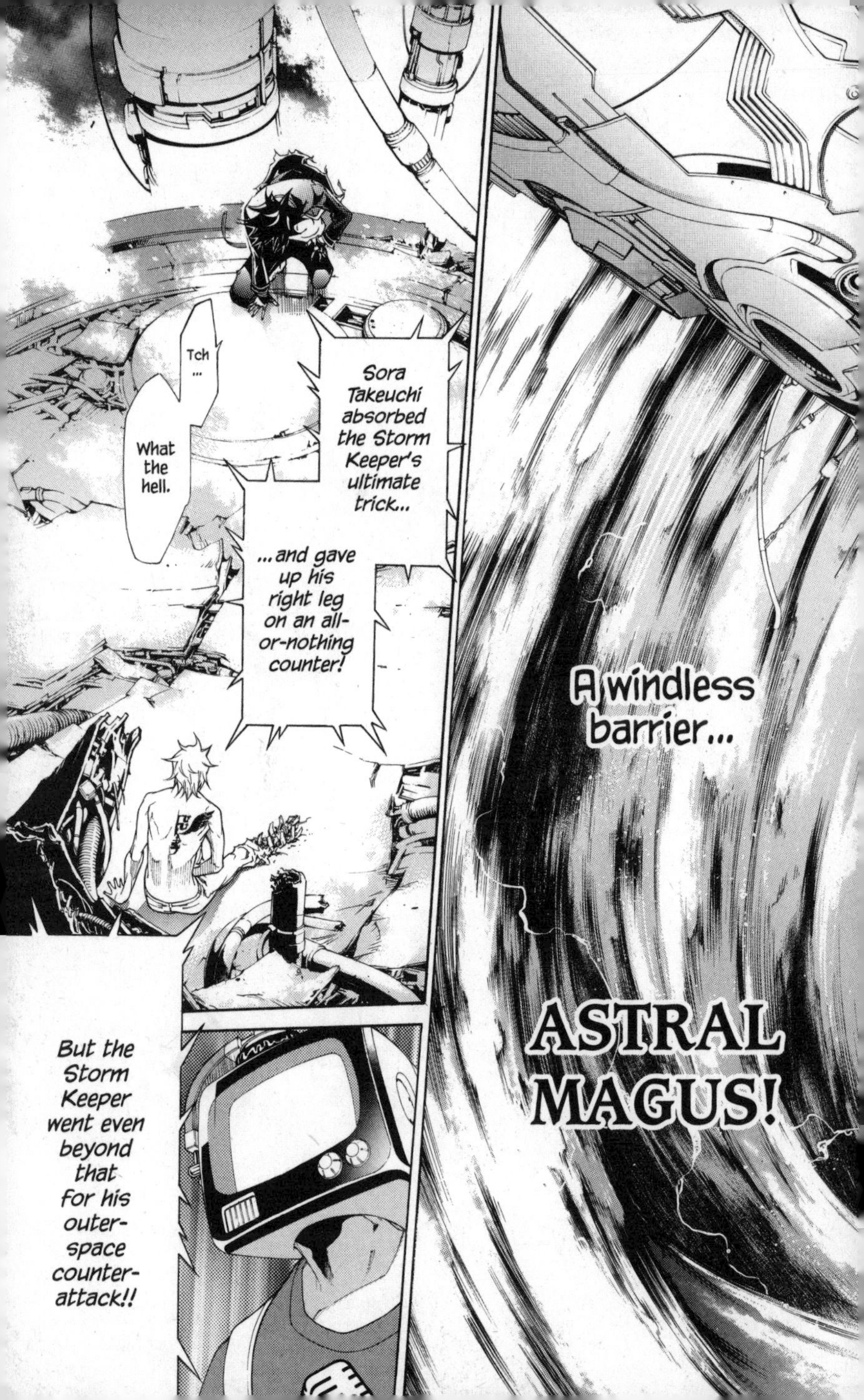
Sora Takeuchi absorbed the Storm Keeper's ultimate trick...
...and gave up his right leg on an all-or-nothing counter!
Tch ...
What the hell.
But the Storm Keeper went even beyond that for his outer-space counter-attack!!
A windless barrier...
ASTRAL MAGUS!

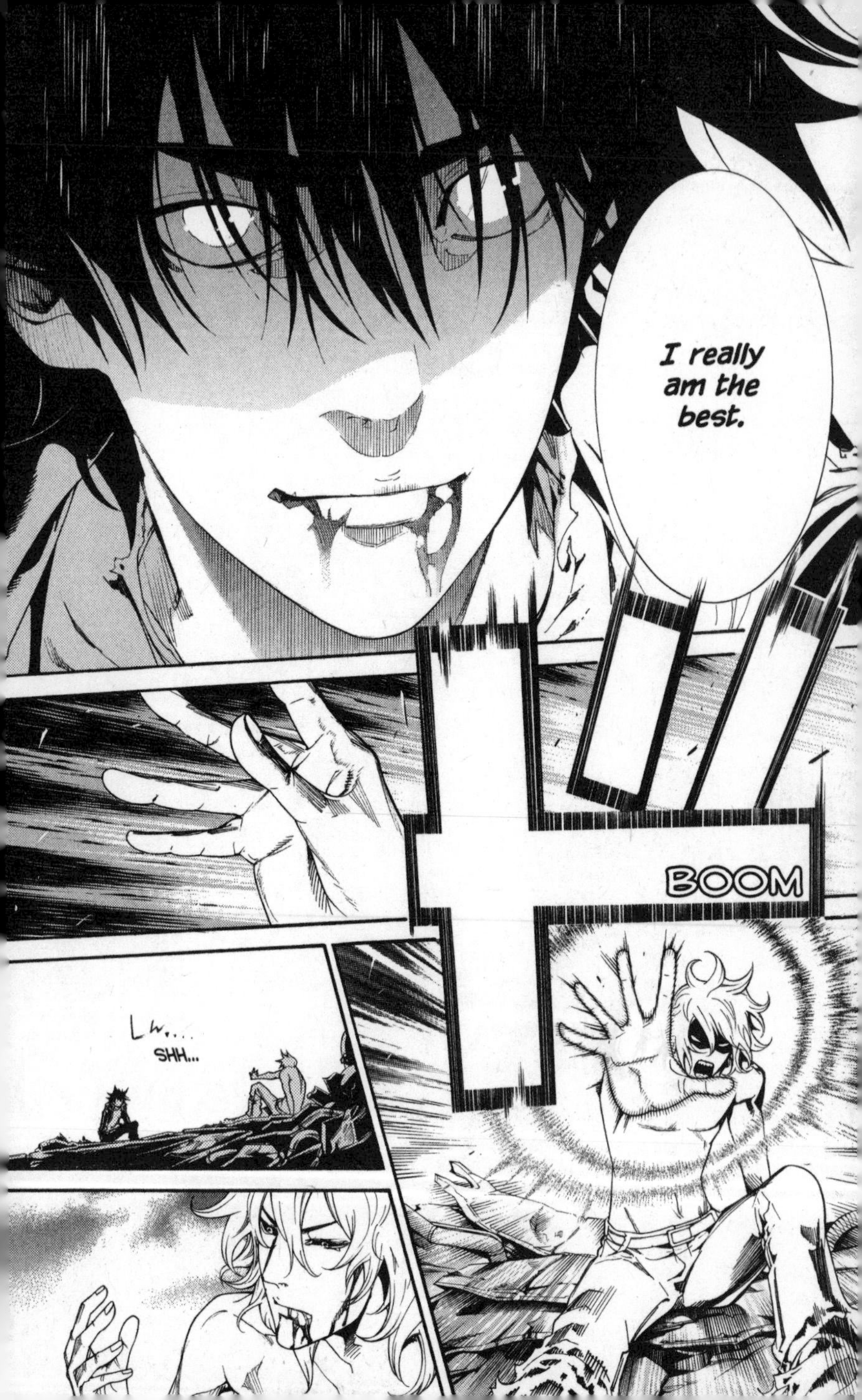
I really am the best.
BOOM
Lw...
SHH...

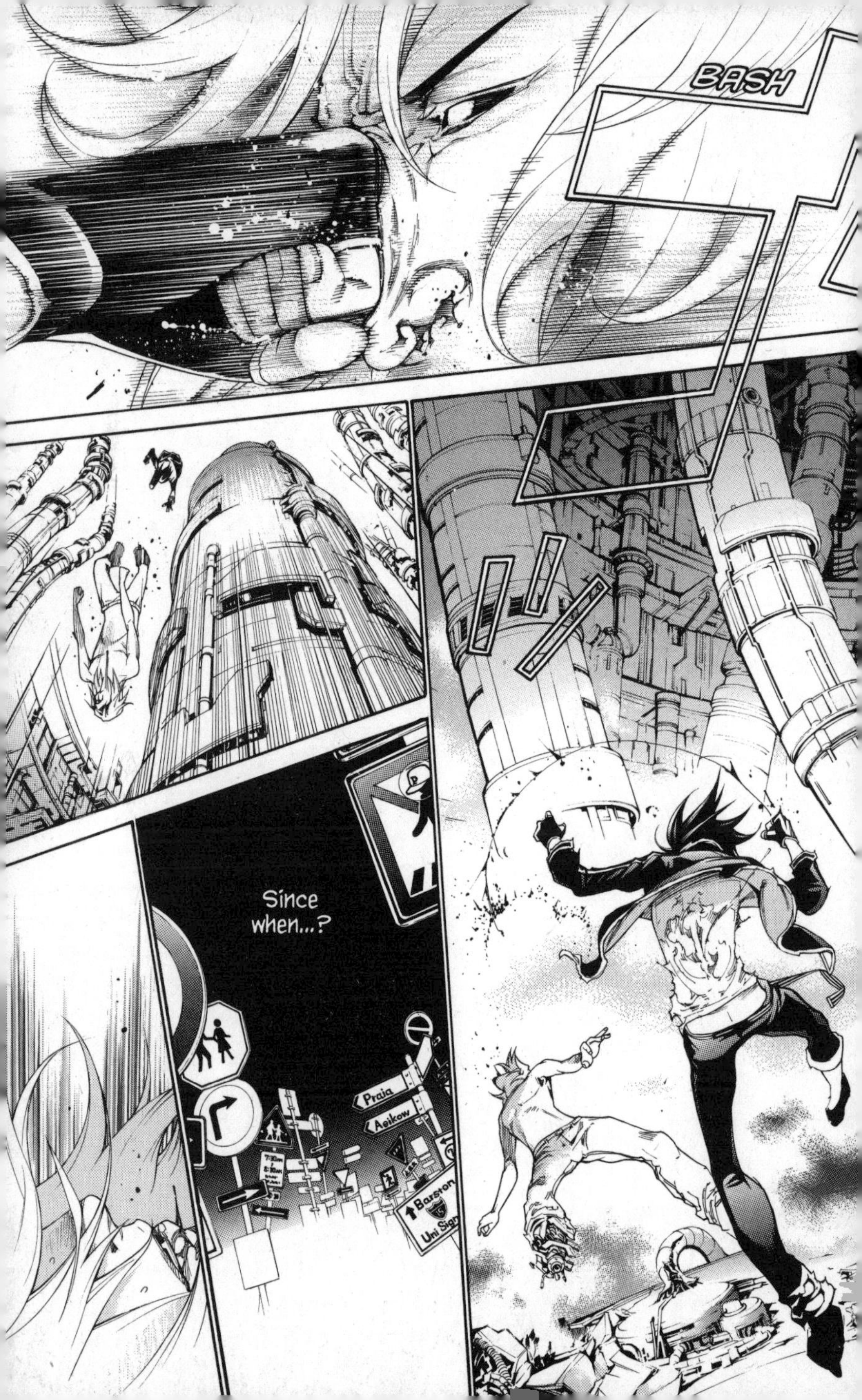
BASH
Since when...?
Praia
Aeikow
Barston
Uni Sign

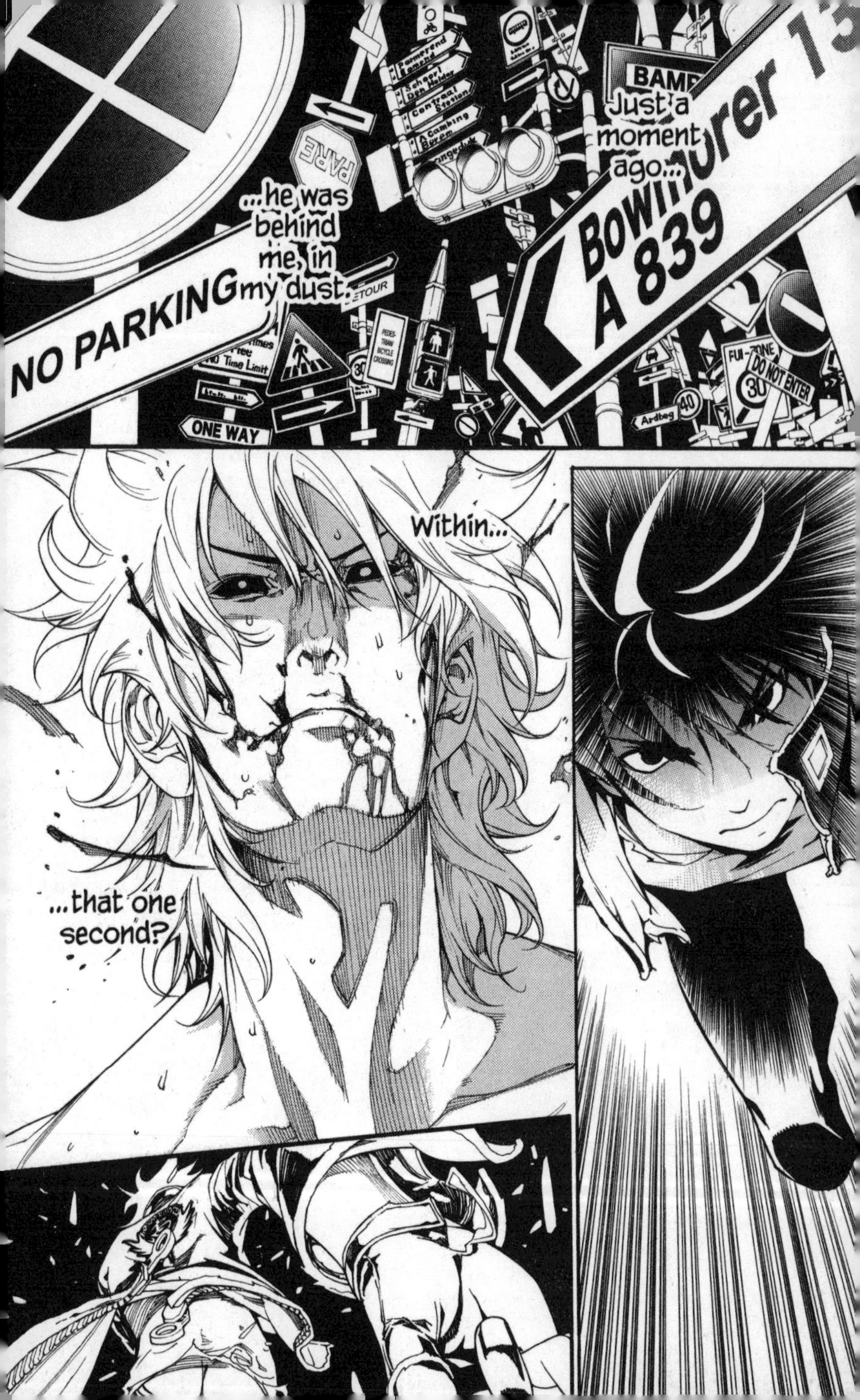
Just a moment ago...
...he was behind me, in my dust.
NO PARKING
ONE WAY
DO NOT ENTER
Within...
...that one second?

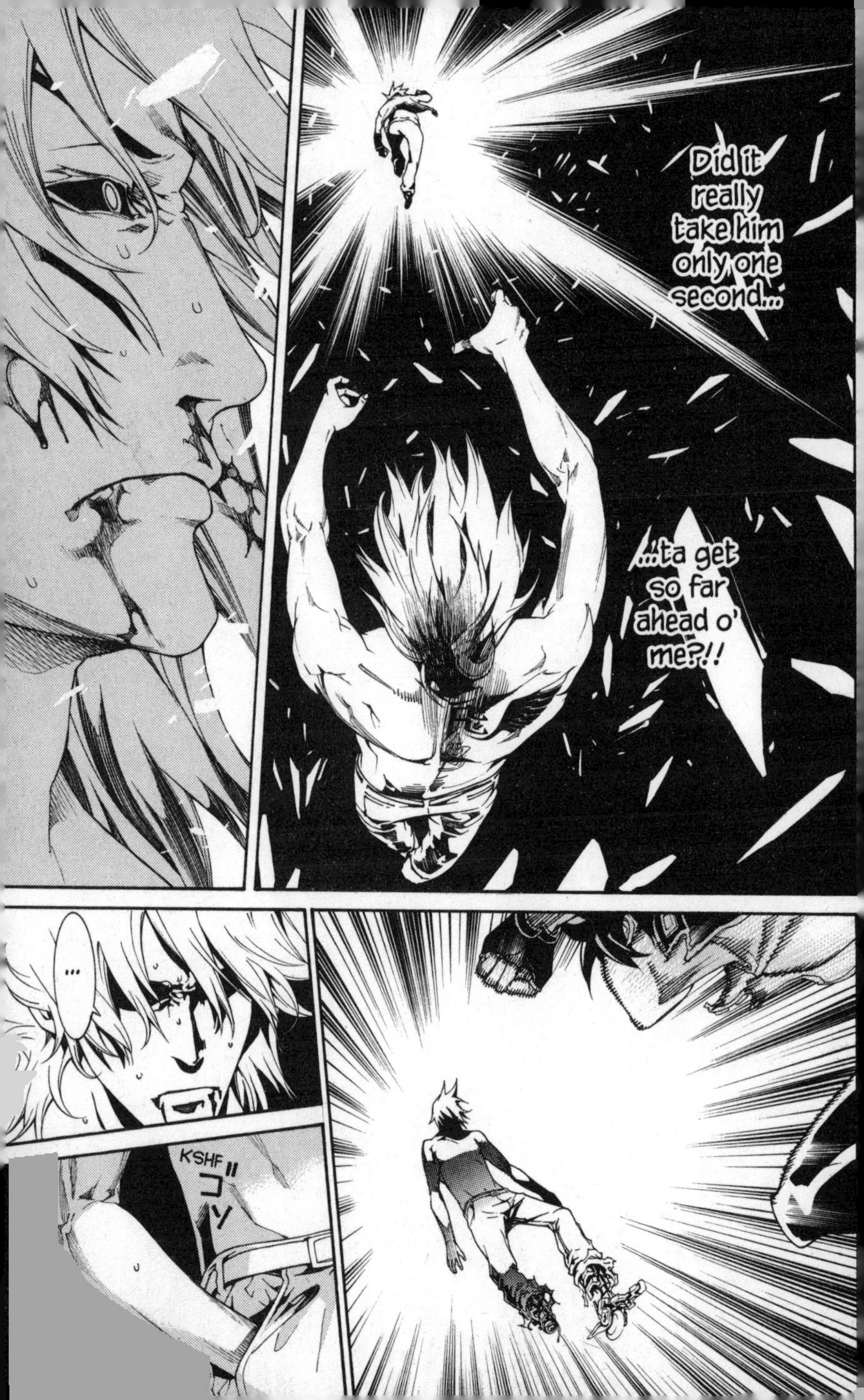
Did it really take him only one second...
...ta get so far ahead o' me?!!
...
KSHF!!
ゴッ

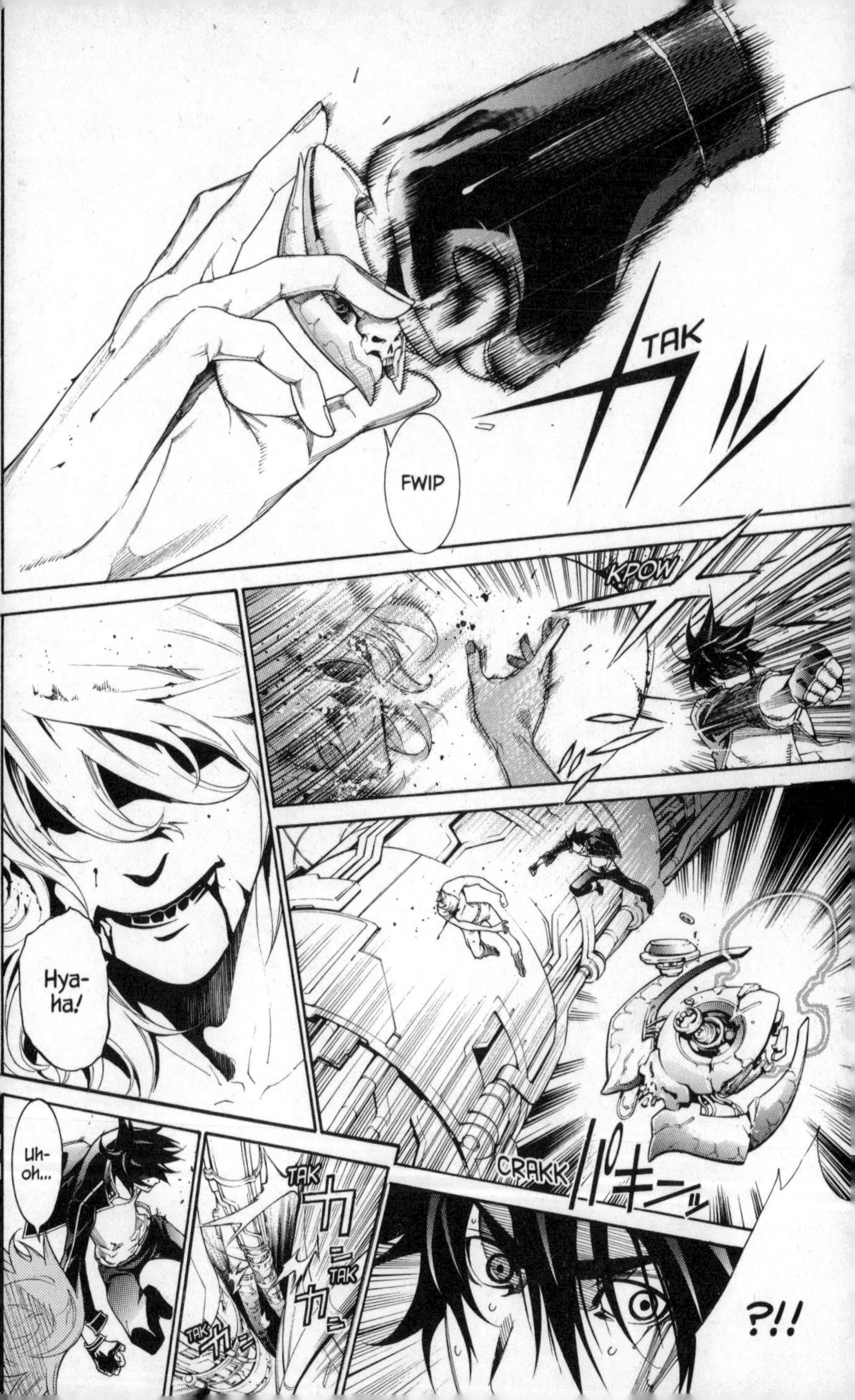
TAK
カッ
FWIP
KPOW
CRAKK
パキーン
Hya-ha!
?!!
TAK
カッ
TAK
カッ
TAK
カッ
Uh-oh...

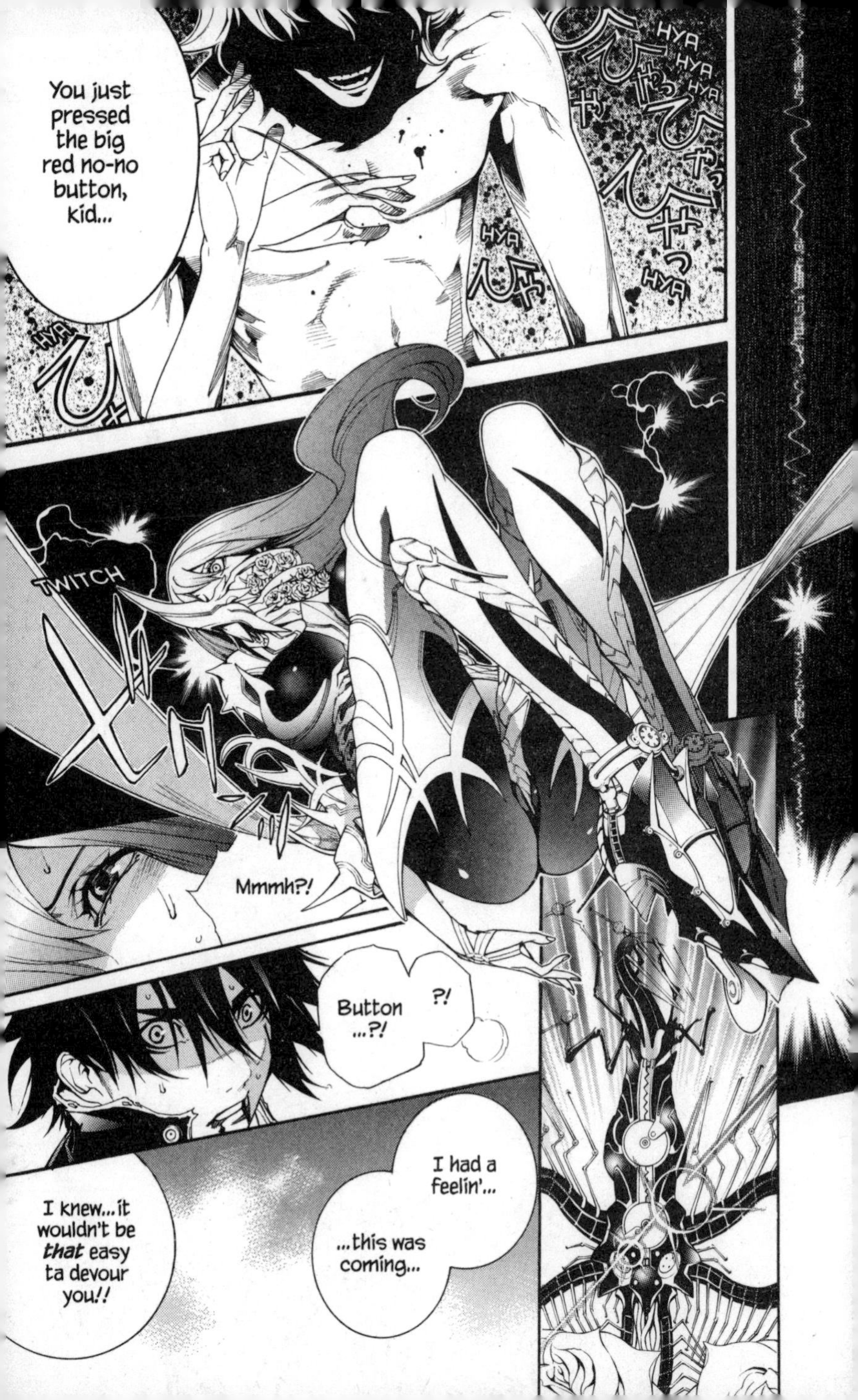
HYA HYA HYA
HYA HYA
You just pressed the big red no-no button, kid...
HYA
TWITCH
Mmmh?!
Button ...?!
?!
I had a feelin'...
...this was coming...
I knew...it wouldn't be *that* easy ta devour you!!

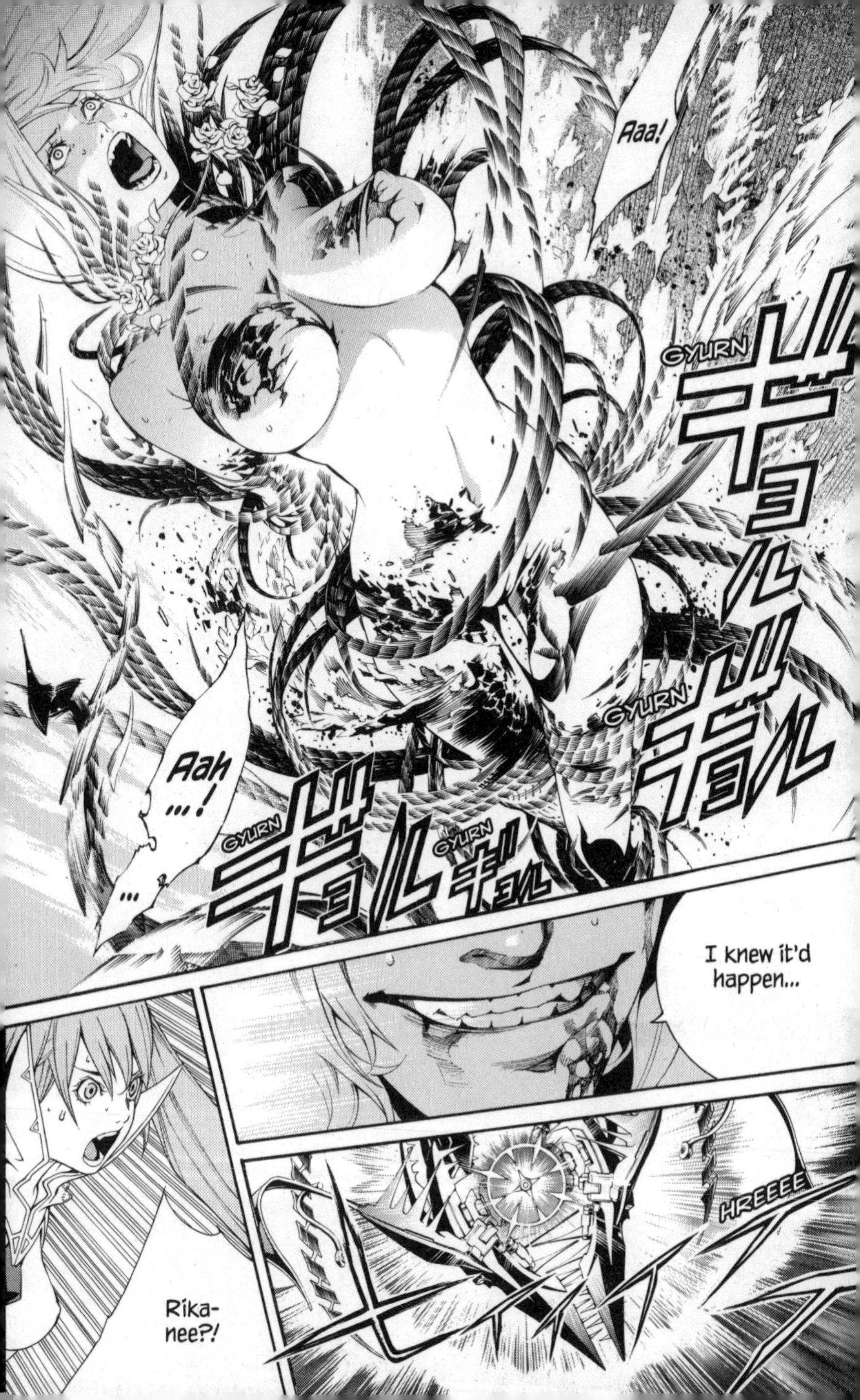
Aaa!
GYURN
GYURN
GYURN
GYURN
Aah ...!
...
I knew it'd happen...
HREEEE
Rika-nee?!

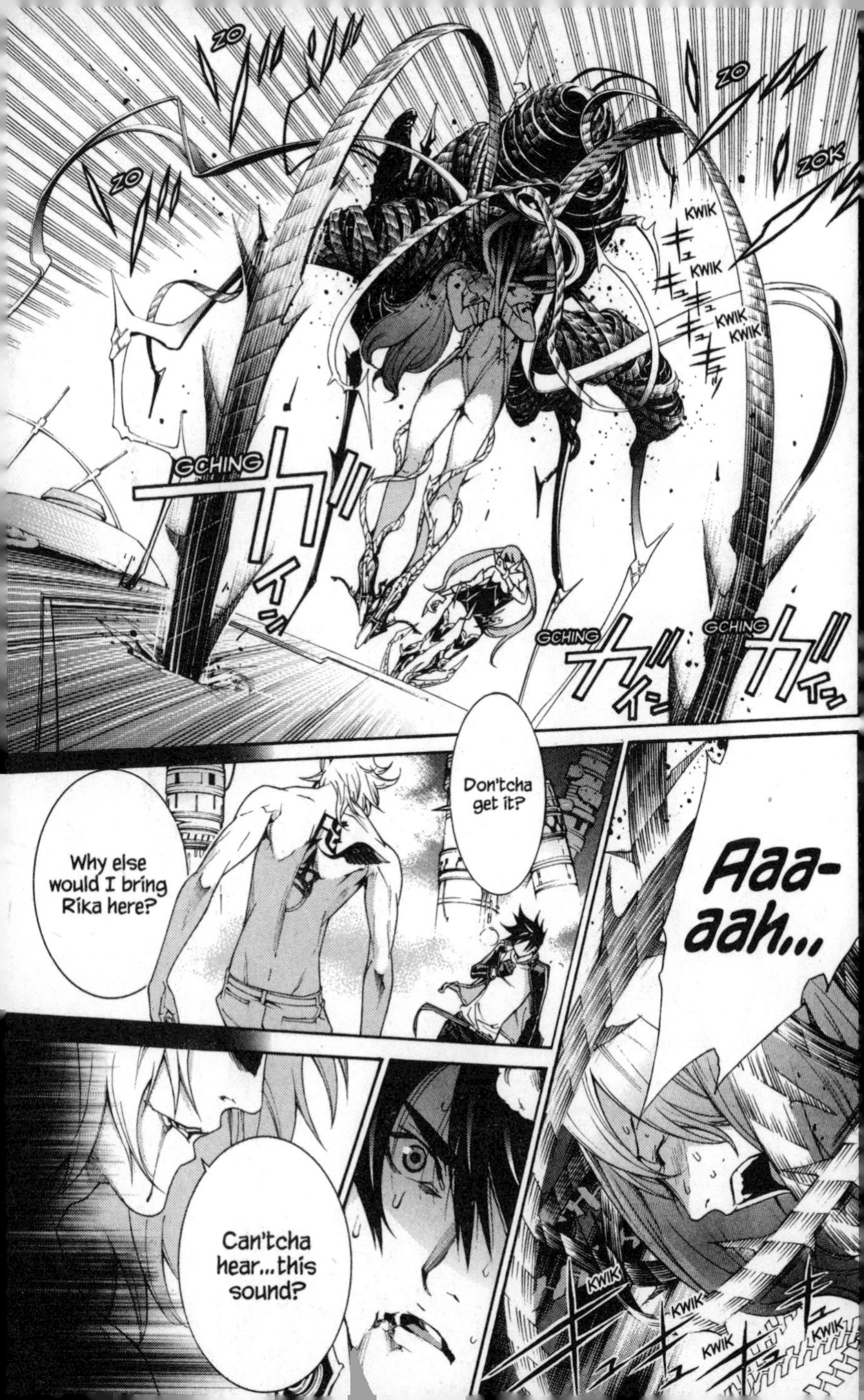
ZO
ZO
ZOK
KWIK
KWIK
KWIK
KWIK
ZO
GCHING
GCHING
GCHING
Aaa-
aah...
Don'tcha get it?
Why else would I bring Rika here?
Can'tcha hear...this sound?
KWIK
KWIK
KWIK
KWIK

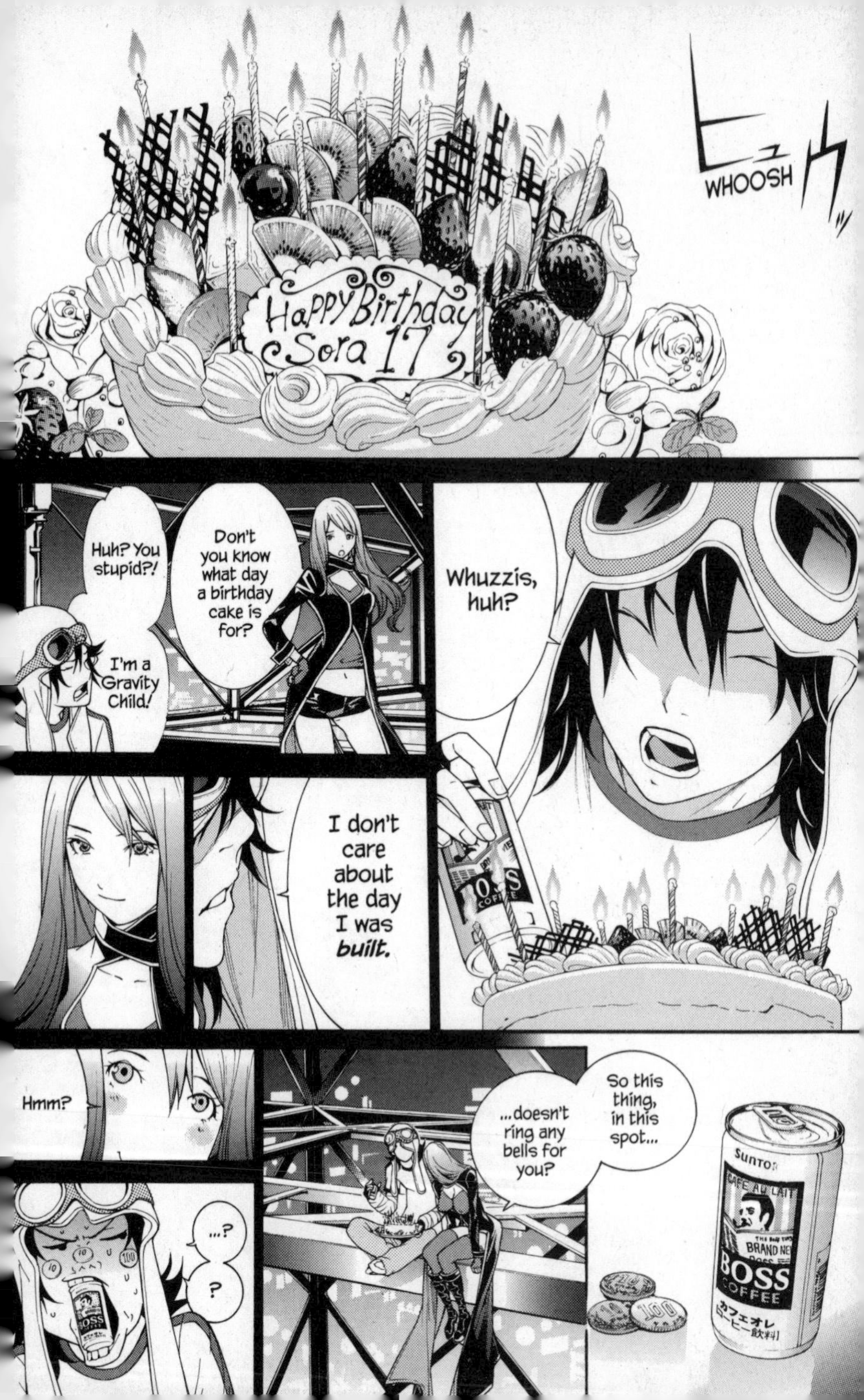
ヒュゥッ
WHOOSH
Happy Birthday Sora 17
Whuzzis, huh?
Don't you know what day a birthday cake is for?
Huh? You stupid?!
I'm a Gravity Child!
I don't care about the day I was built.
So this thing, in this spot...
...doesn't ring any bells for you?
Hmm?
...?
?
Suntory
CAFE AU LAIT
BRAND NEW
BOSS COFFEE
カフェオレ
コーヒー飲料

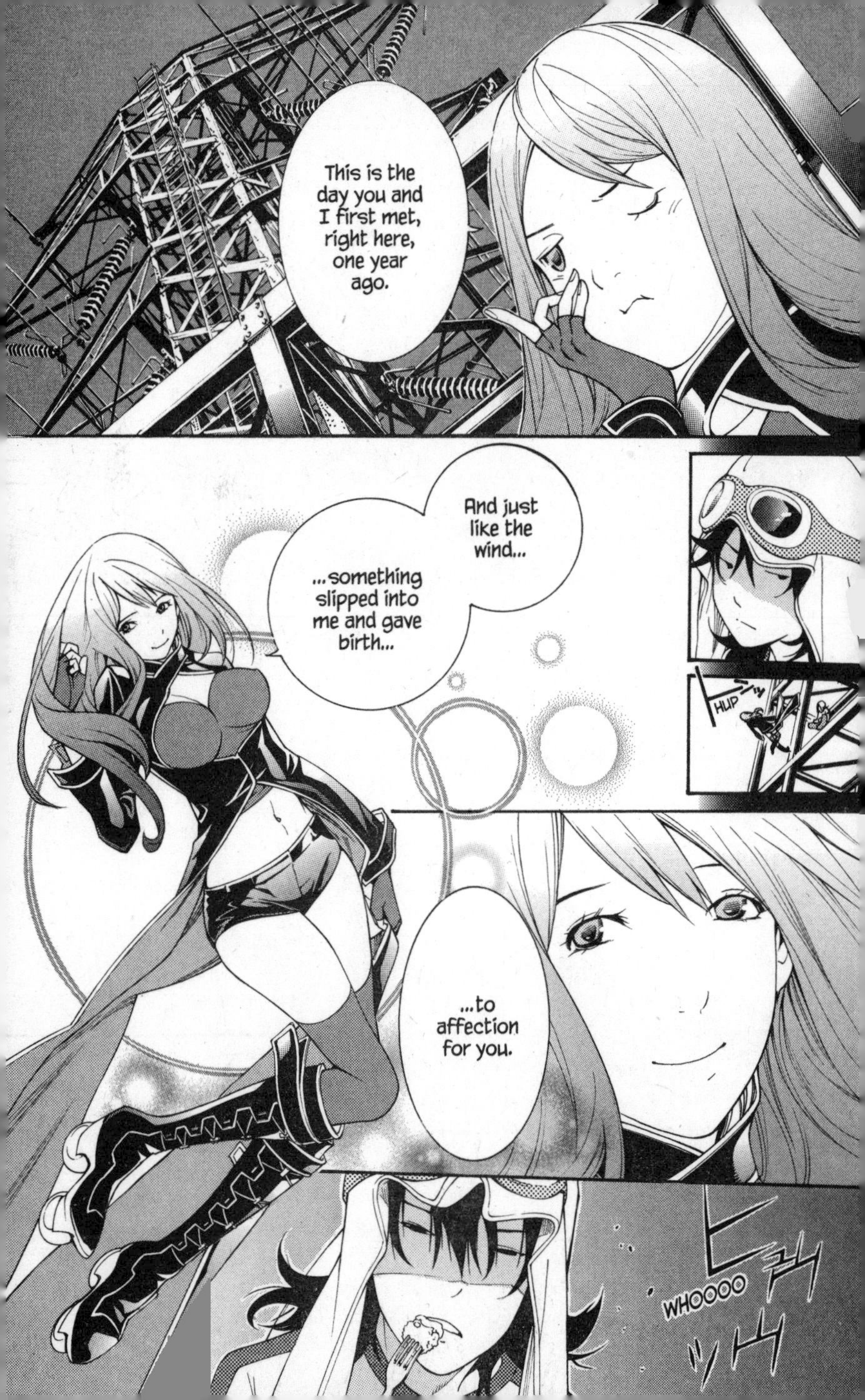
This is the day you and I first met, right here, one year ago.
HUP
And just like the wind...
...something slipped into me and gave birth...
...to affection for you.
WHOOOO

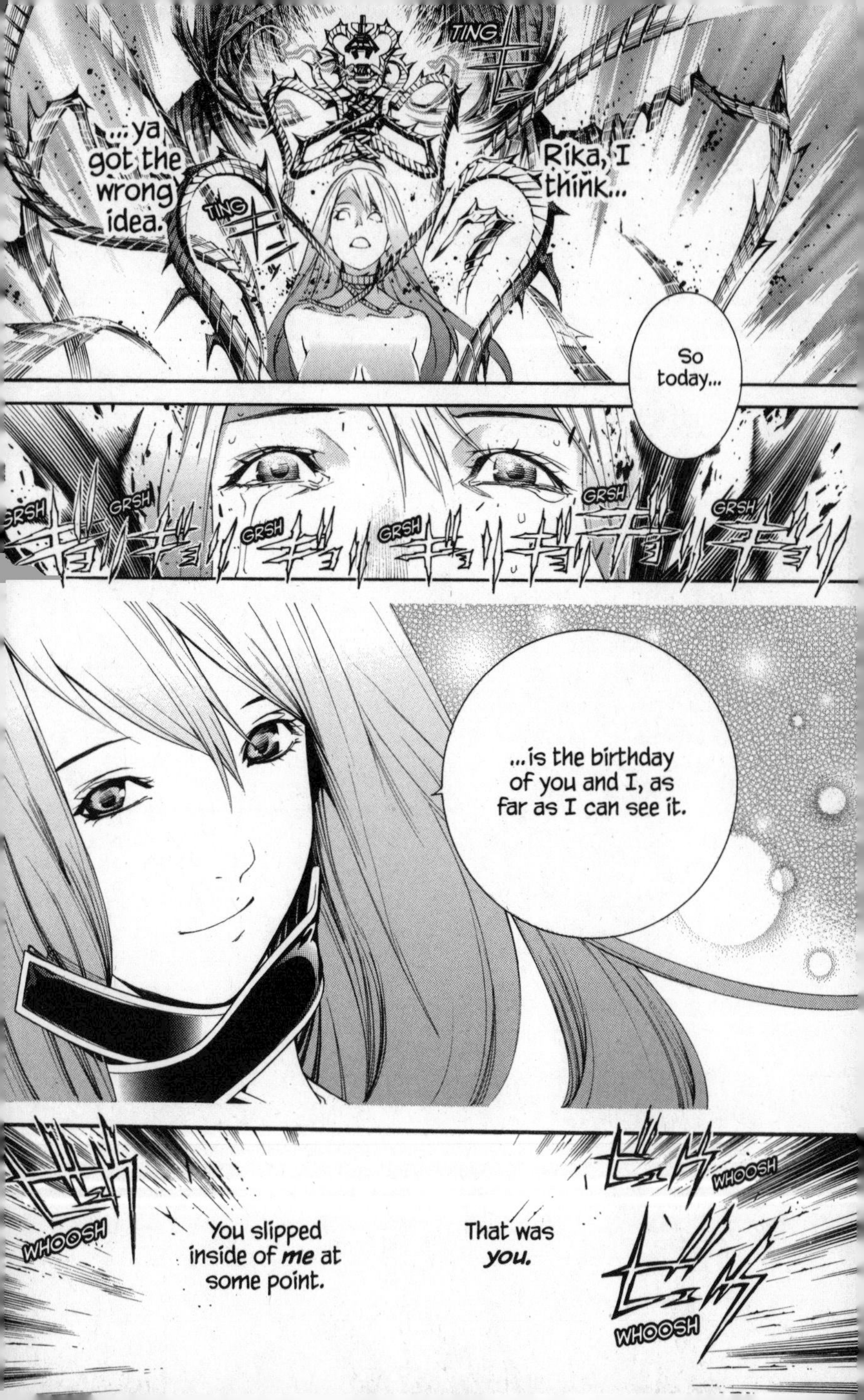
TING
Rika, I think...
...ya got the wrong idea.
TING
So today...
GRSH
GRSH
GRSH
GRSH
GRSH
GRSH
...is the birthday of you and I, as far as I can see it.
WHOOSH
WHOOSH
That was *you.*
You slipped inside of *me* at some point.
WHOOSH

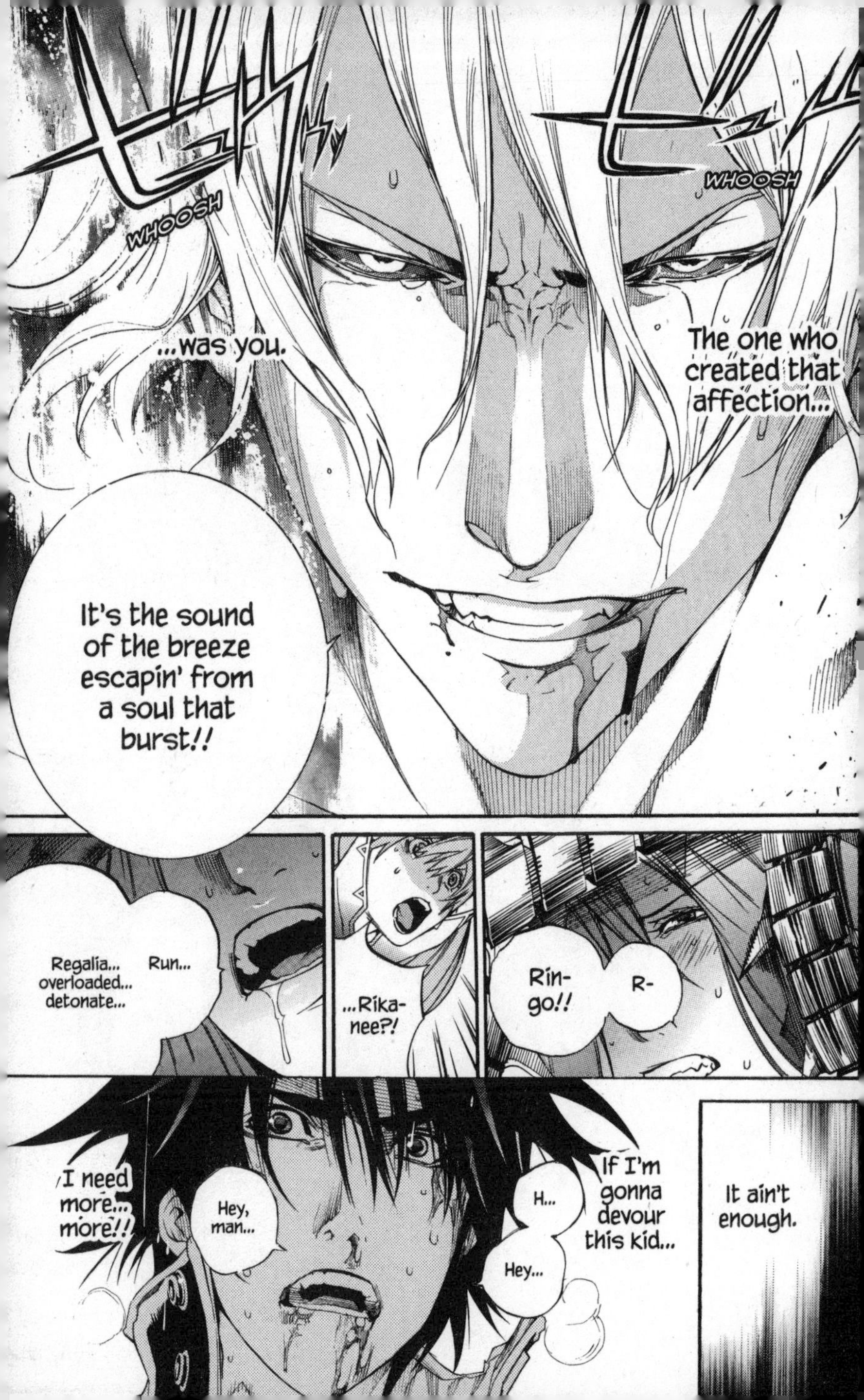
WHOOSH
WHOOSH
The one who created that affection...
...was you.
It's the sound of the breeze escapin' from a soul that burst!!
R-
Rin-go!!
...Rika-nee?!
Run...
Regalia... overloaded... detonate...
It ain't enough.
If I'm gonna devour this kid...
H...
Hey...
Hey, man...
I need more... more!!

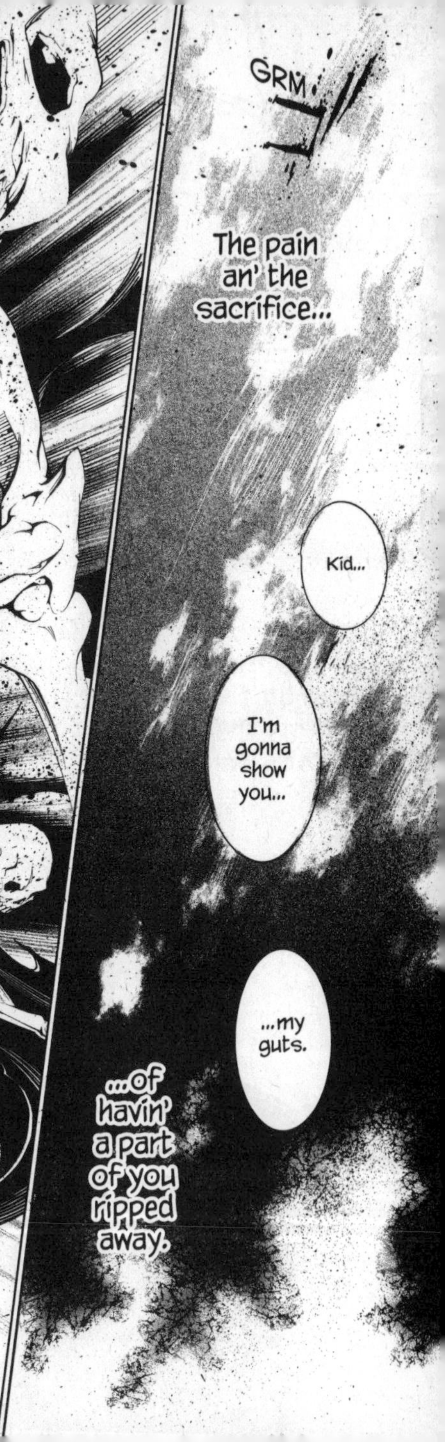
GRM
The pain an' the sacrifice...
Kid...
I'm gonna show you...
...my guts.
...of havin' a part of you ripped away.
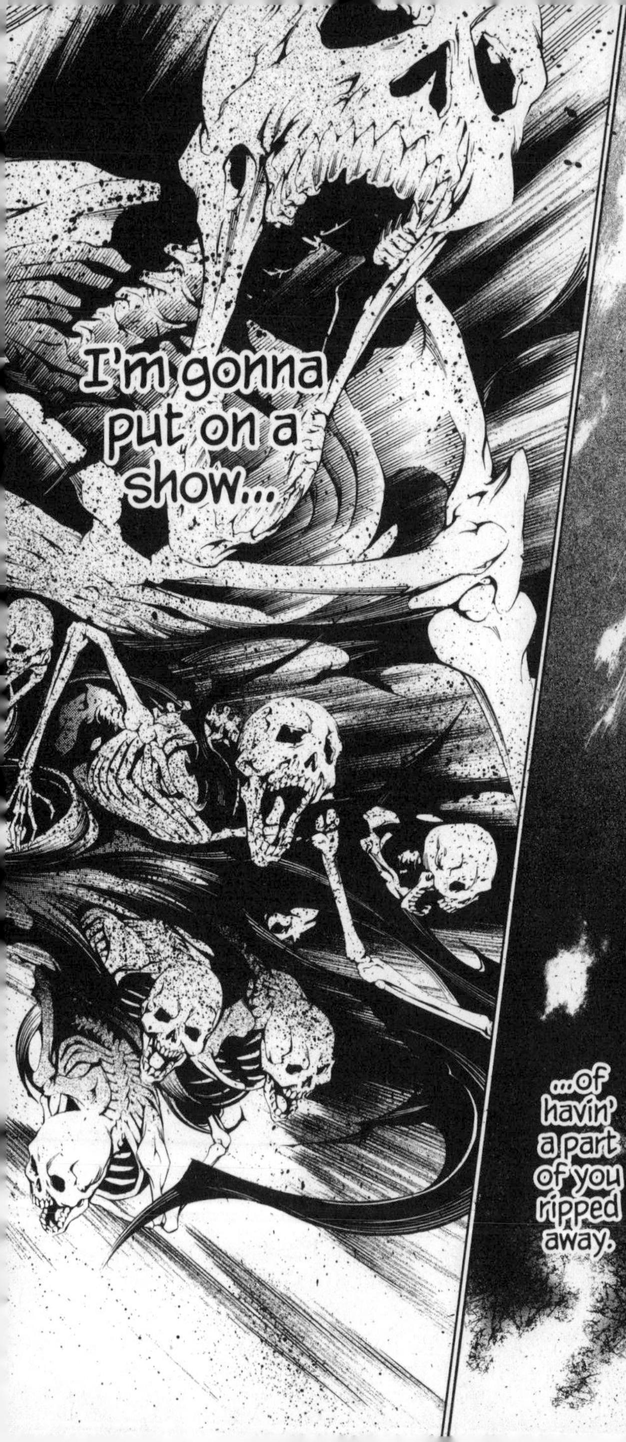
I'm gonna put on a show...

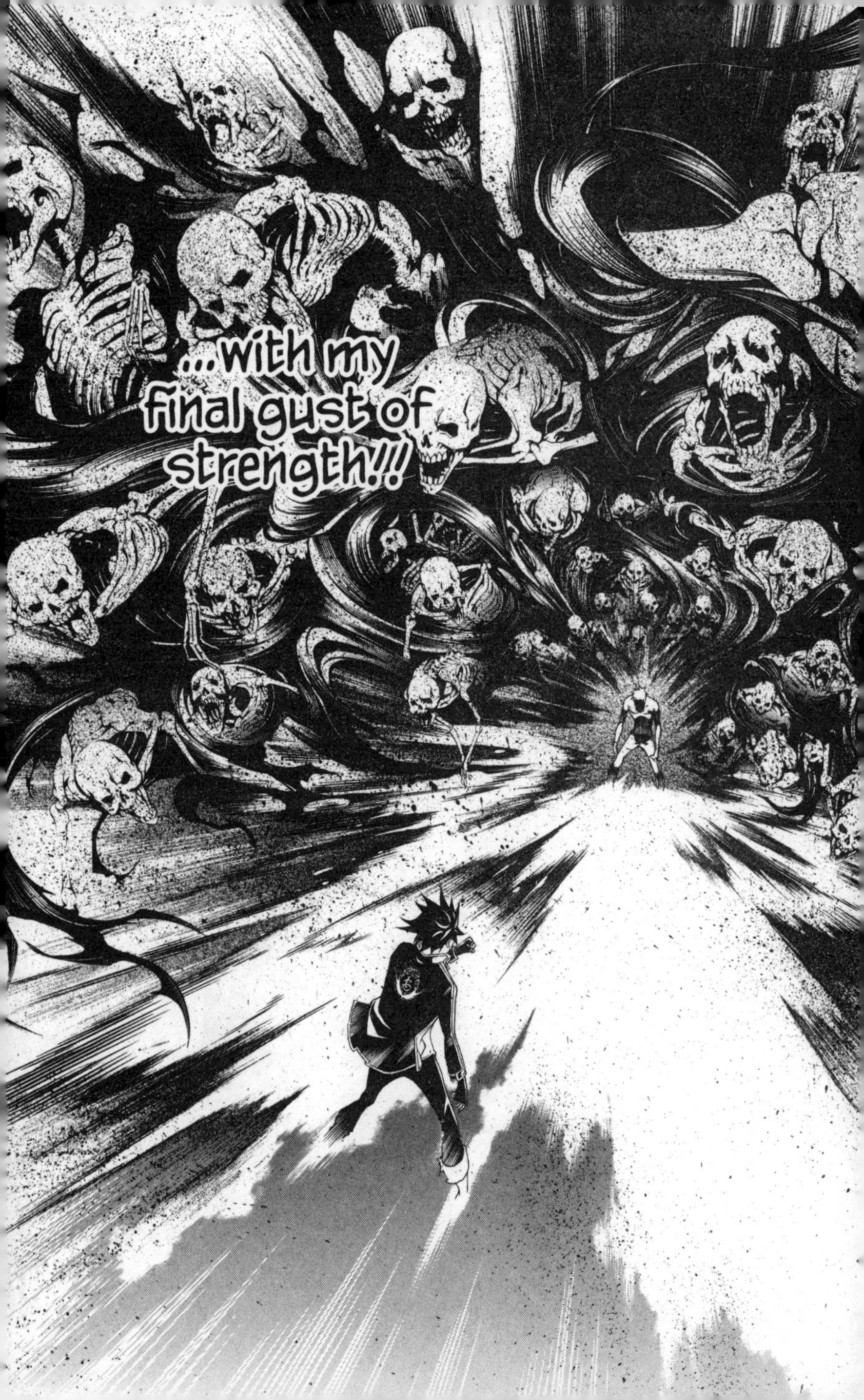
...with my final gust of strength!!

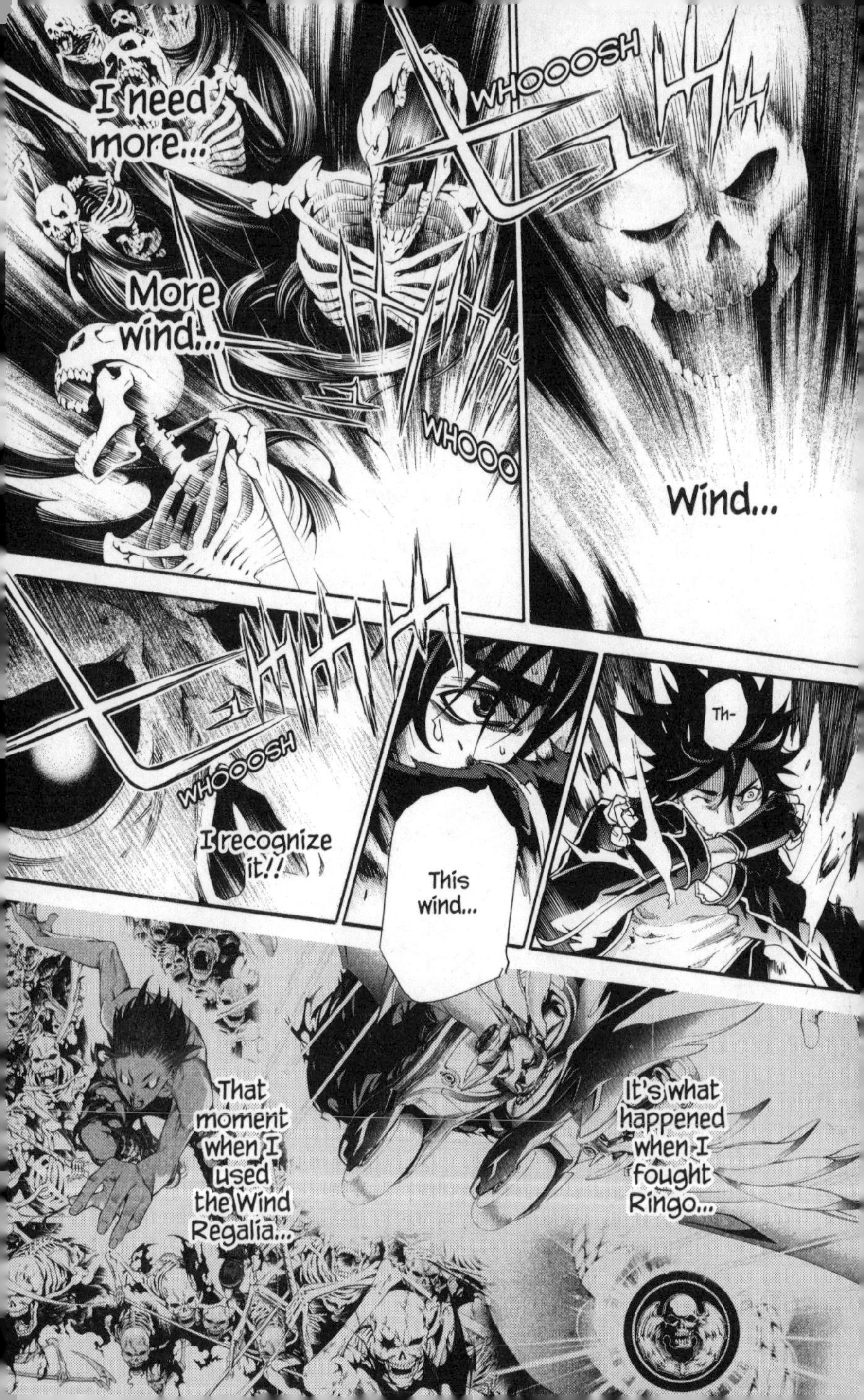
WHOOOSH
Wind...
I need more...
More wind...
WHOOO
Th-
This wind...
WHOOOSH
I recognize it!!
It's what happened when I fought Ringo...
That moment when I used the Wind Regalia...

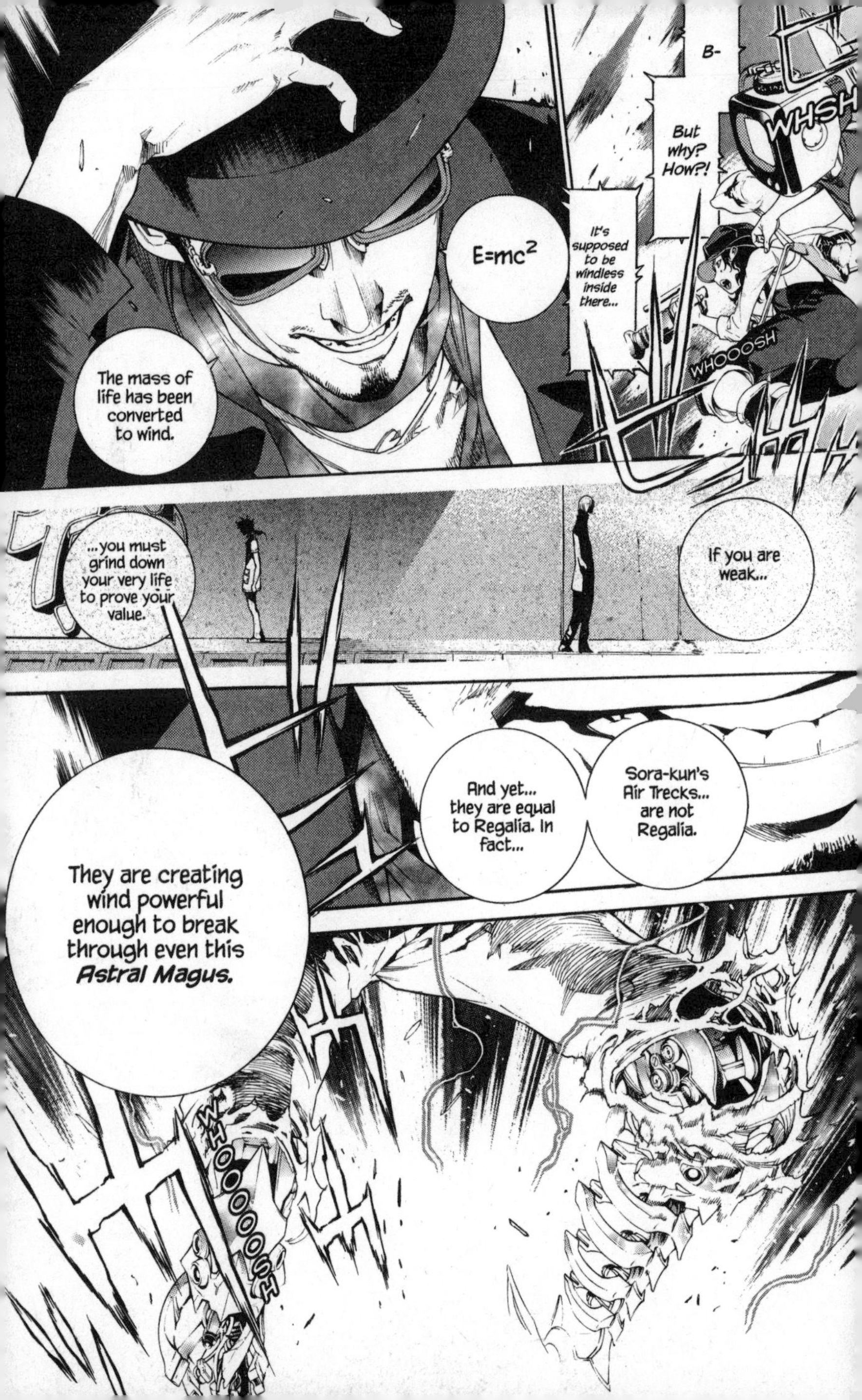
WHSH
B-
But why? How?!
It's supposed to be windless inside there...
WHOOOSH
E=mc²
The mass of life has been converted to wind.
If you are weak...
...you must grind down your very life to prove your value.
Sora-kun's Air Trecks... are not Regalia.
And yet... they are equal to Regalia. In fact...
They are creating wind powerful enough to break through even this *Astral Magus.*
WHOOOOOOSH

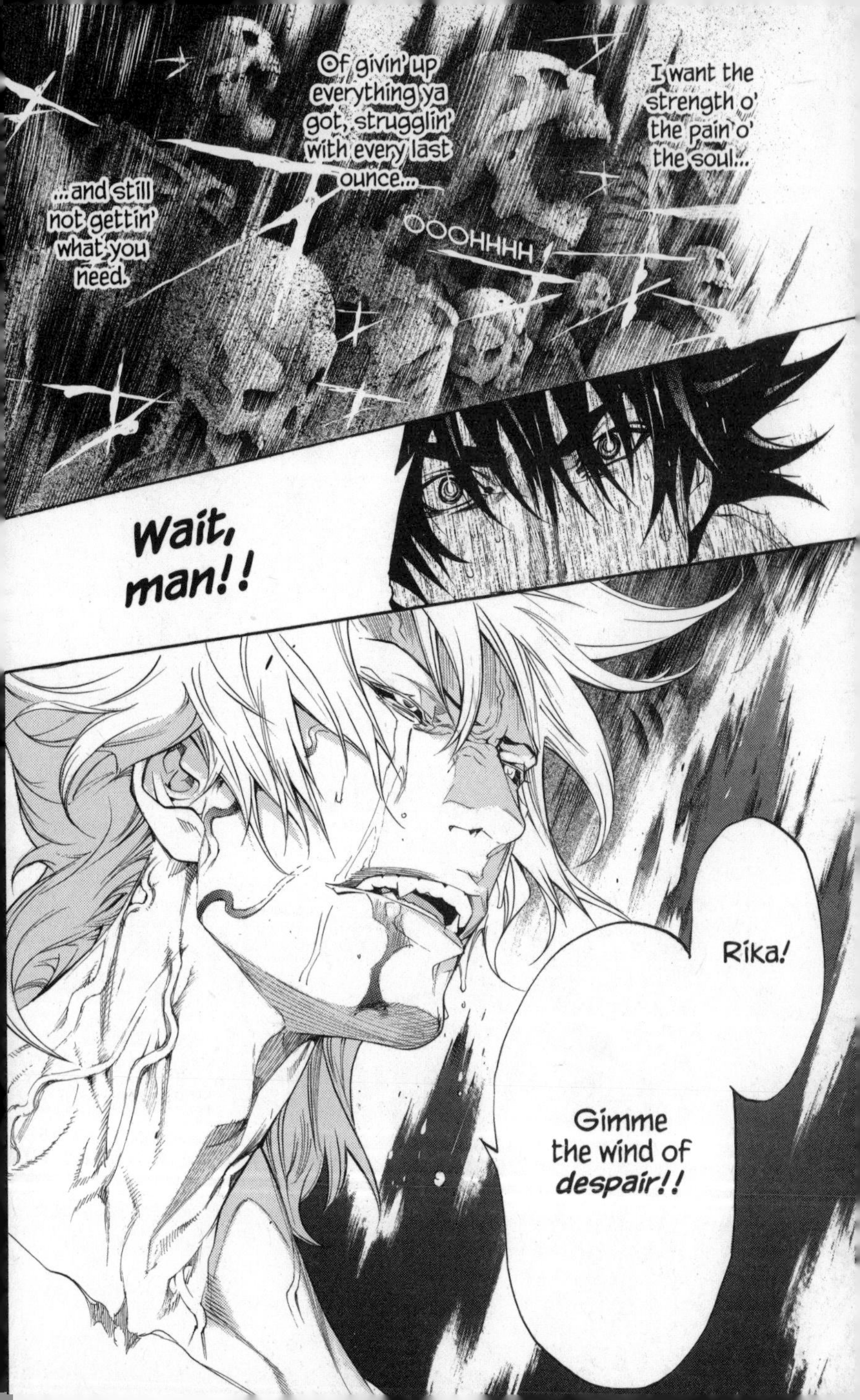
I want the strength o' the pain o' the soul...
Of givin' up everything ya got, strugglin' with every last ounce...
OOOHHHH
...and still not gettin' what you need.
Wait, man!!
Rika!
Gimme the wind of *despair!!*

Trick:353

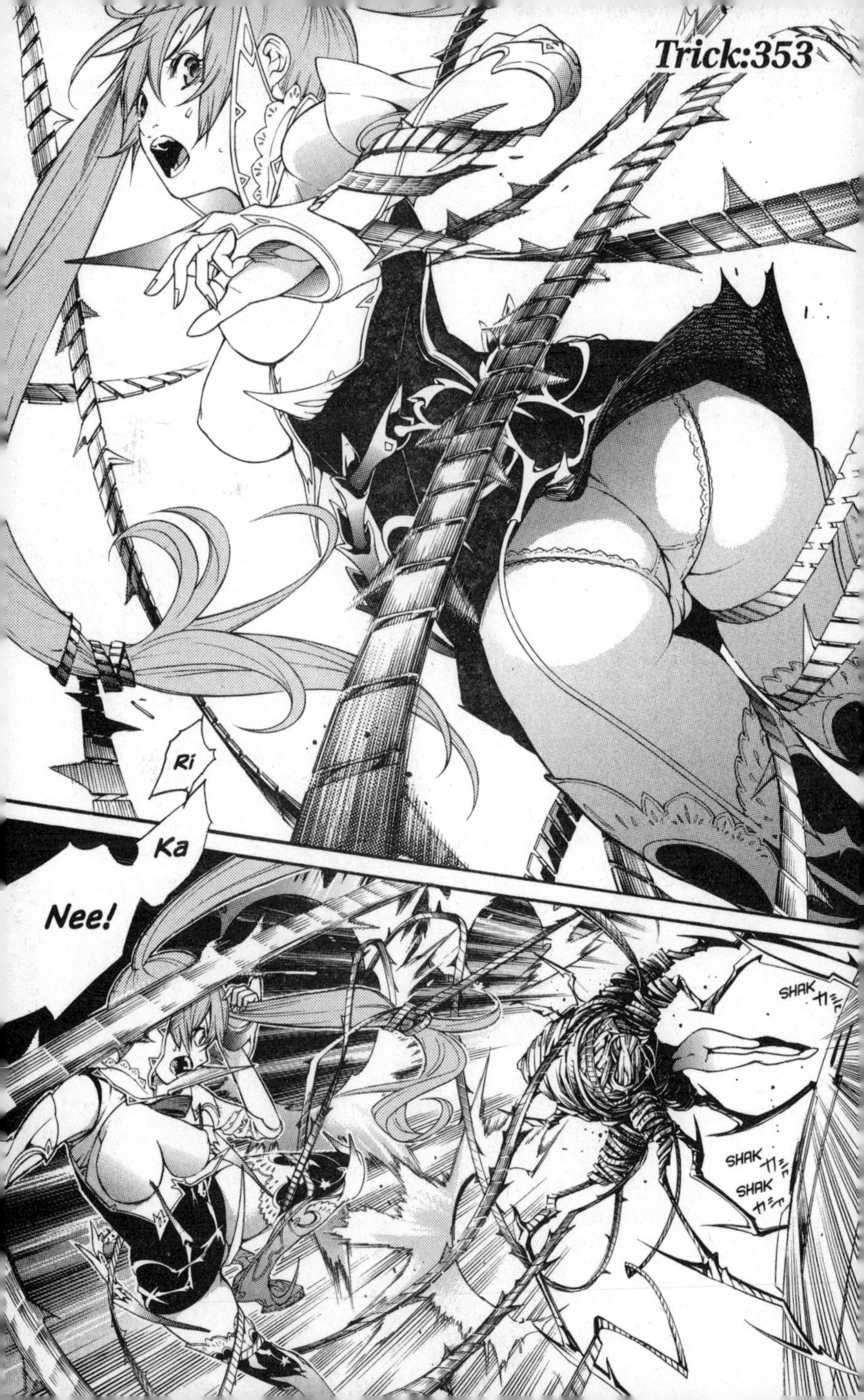

Ri
Ka
Nee!
SHAK
SHAK
SHAK

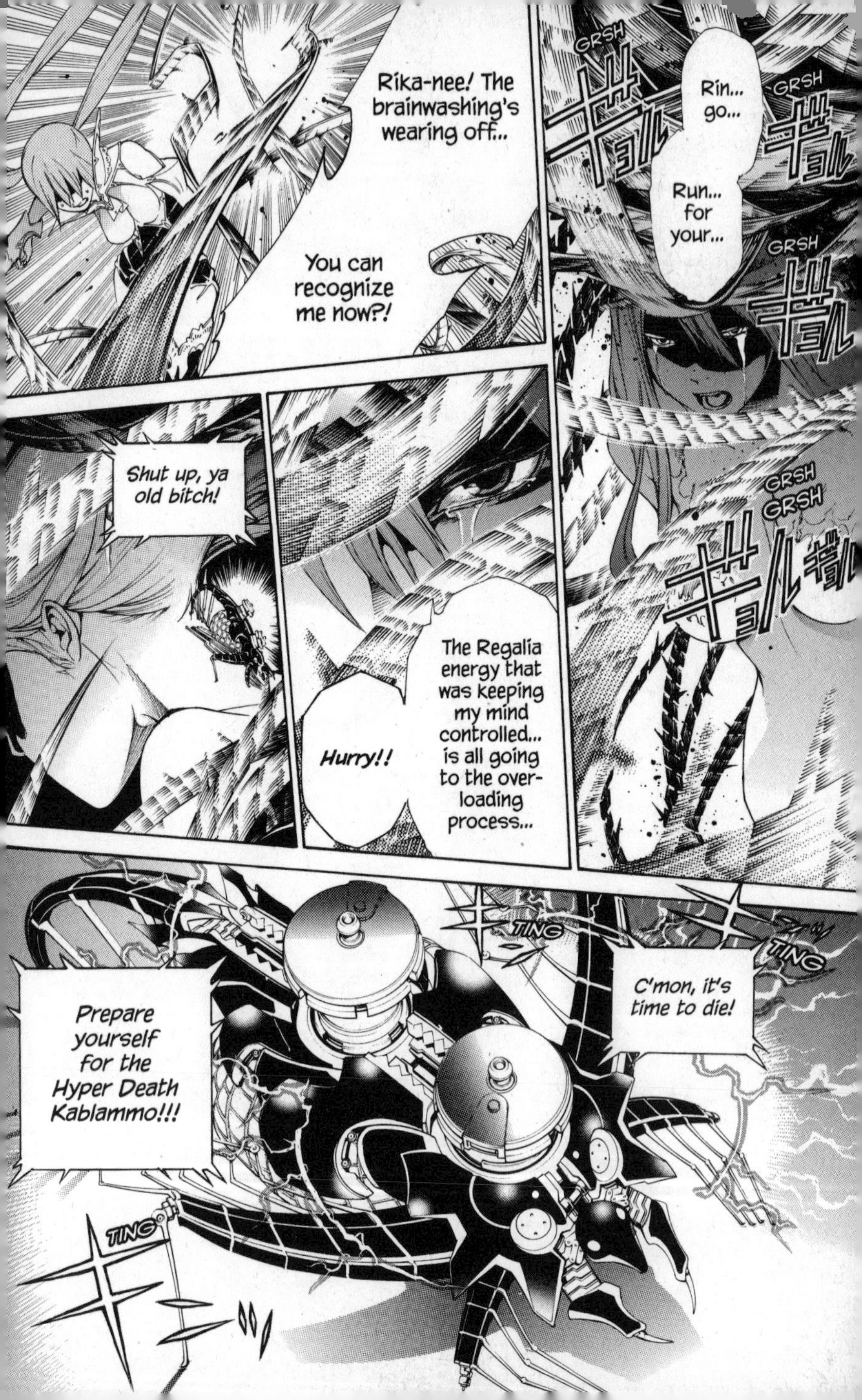
GRSH
Rin... go...
GRSH
Run... for your...
GRSH
Rika-nee! The brainwashing's wearing off...
You can recognize me now?!
GRSH
GRSH
The Regalia energy that was keeping my mind controlled... is all going to the over-loading process...
Hurry!!
Shut up, ya old bitch!
TING
TING
C'mon, it's time to die!
TING
Prepare yourself for the Hyper Death Kablammo!!!

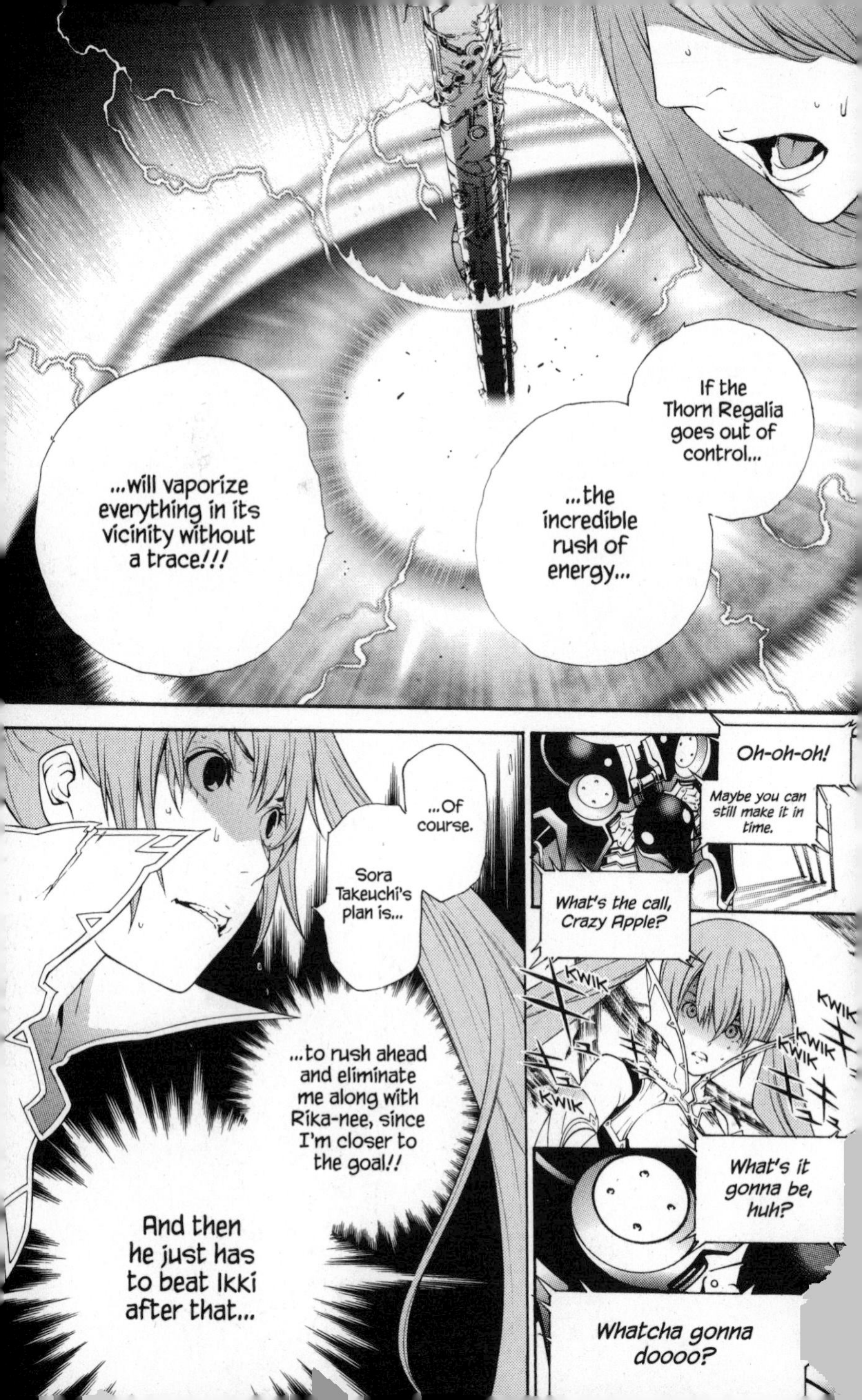
If the Thorn Regalia goes out of control...
...the incredible rush of energy...
...will vaporize everything in its vicinity without a trace!!!
Oh-oh-oh!
Maybe you can still make it in time.
What's the call, Crazy Apple?
KWIK
KWIK
KWIK
KWIK
What's it gonna be, huh?
Whatcha gonna doooo?
...Of course.
Sora Takeuchi's plan is...
...to rush ahead and eliminate me along with Rika-nee, since I'm closer to the goal!!
And then he just has to beat Ikki after that...

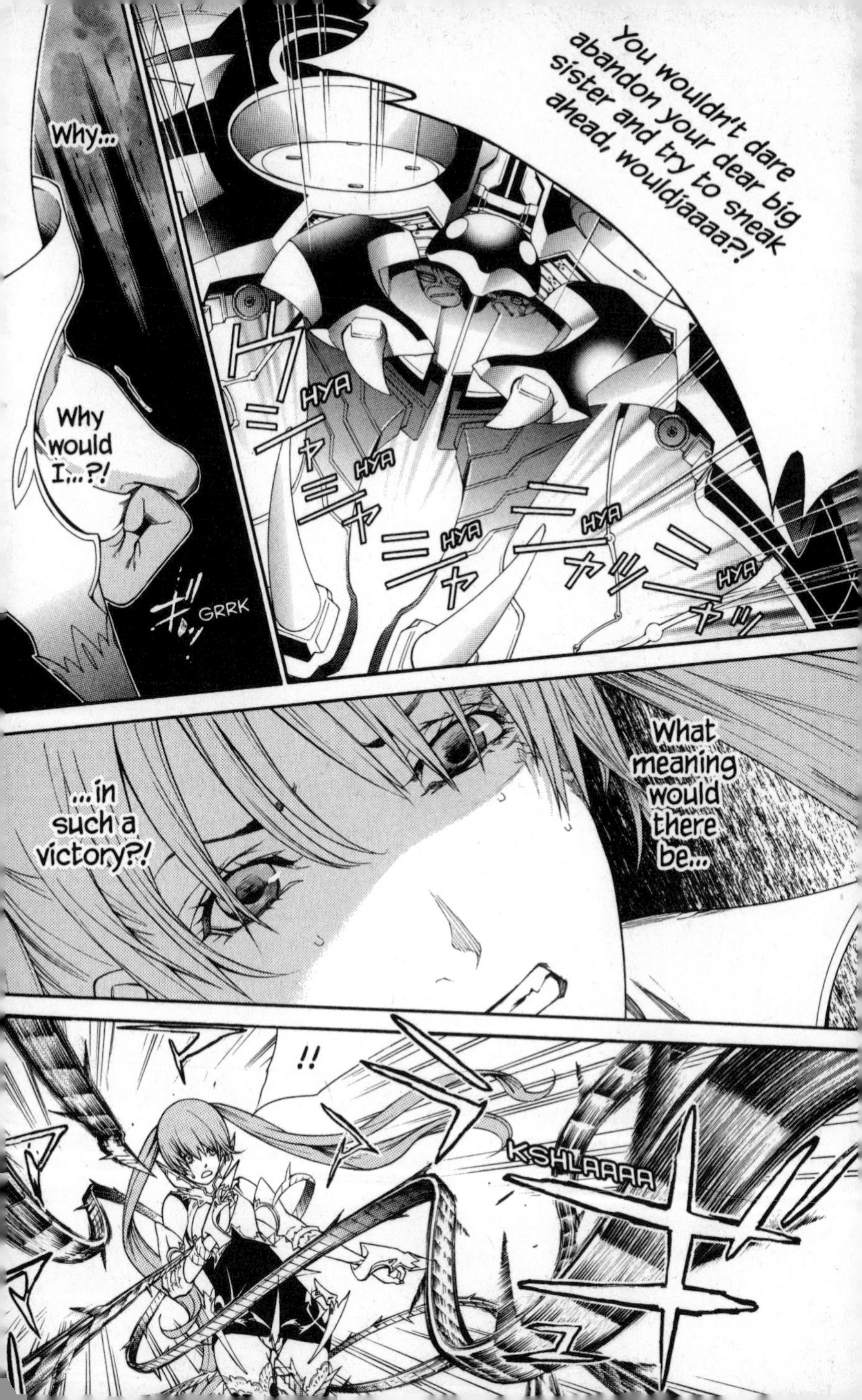
You wouldn't dare abandon your dear big sister and try to sneak ahead, wouldjaaaa?!
HYA
HYA
HYA
HYA
HYA
Why...
Why would I...?!
GRRK
What meaning would there be...
...in such a victory?!
!!
KSHLAAAA

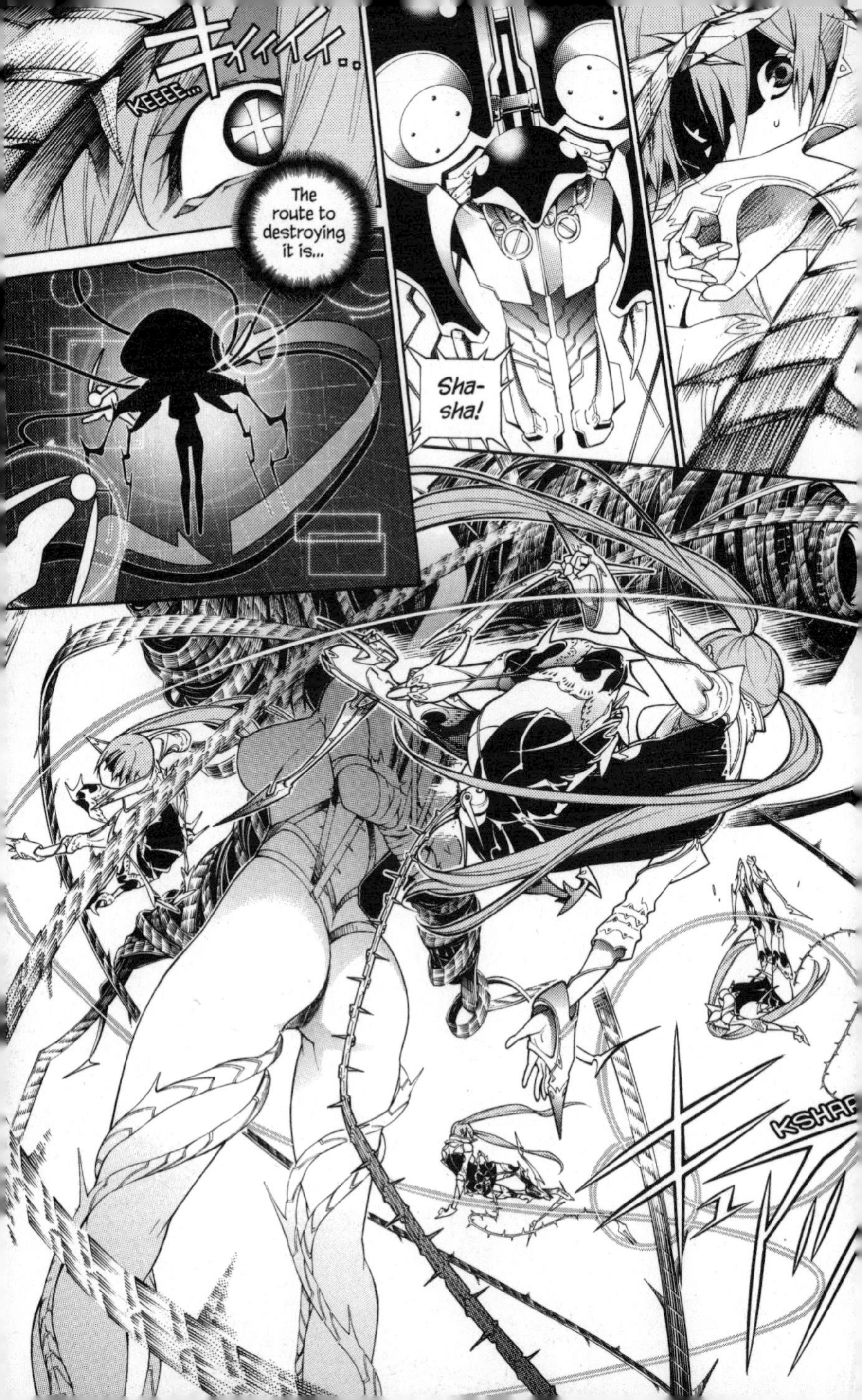
Sha-sha!
キイイイイ..
KEEEE...
The route to destroying it is...
KSHA

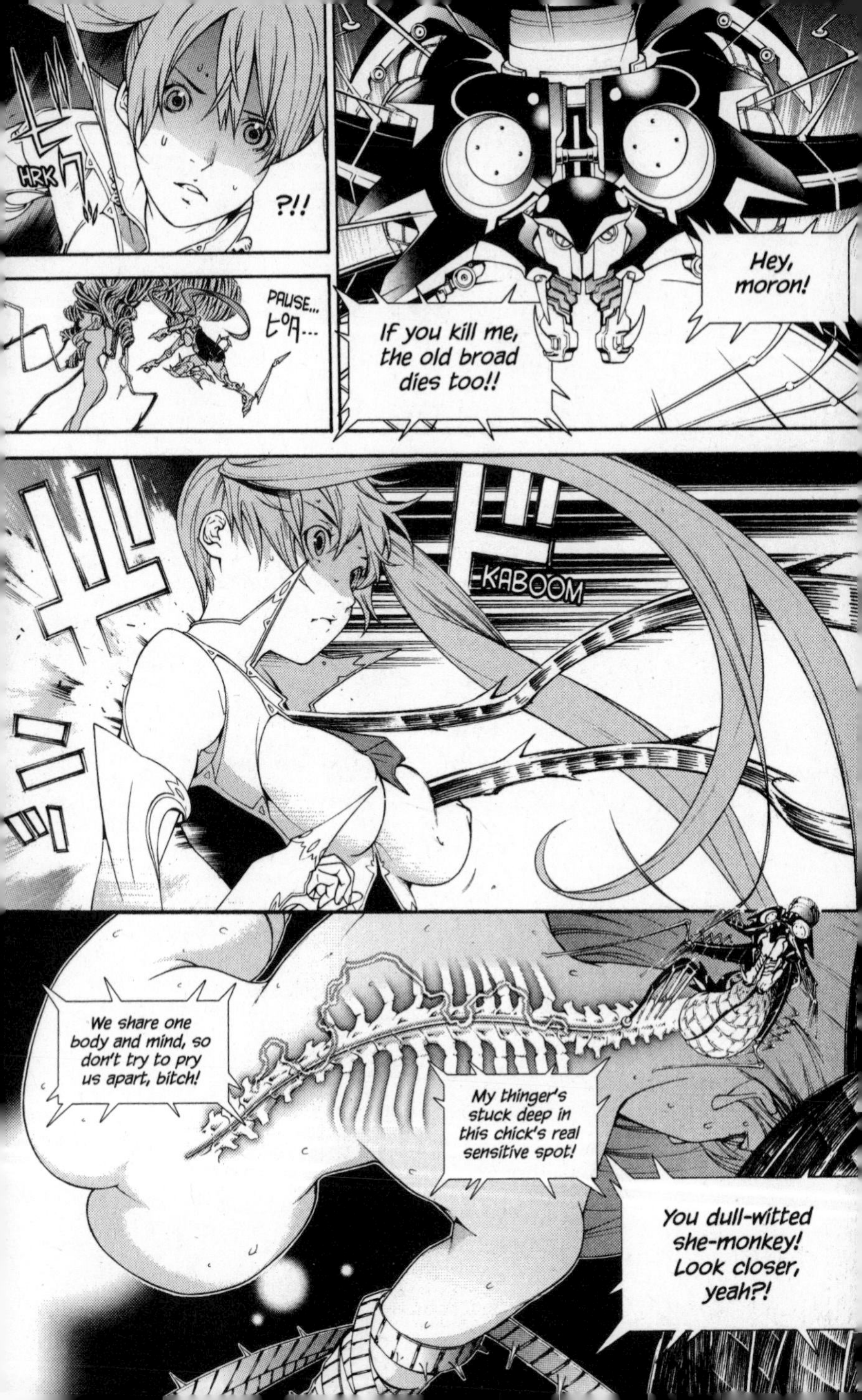
Hey, moron!
If you kill me, the old broad dies too!!
HRK
?!!
PAUSE...
KABOOM
You dull-witted she-monkey! Look closer, yeah?!
My thinger's stuck deep in this chick's real sensitive spot!
We share one body and mind, so don't try to pry us apart, bitch!

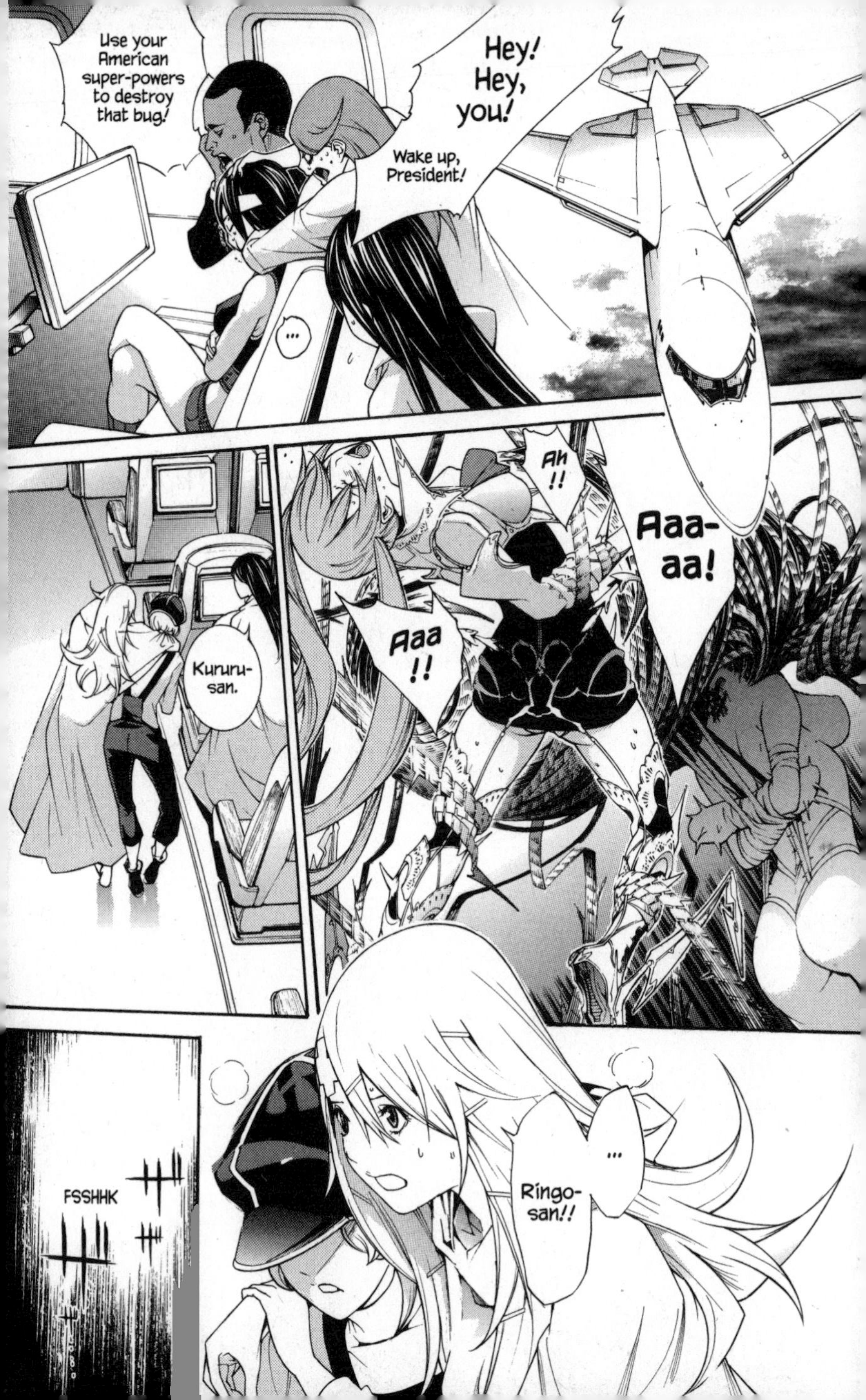
Hey! Hey, you!
Wake up, President!
Use your American super-powers to destroy that bug!
...
Aaa-aa!
Ah!!
Aaa!!
Kururu-san.
...
Ringo-san!!
FSSHHK

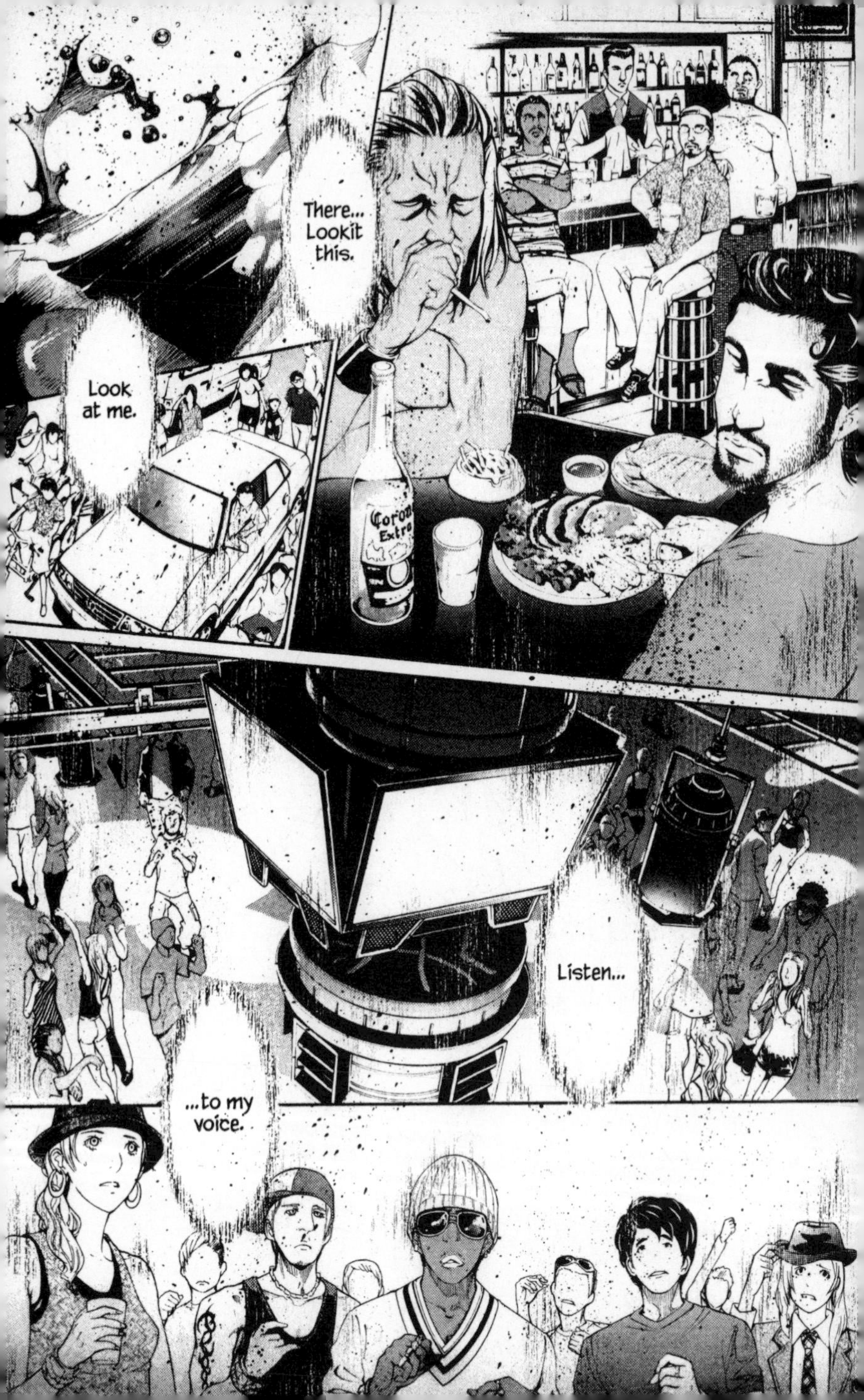
There... Lookit this.
Look at me.
Listen...
...to my voice.

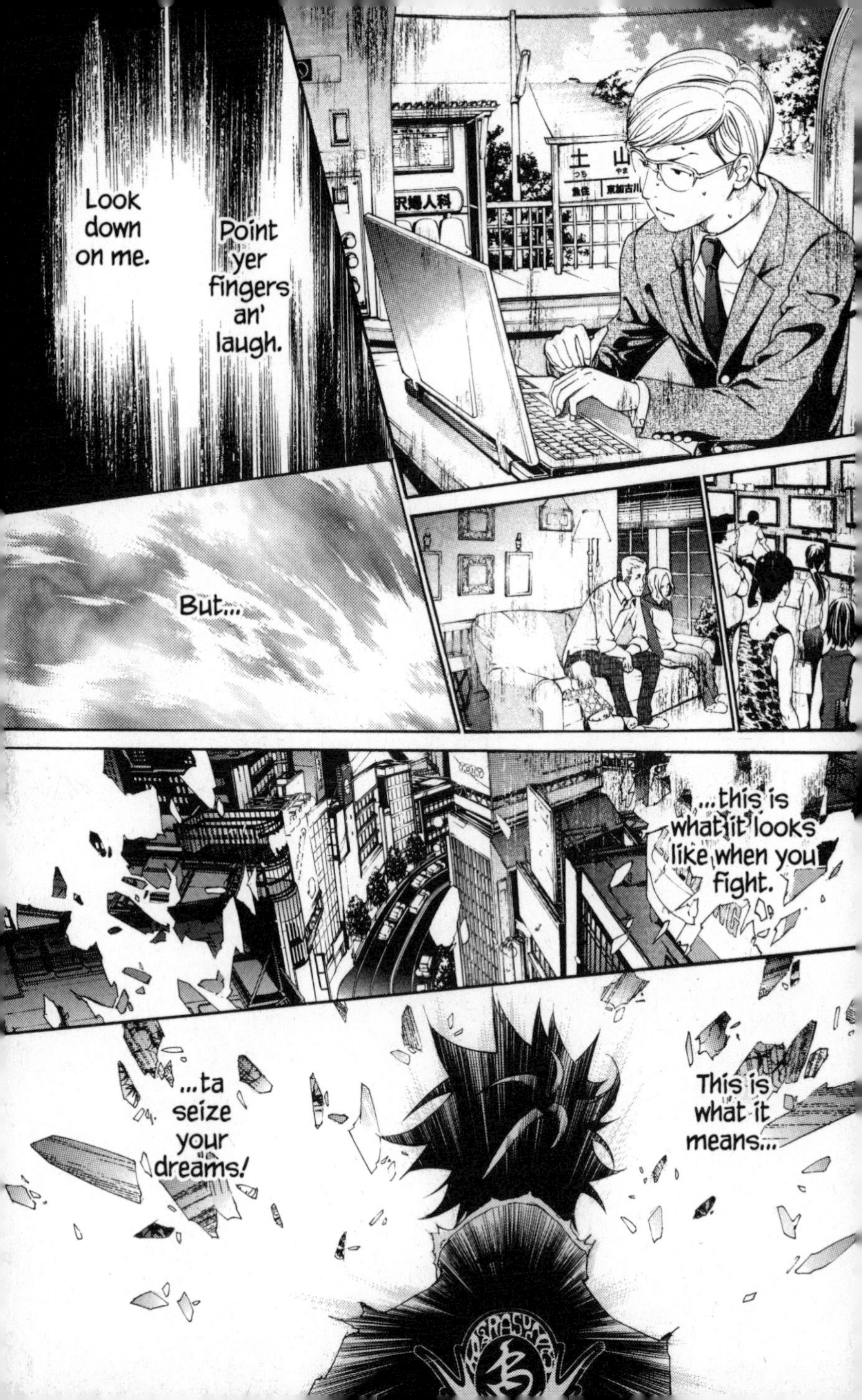
土山
Point yer fingers an' laugh.
Look down on me.
But...
...this is what it looks like when you fight.
This is what it means...
...ta seize your dreams!

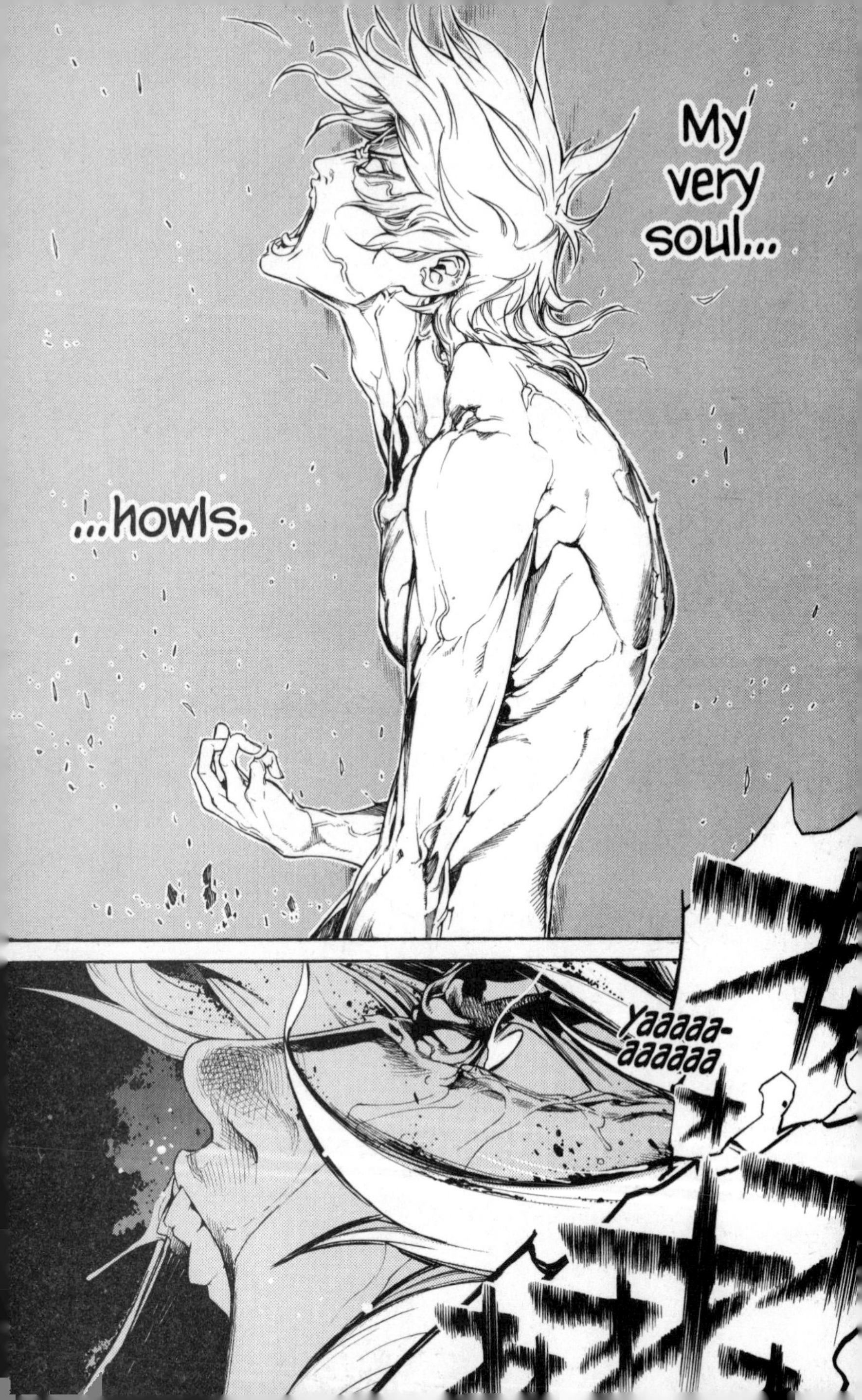
My very soul...
...howls.
Yaaaaa-aaaaaa

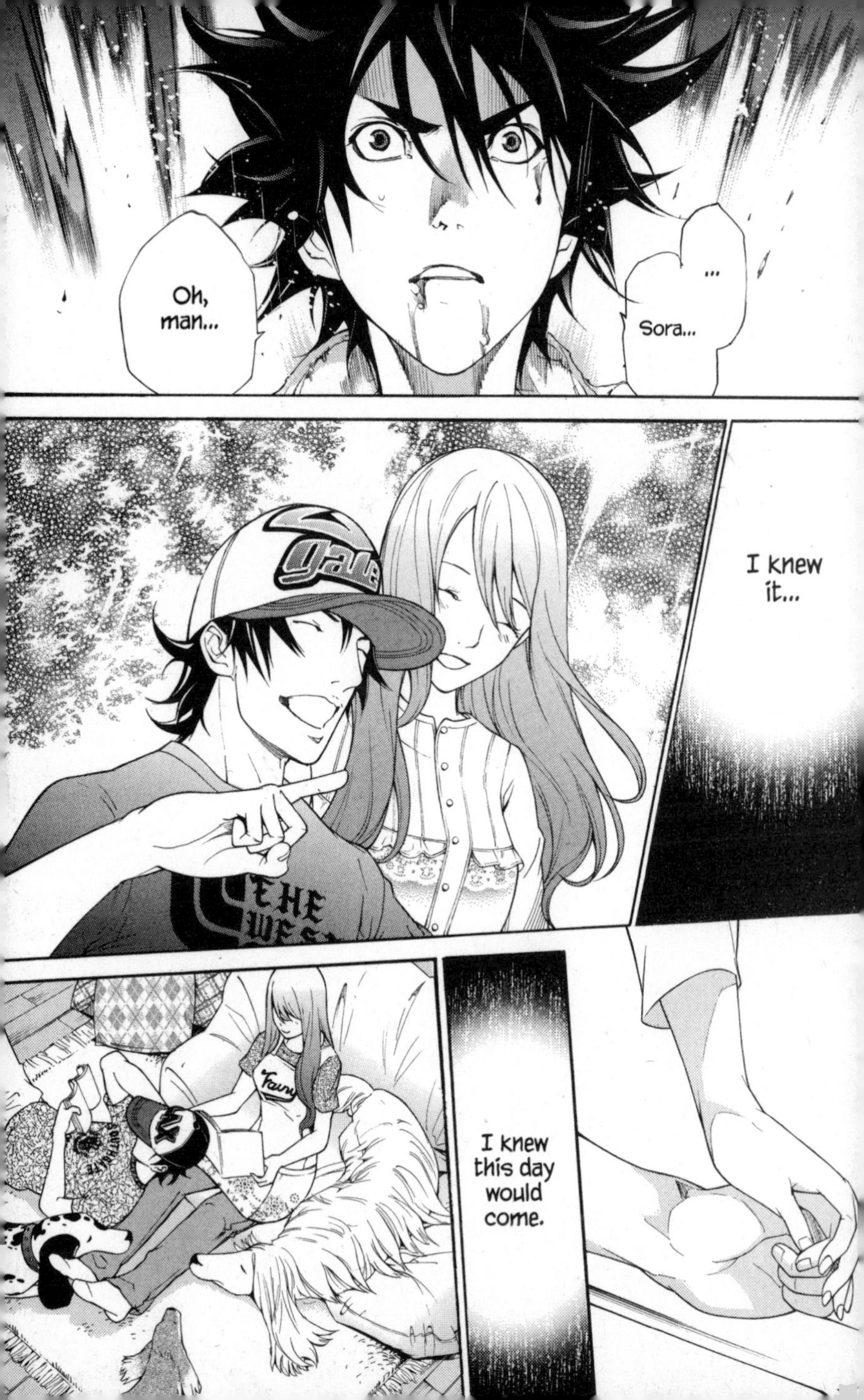
...
Sora...
Oh, man...
I knew it...
I knew this day would come.

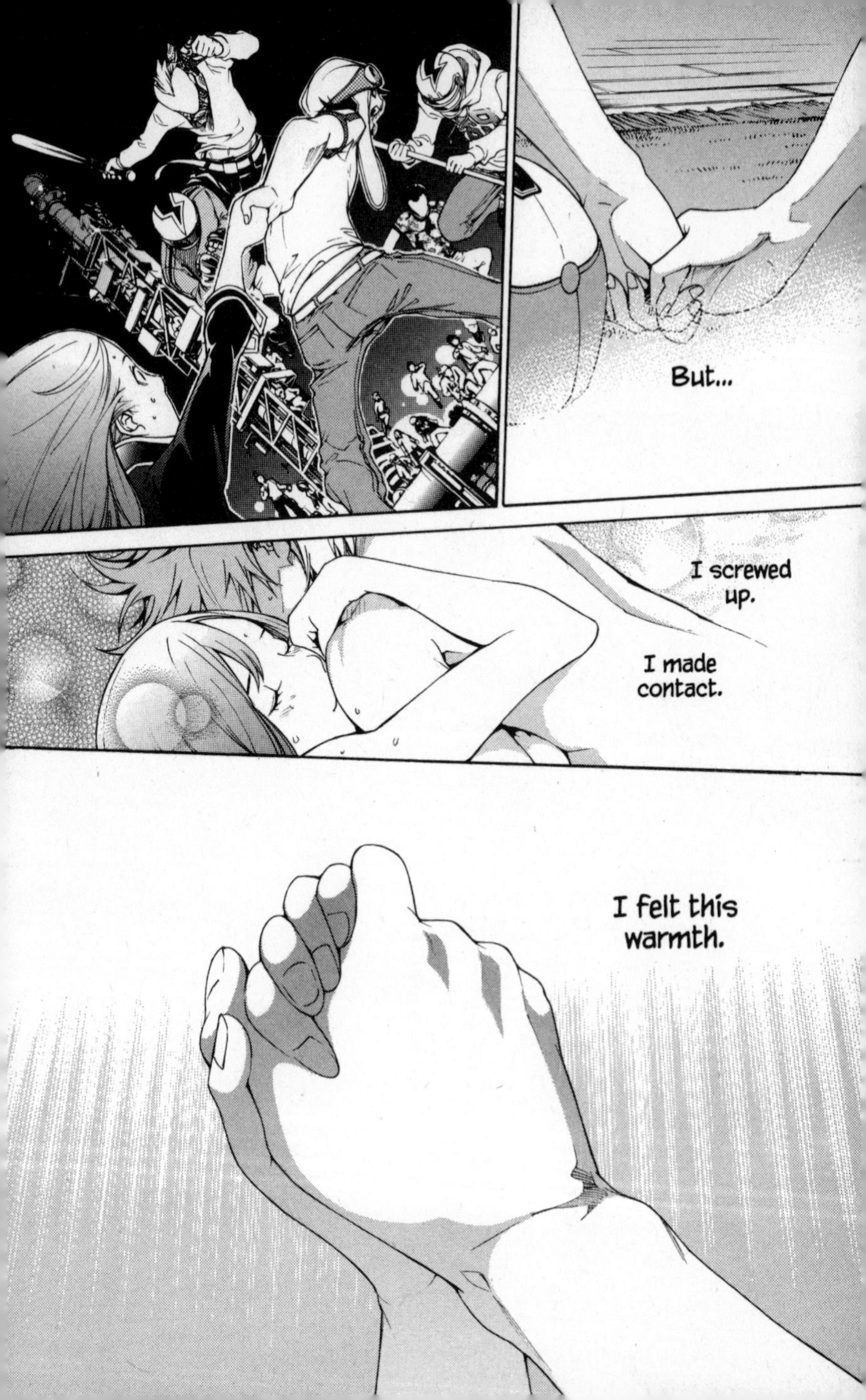
But...
I screwed up.
I made contact.
I felt this warmth.

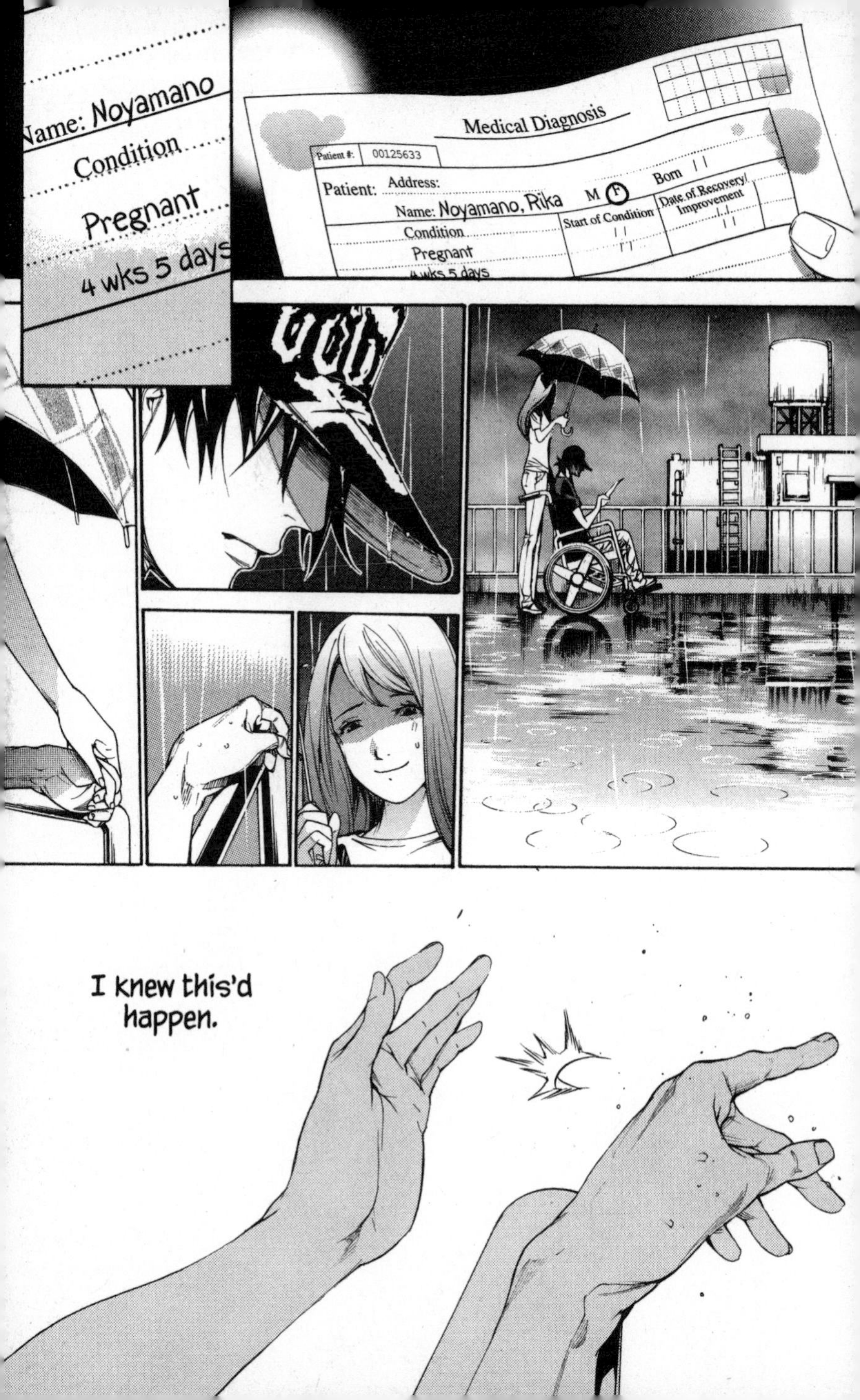
Medical Diagnosis
Patient #: 00125633
Patient: Address:
Born / /
Name: Noyamano, Rika M (F)
Start of Condition / /
Date of Recovery/ Improvement / /
Condition
Pregnant
4 wks 5 days
Name: Noyamano
Condition
Pregnant
4 wks 5 days
I knew this'd happen.

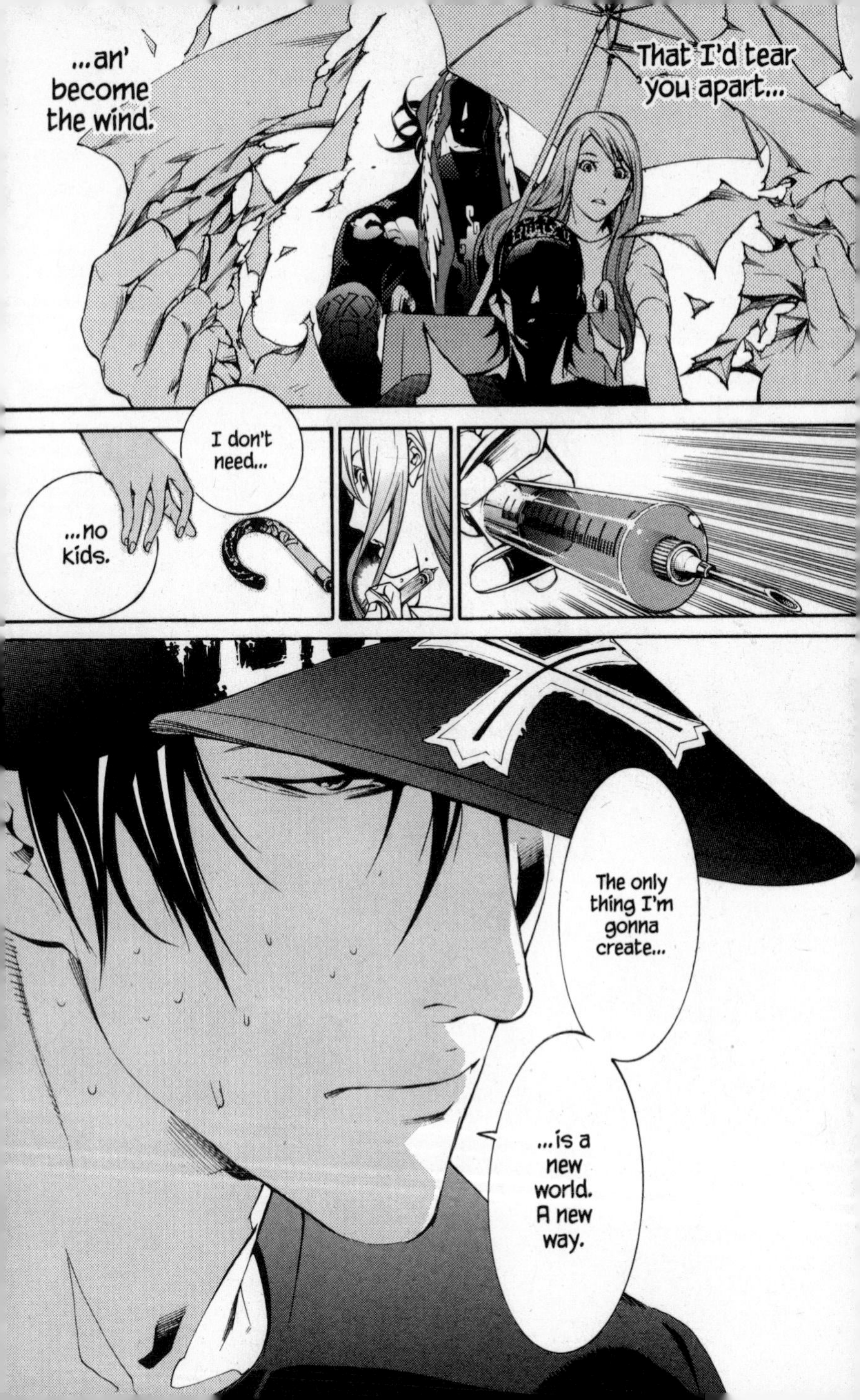
That I'd tear you apart...
...an' become the wind.
I don't need...
...no kids.
The only thing I'm gonna create...
...is a new world. A new way.

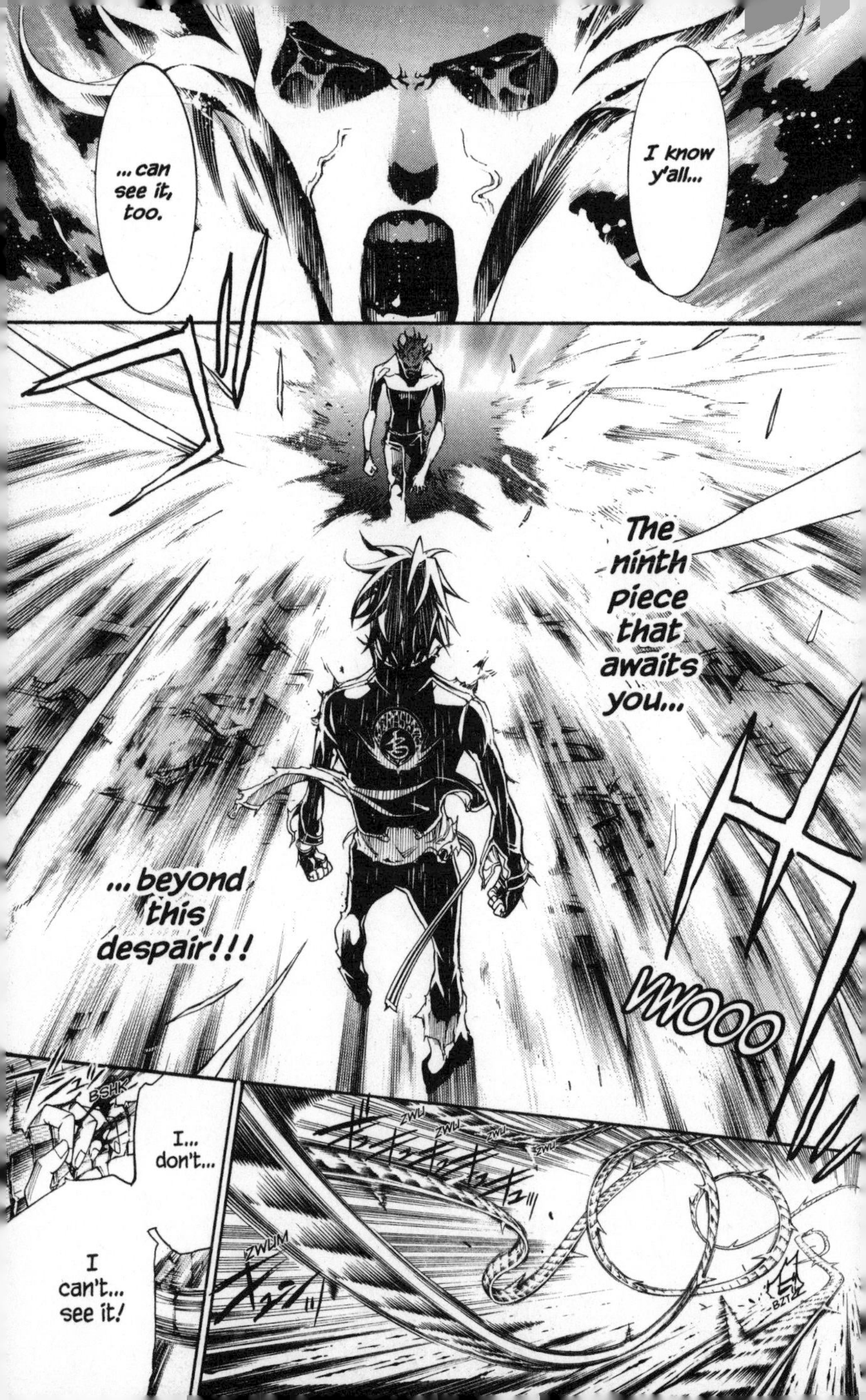
I know y'all...
...can see it, too.
The ninth piece that awaits you...
VWOOO
...beyond this despair!!!
ZWU
ZWU
ZWU
ZWU
BZT
ZWUM
BSHK
I... don't...
I can't... see it!

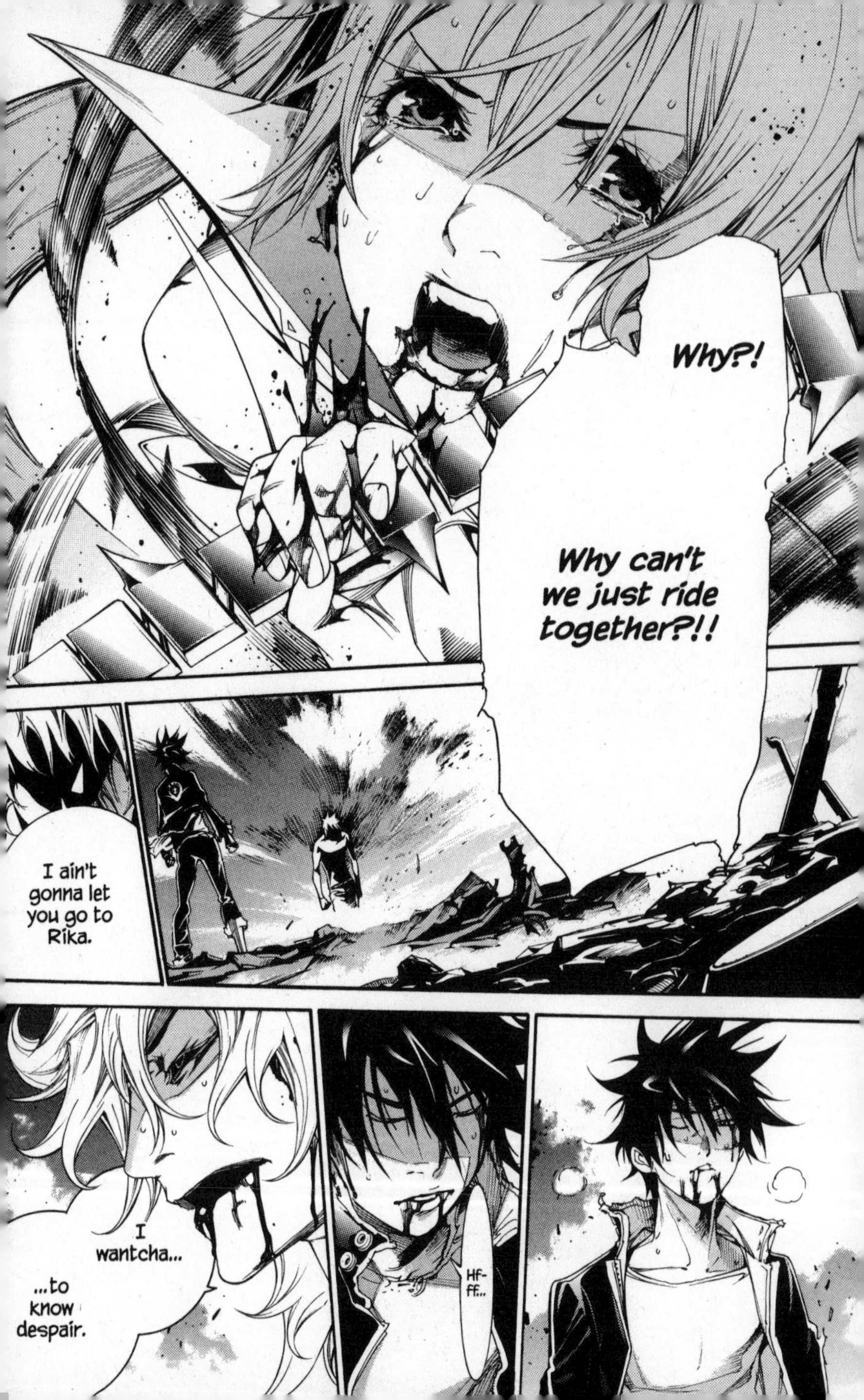
Why?!
Why can't we just ride together?!!
I ain't gonna let you go to Rika.
Hf-ff...
I wantcha...
...to know despair.

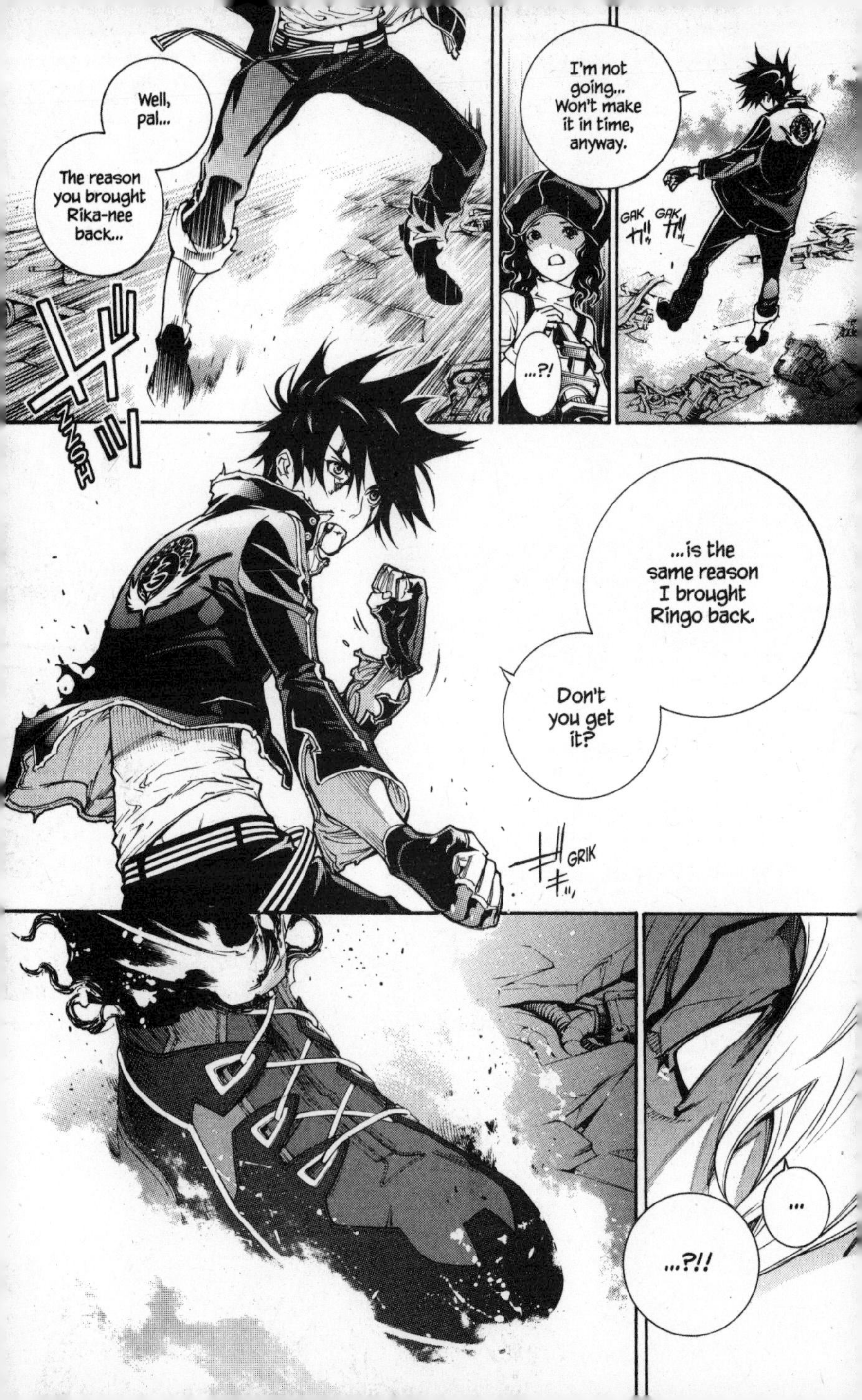
I'm not going... Won't make it in time, anyway.
GAK GAK
...?!
Well, pal...
The reason you brought Rika-nee back...
FOOSH
...is the same reason I brought Ringo back.
Don't you get it?
GRIK
...
...?!!

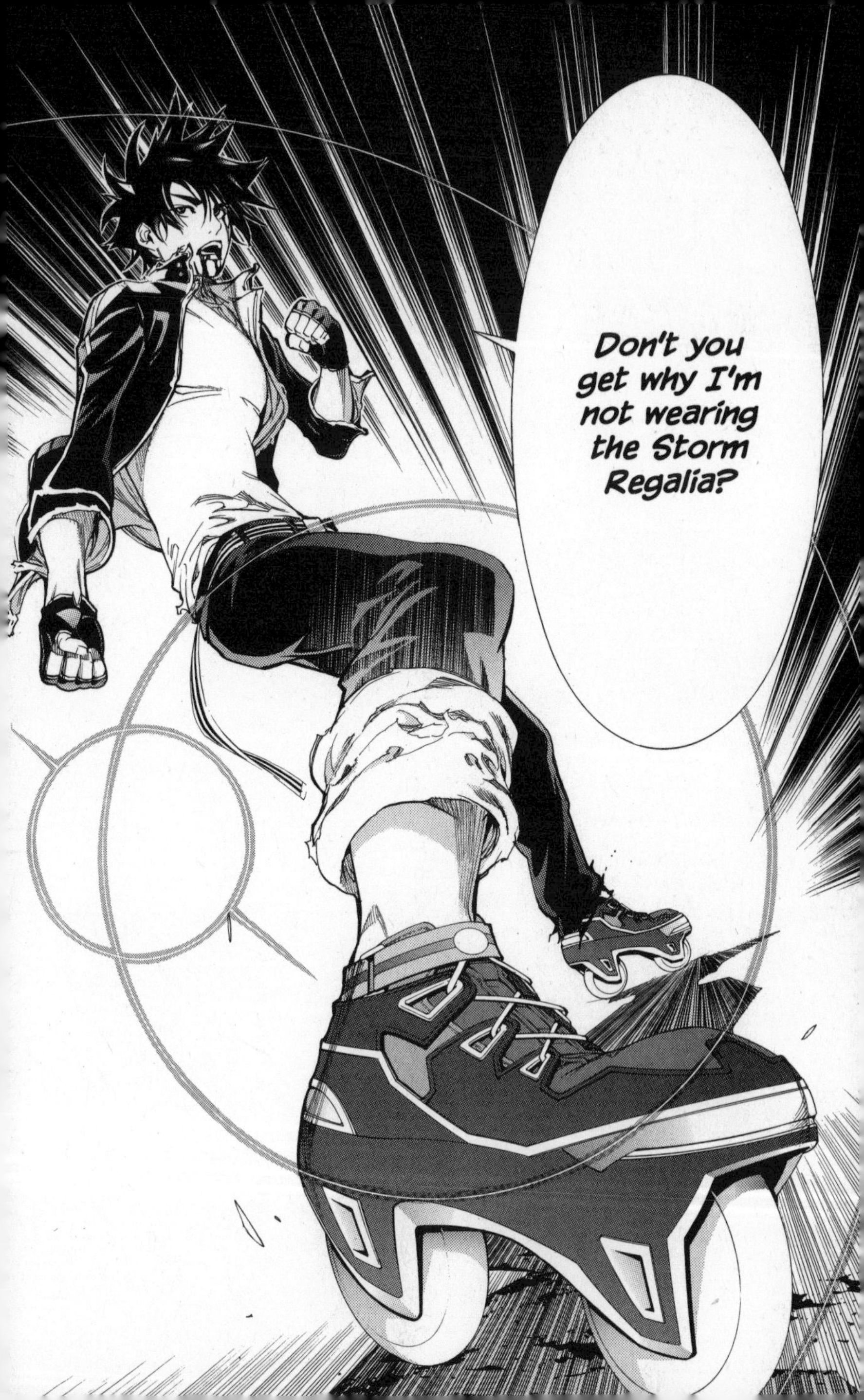
Don't you get why I'm not wearing the Storm Regalia?

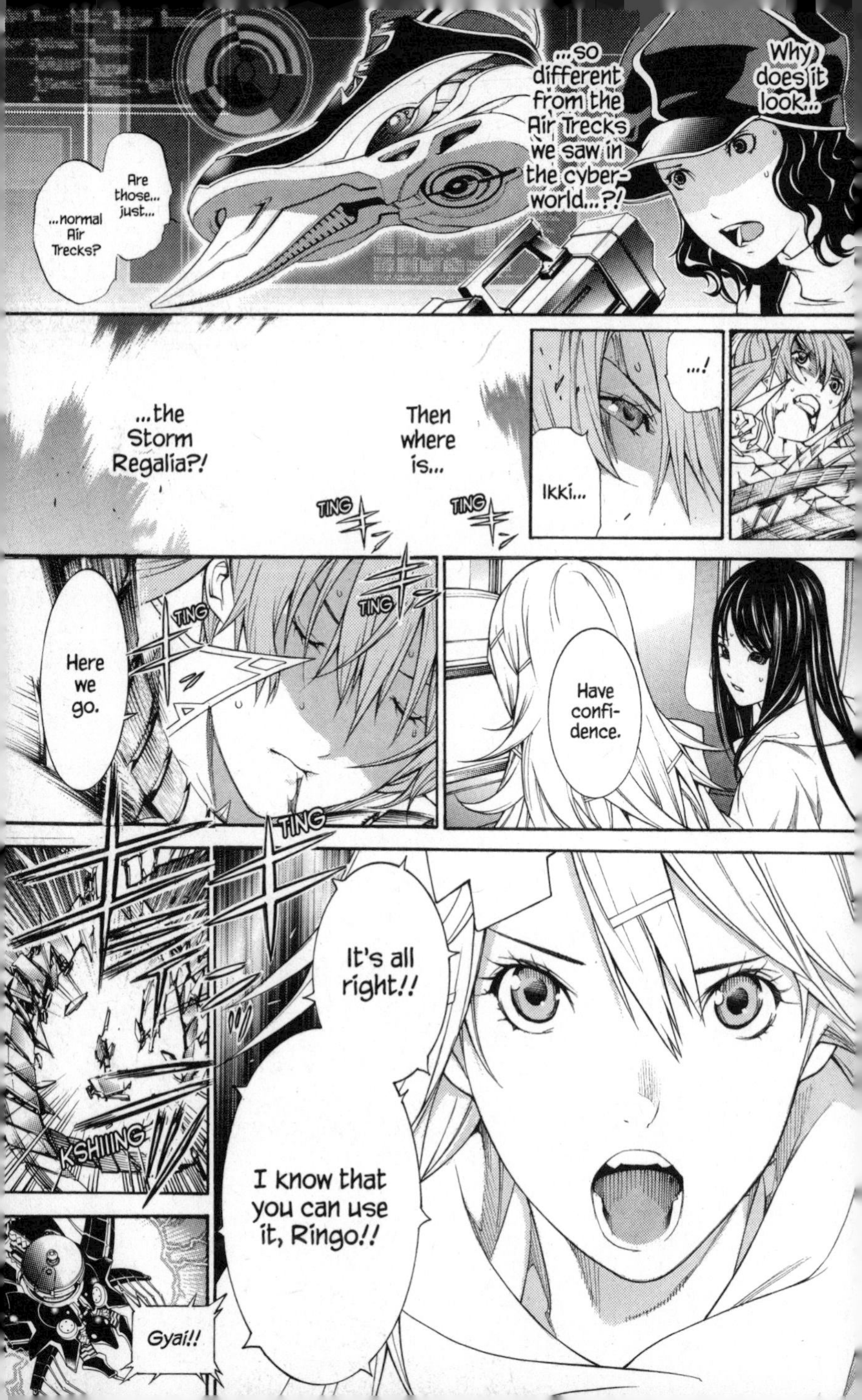
Why does it look...
...so different from the Air Trecks we saw in the cyber-world...?!
Are those... just...
...normal Air Trecks?
...!
Ikki...
Then where is...
...the Storm Regalia?!
TING
TING
TING
TING
Have confi-dence.
Here we go.
TING
It's all right!!
I know that you can use it, Ringo!!
KSHIIING
Gyai!!

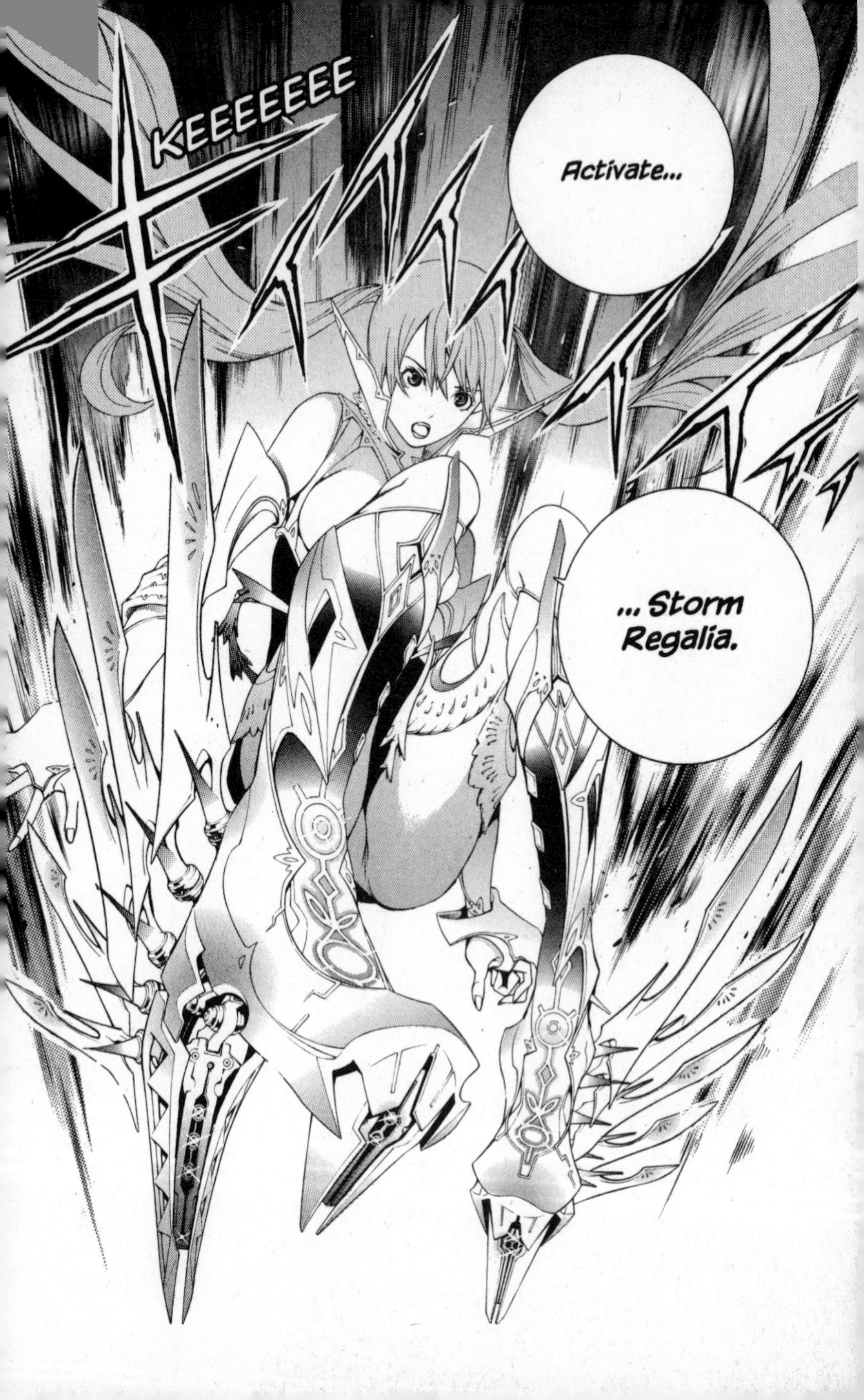
Activate...
KEEEEEEE
...Storm Regalia.

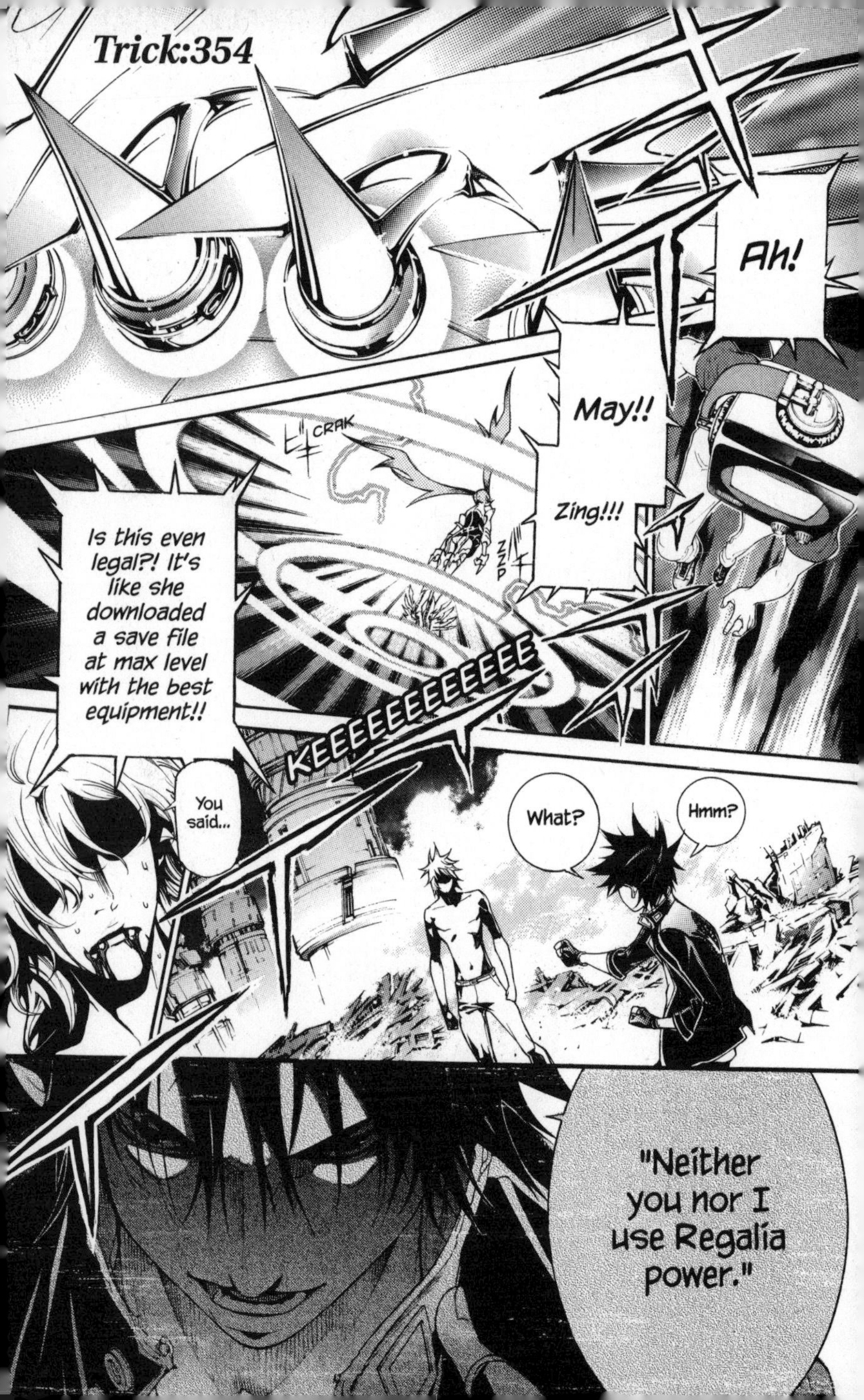
Trick:354
Ah!
May!!
Zing!!!
CRAK
ZZP
Is this even legal?! It's like she downloaded a save file at max level with the best equipment!!
KEEEEEEEEEEEEE
You said...
Hmm?
What?
"Neither you nor I use Regalia power."

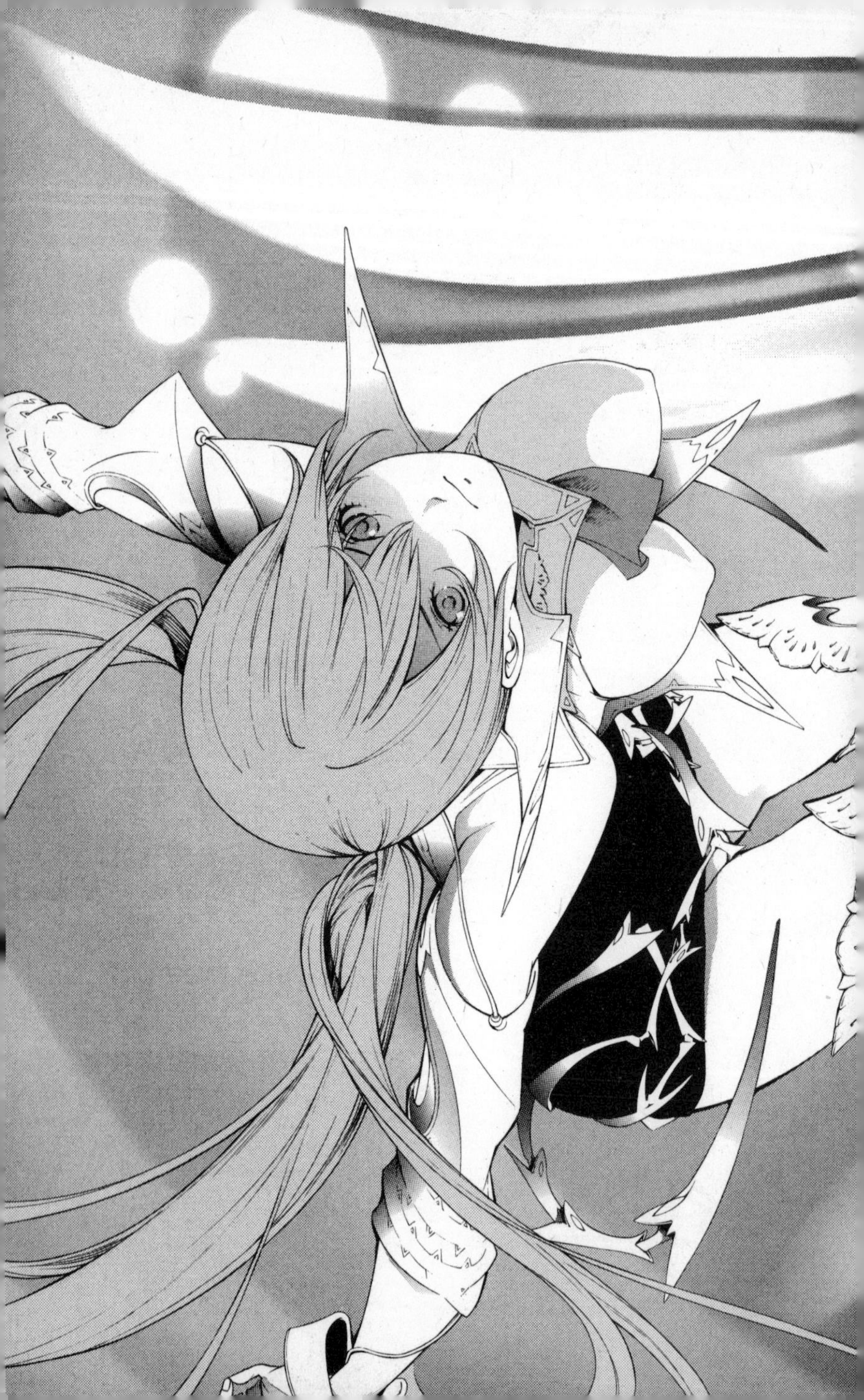

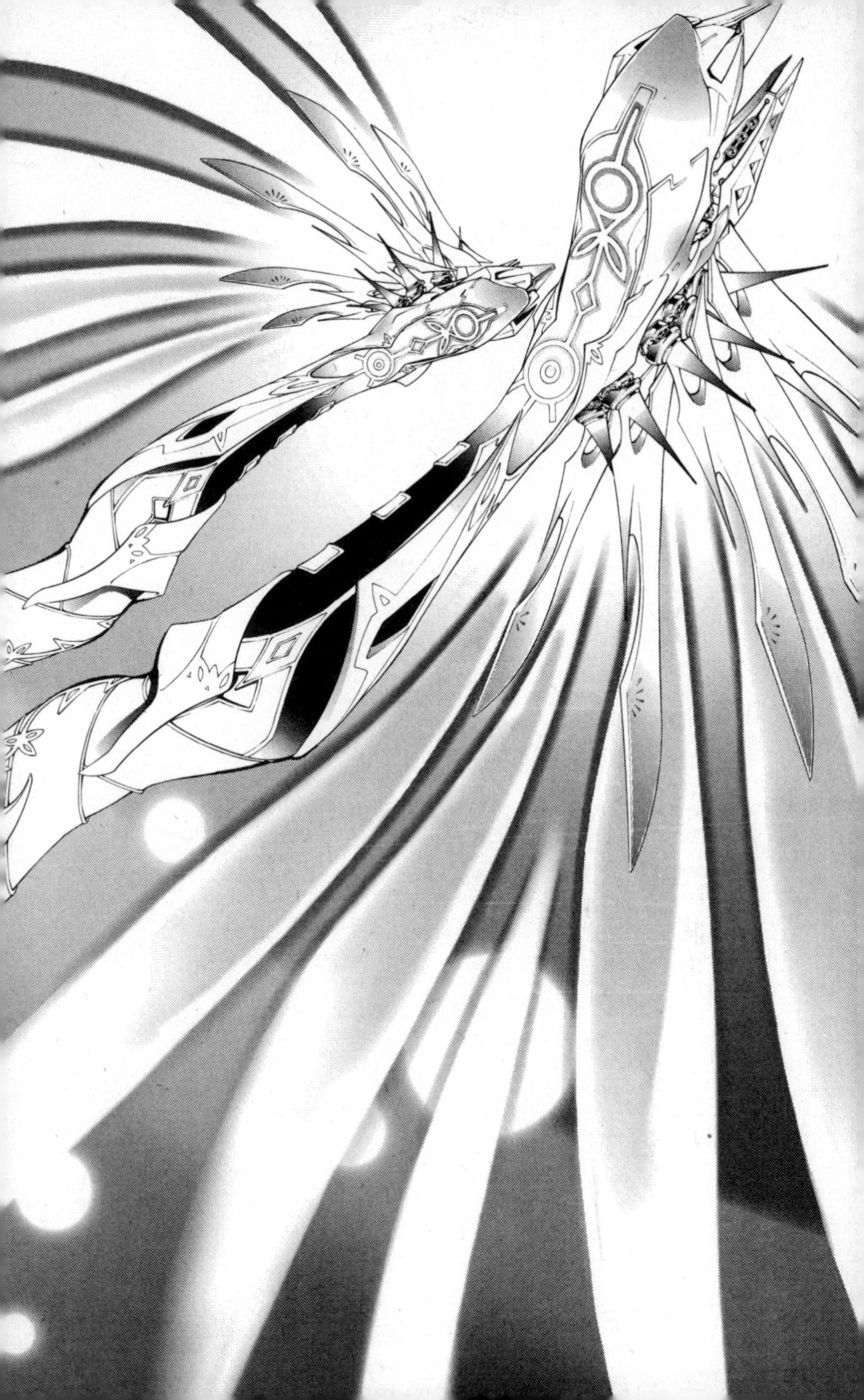

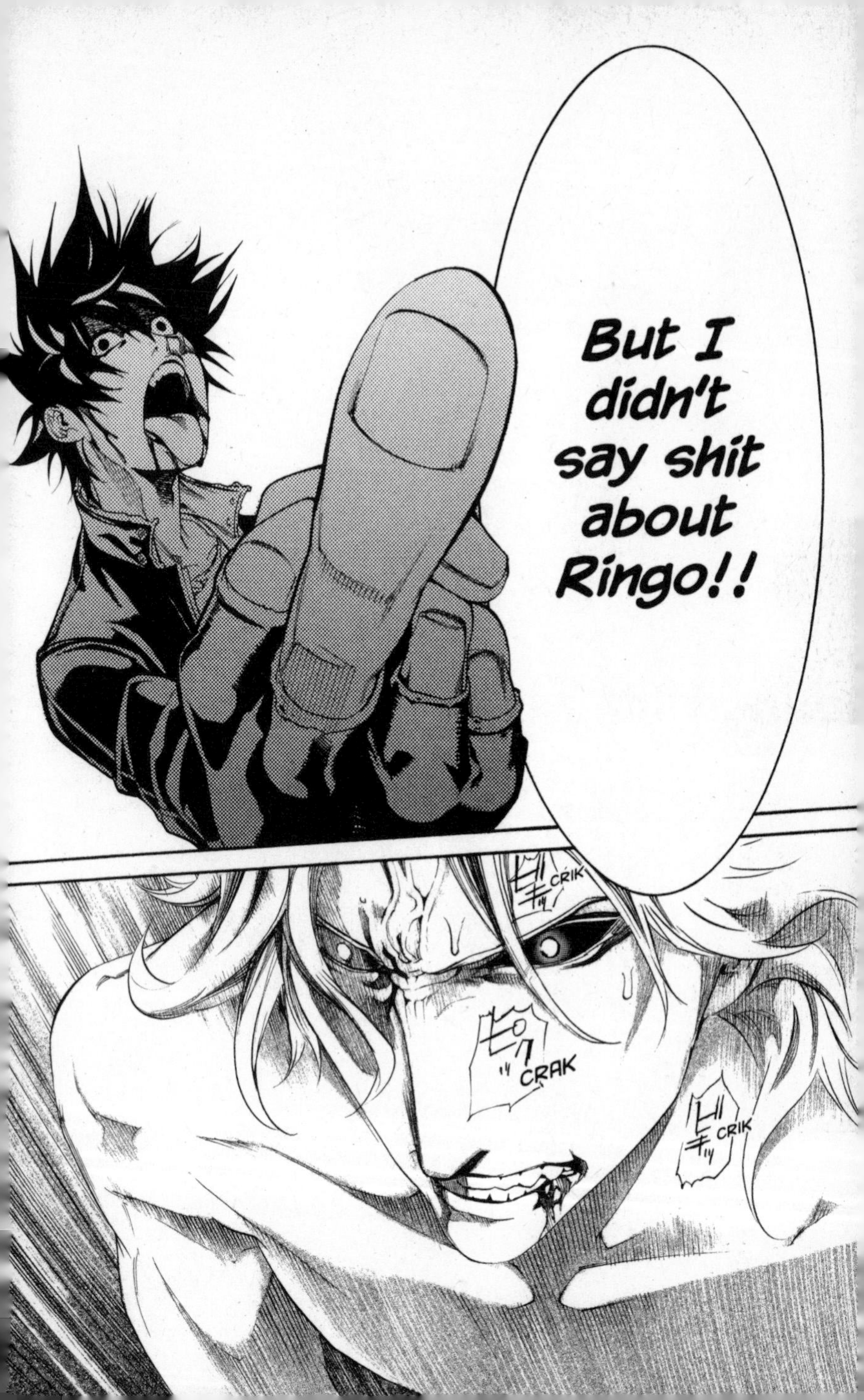
But I didn't say shit about Ringo!!
CRIK
CRAK
CRIK

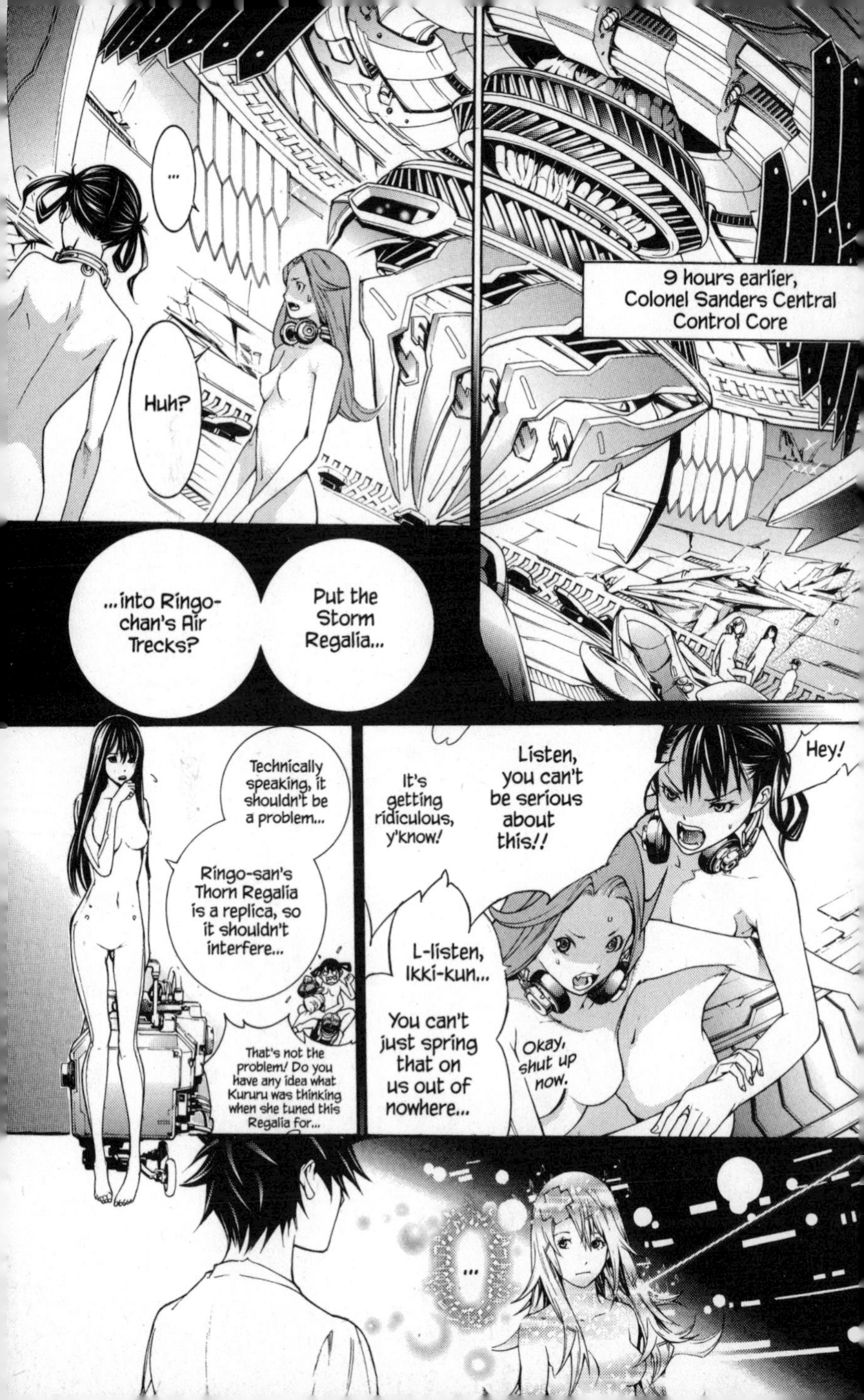
9 hours earlier, Colonel Sanders Central Control Core
...
Huh?
Put the Storm Regalia...
...into Ringo-chan's Air Trecks?
Hey!
Listen, you can't be serious about this!!
It's getting ridiculous, y'know!
L-listen, Ikki-kun...
You can't just spring that on us out of nowhere...
Okay, shut up now.
Technically speaking, it shouldn't be a problem...
Ringo-san's Thorn Regalia is a replica, so it shouldn't interfere...
That's not the problem! Do you have any idea what Kururu was thinking when she tuned this Regalia for...
...

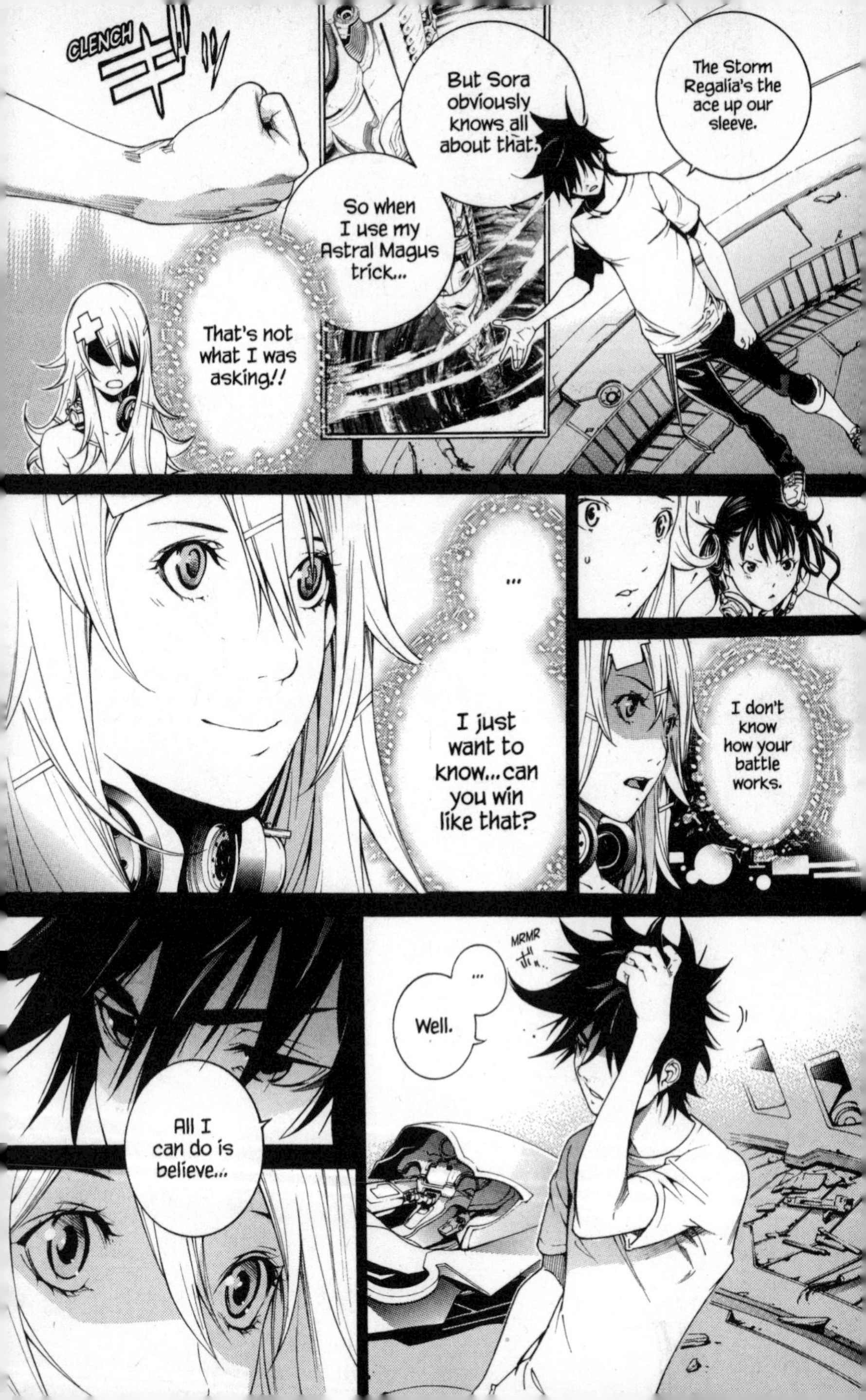
The Storm Regalia's the ace up our sleeve.
But Sora obviously knows all about that.
So when I use my Astral Magus trick...
CLENCH
That's not what I was asking!!
I don't know how your battle works.
...
I just want to know...can you win like that?
MRMR
...
Well.
All I can do is believe...

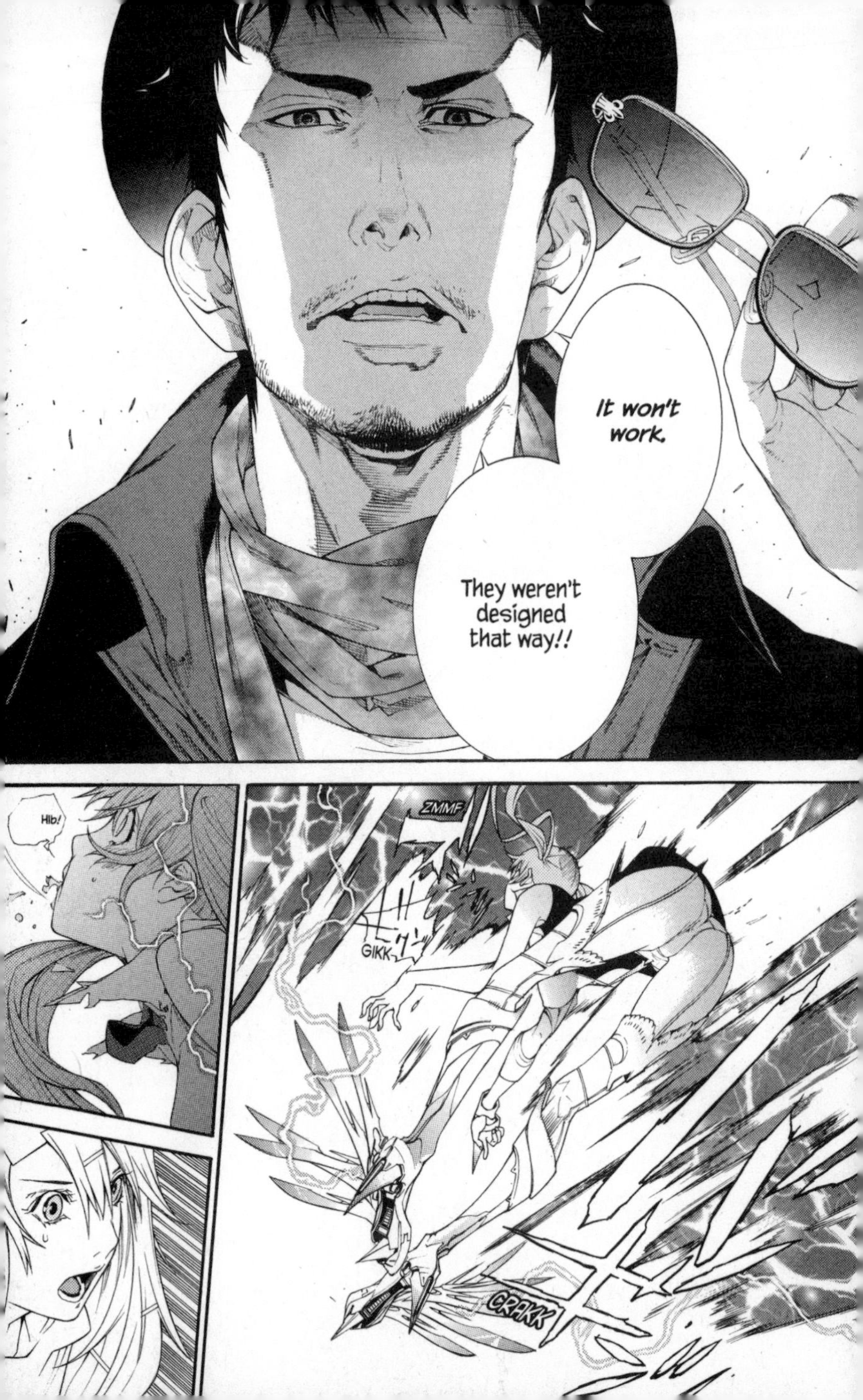
It won't work.
They weren't designed that way!!
ZMMF
GIKK
CRAKK
Hib!

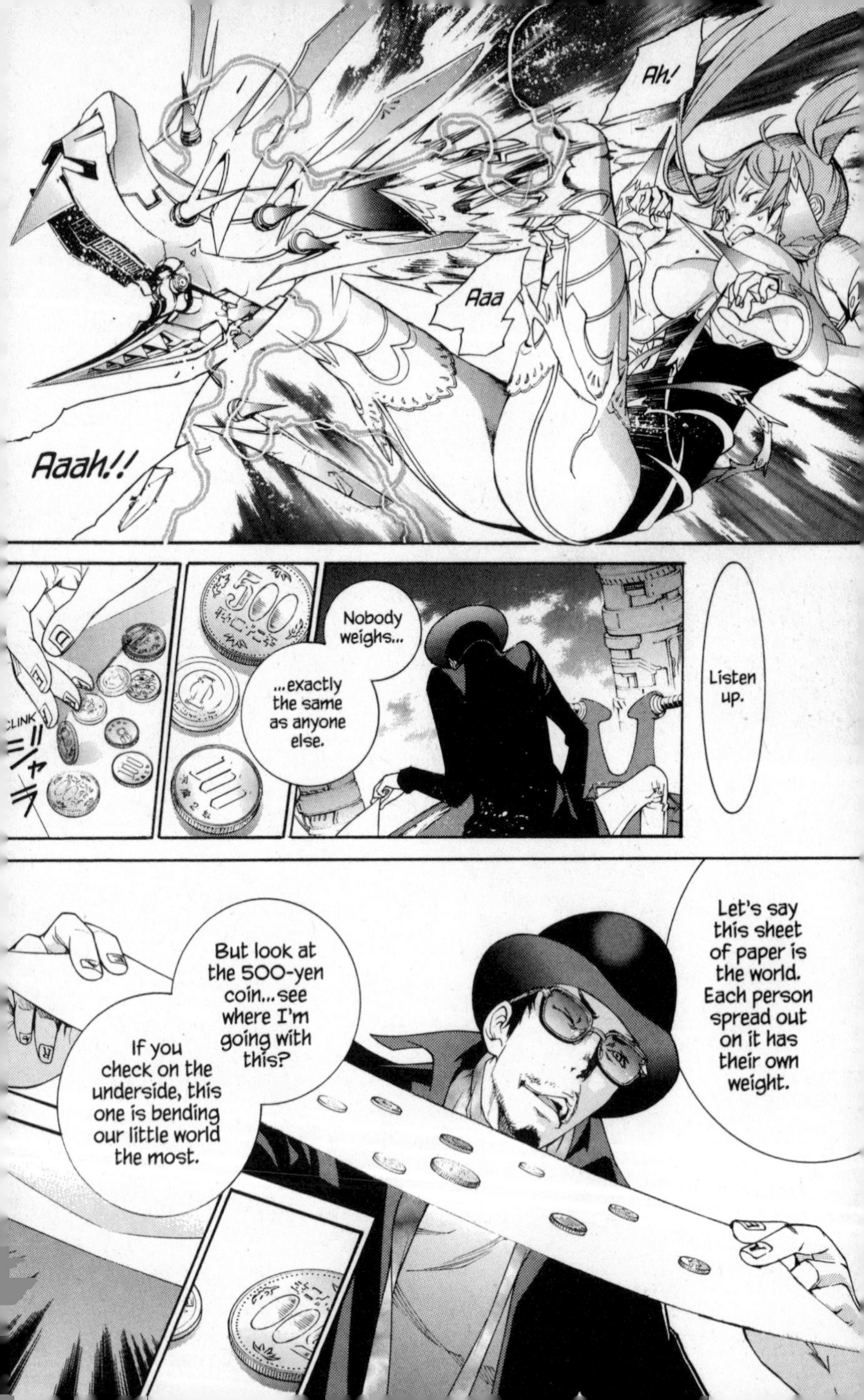
Ah!
Aaa
Aaah!!
Listen up.
Nobody weighs...
...exactly the same as anyone else.
CLINK
Let's say this sheet of paper is the world. Each person spread out on it has their own weight.
But look at the 500-yen coin...see where I'm going with this?
If you check on the underside, this one is bending our little world the most.

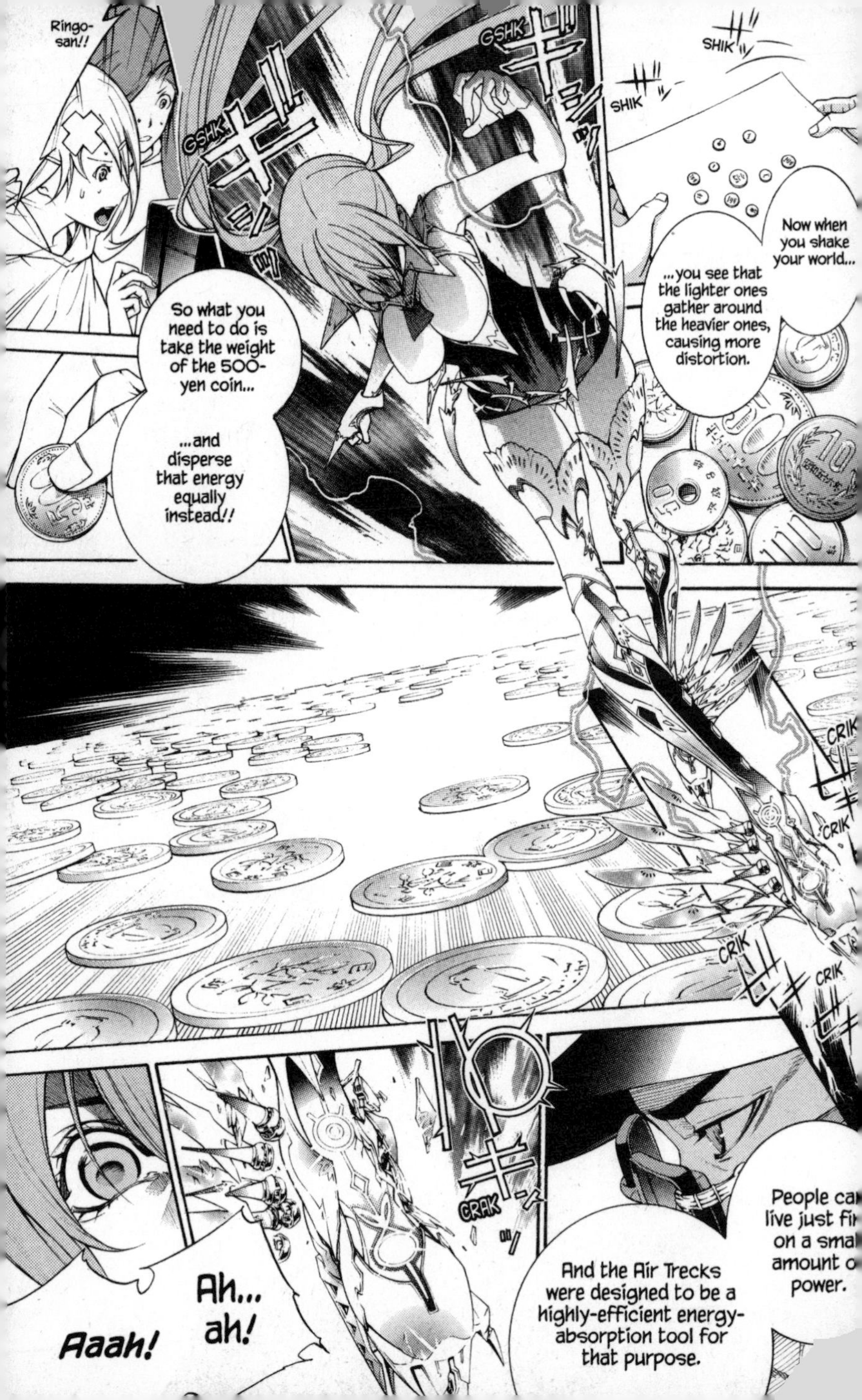
SHIK
SHIK
Now when you shake your world...
...you see that the lighter ones gather around the heavier ones, causing more distortion.
GSHK
GSHK
So what you need to do is take the weight of the 500-yen coin...
...and disperse that energy equally instead!!
Ringo-san!!
CRIK
CRIK
CRIK
CRIK
People ca
live just fi
on a sma
amount o
power.
And the Air Trecks were designed to be a highly-efficient energy-absorption tool for that purpose.
CRAK
Ah... ah!
Aaah!

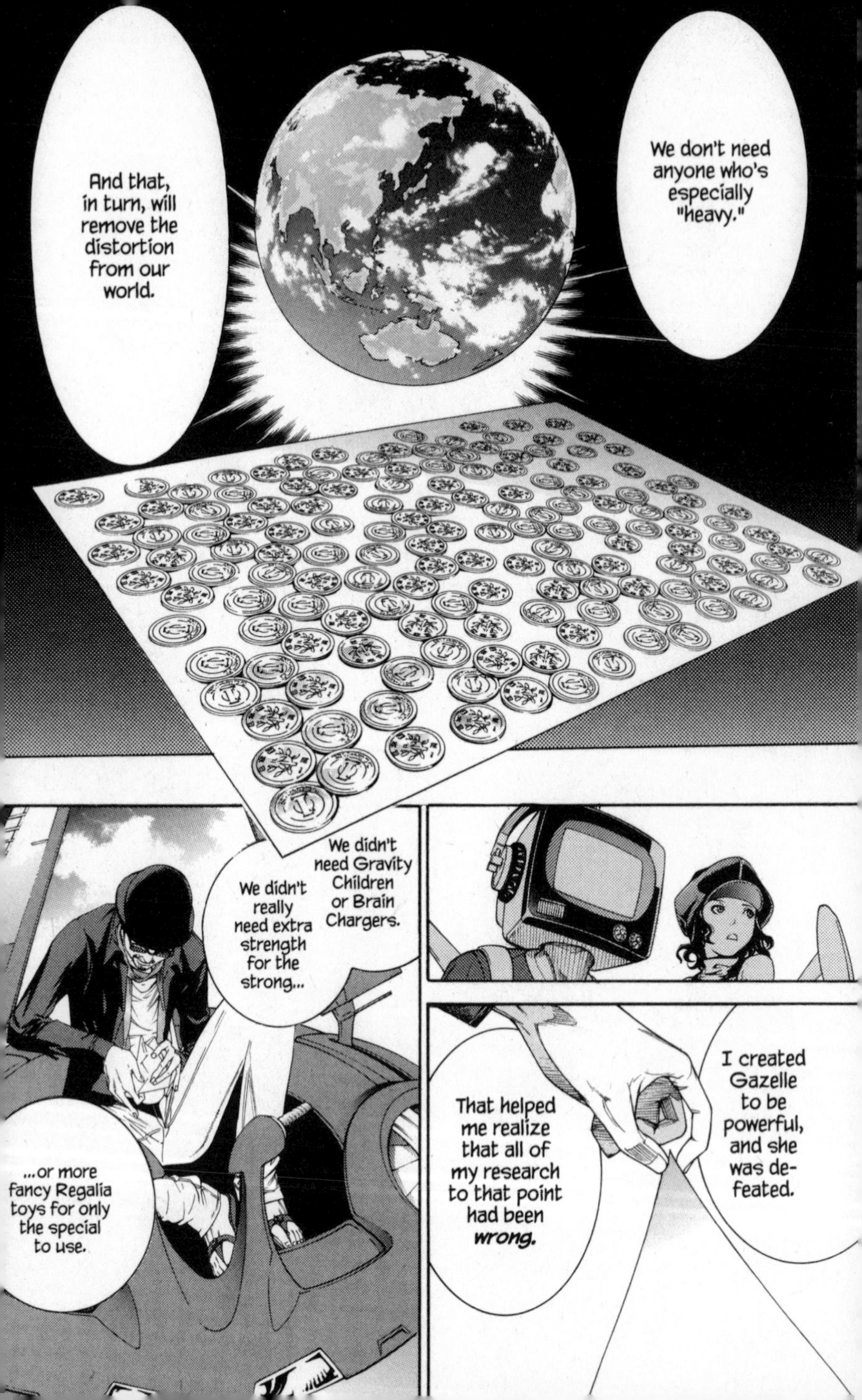
We don't need anyone who's especially "heavy."
And that, in turn, will remove the distortion from our world.
I created Gazelle to be powerful, and she was de-feated.
That helped me realize that all of my research to that point had been *wrong.*
We didn't need Gravity Children or Brain Chargers.
We didn't really need extra strength for the strong...
...or more fancy Regalia toys for only the special to use.

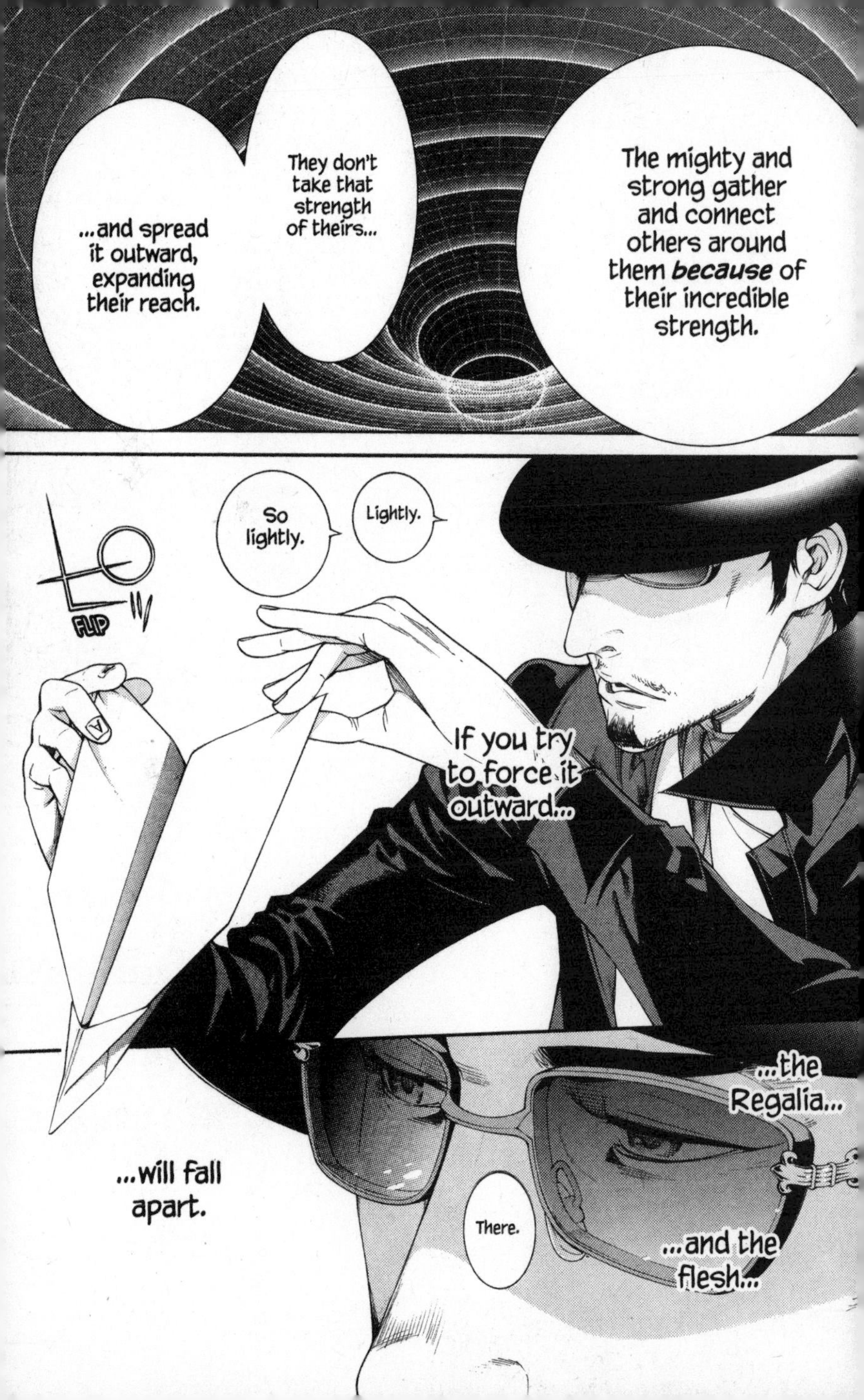
The mighty and strong gather and connect others around them *because* of their incredible strength.
They don't take that strength of theirs...
...and spread it outward, expanding their reach.
Lightly.
So lightly.
FLIP
If you try to force it outward...
...the Regalia...
...and the flesh...
There.
...will fall apart.

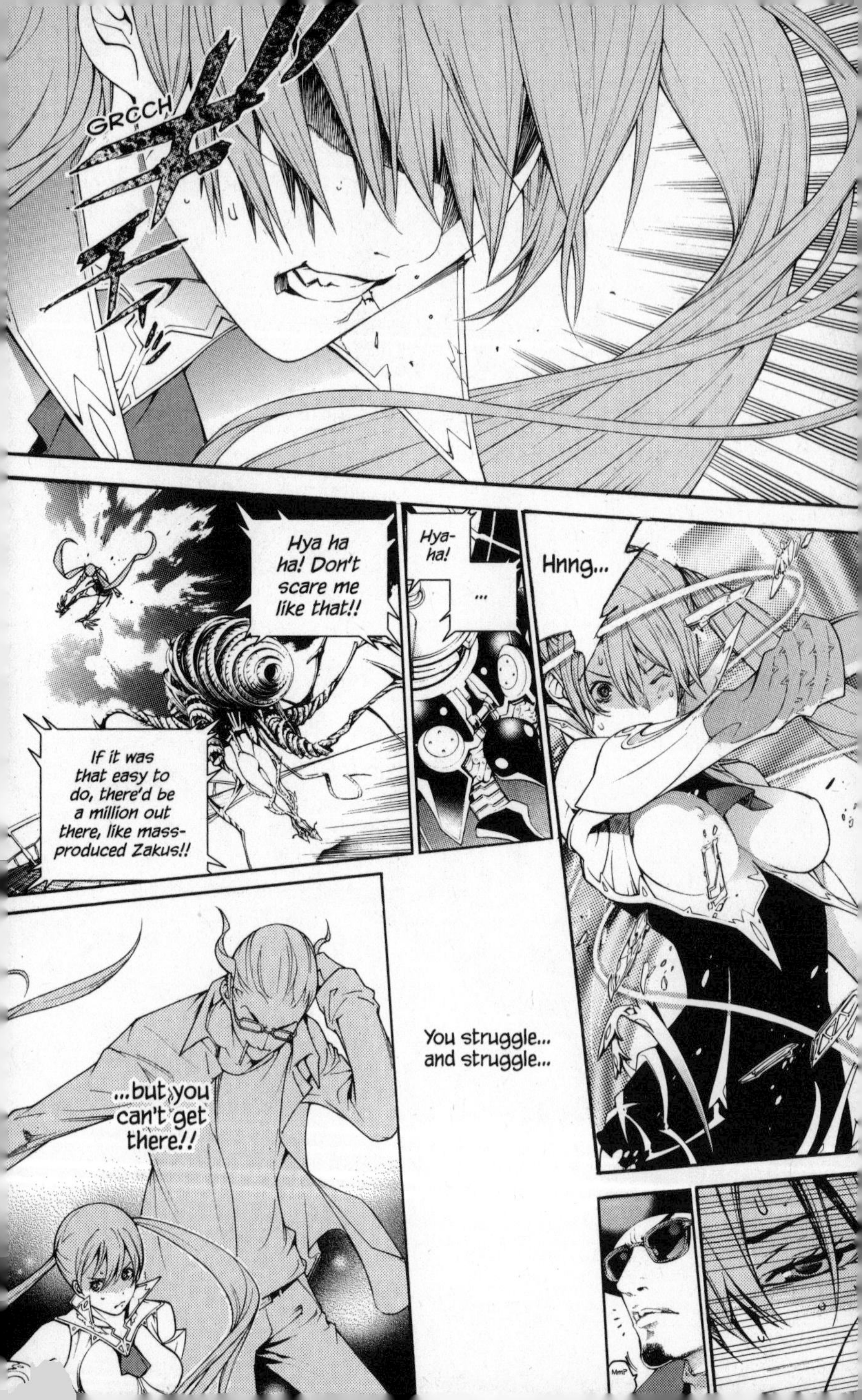
GRCCH
Hnng...
Hya-
ha!
...
Hya ha ha! Don't scare me like that!!
If it was that easy to do, there'd be a million out there, like mass-produced Zakus!!
You struggle... and struggle...
...but you can't get there!!
Mmp

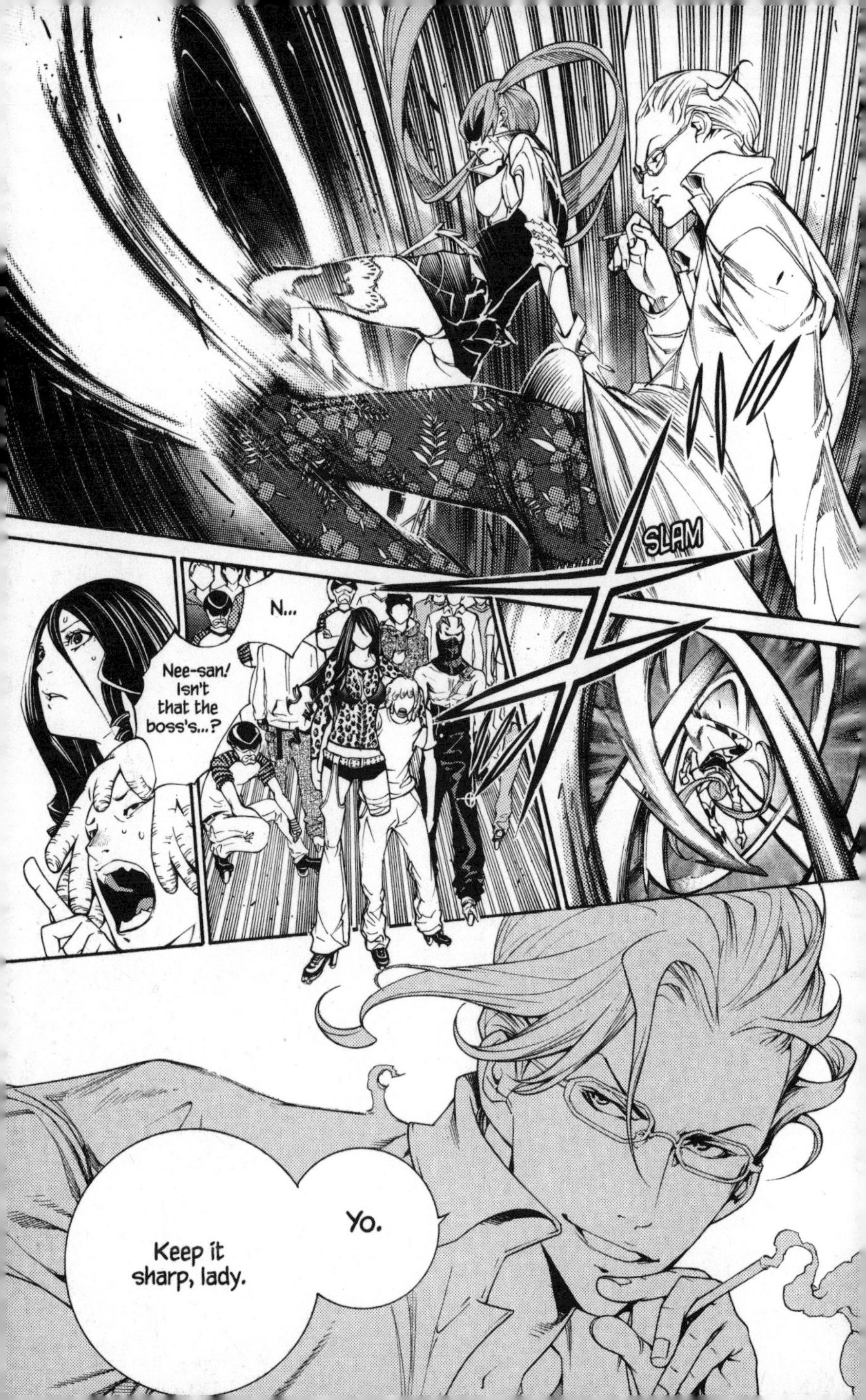
SLAM
N...
Nee-san! Isn't that the boss's...?
Yo.
Keep it sharp, lady.

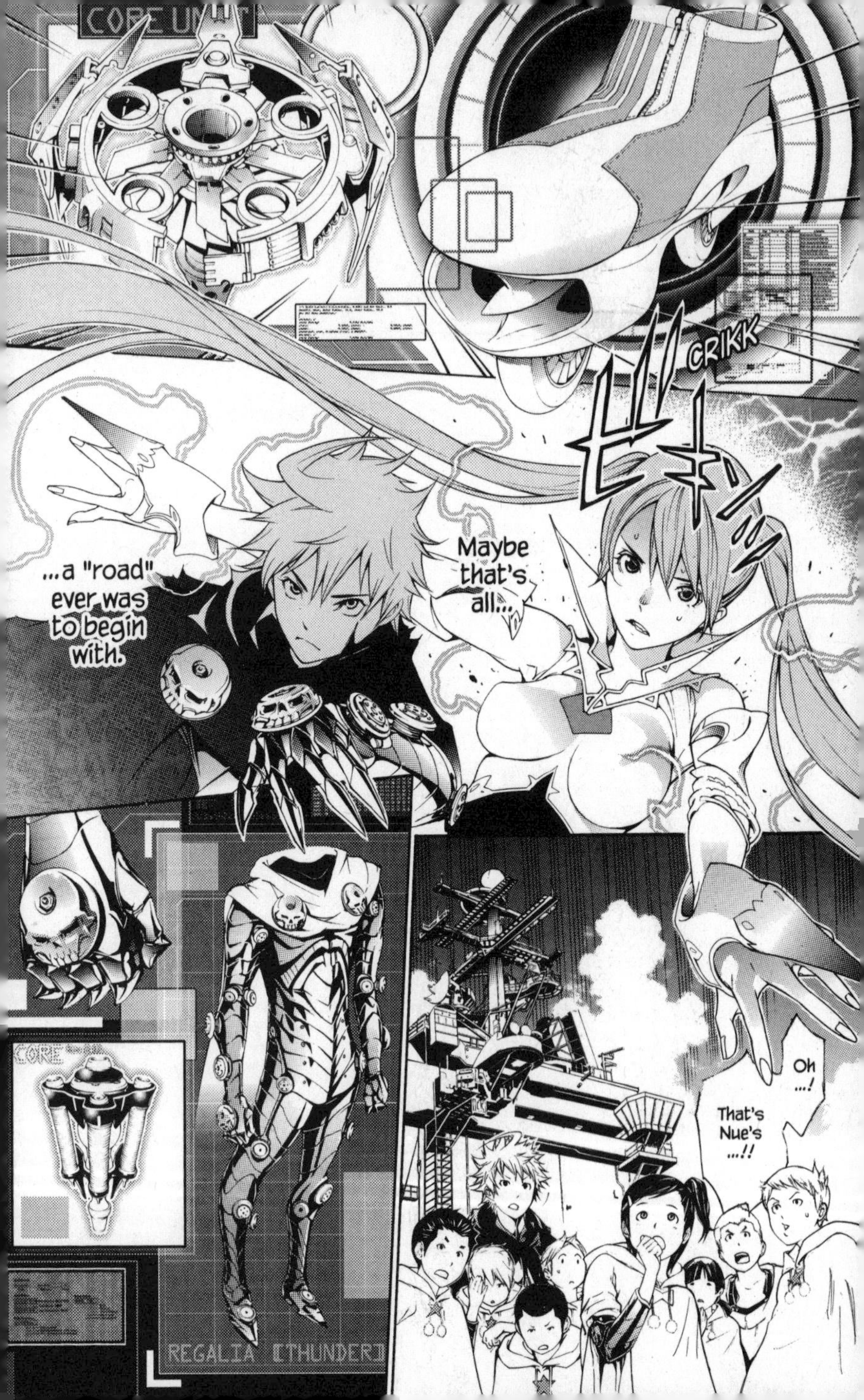
CORE UNIT
CRIKK
Maybe that's all...
...a "road" ever was to begin with.
Oh ...!
That's Nue's ...!!
CORE
REGALIA [THUNDER]

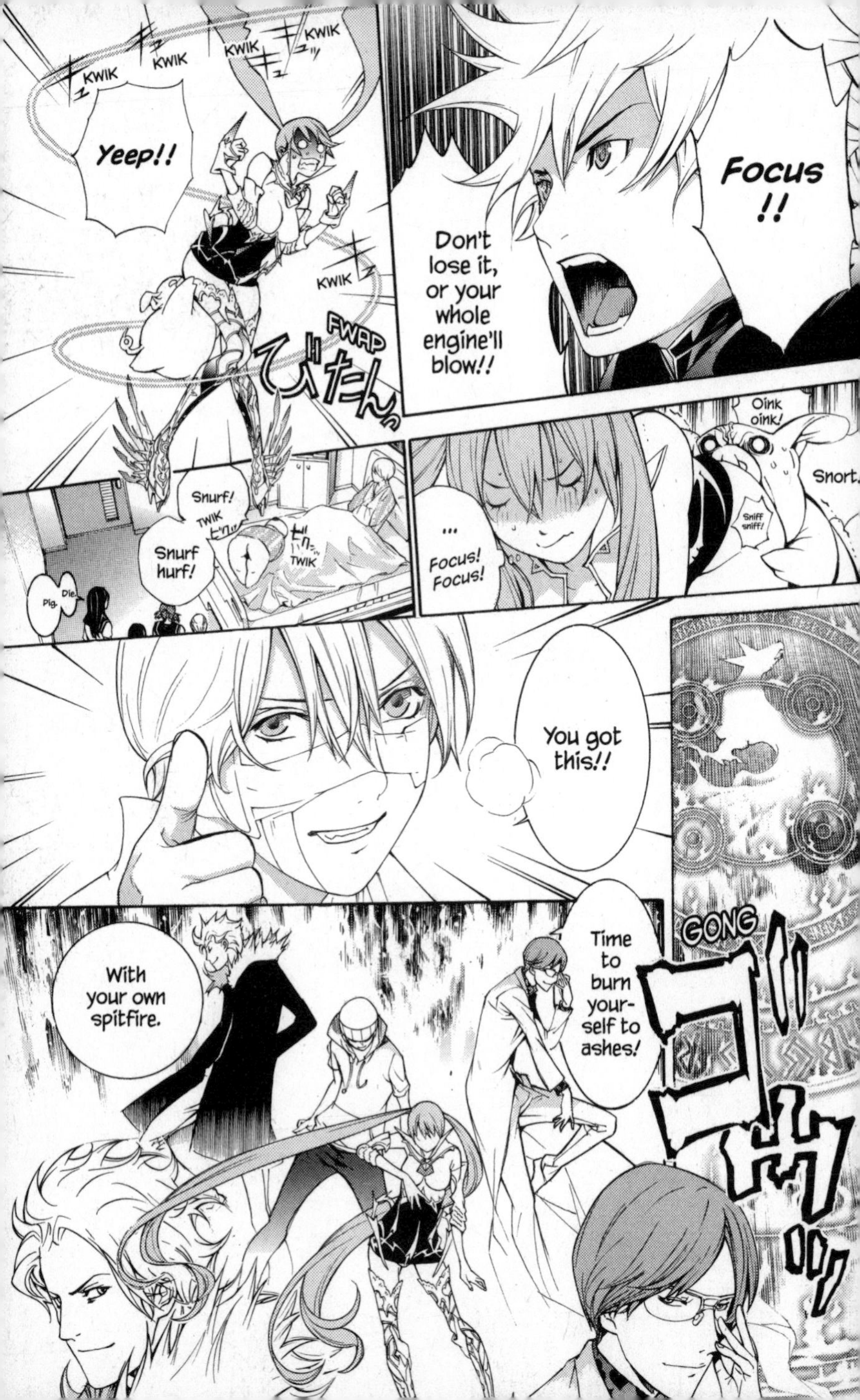
Focus!!
Don't lose it, or your whole engine'll blow!!
KWIK
KWIK
KWIK
KWIK
KWIK
Yeep!!
FWAP
びたん
Oink oink!
Snort.
Sniff sniff!
...
Focus! Focus!
Snurf!
TWIK
Snurf hurf!
TWIK
Die.
Pig.
GONG
You got this!!
Time to burn your-self to ashes!
With your own spitfire.

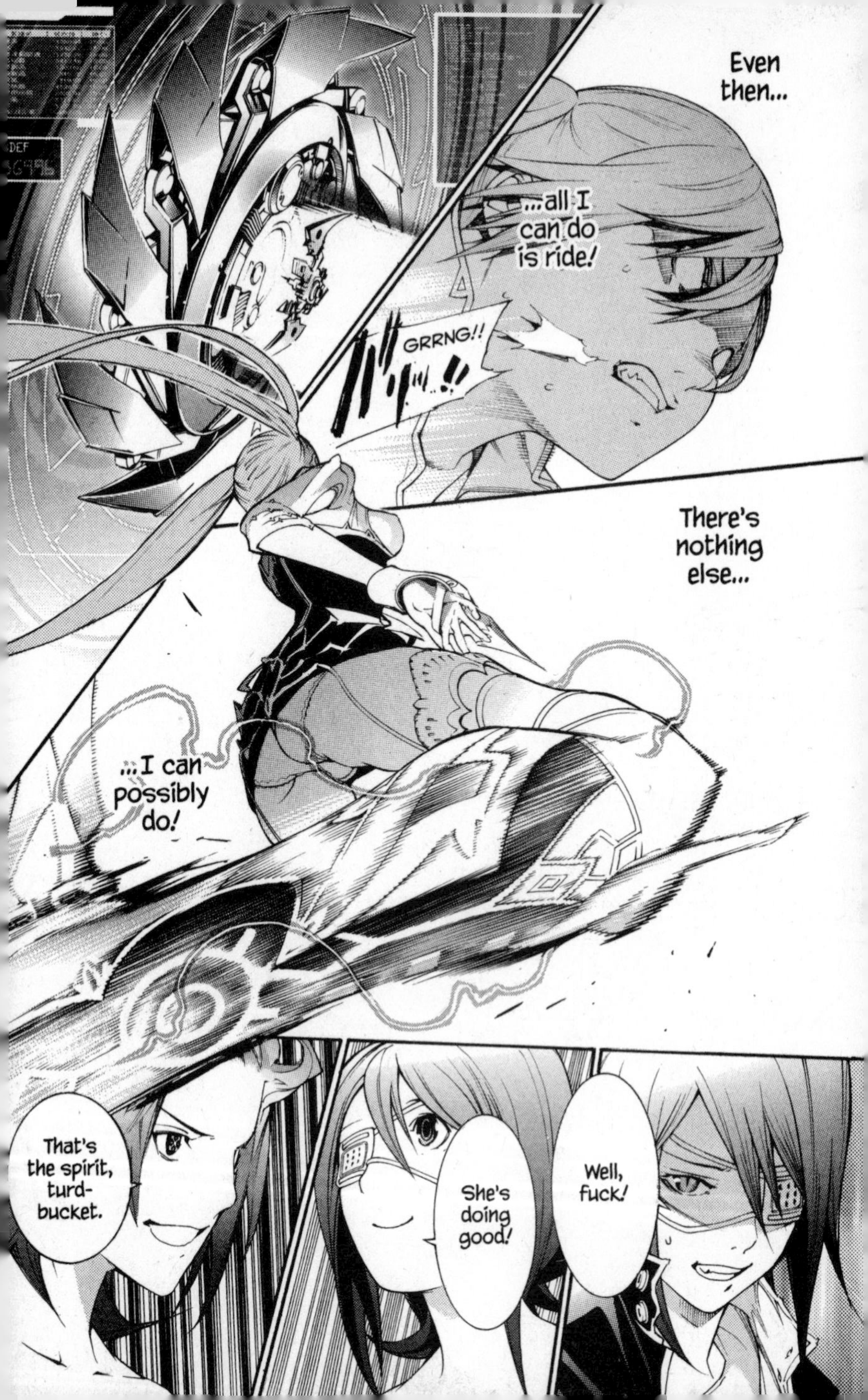
Even then...
...all I can do is ride!
GRRNG!!
There's nothing else...
...I can possibly do!
Well, fuck!
She's doing good!
That's the spirit, turd-bucket.

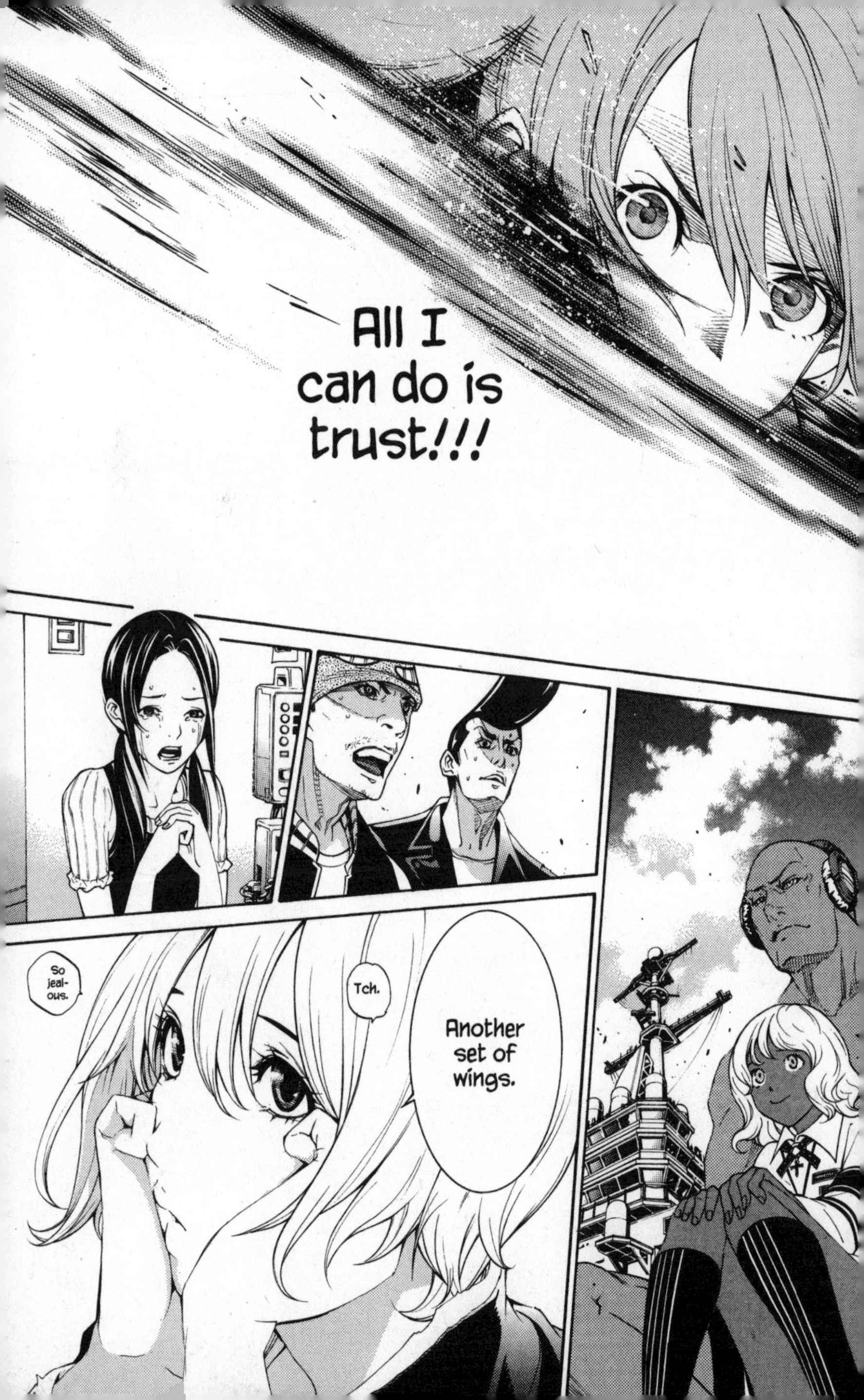
All I can do is trust!!!
Another set of wings.
Tch.
So jeal-ous.

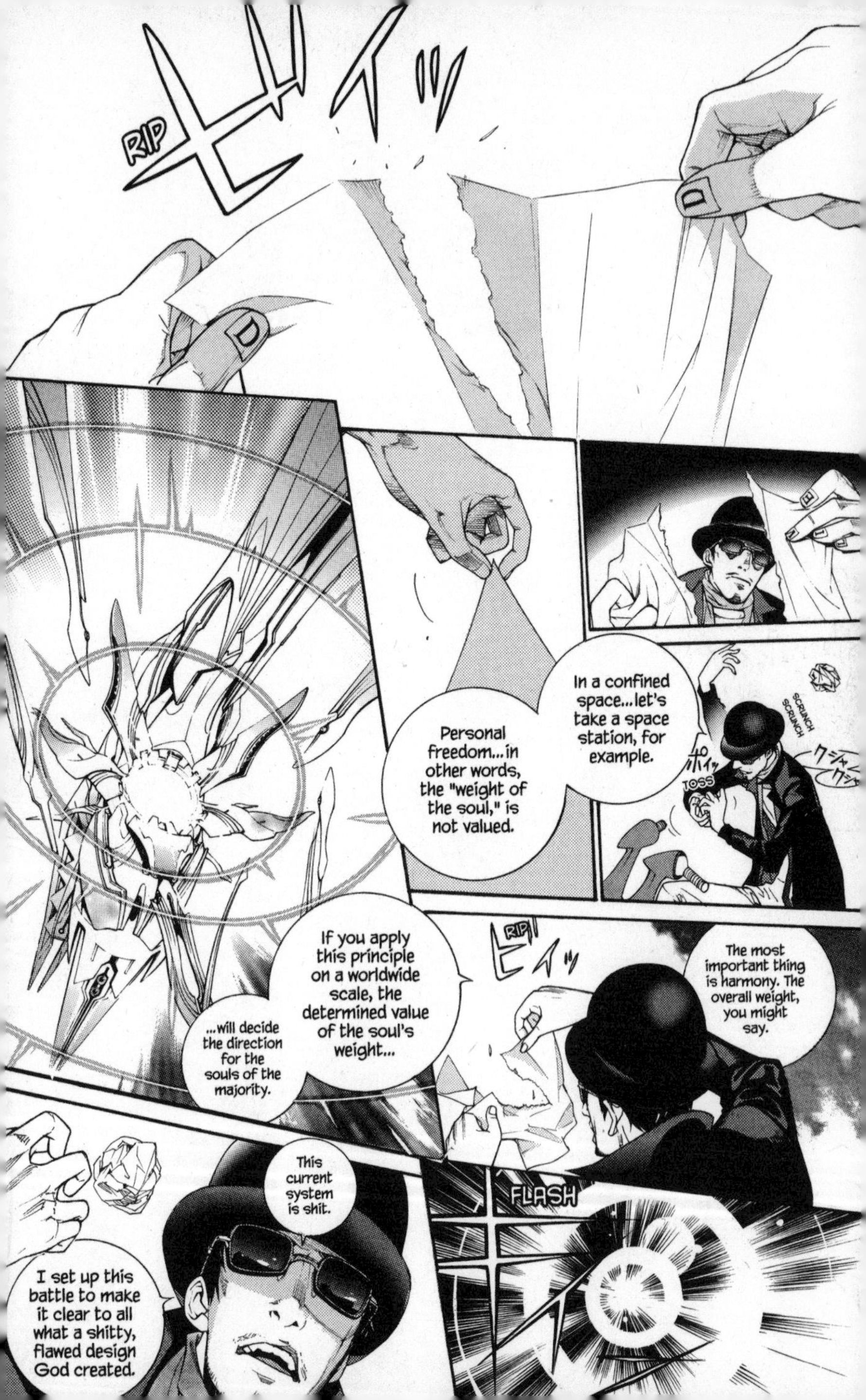
RIP
In a confined space...let's take a space station, for example.
SCRUNCH SCRUNCH
TOSS
Personal freedom...in other words, the "weight of the soul," is not valued.
The most important thing is harmony. The overall weight, you might say.
RIP
If you apply this principle on a worldwide scale, the determined value of the soul's weight...
...will decide the direction for the souls of the majority.
FLASH
This current system is shit.
I set up this battle to make it clear to all what a shitty, flawed design God created.

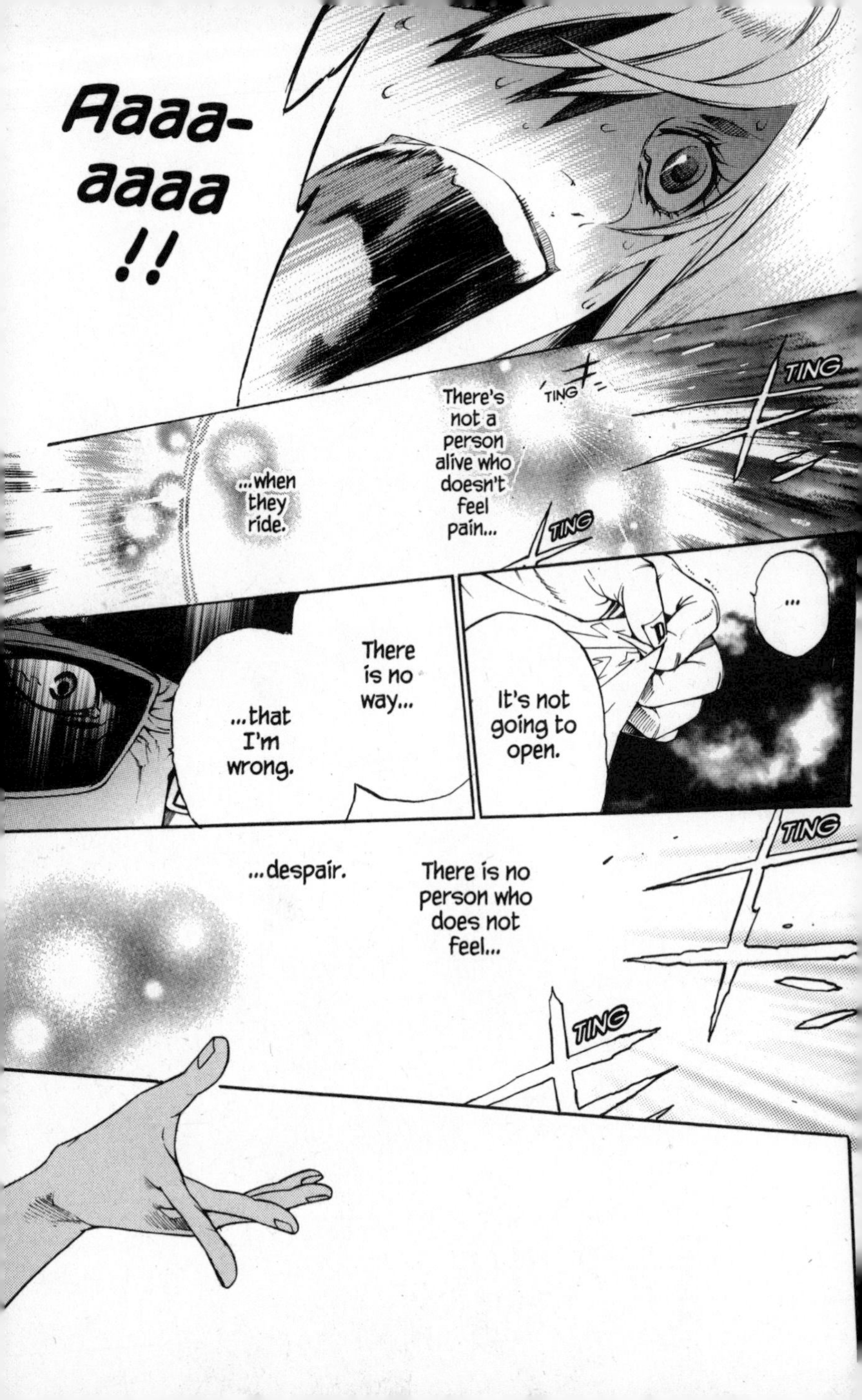
Aaaa-aaaa!!
TING
TING
There's not a person alive who doesn't feel pain...
...when they ride.
TING
...
It's not going to open.
There is no way...
...that I'm wrong.
TING
There is no person who does not feel...
...despair.
TING

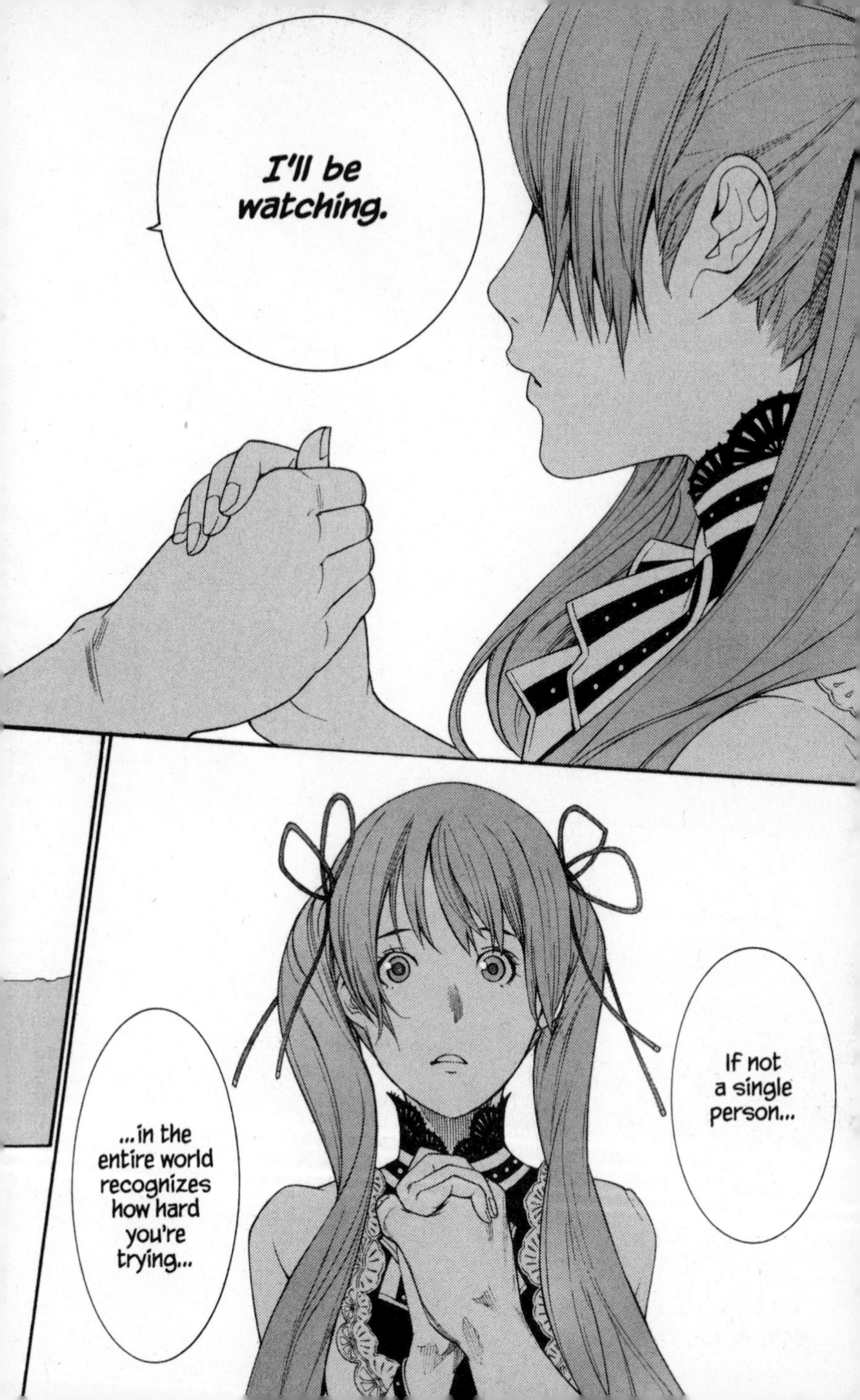
I'll be watching.
If not a single person...
...in the entire world recognizes how hard you're trying...

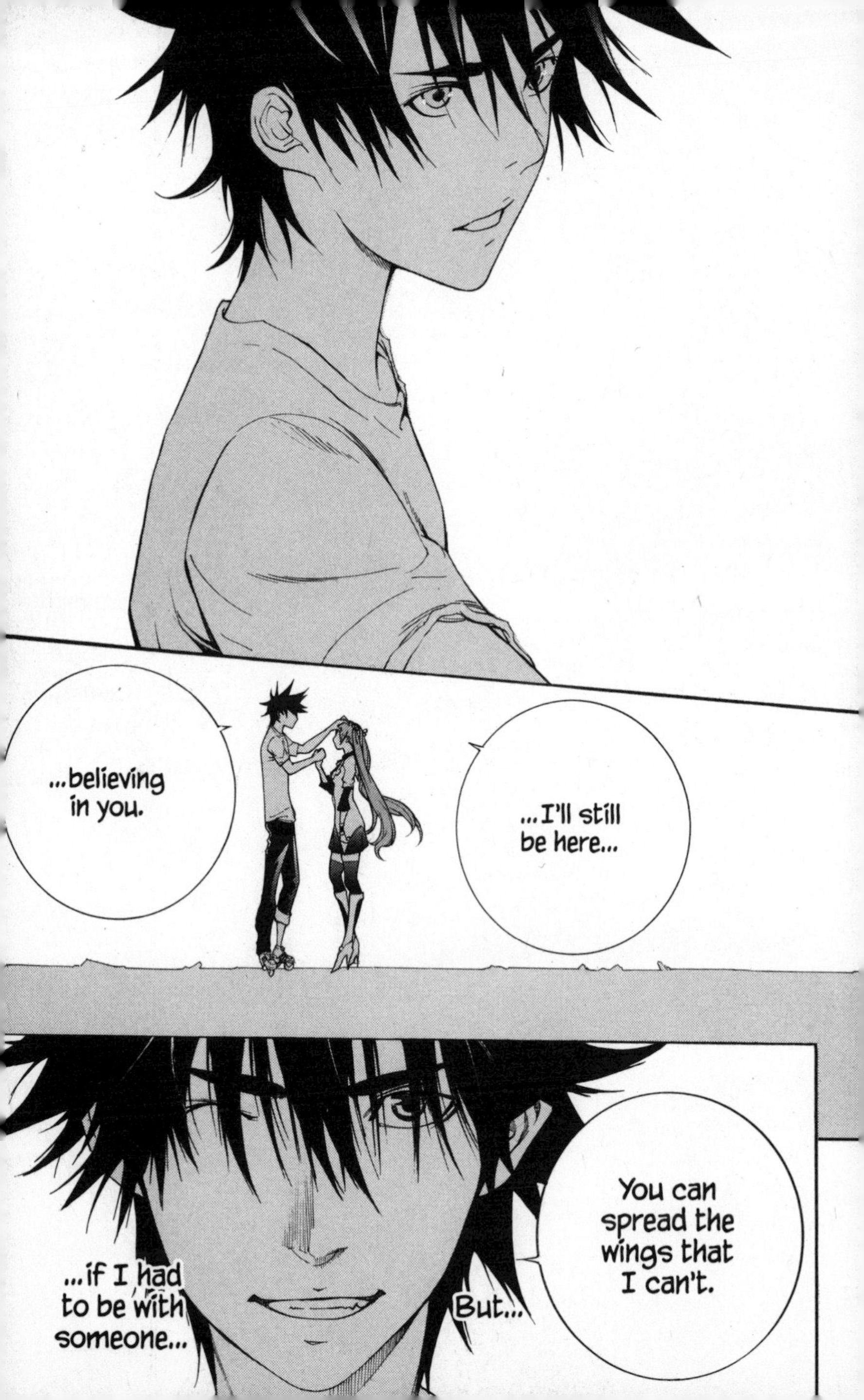
...I'll still be here...
...believing in you.
You can spread the wings that I can't.
But...
...if I had to be with someone...

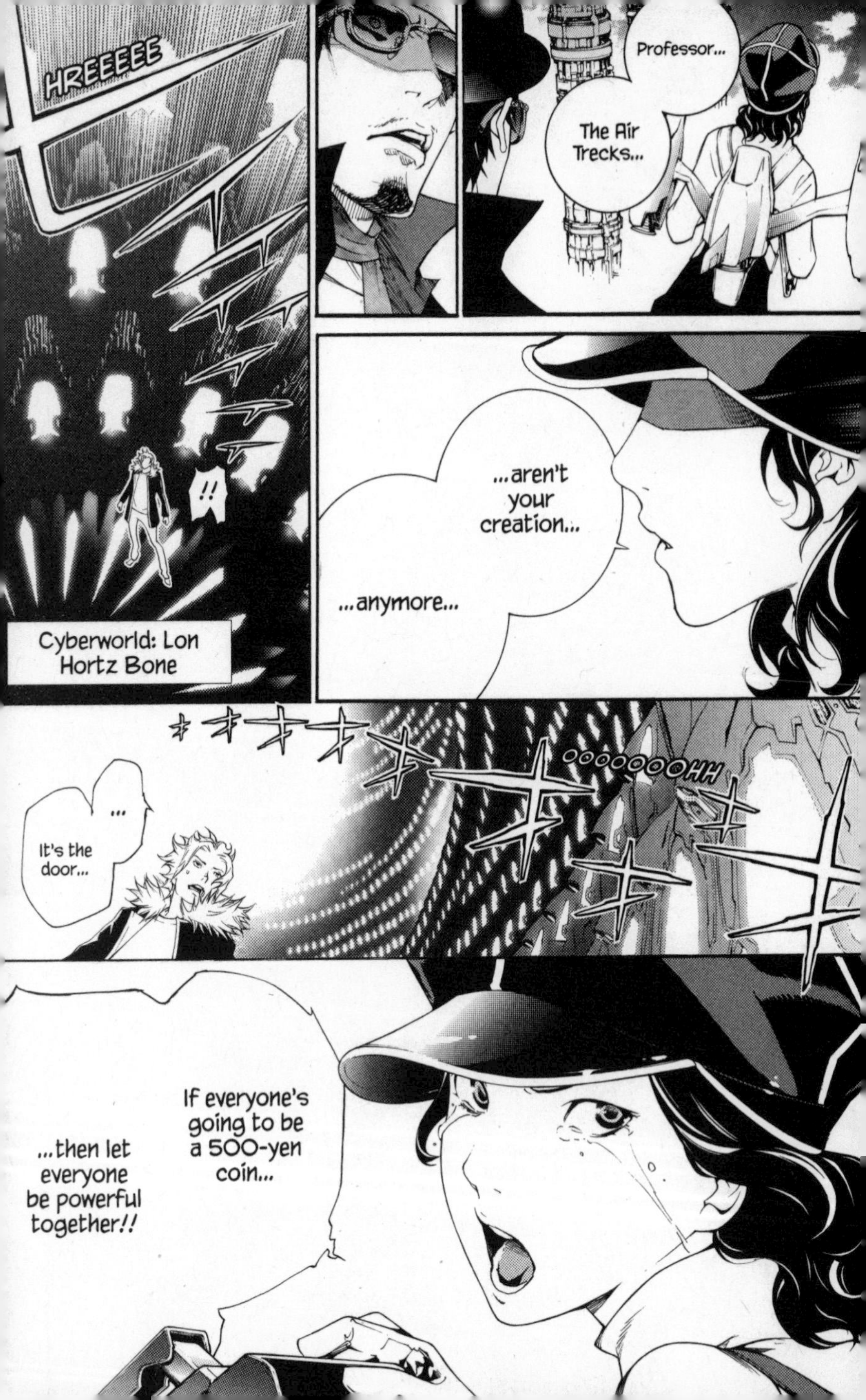
Professor...
The Air Trecks...
HREEEEE
...aren't your creation...
...anymore...
Cyberworld: Lon Hortz Bone
!!
OOOOOOOOHH
...
It's the door...
If everyone's going to be a 500-yen coin...
...then let everyone be powerful together!!

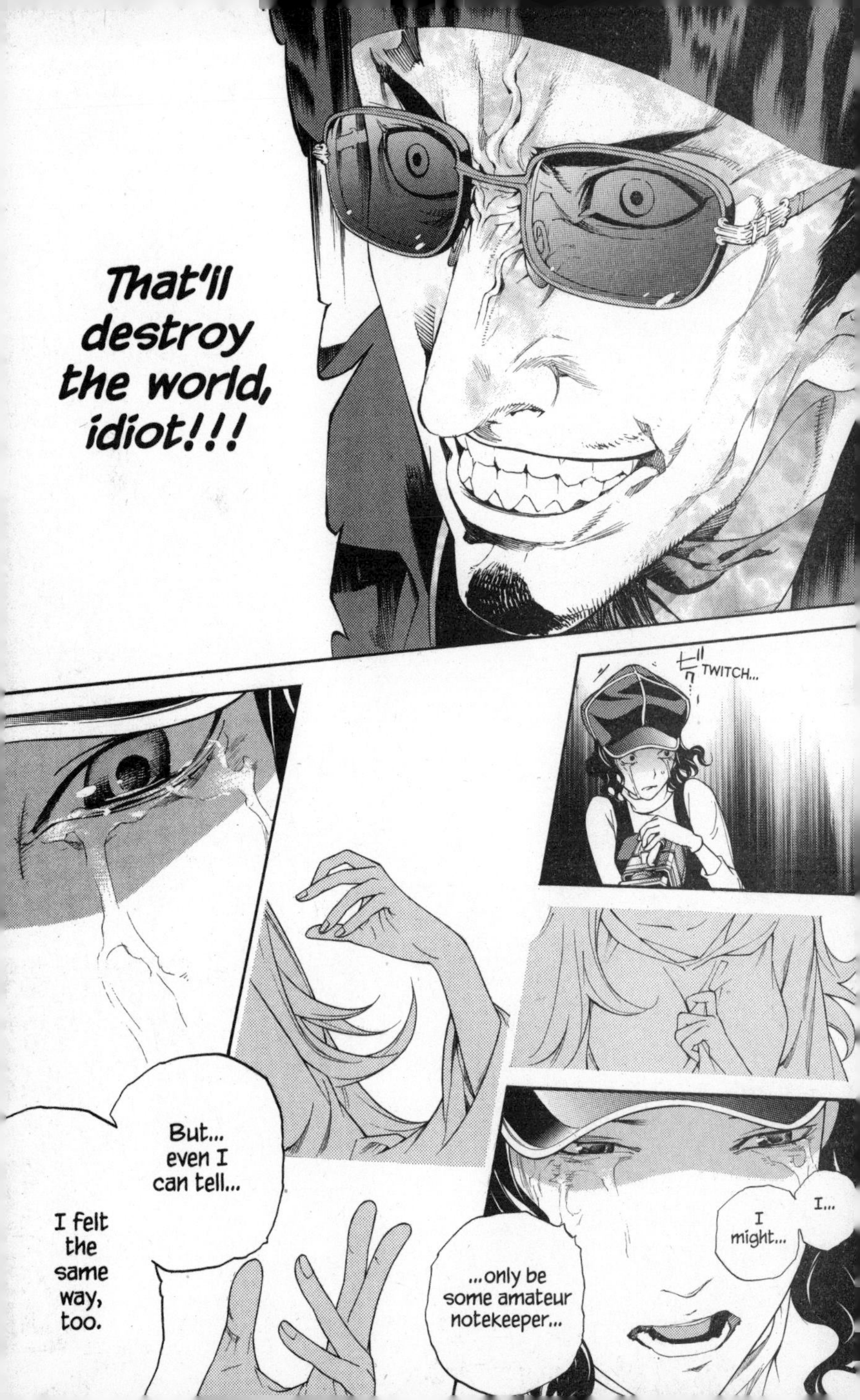
That'll destroy the world, idiot!!!
TWITCH...
I...
I might...
...only be some amateur notekeeper...
But... even I can tell...
I felt the same way, too.

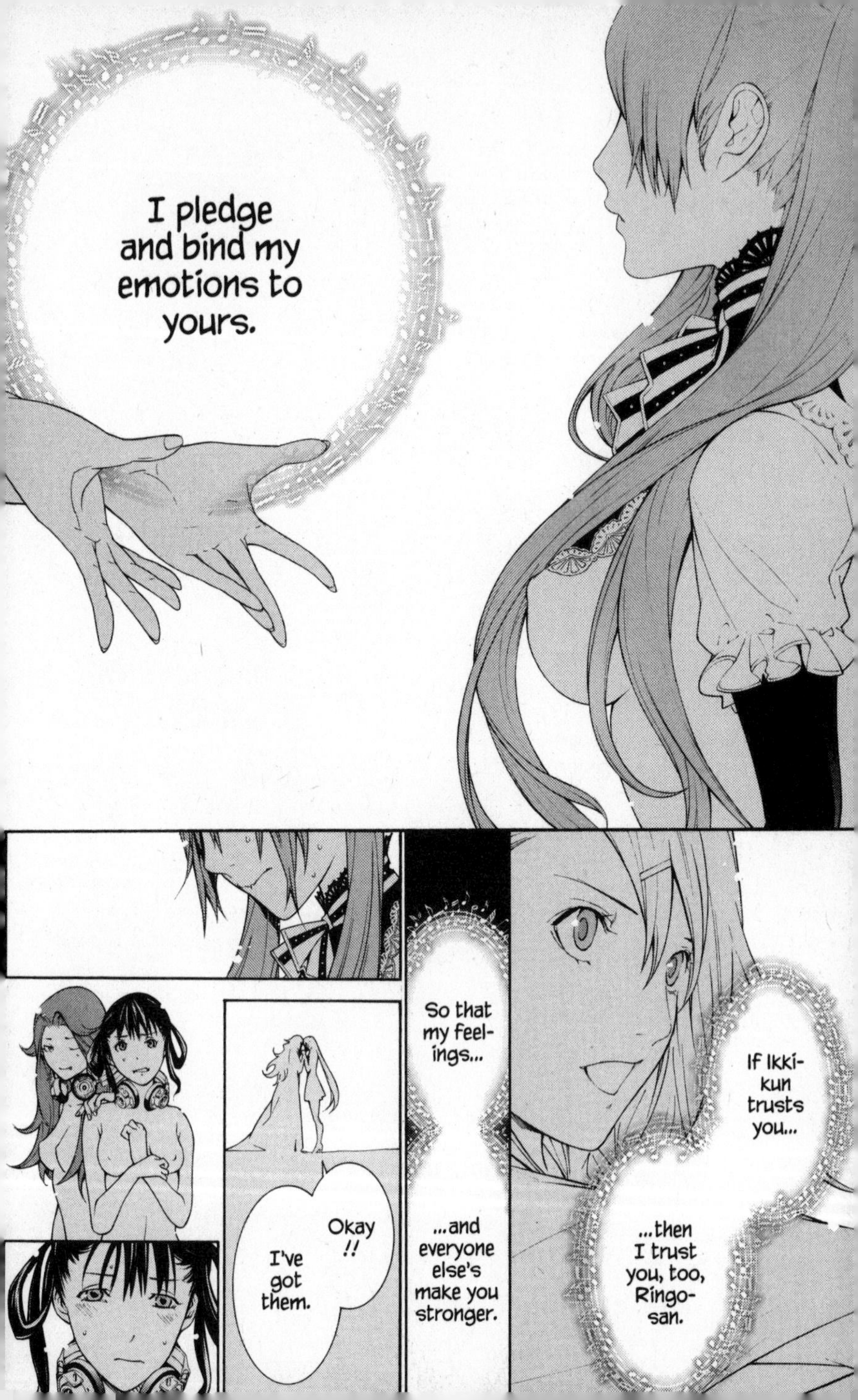
I pledge and bind my emotions to yours.
If Ikki-kun trusts you...
...then I trust you, too, Ringo-san.
So that my feelings...
...and everyone else's make you stronger.
Okay !!
I've got them.

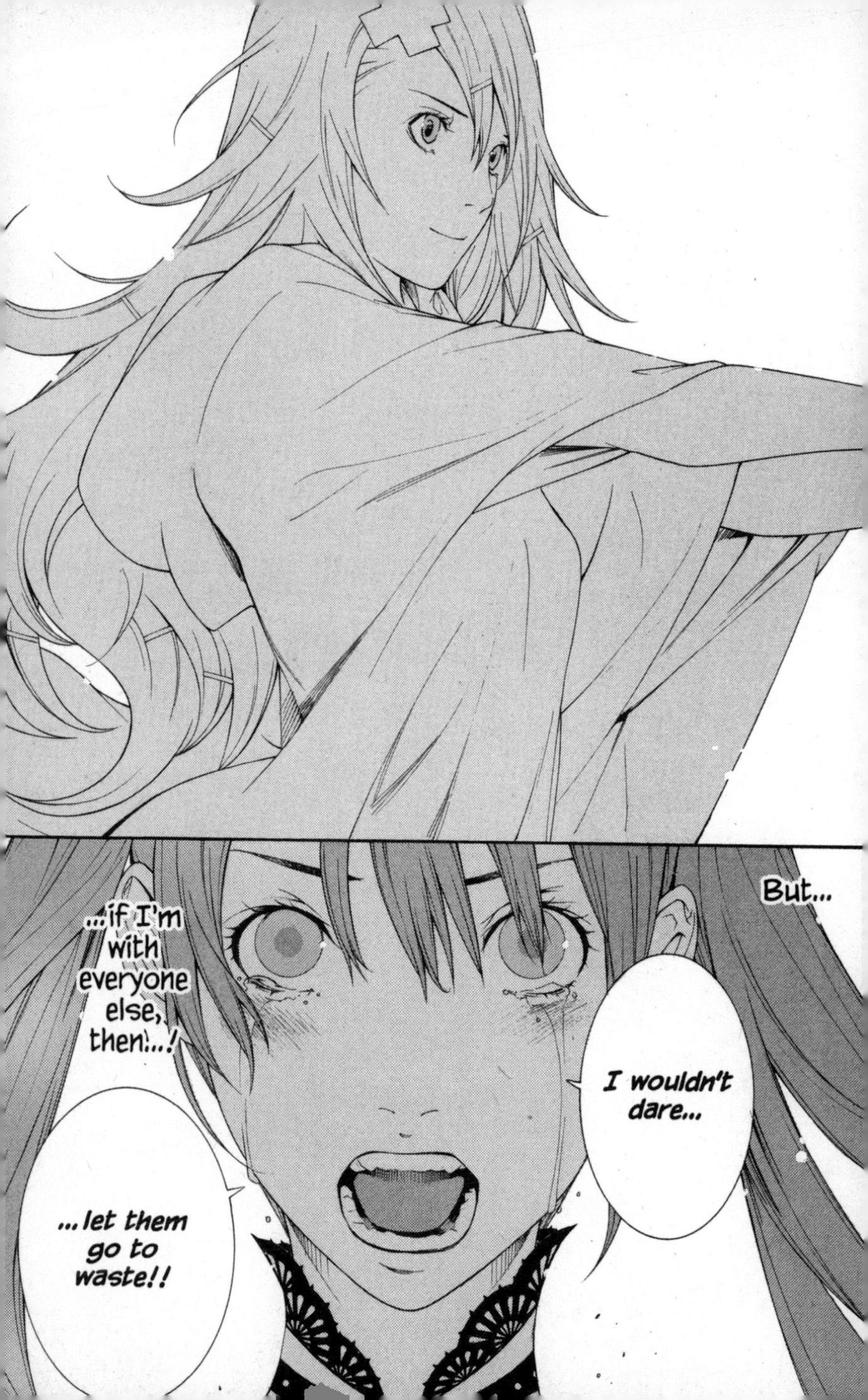
But...
I wouldn't dare...
...if I'm with everyone else, then!...!
...let them go to waste!!

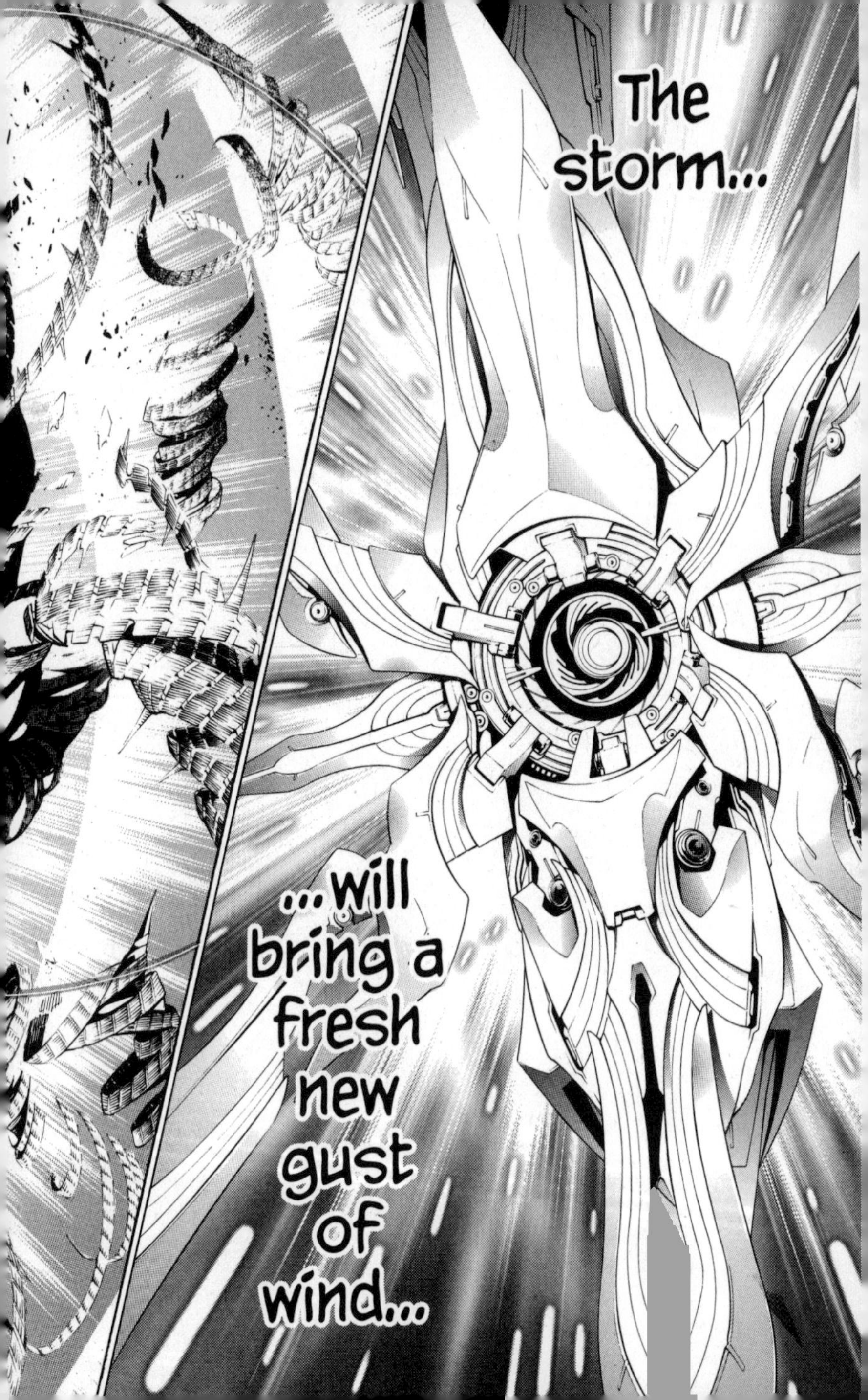
The storm...
...will bring a fresh new gust of wind...

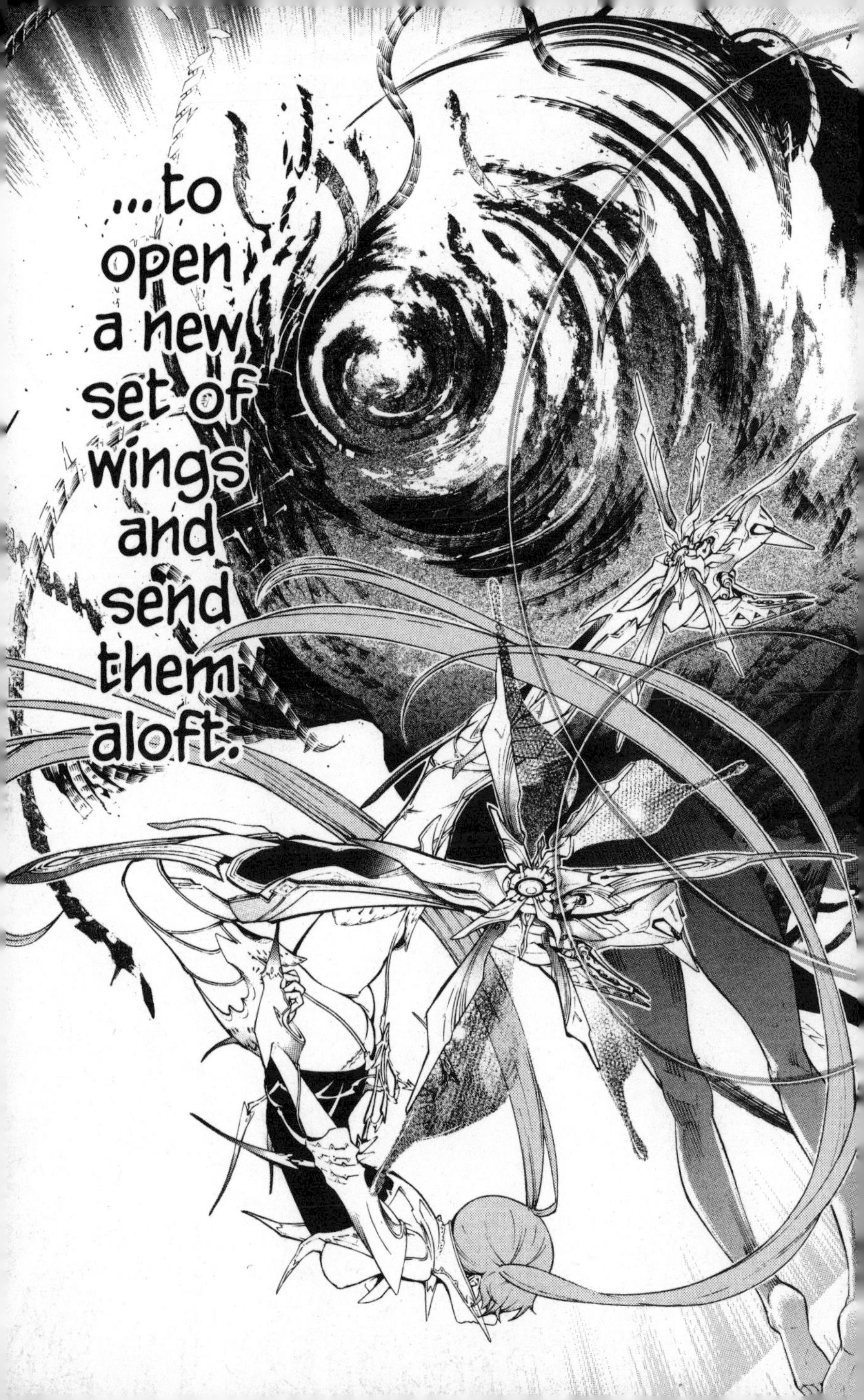
...to open a new set of wings and send them aloft.

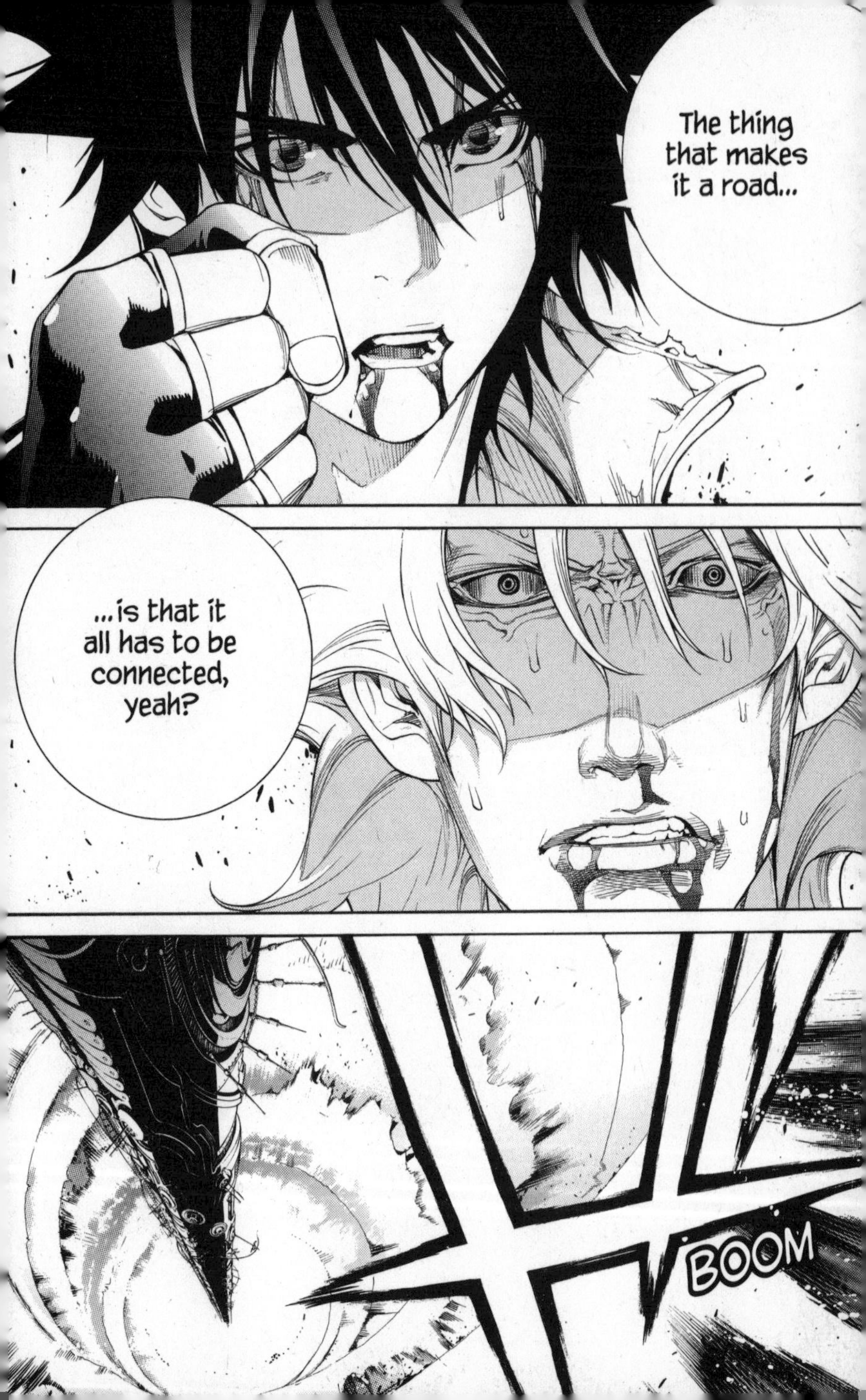
The thing that makes it a road...
...is that it all has to be connected, yeah?
BOOM

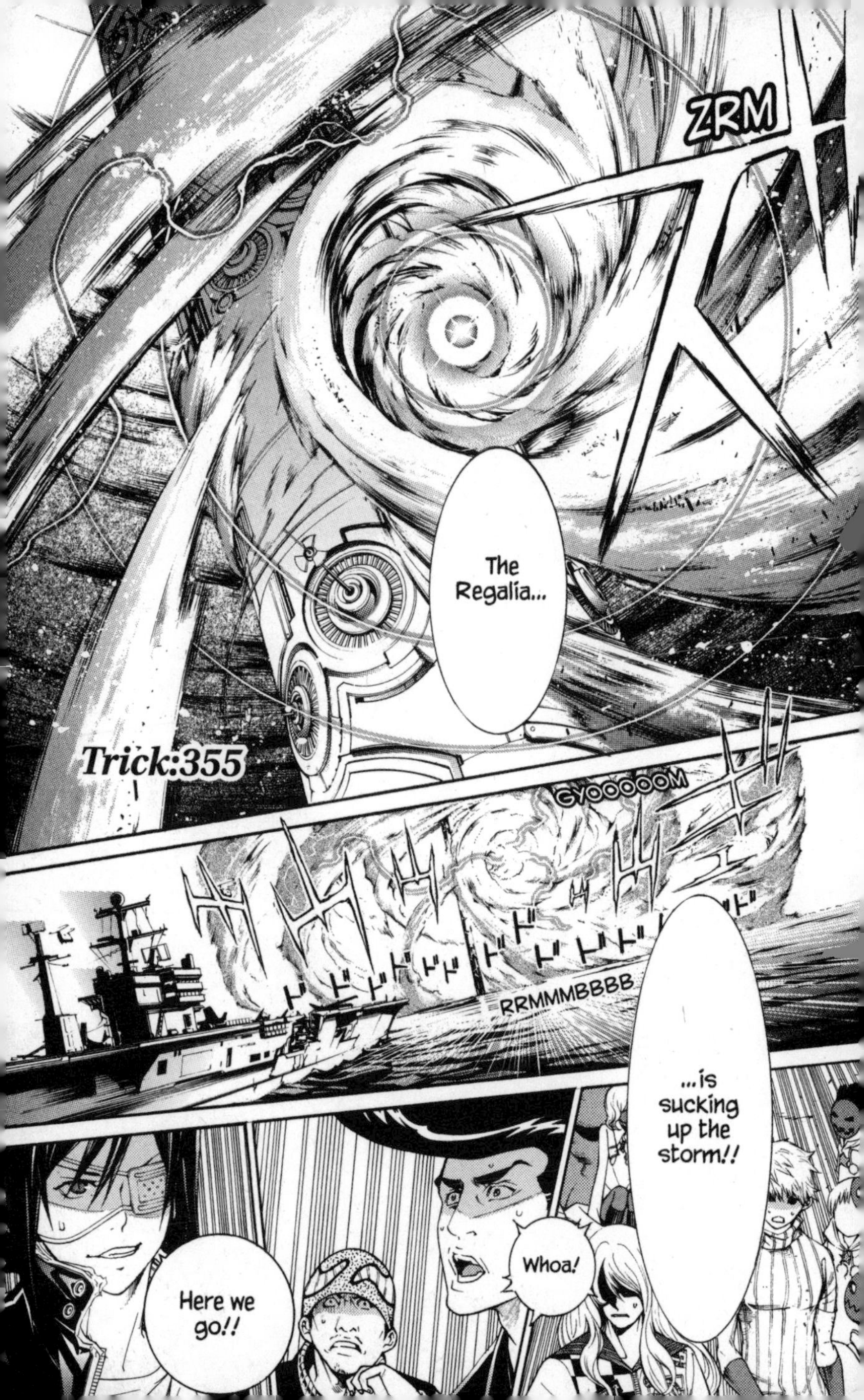
ZRM
The Regalia...
Trick:355
GYOOOOOM
RRMMMBBBB
...is sucking up the storm!!
Whoa!
Here we go!!

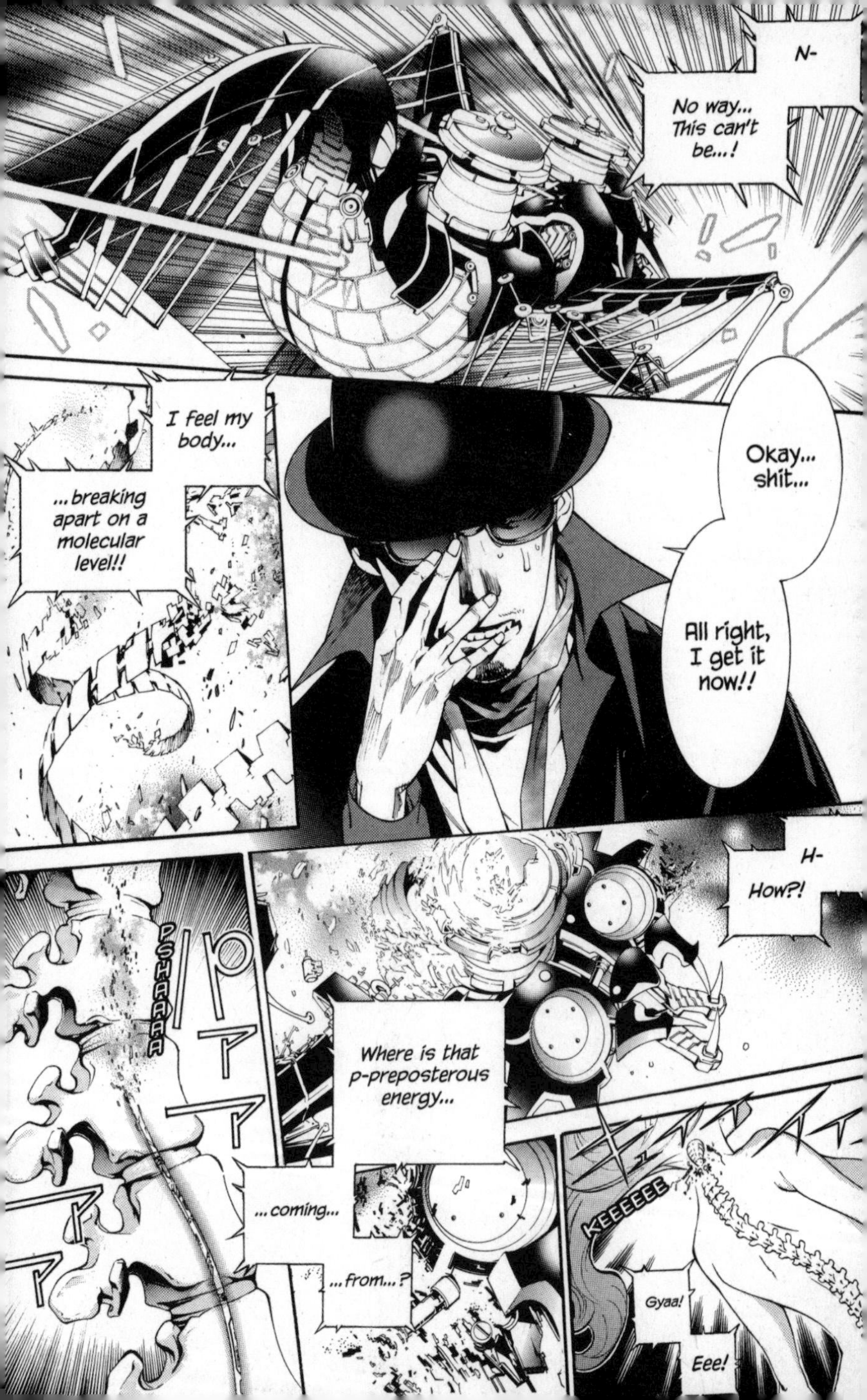
N-
No way... This can't be...!
Okay... shit...
All right, I get it now!!
I feel my body...
...breaking apart on a molecular level!!
H- How?!
Where is that p-preposterous energy...
...coming...
...from...?
PSHAAAAA
KEEEEEE
Gyaa!
Eee!

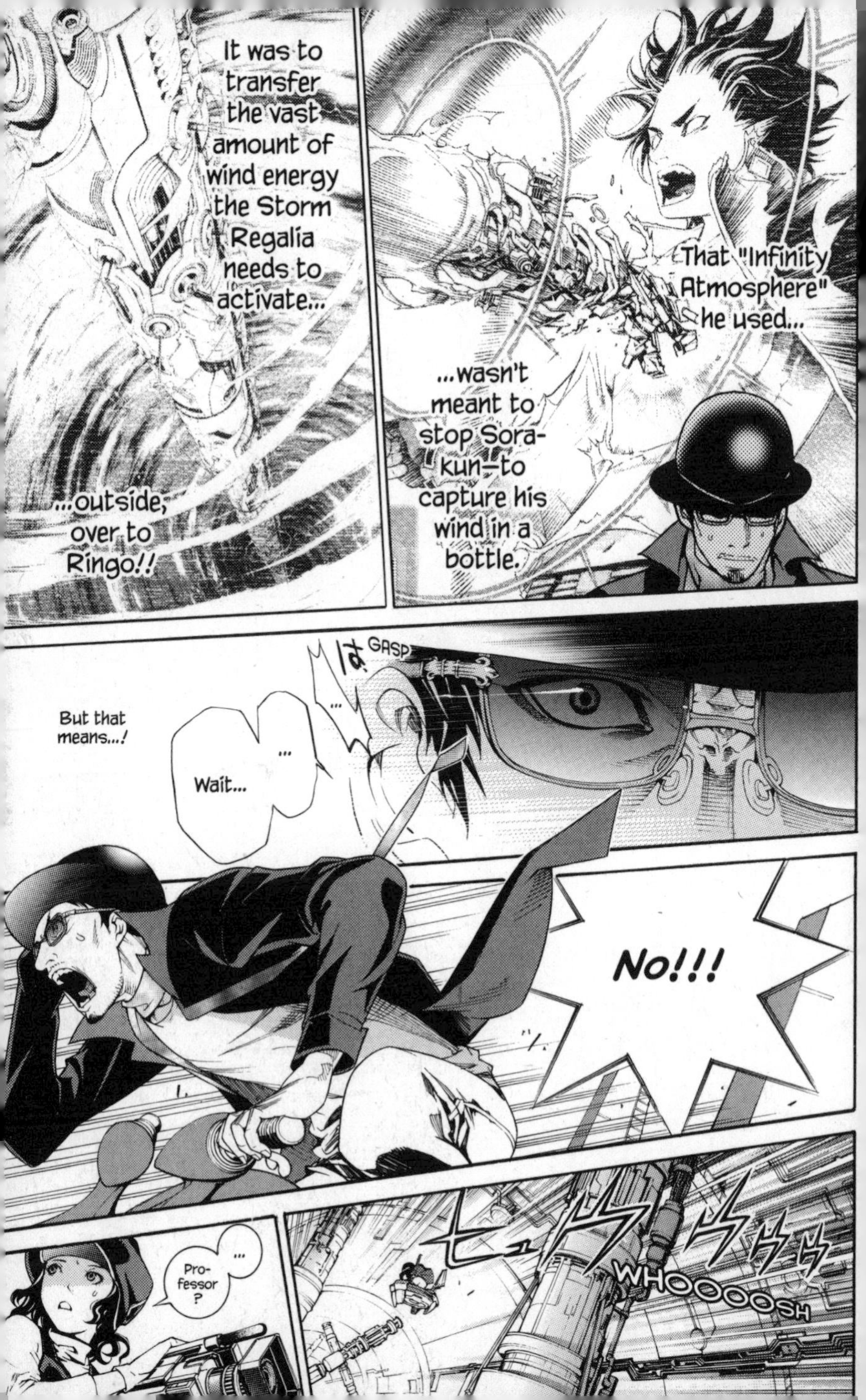
That "Infinity Atmosphere" he used...
...wasn't meant to stop Sora-kun—to capture his wind in a bottle.
It was to transfer the vast amount of wind energy the Storm Regalia needs to activate...
...outside, over to Ringo!!
は GASP
...
...
Wait...
But that means...!
No!!!
WHOOOOOSH
...
Pro-fessor?

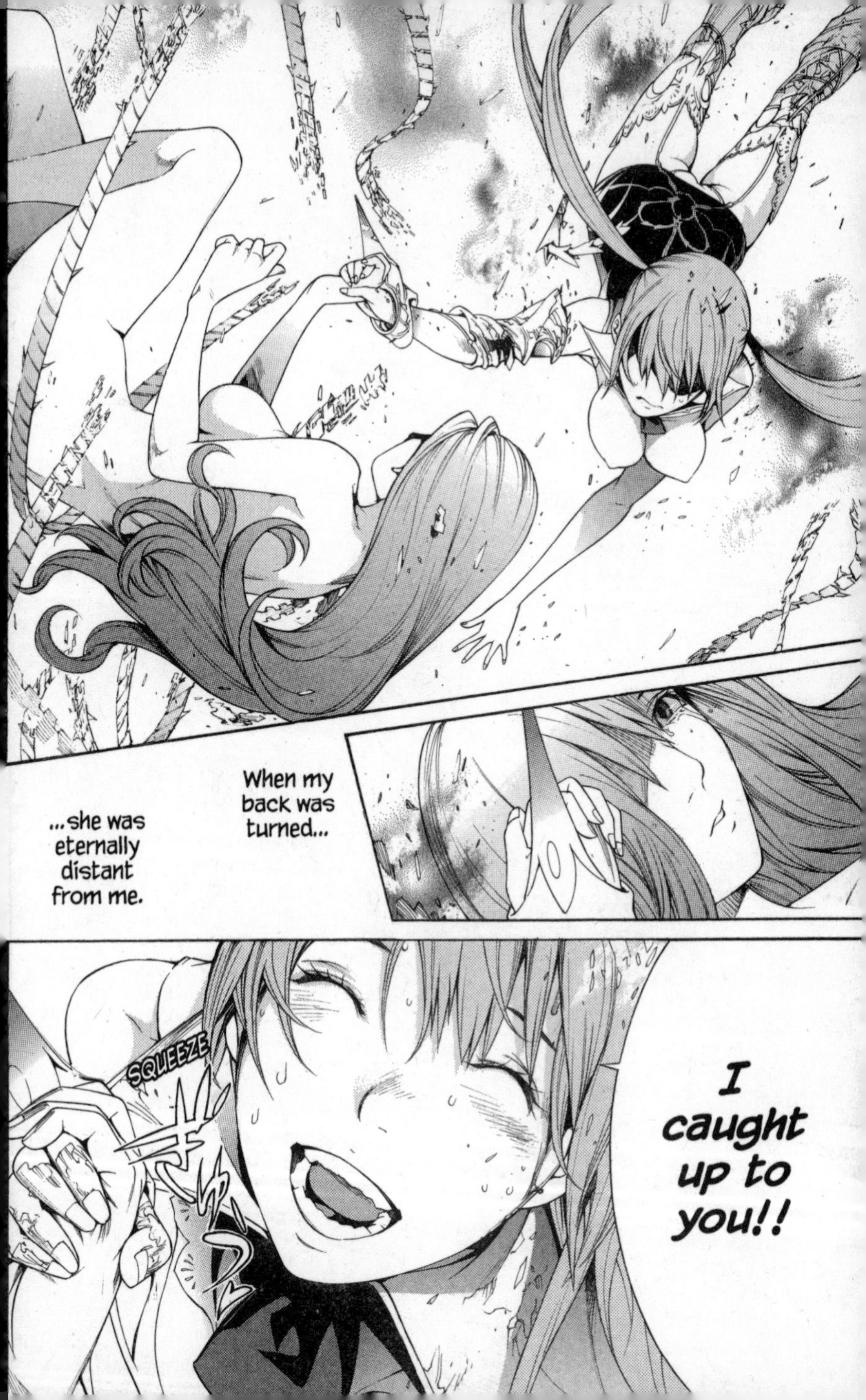
When my back was turned...
...she was eternally distant from me.
SQUEEZE
I caught up to you!!

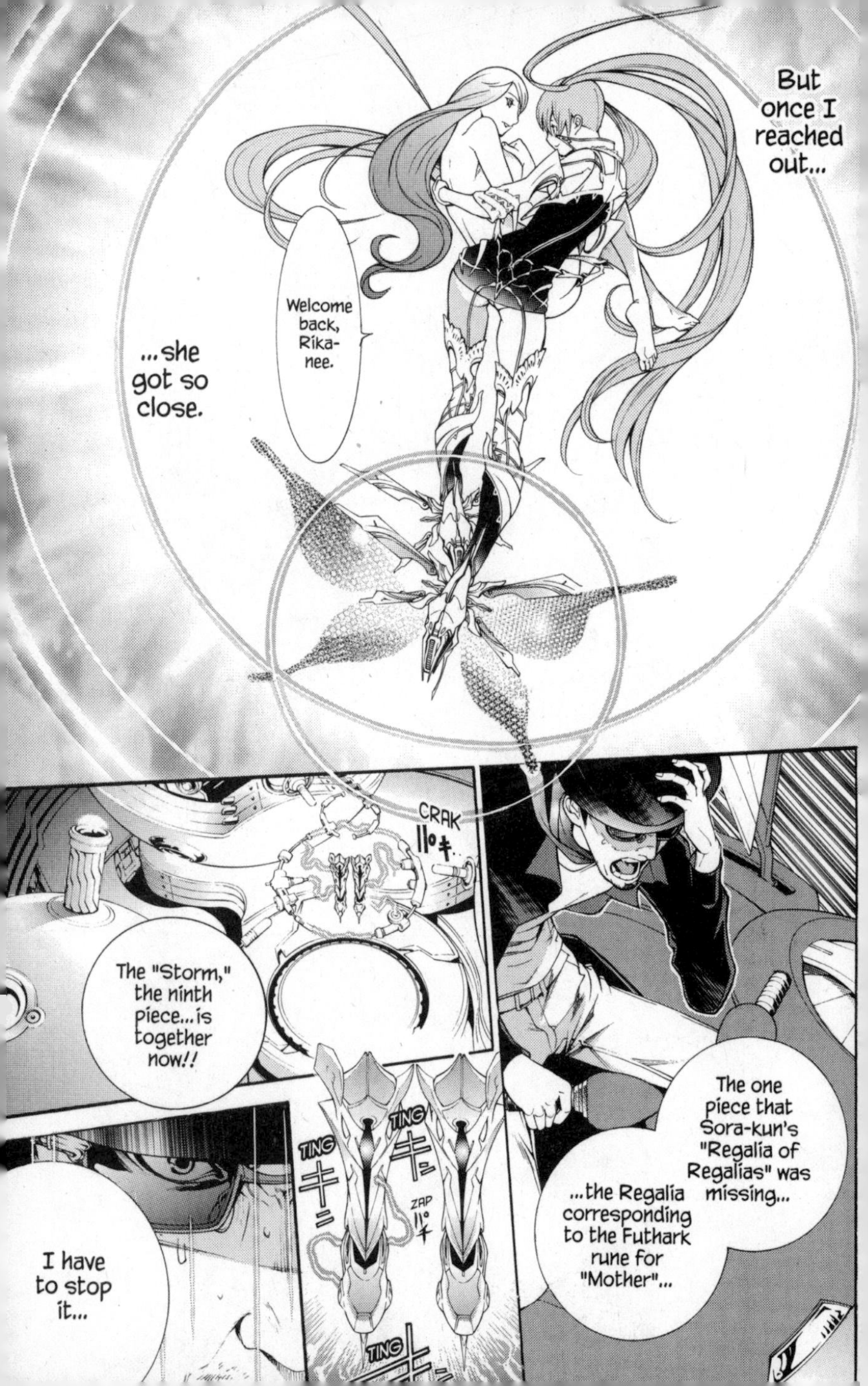
But once I reached out...
Welcome back, Rika-nee.
...she got so close.
CRAK
The one piece that Sora-kun's "Regalia of Regalias" was missing...
...the Regalia corresponding to the Futhark rune for "Mother"...
The "Storm," the ninth piece...is together now!!
TING
TING
ZAP
TING
I have to stop it...

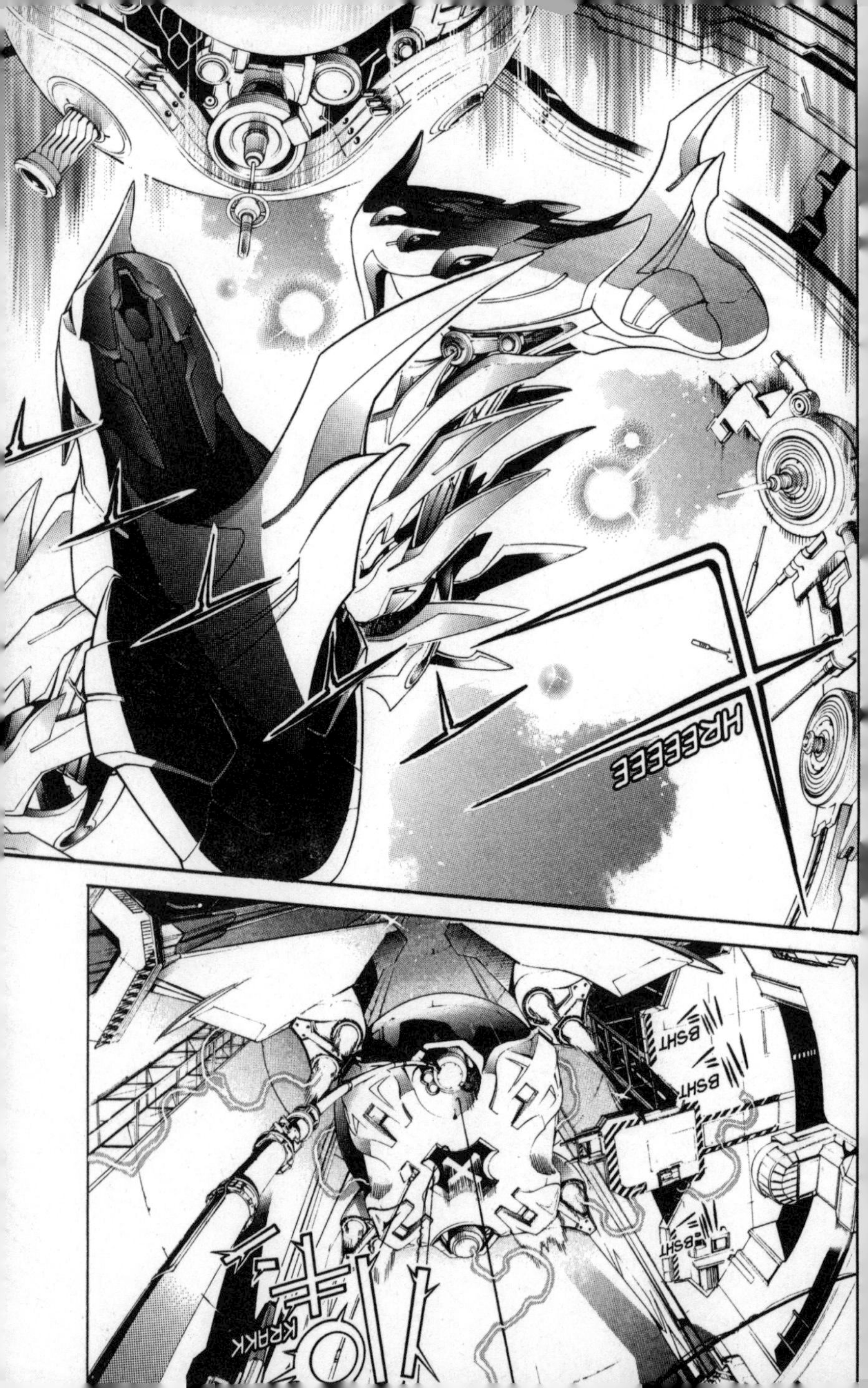
HREEEEE
BSHT
BSHT
BSHT
KRAKK

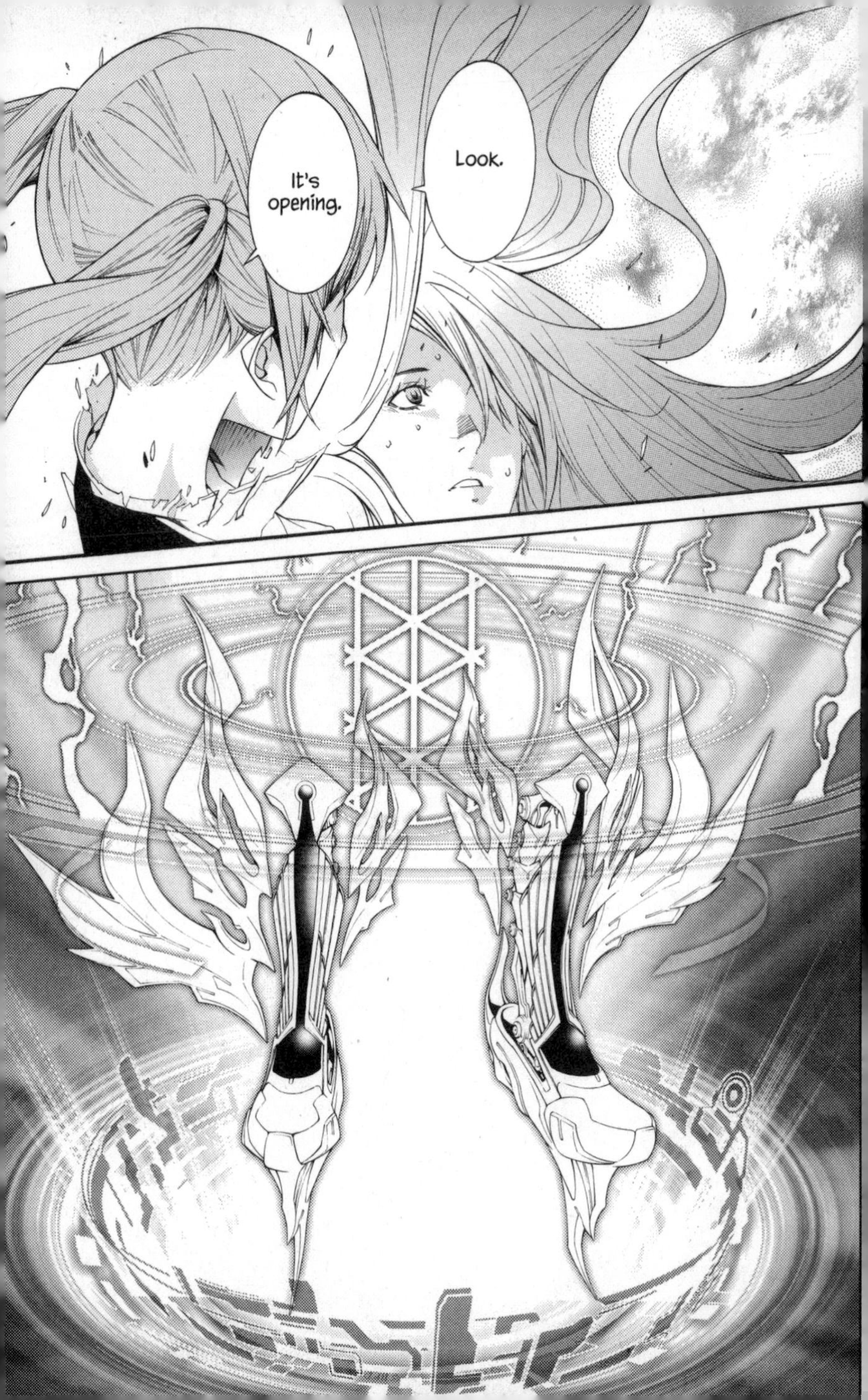
Look.
It's opening.

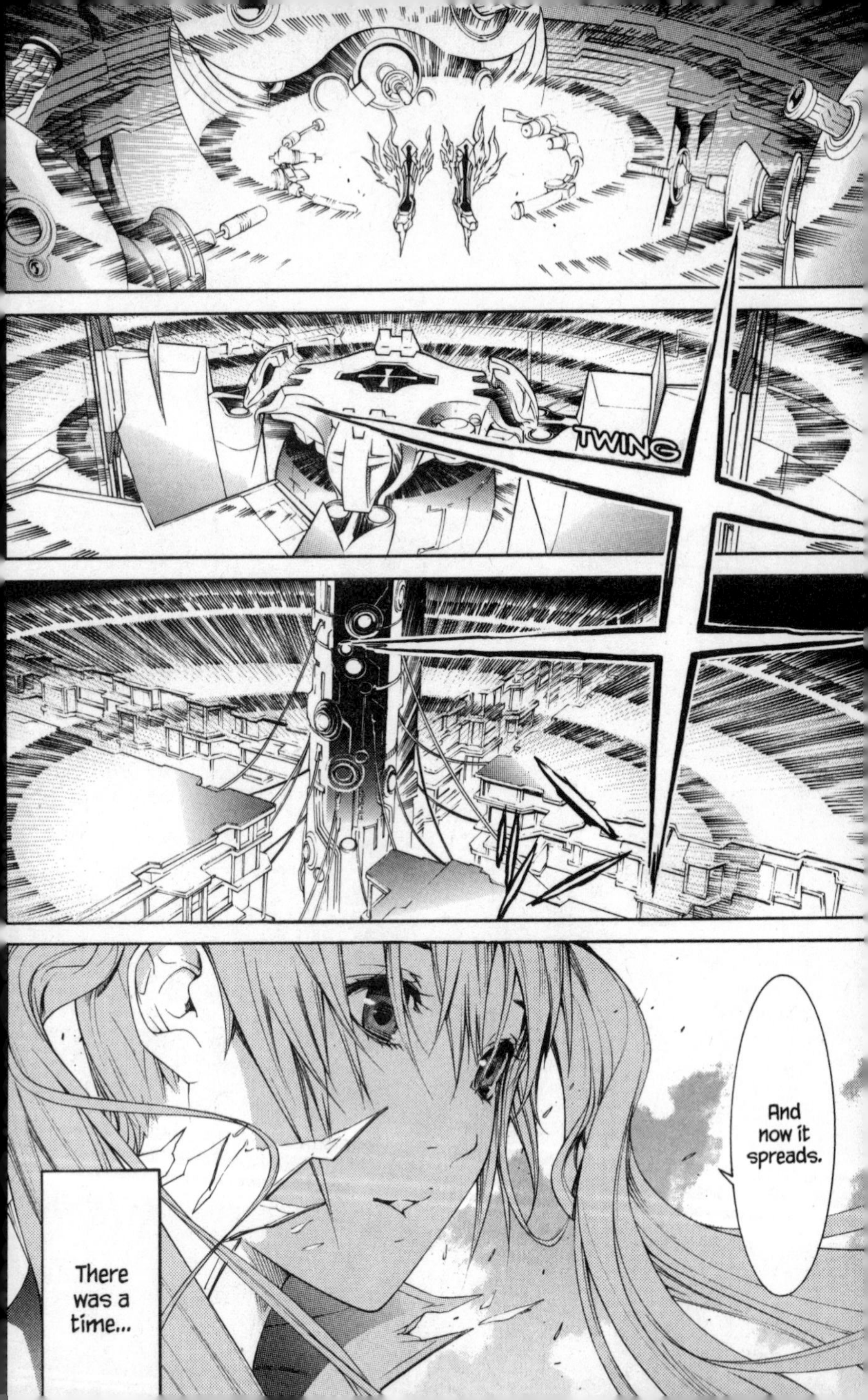
TWING
And now it spreads.
There was a time...

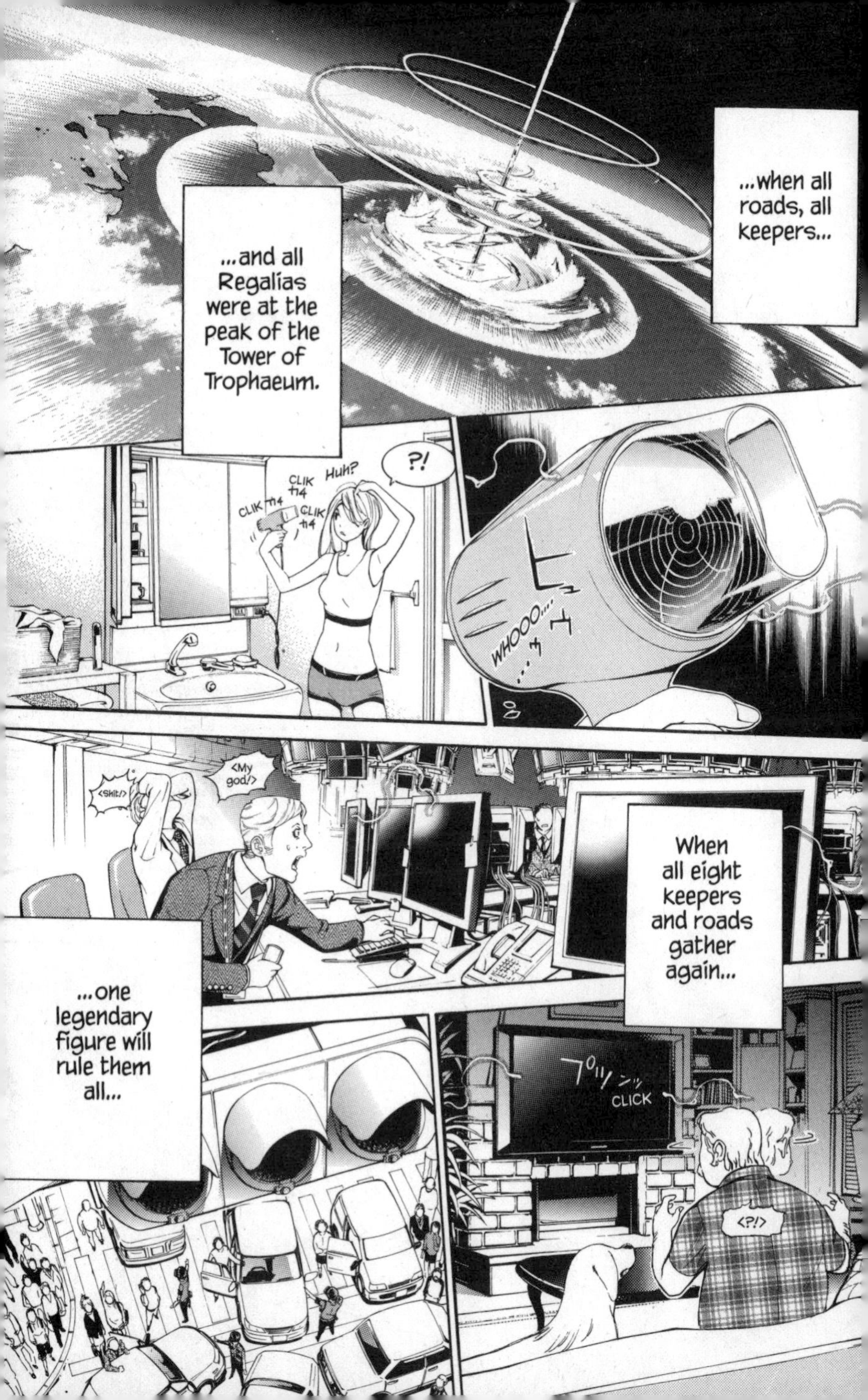
...when all roads, all keepers...
...and all Regalias were at the peak of the Tower of Trophaeum.
WHOOO....
?!
Huh?
CLIK
CLIK
CLIK
<Shit!/>
<My god!/>
When all eight keepers and roads gather again...
<?!/>
CLICK
...one legendary figure will rule them all...

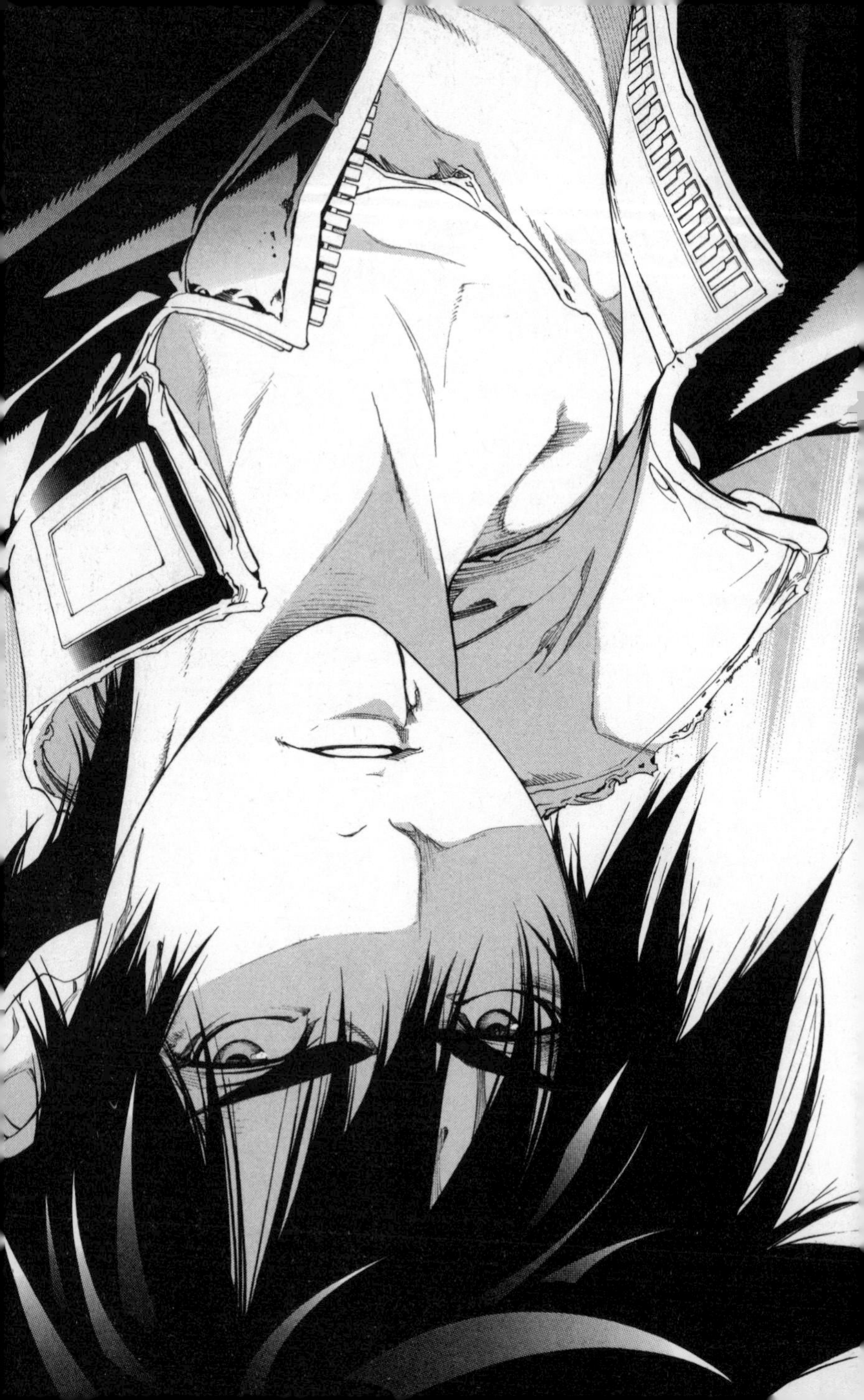

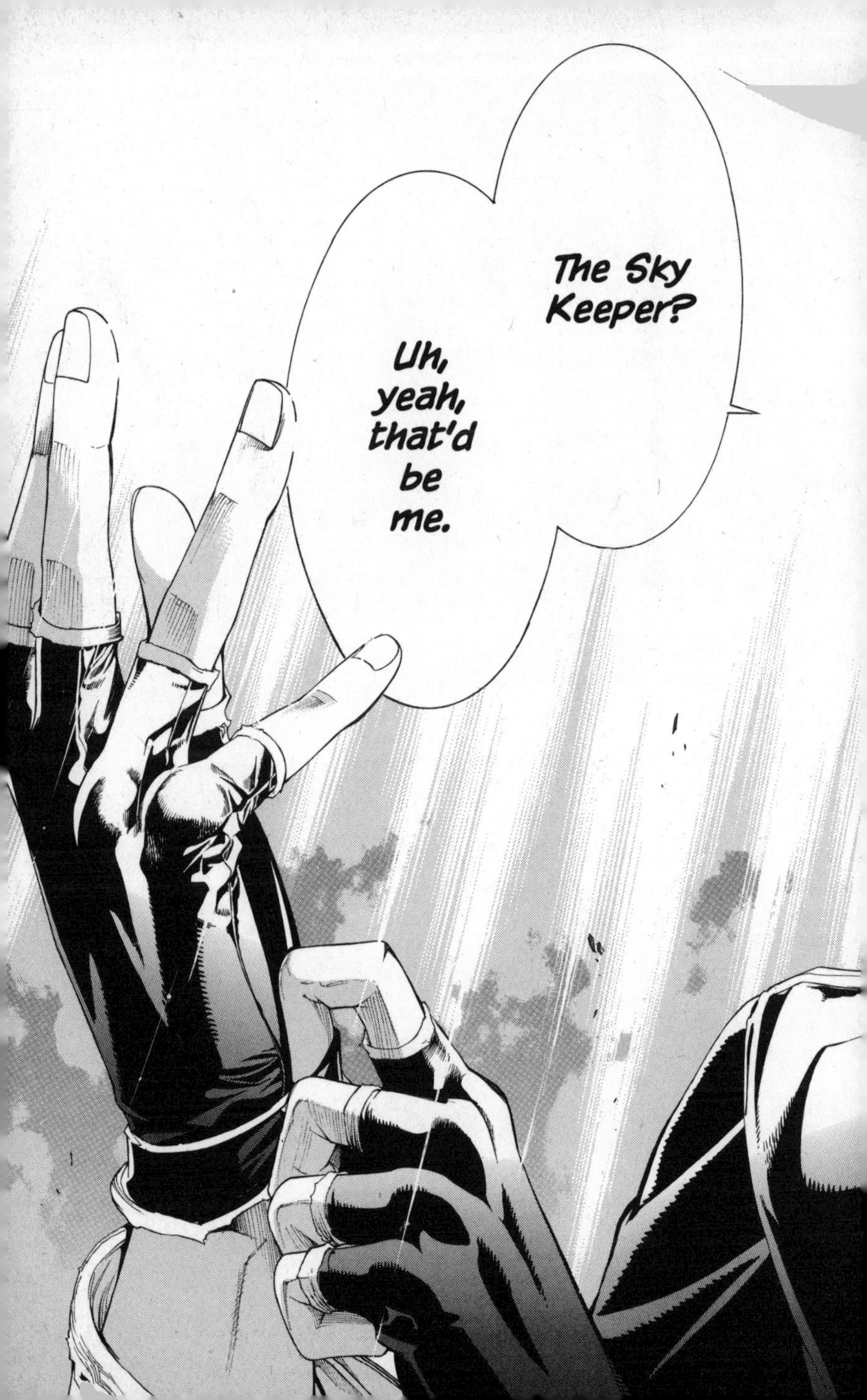
The Sky Keeper?
Uh, yeah, that'd be me.

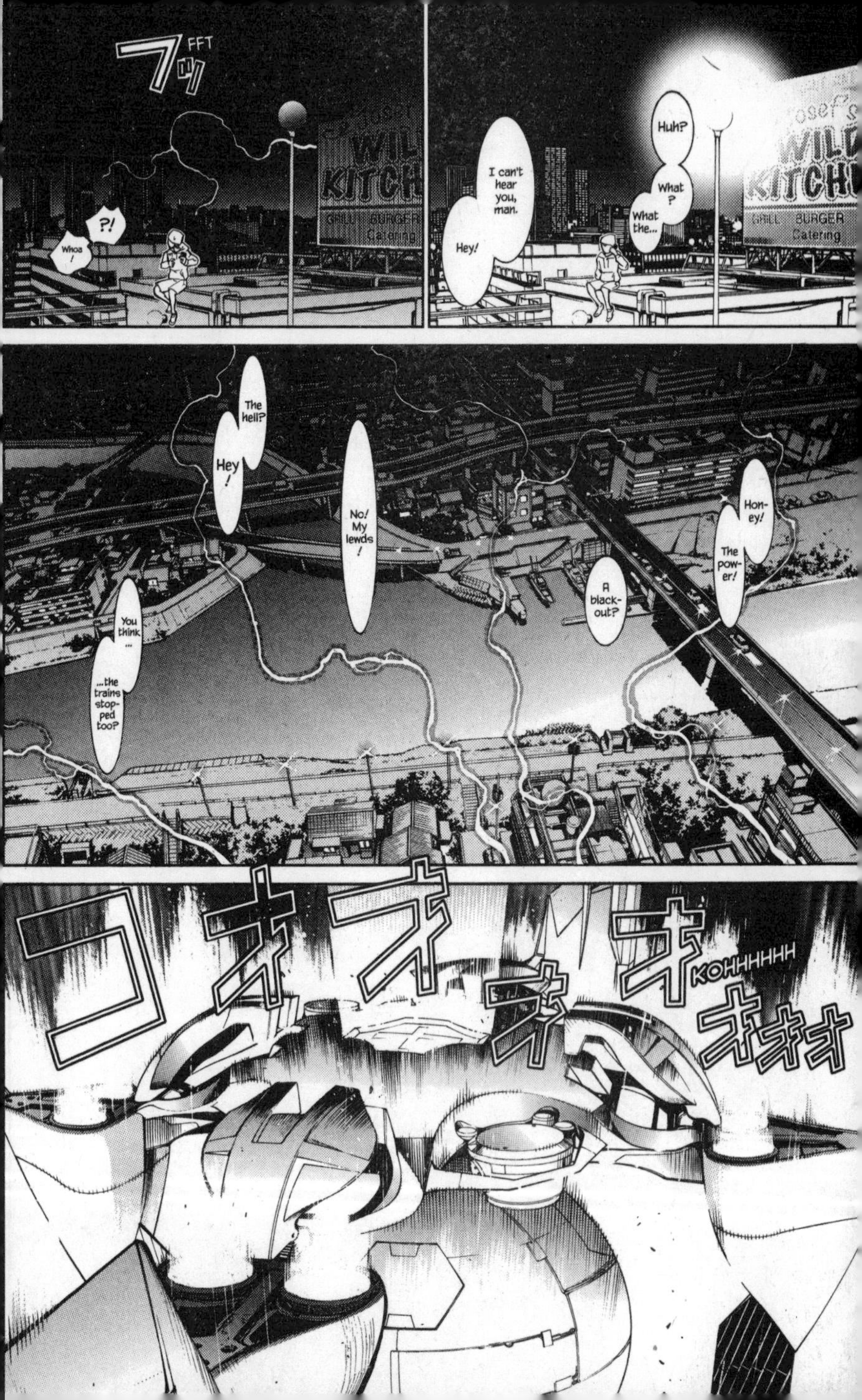
WILD KITCH
GRILL BURGER
Catering
Huh?
What?
What the...
I can't hear you, man.
Hey!
FFT
Whoa!
?!
WILD KITCH
GRILL BURGER
Catering
Honey!
The power!
A blackout?
No! My lewds!
Hey!
The hell?
You think...
...the trains stopped too?
KOHHHHHH

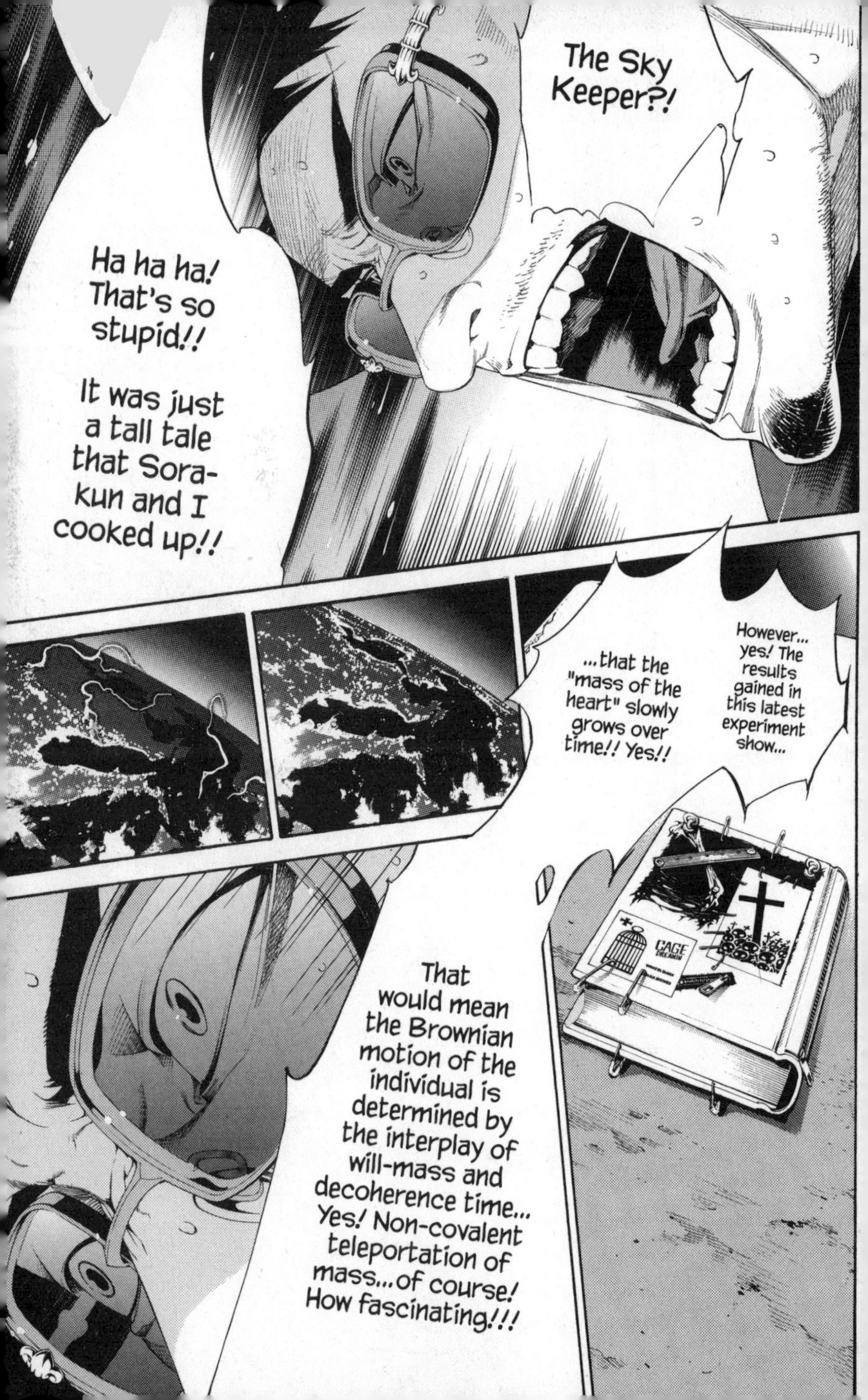
The Sky Keeper?!
Ha ha ha! That's so stupid!!
It was just a tall tale that Sora-kun and I cooked up!!
However... yes! The results gained in this latest experiment show...
...that the "mass of the heart" slowly grows over time!! Yes!!
CAGE
That would mean the Brownian motion of the individual is determined by the interplay of will-mass and decoherence time... Yes! Non-covalent teleportation of mass...of course! How fascinating!!!

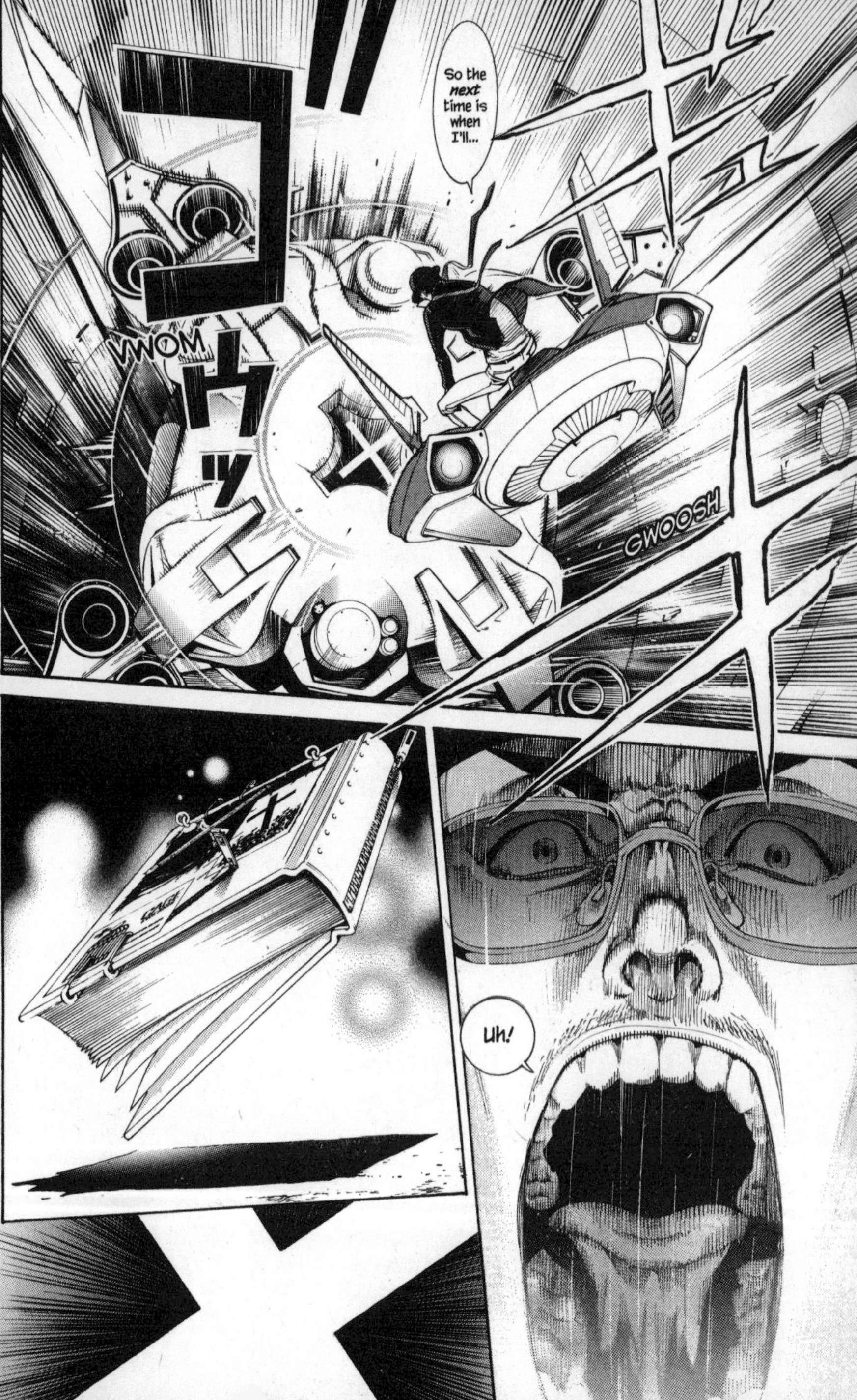
So the *next* time is when I'll...
GWOOSH
VWOM
Uh!

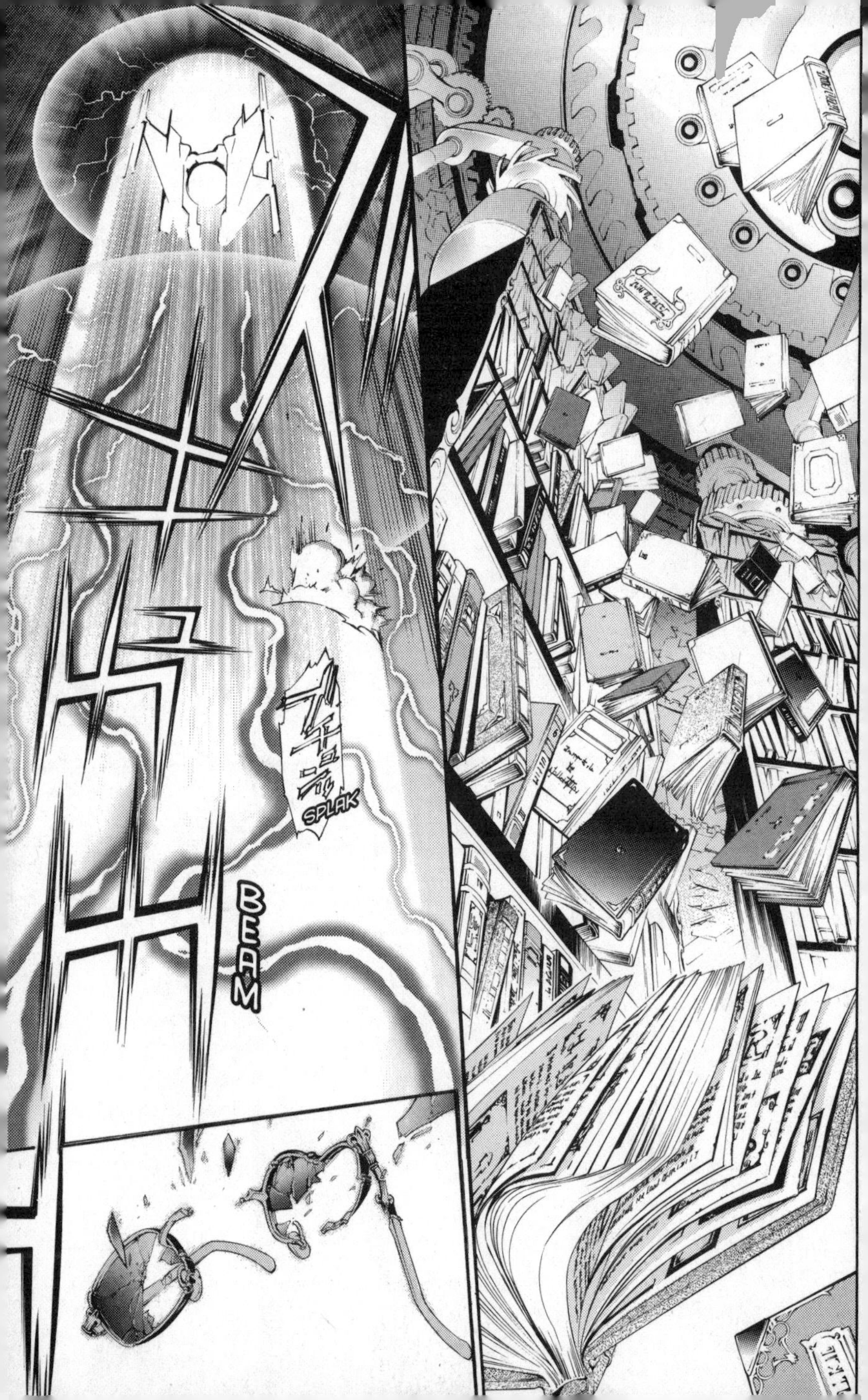
BEAM
SPLAK

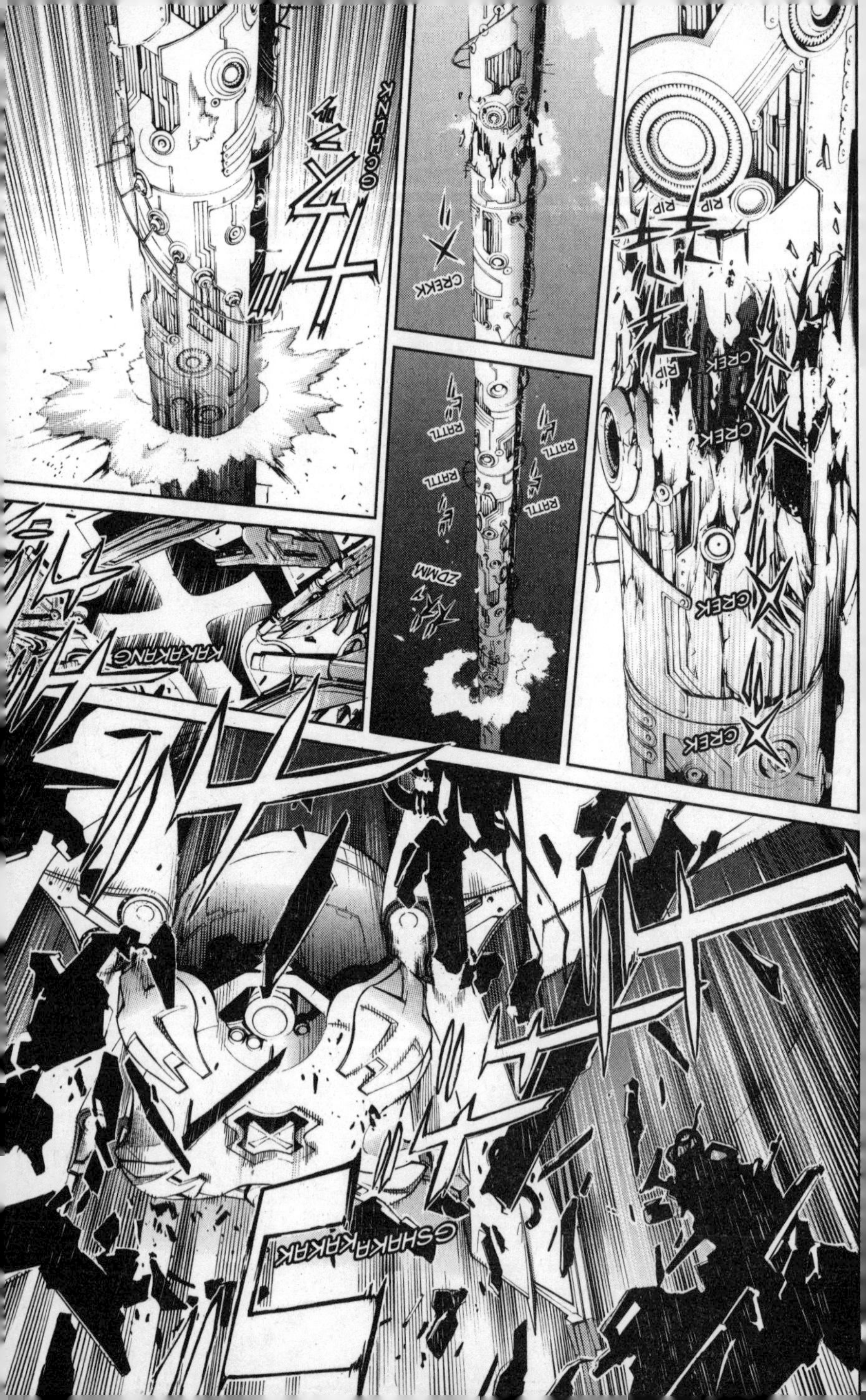
RIP
RIP
RIP
CREK
CREK
CREK
CREK
CREKK
RATTL
RATTL
RATTL
ZDMM
KAKAKANG
GSHAKAKAKAK

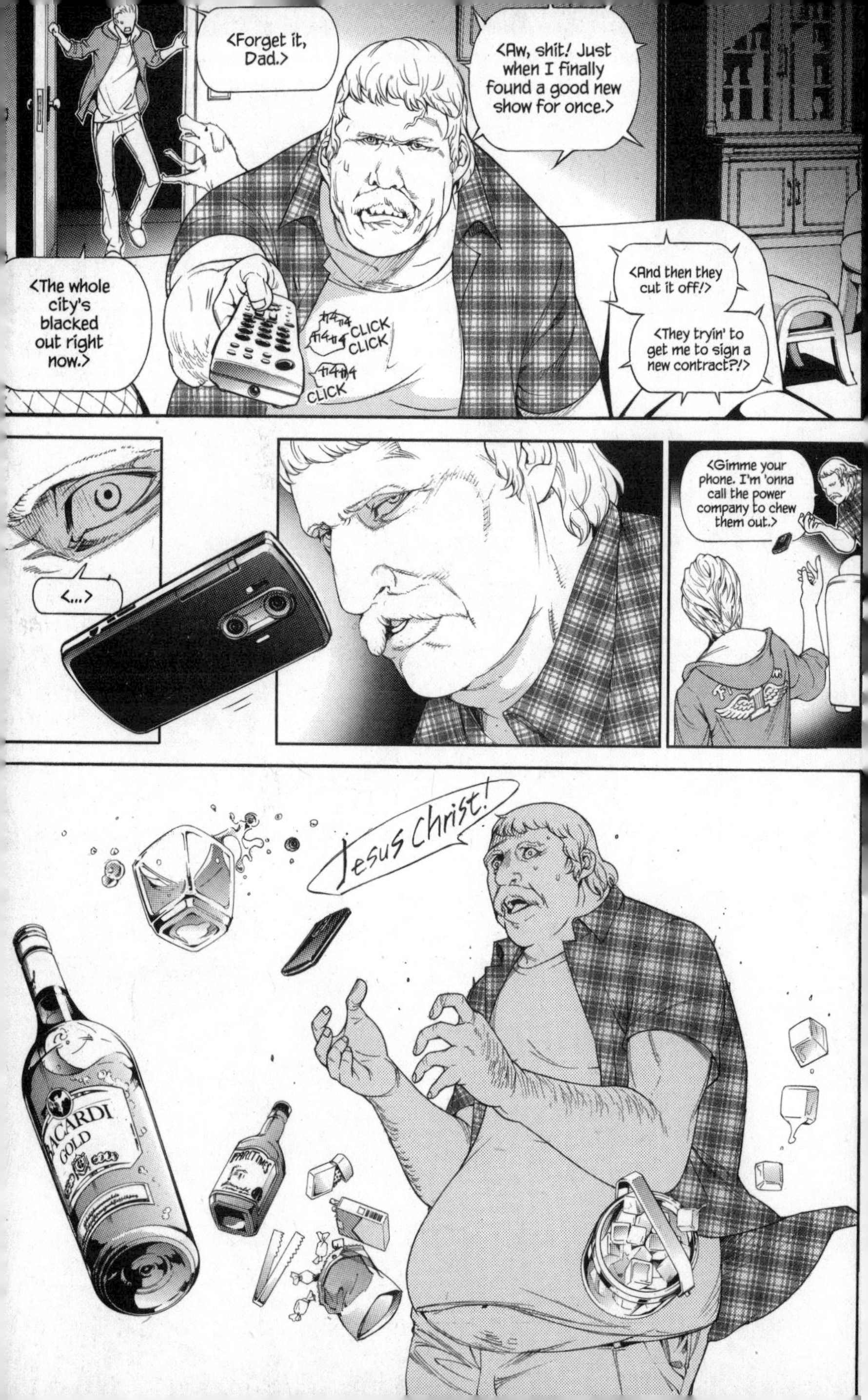
<Aw, shit! Just when I finally found a good new show for once.>
<Forget it, Dad.>
<And then they cut it off!>
<They tryin' to get me to sign a new contract?!>
CLICK
CLICK
CLICK
<The whole city's blacked out right now.>
<Gimme your phone. I'm 'onna call the power company to chew them out.>
<...>
Jesus Christ!
BACARDI
GOLD

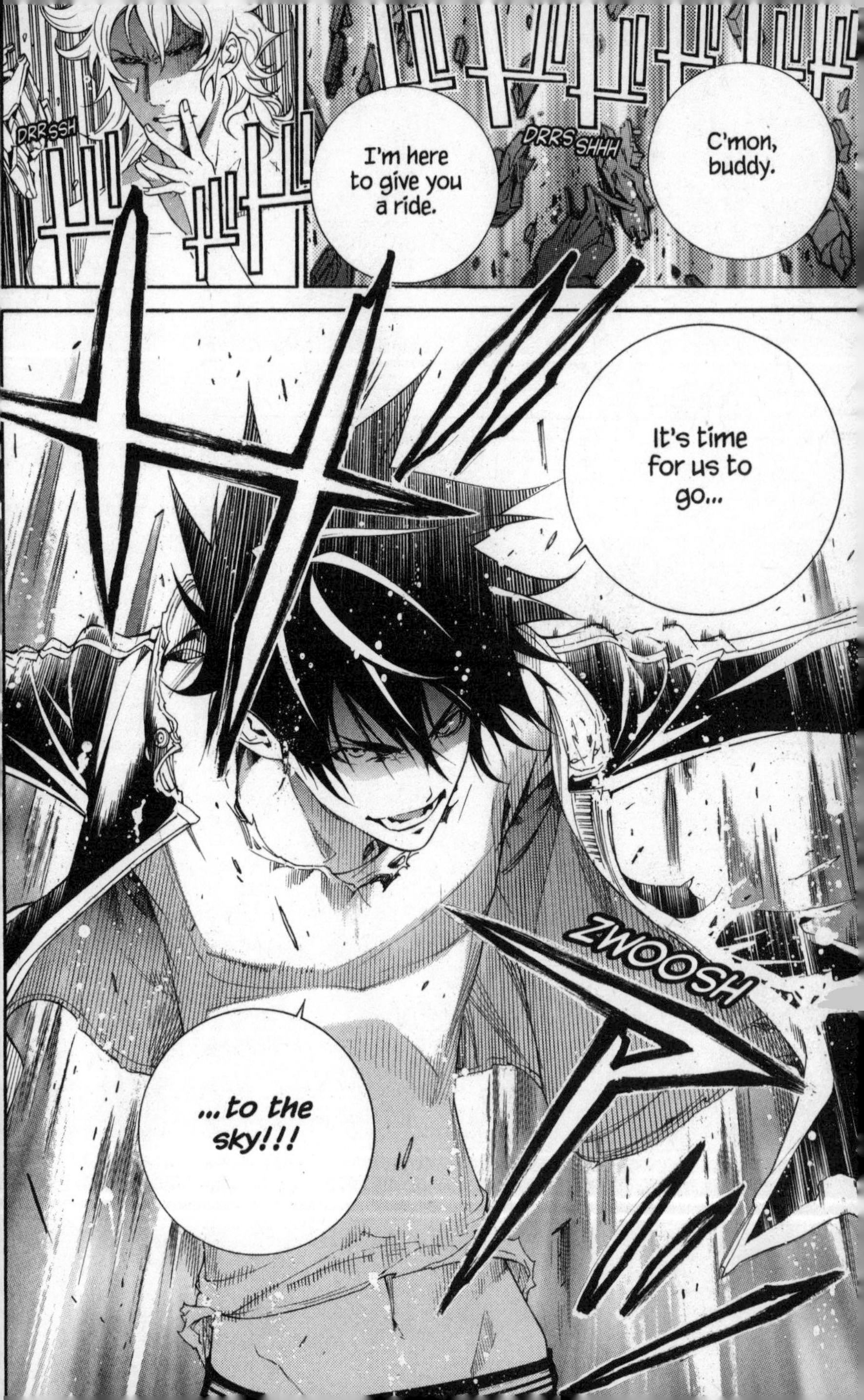
C'mon, buddy.
DRRS SHHH
I'm here to give you a ride.
DRRSSH
It's time for us to go...
ZWOOSH
...to the sky!!!

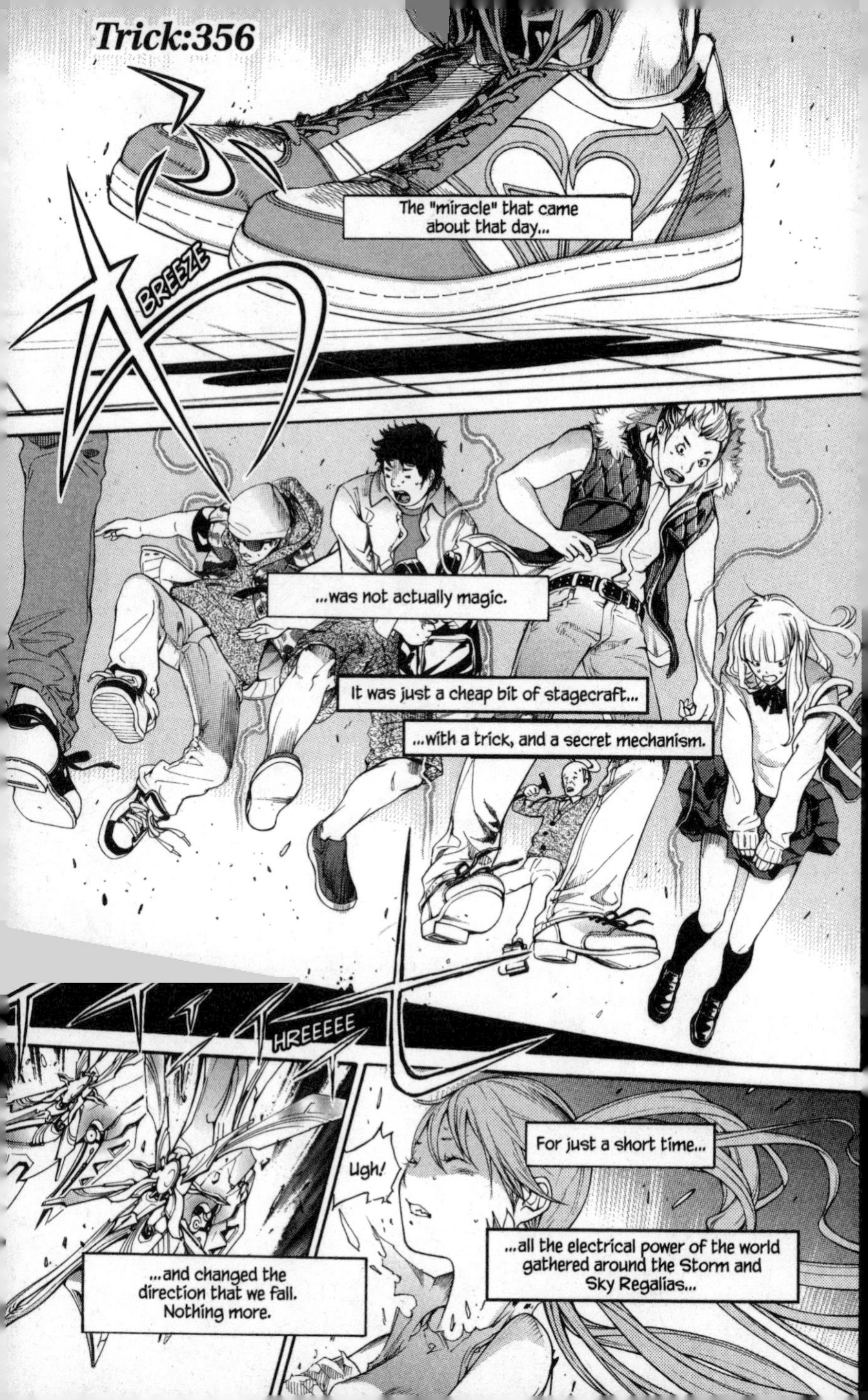
Trick:356
BREEZE
The "miracle" that came about that day...
...was not actually magic.
It was just a cheap bit of stagecraft...
...with a trick, and a secret mechanism.
HREEEEE
For just a short time...
...all the electrical power of the world gathered around the Storm and Sky Regalias...
Ugh!
...and changed the direction that we fall. Nothing more.

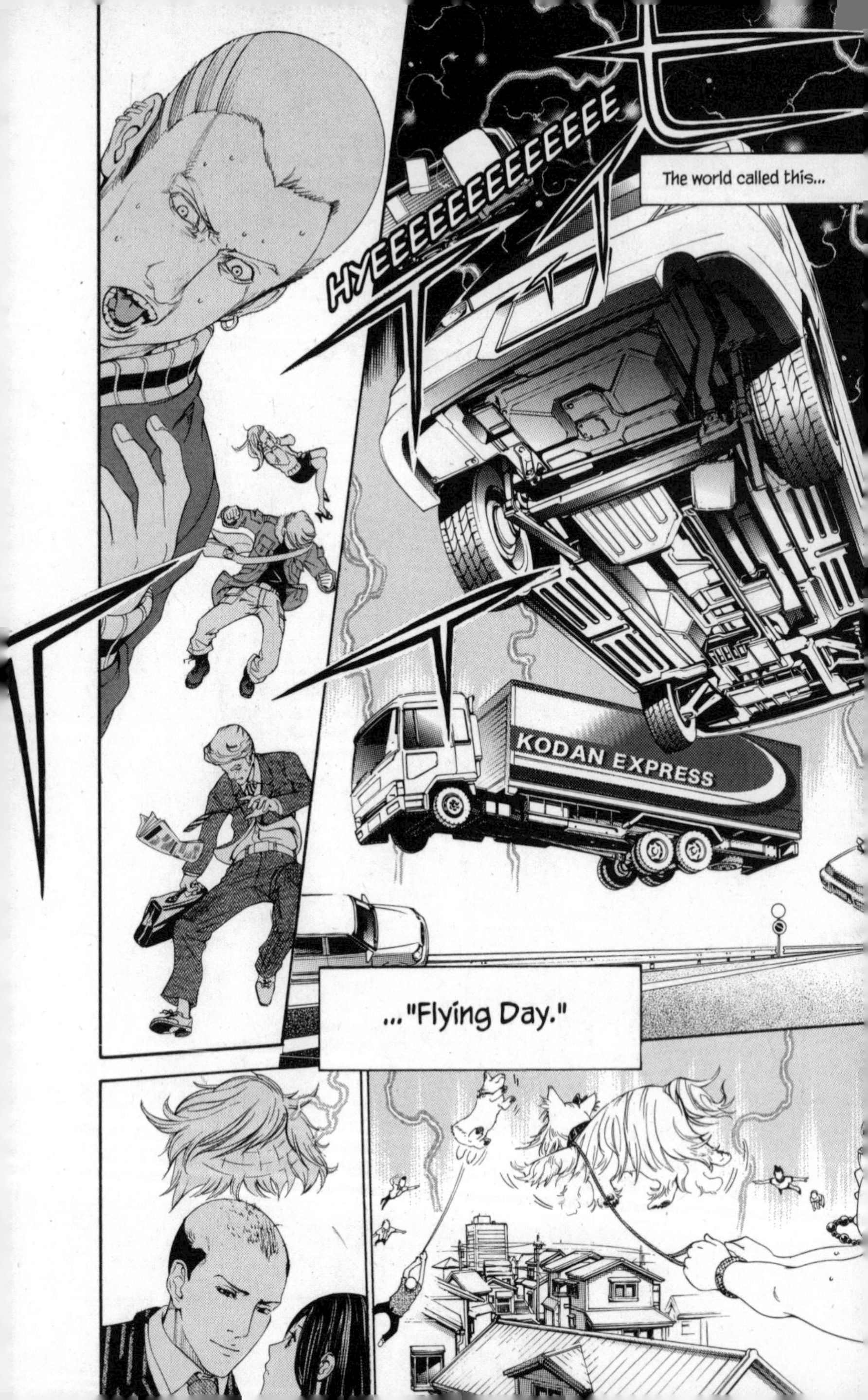
The world called this...
HYEEEEEEEEEEEEEE
KODAN EXPRESS
..."Flying Day."

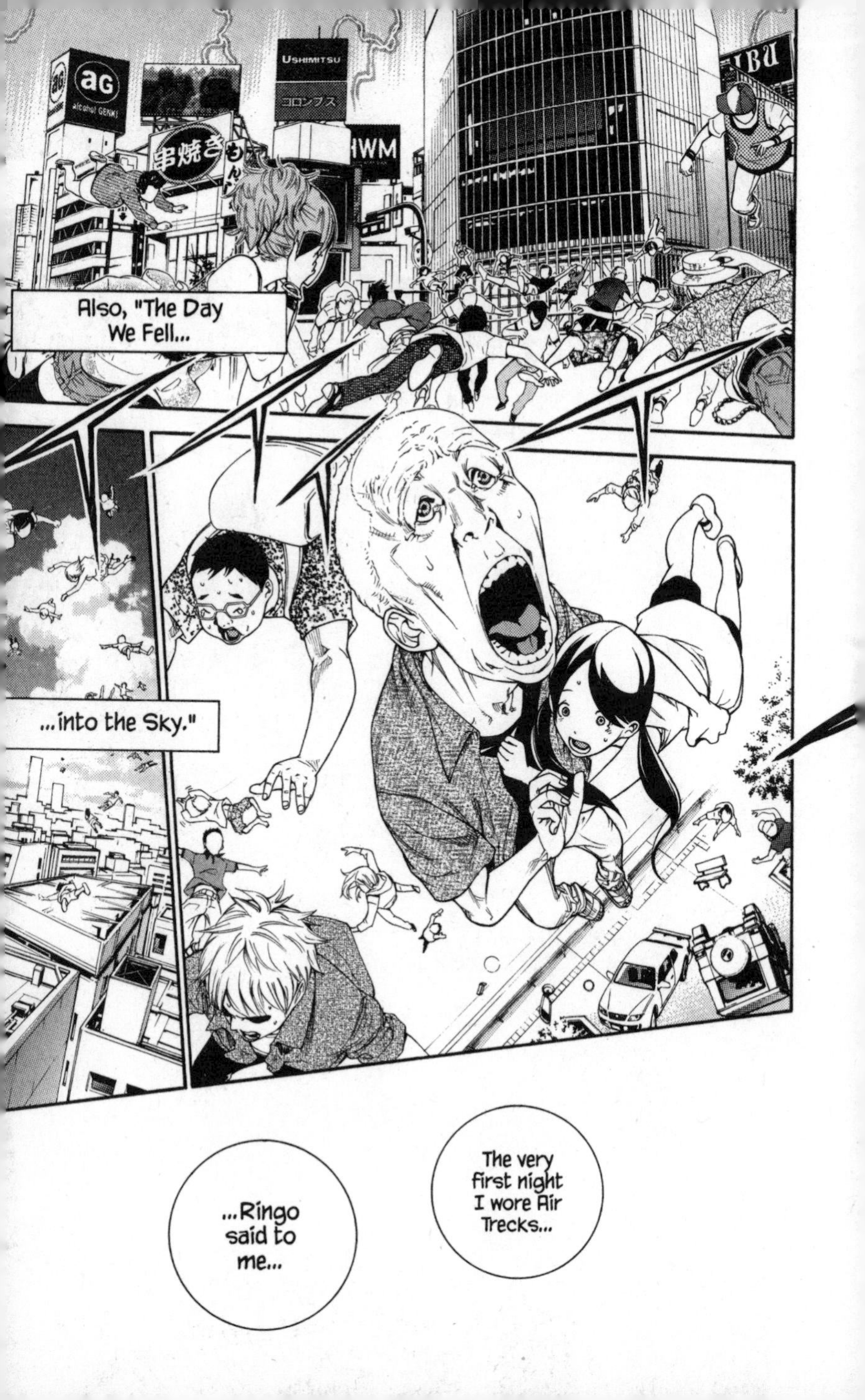
aG
USHIMITSU
コロンブス
串焼き
Also, "The Day We Fell...
...into the Sky."
The very first night I wore Air Trecks...
...Ringo said to me...

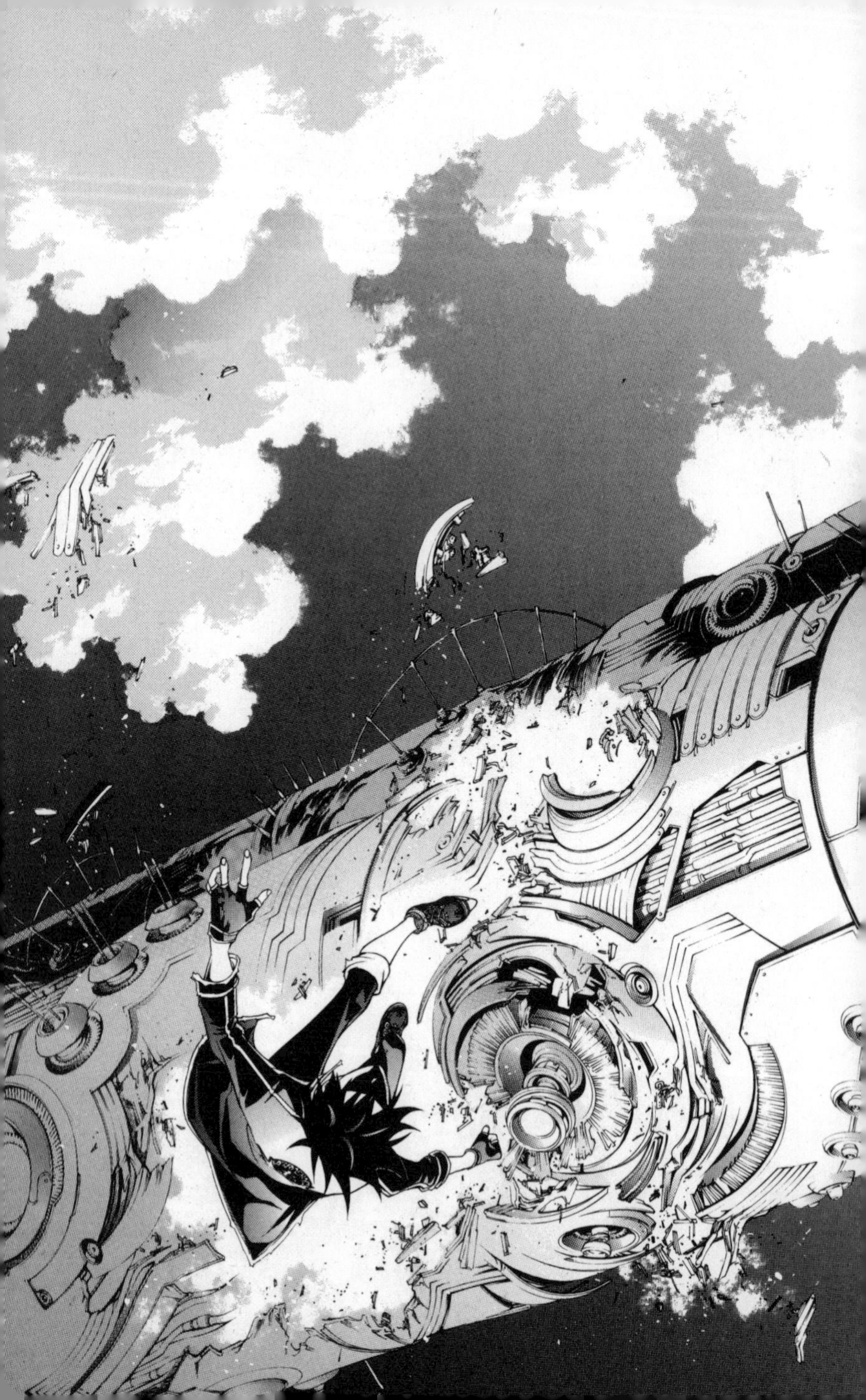

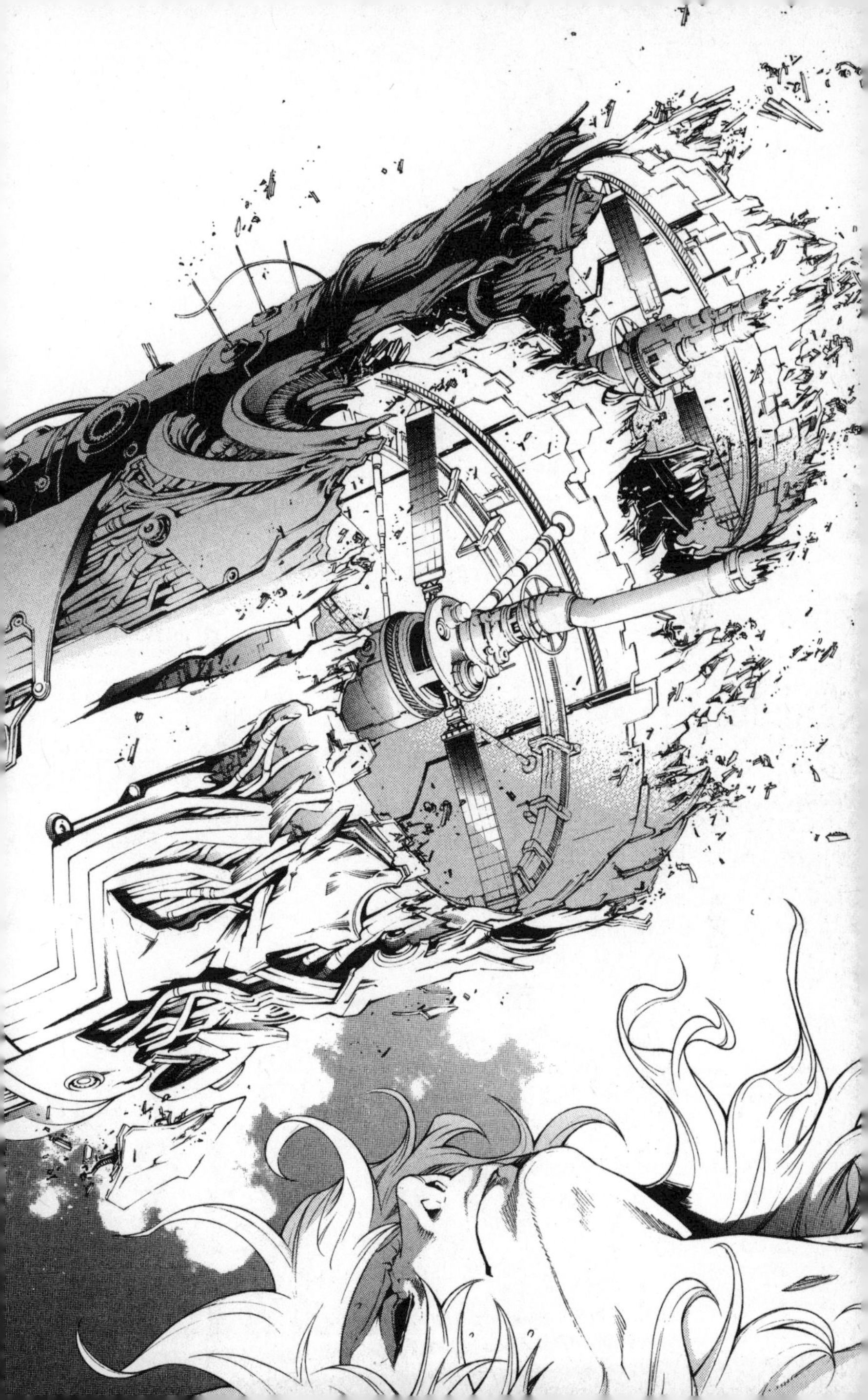

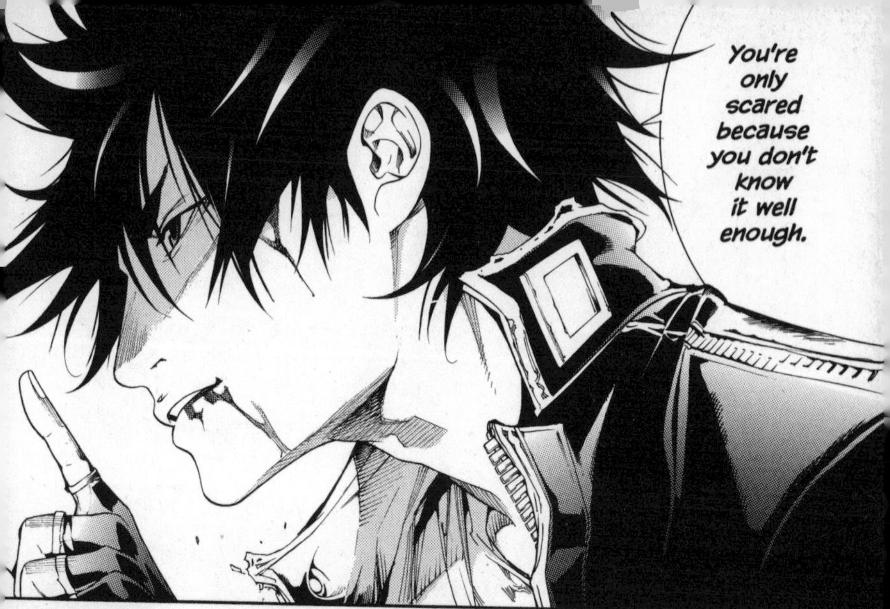
You're only scared because you don't know it well enough.

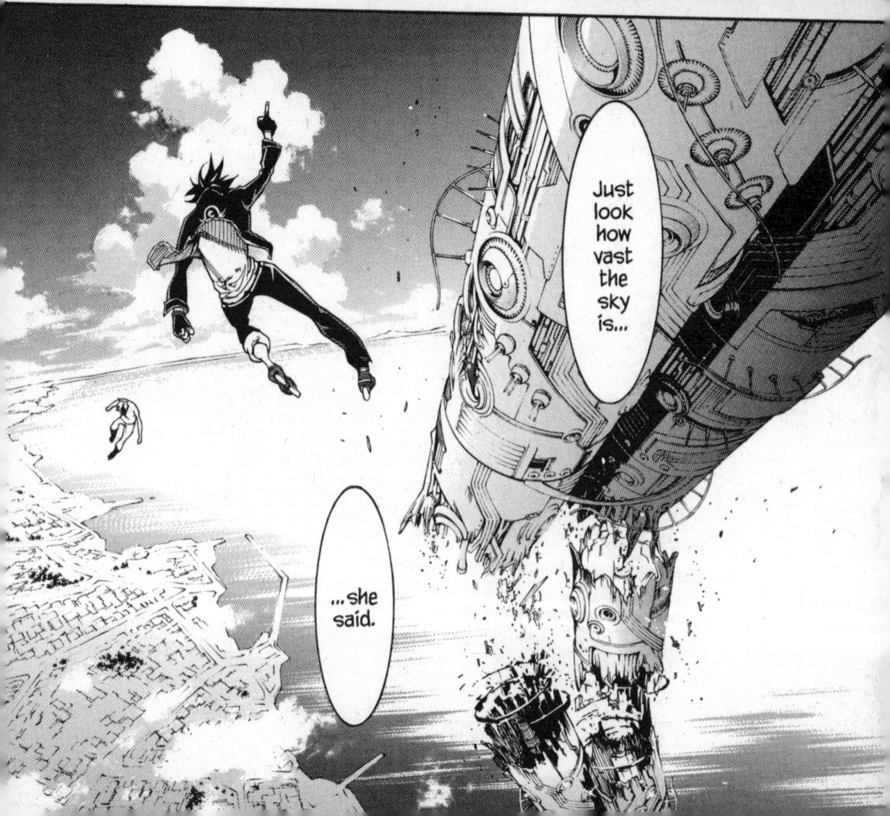
Just look how vast the sky is...
...she said.

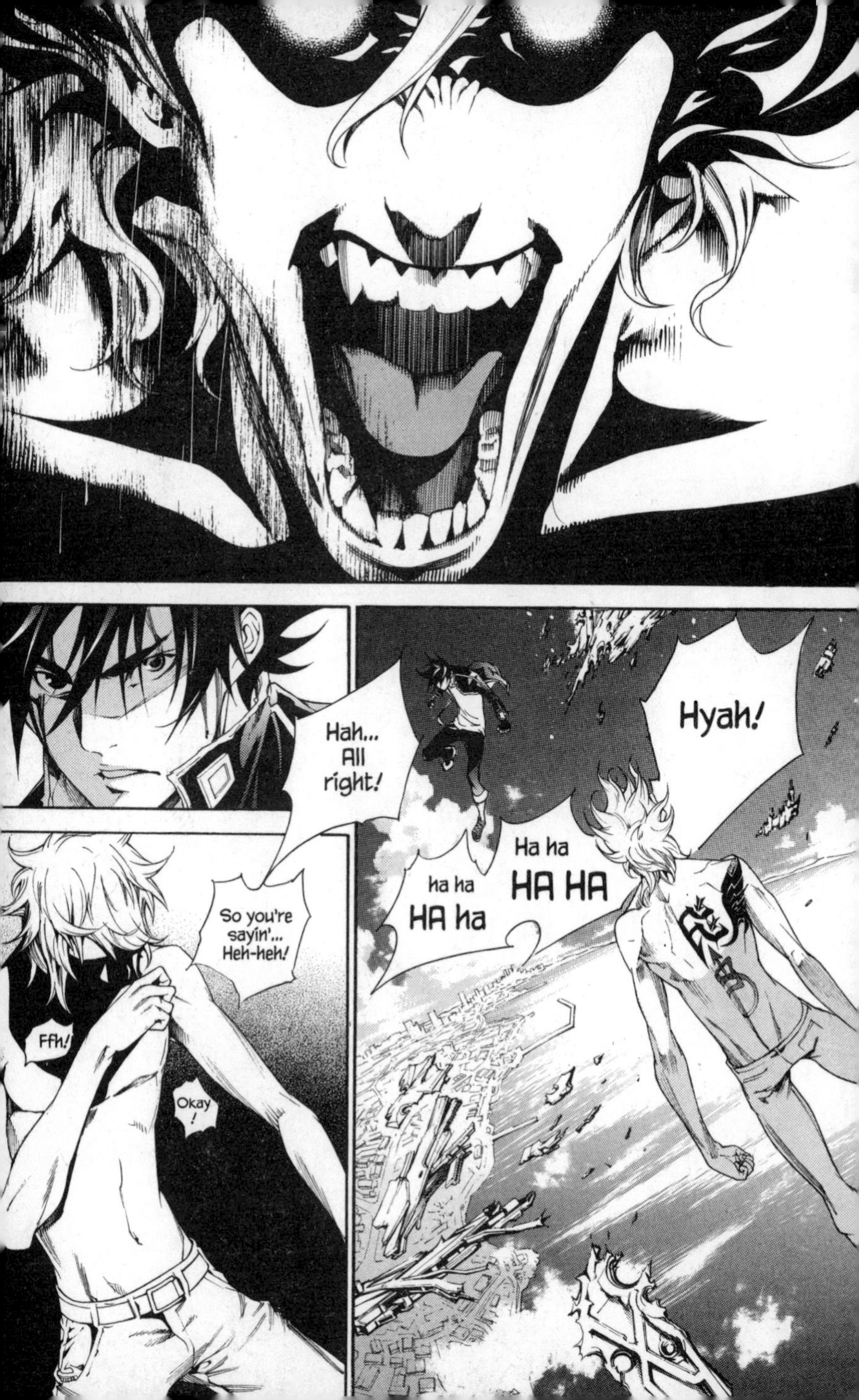
Hyah!
Ha ha
HA HA
ha ha
HA ha
Hah... All right!
So you're sayin'... Heh-heh!
Ffh!
Okay!

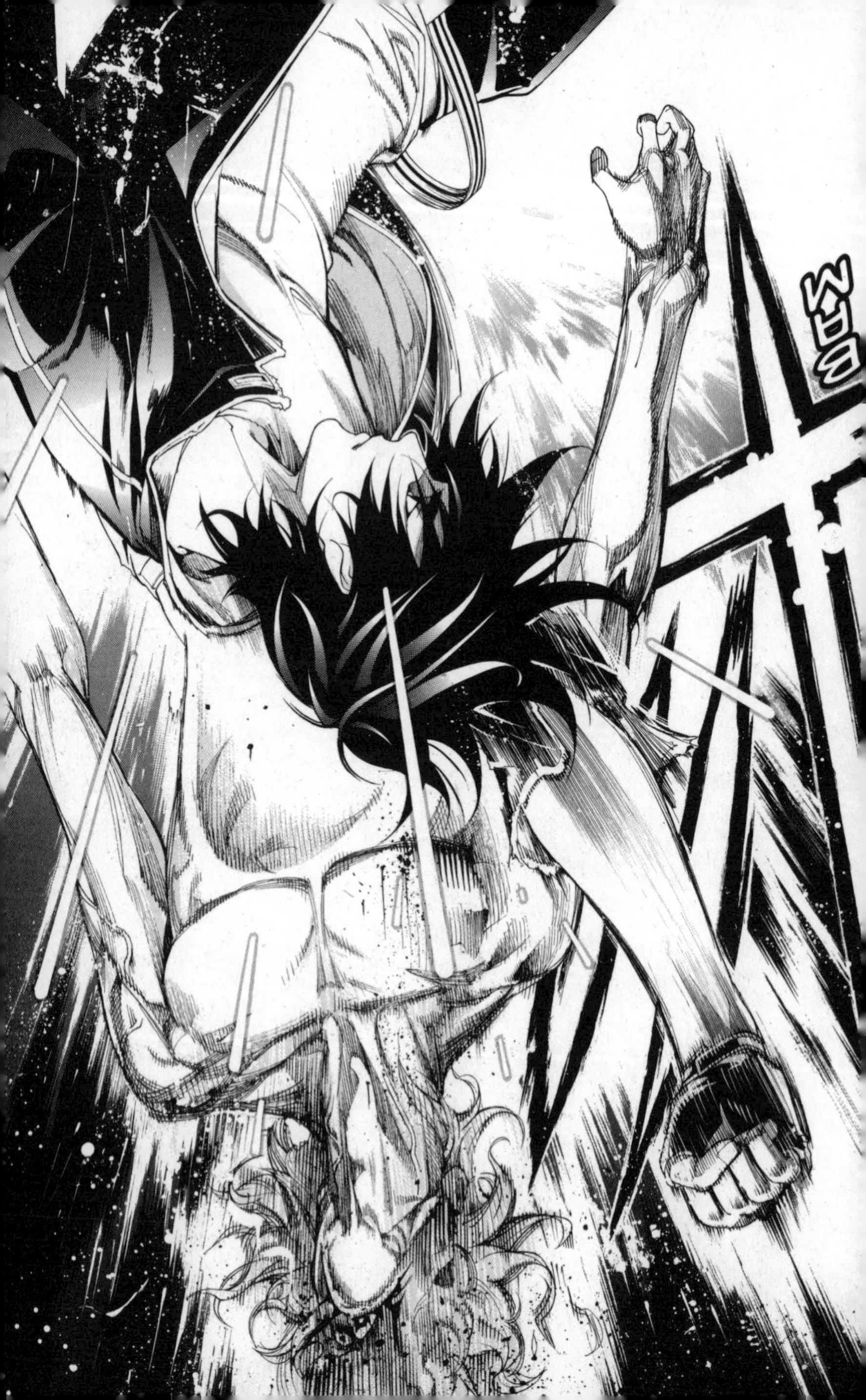
BAM

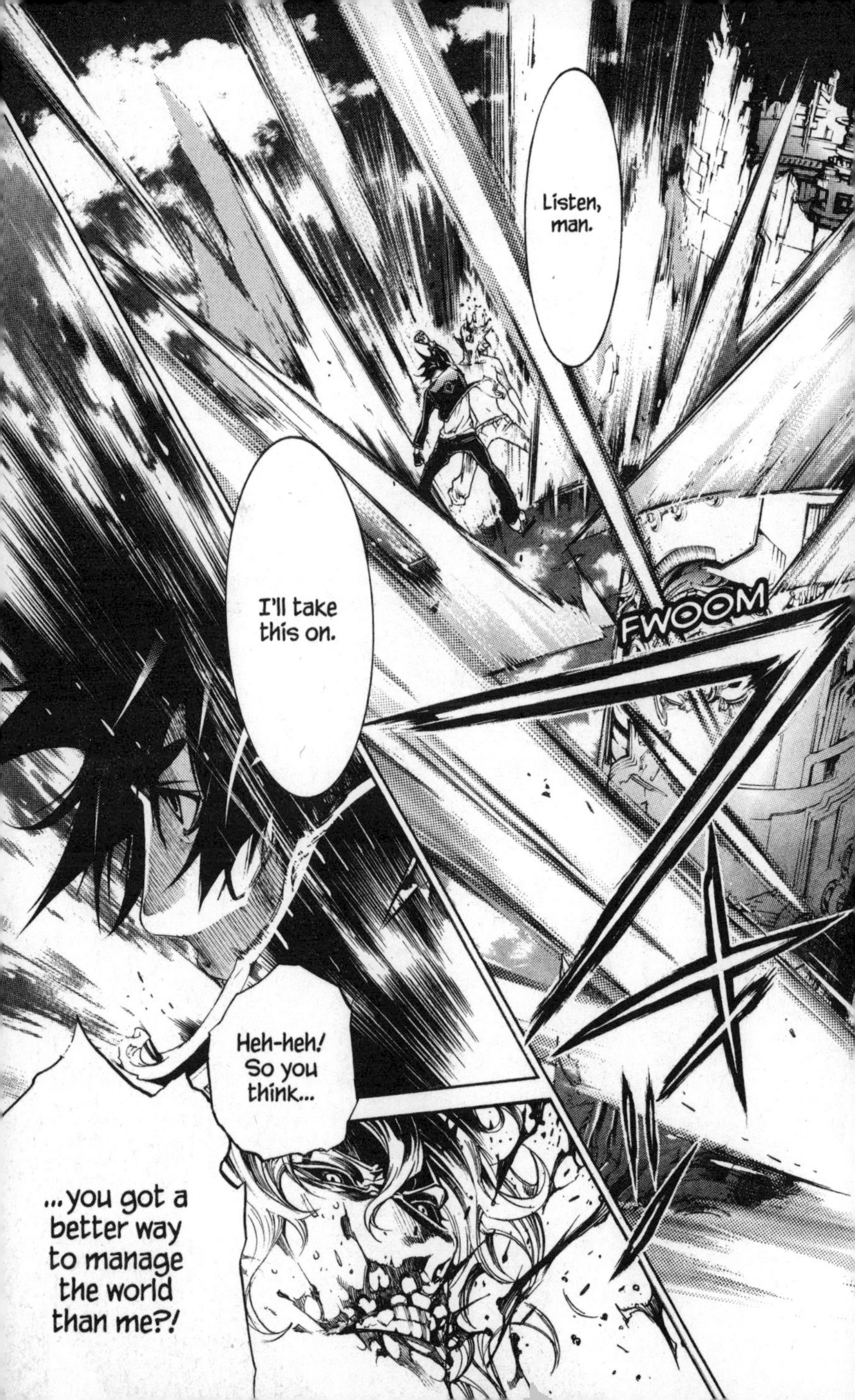
Listen, man.
I'll take this on.
FWOOM
Heh-heh! So you think...
...you got a better way to manage the world than me?!

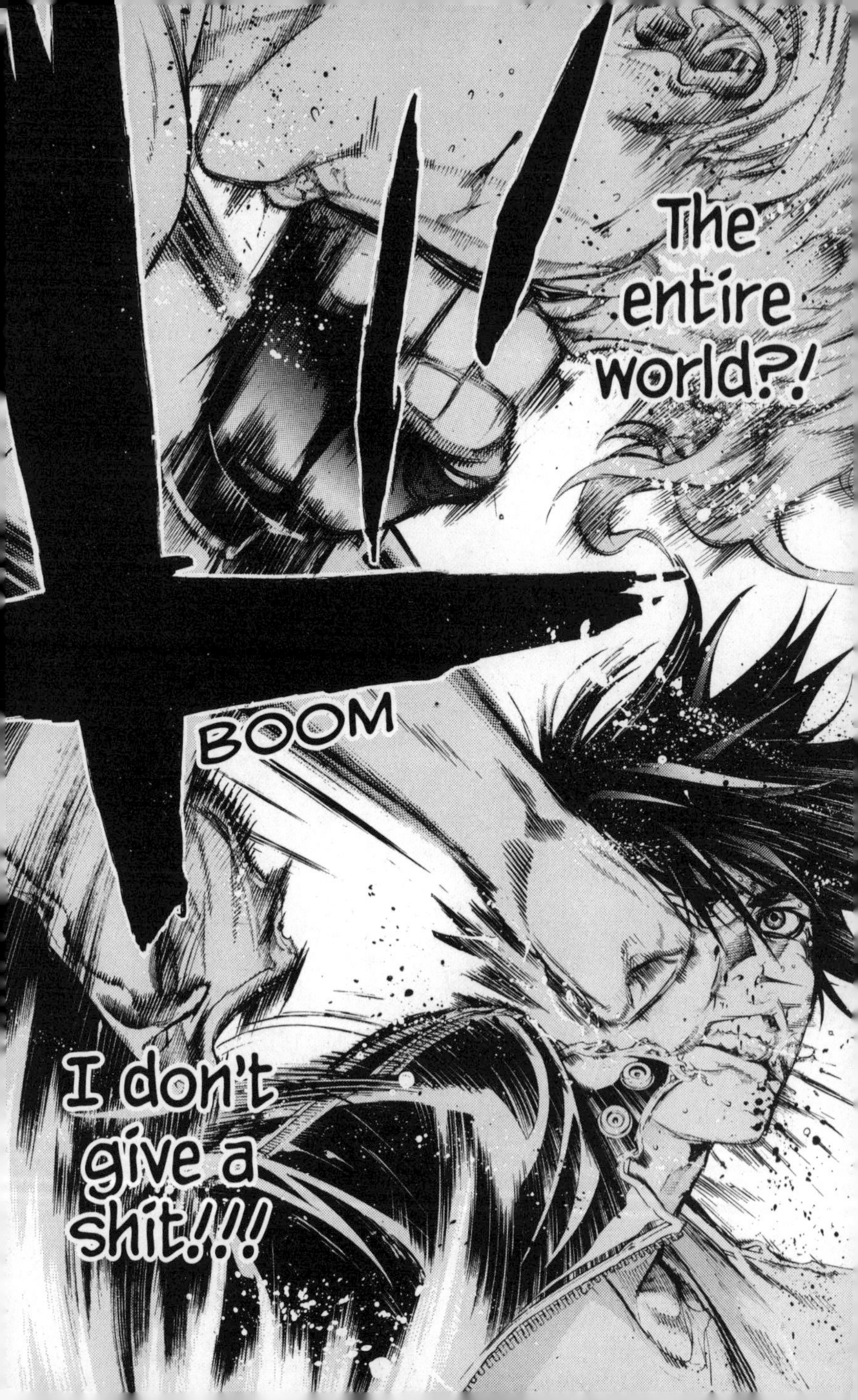
The entire world?!
BOOM
I don't give a shit!!!

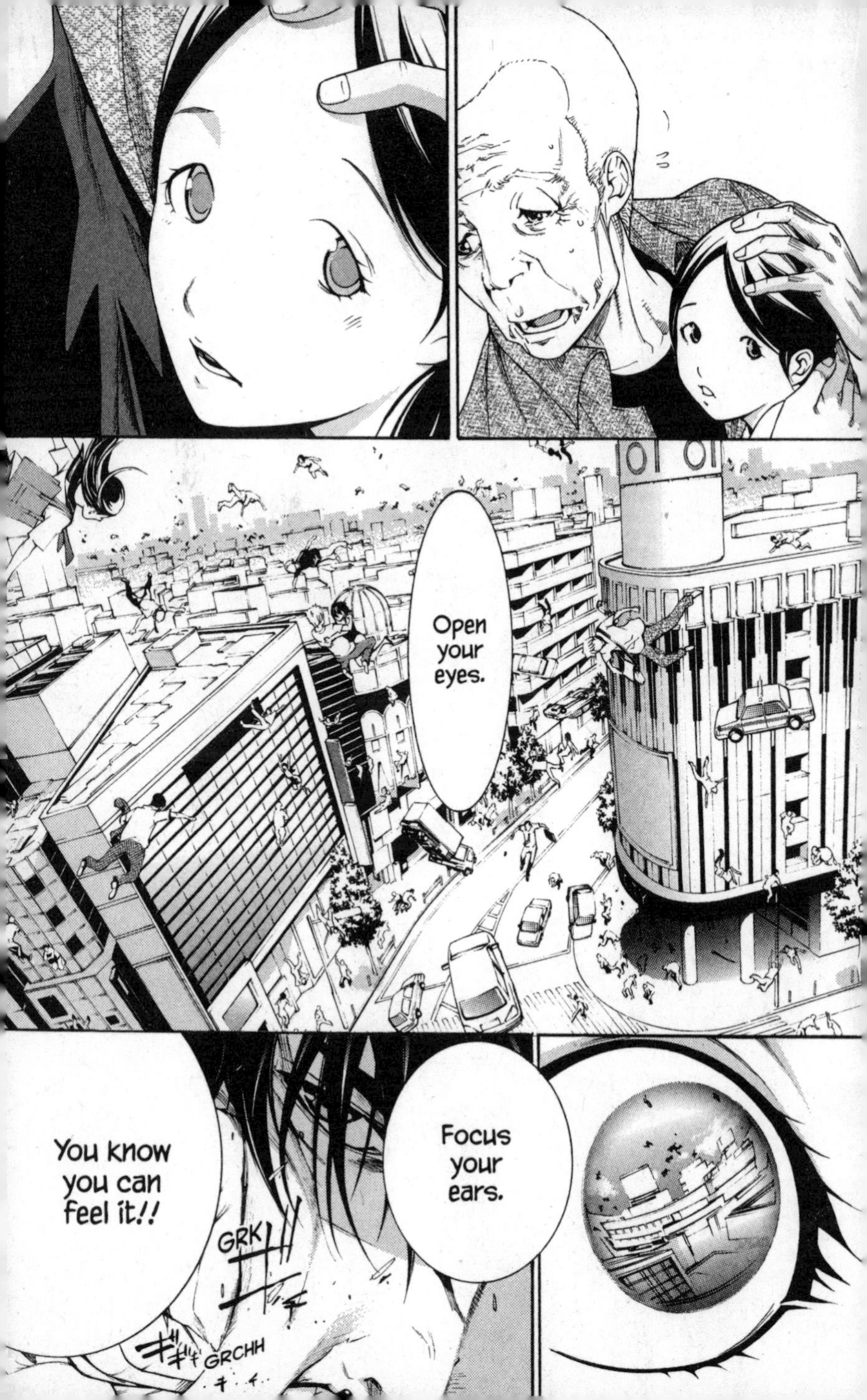
Open your eyes.
Focus your ears.
You know you can feel it!!
GRK
GRCHH

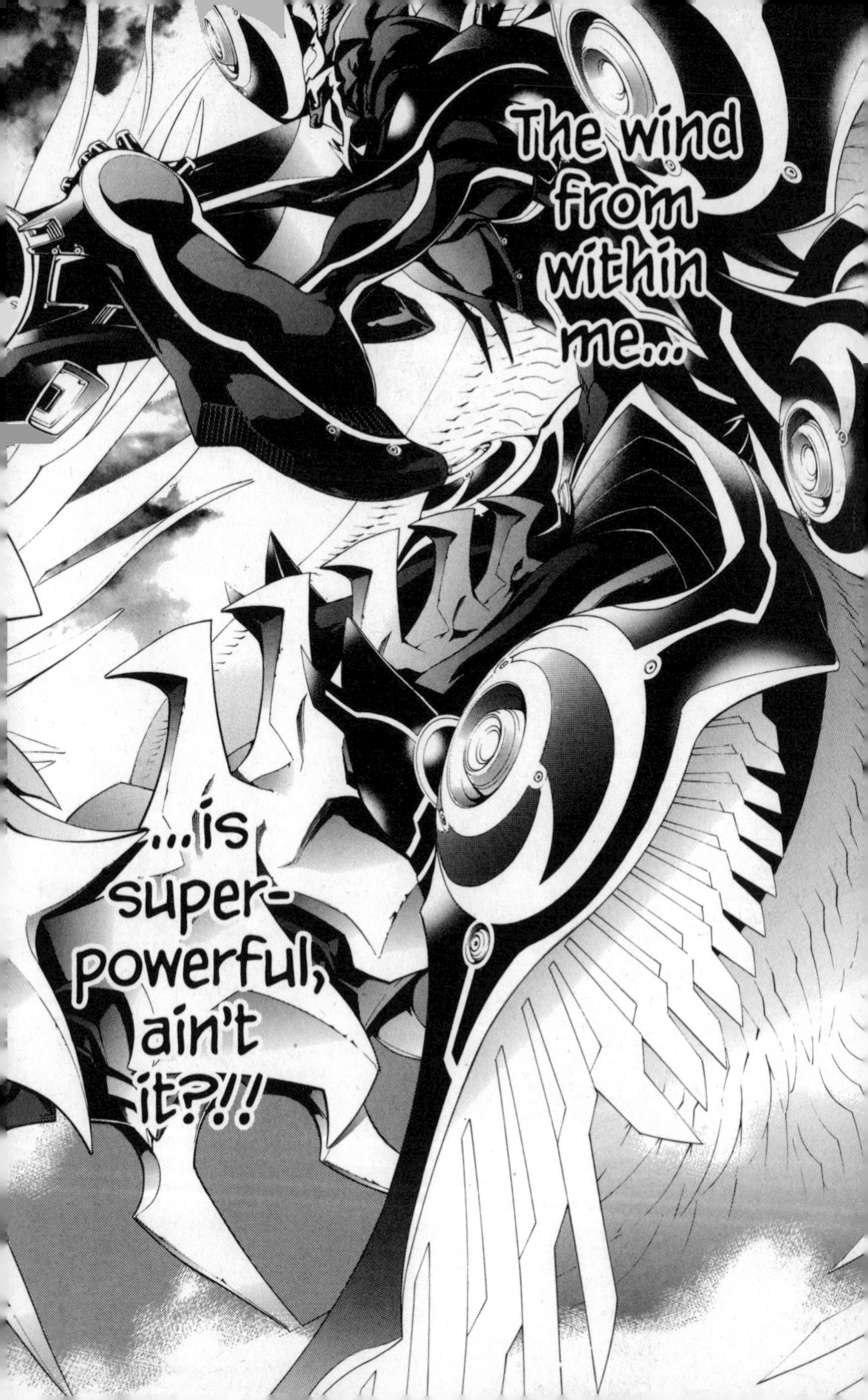
The wind from within me...
...is super-powerful, ain't it?!!

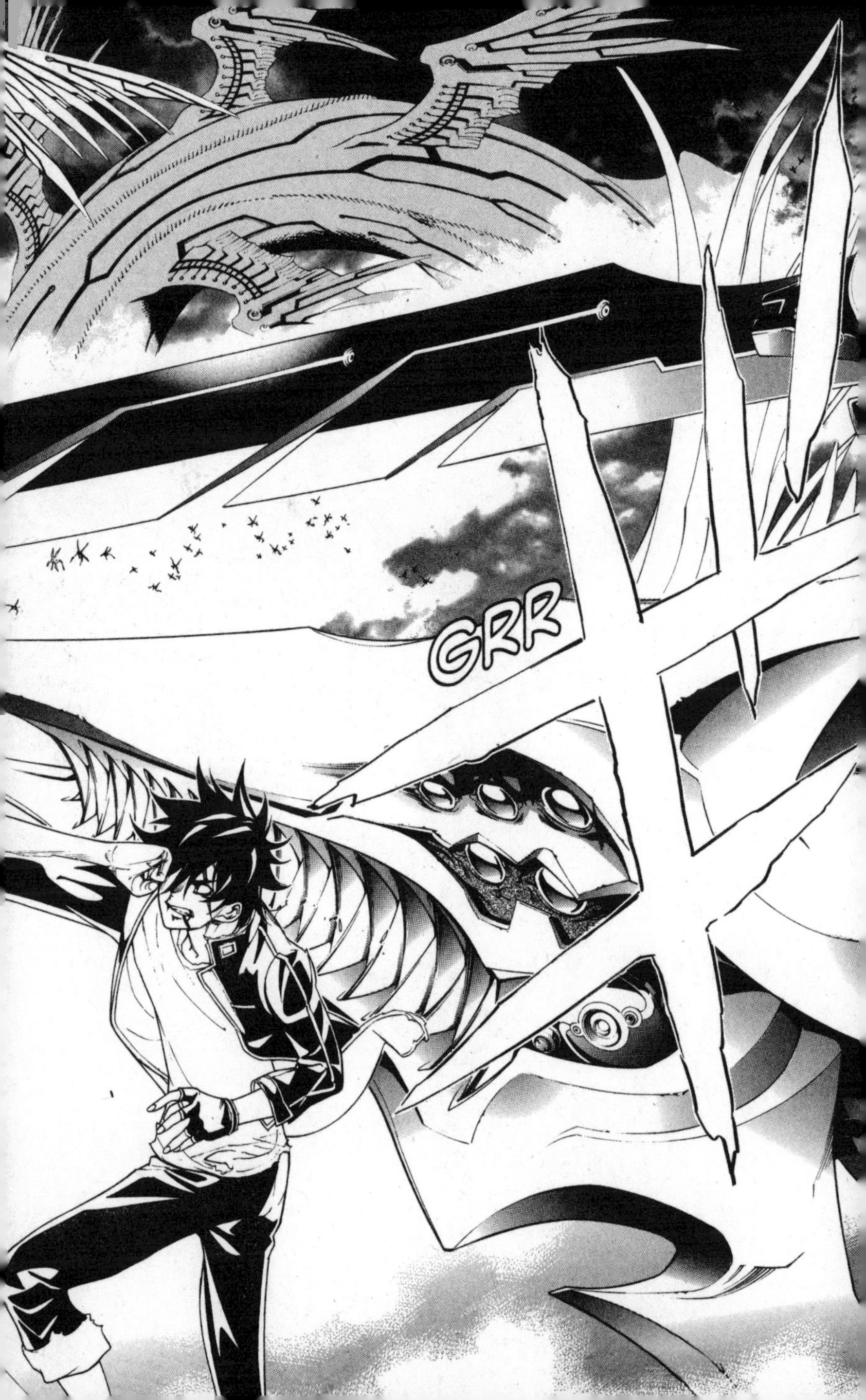
GRR

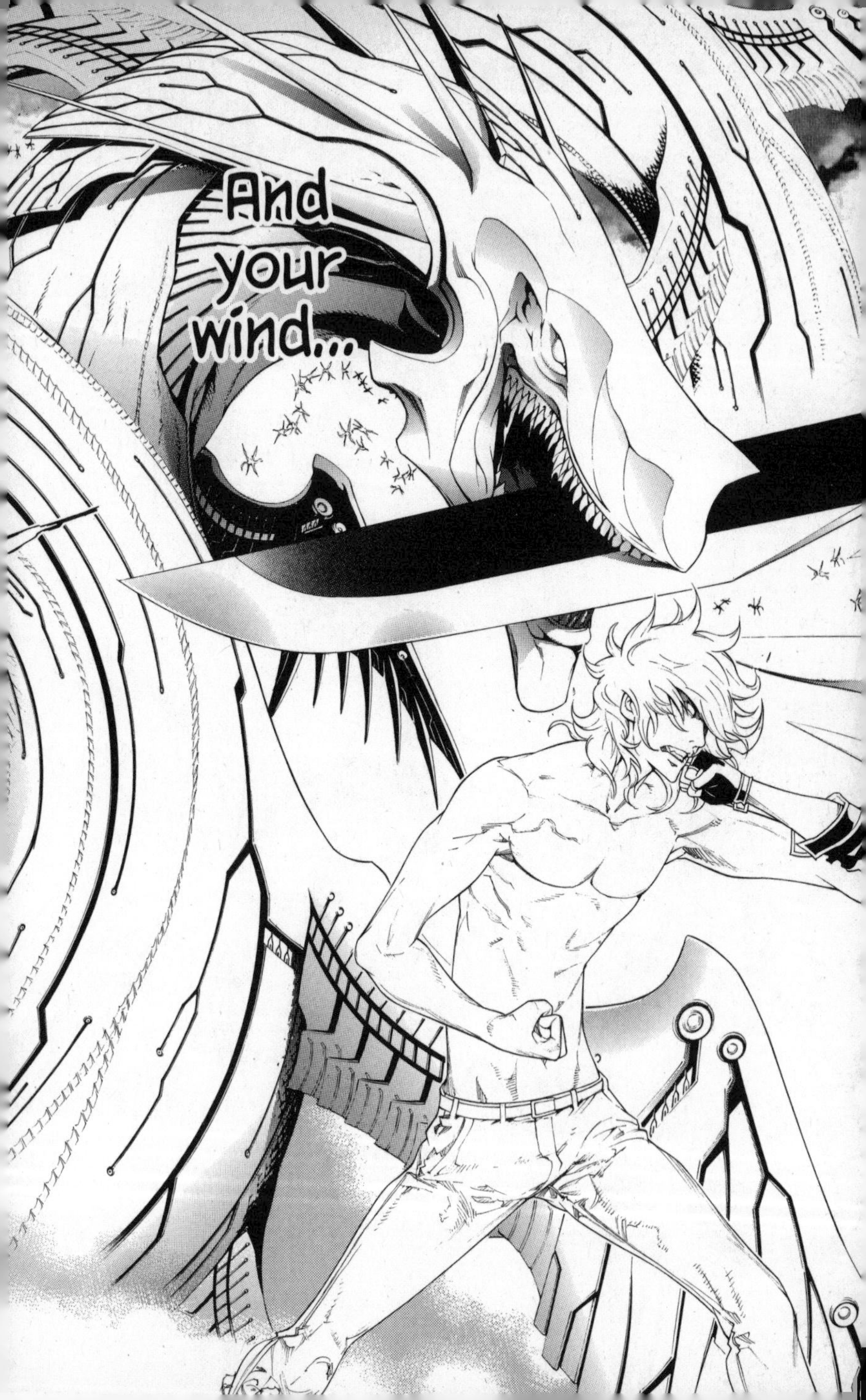
And your wind...

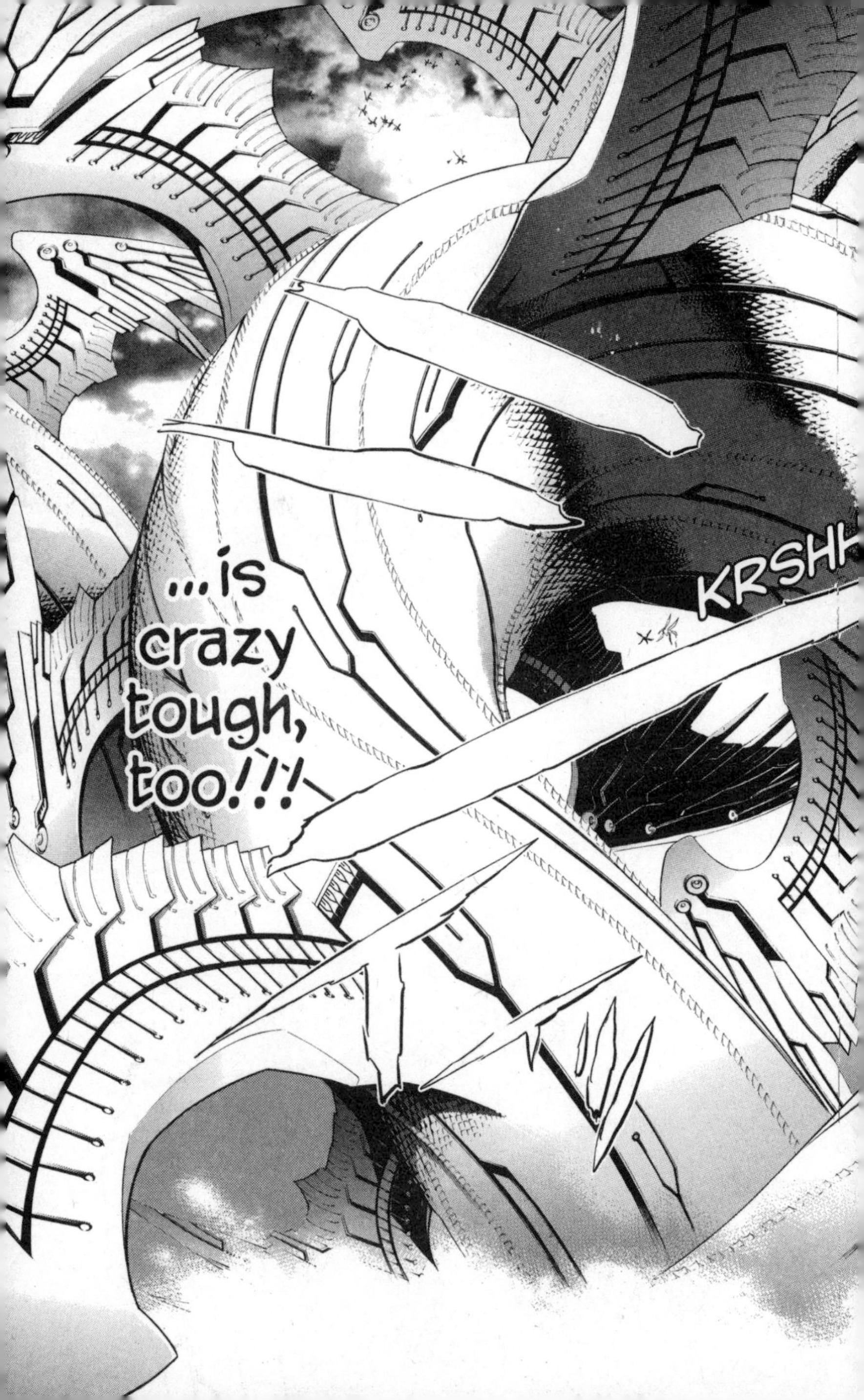
KRSHH
...is crazy tough, too!!!

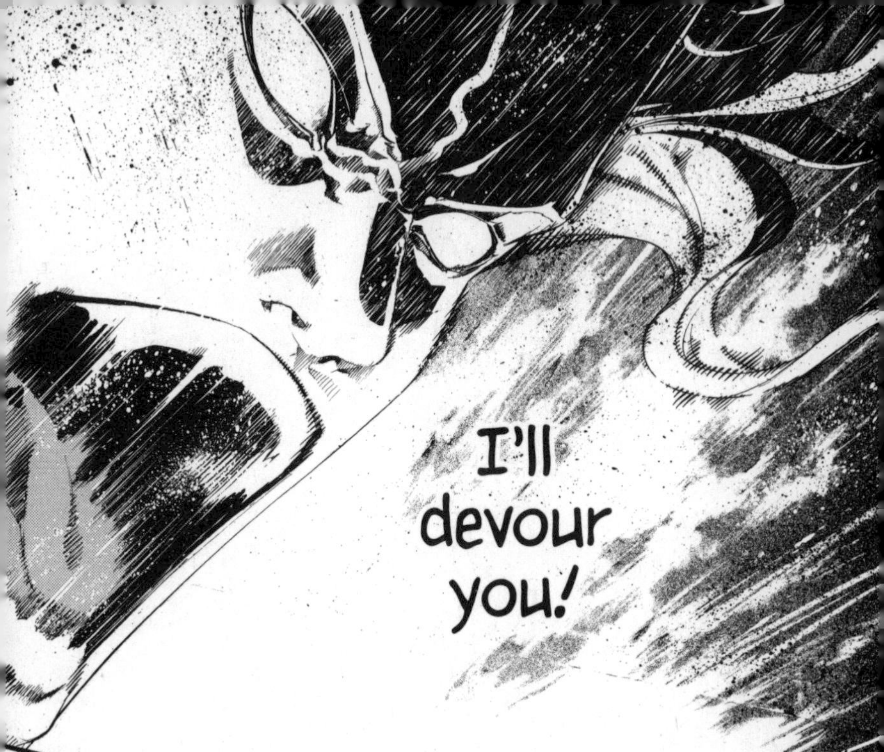
I'll devour you!
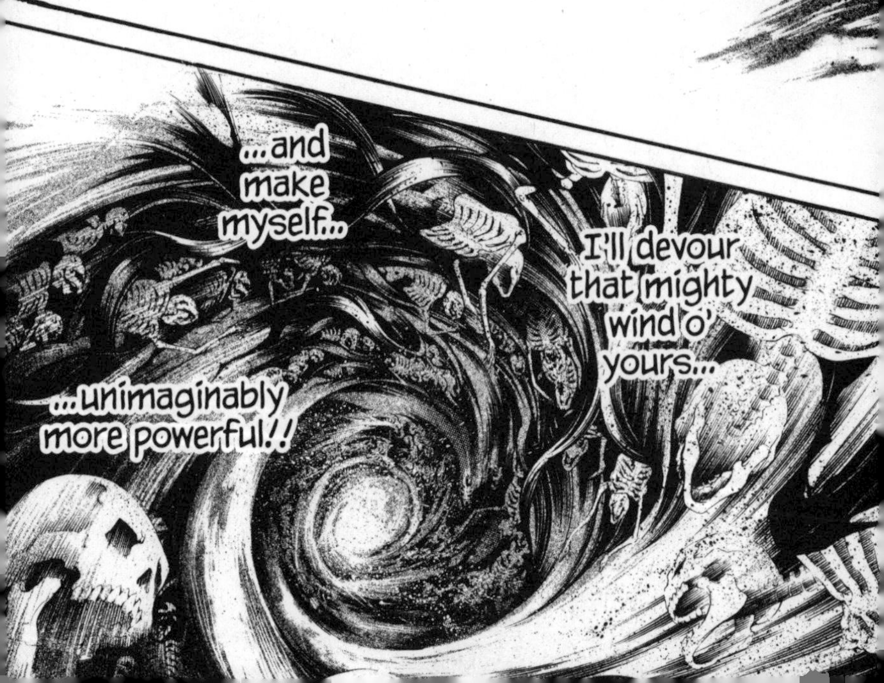
I'll devour that mighty wind o' yours...
...and make myself...
...unimaginably more powerful!!

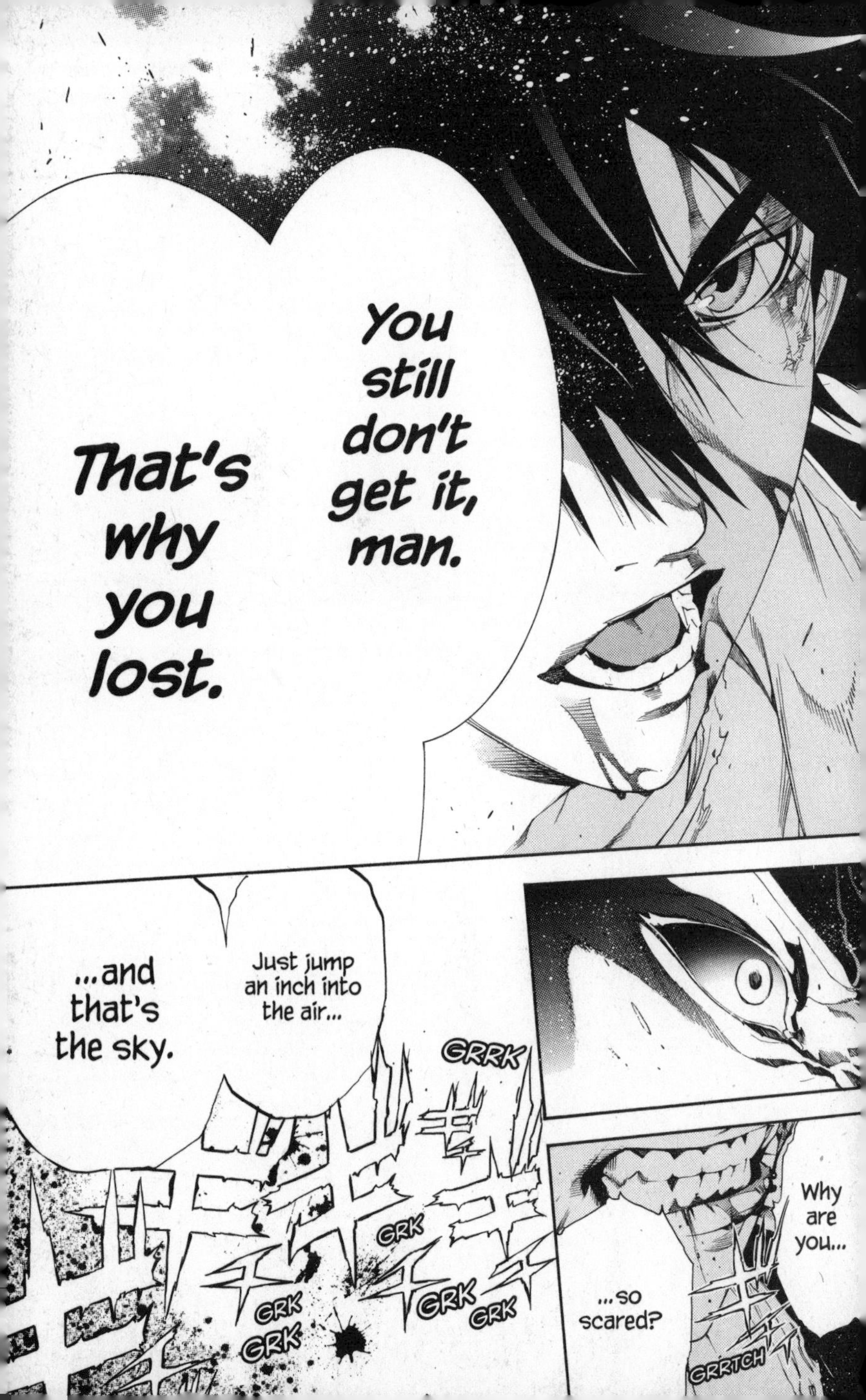
You still don't get it, man.
That's why you lost.
Just jump an inch into the air...
...and that's the sky.
GRRK
GRK
GRK
GRK
GRK
GRK
Why are you...
...so scared?
GRRTCH

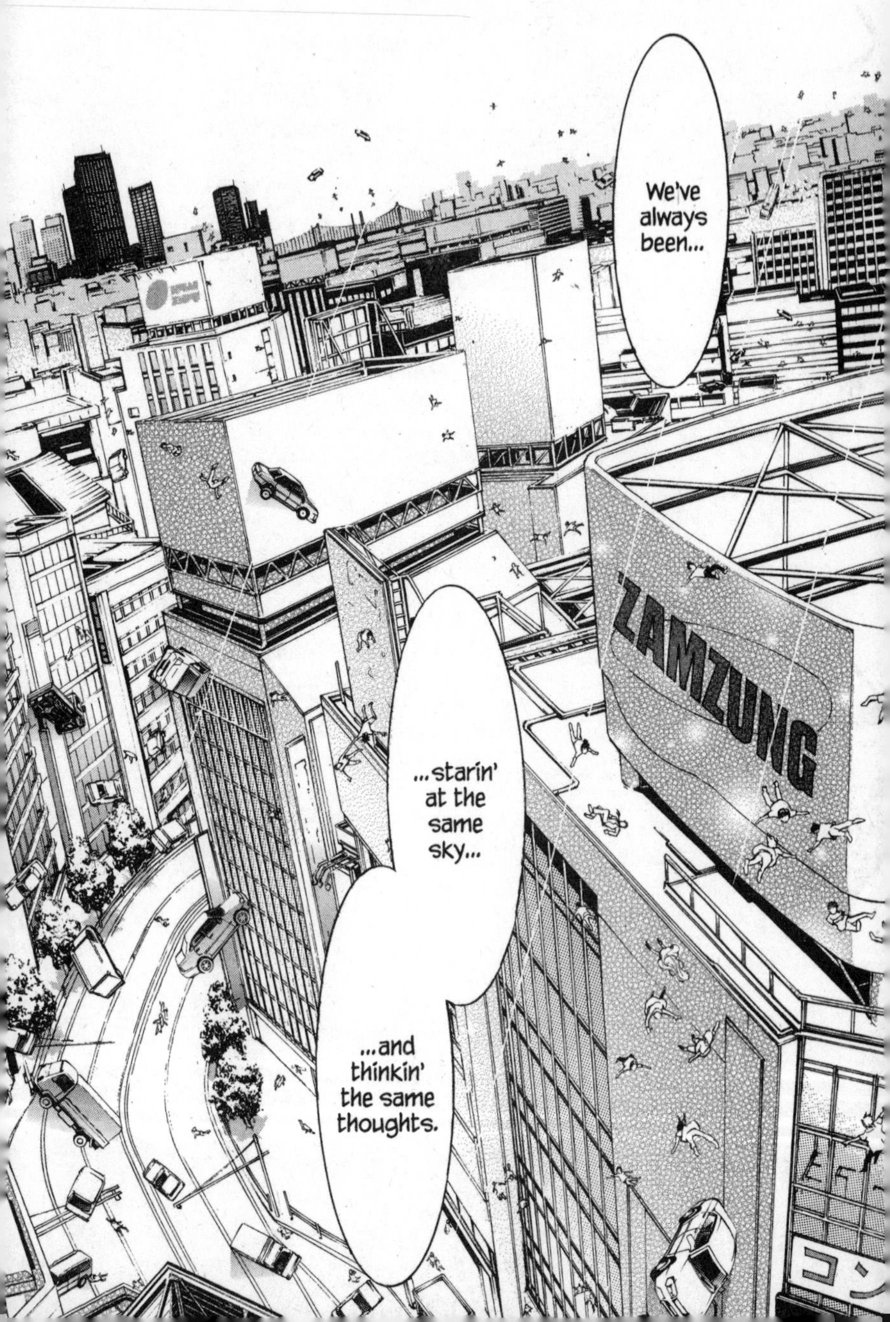
We've always been...
...starin' at the same sky...
...and thinkin' the same thoughts.
ZAMZUNG

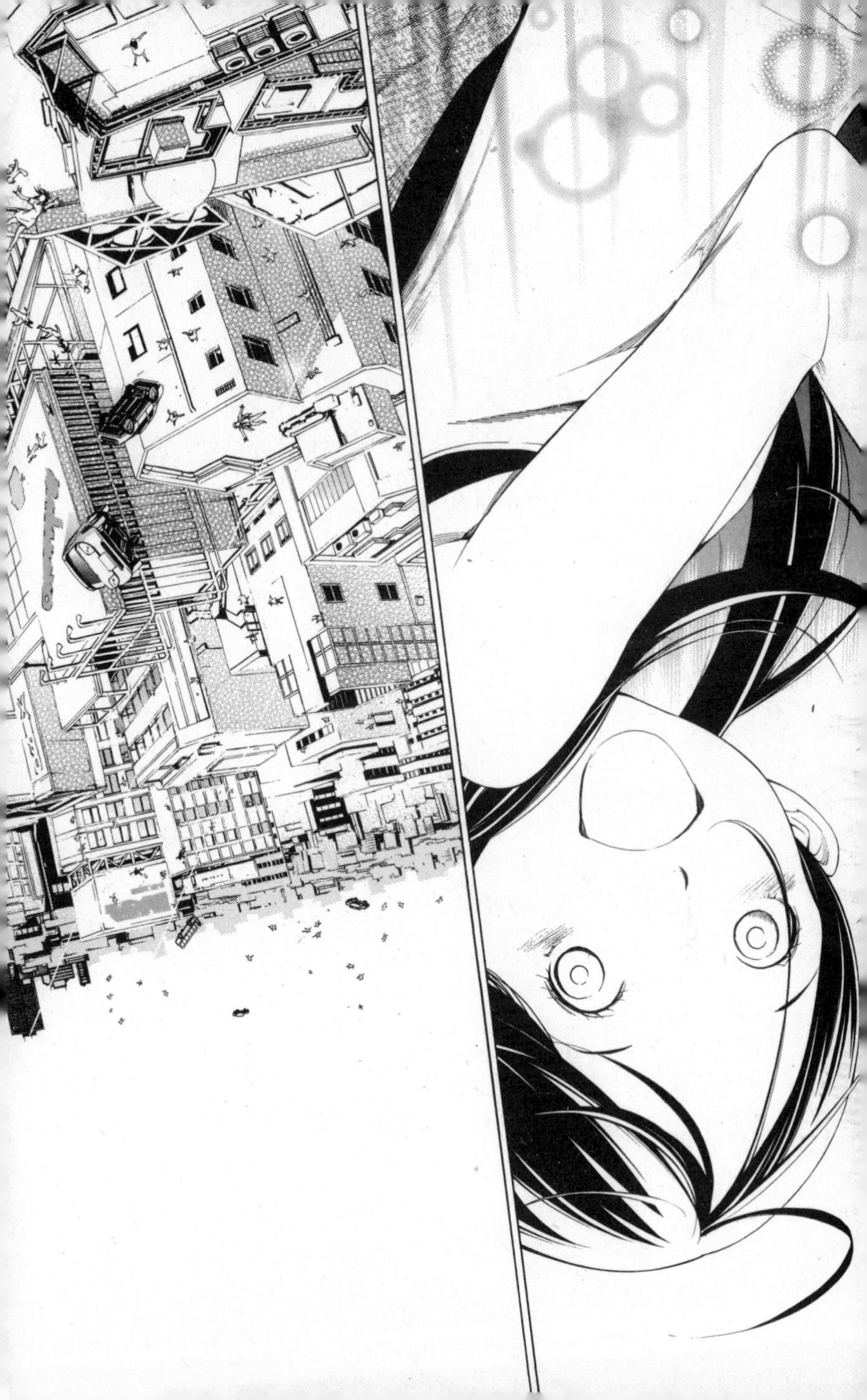

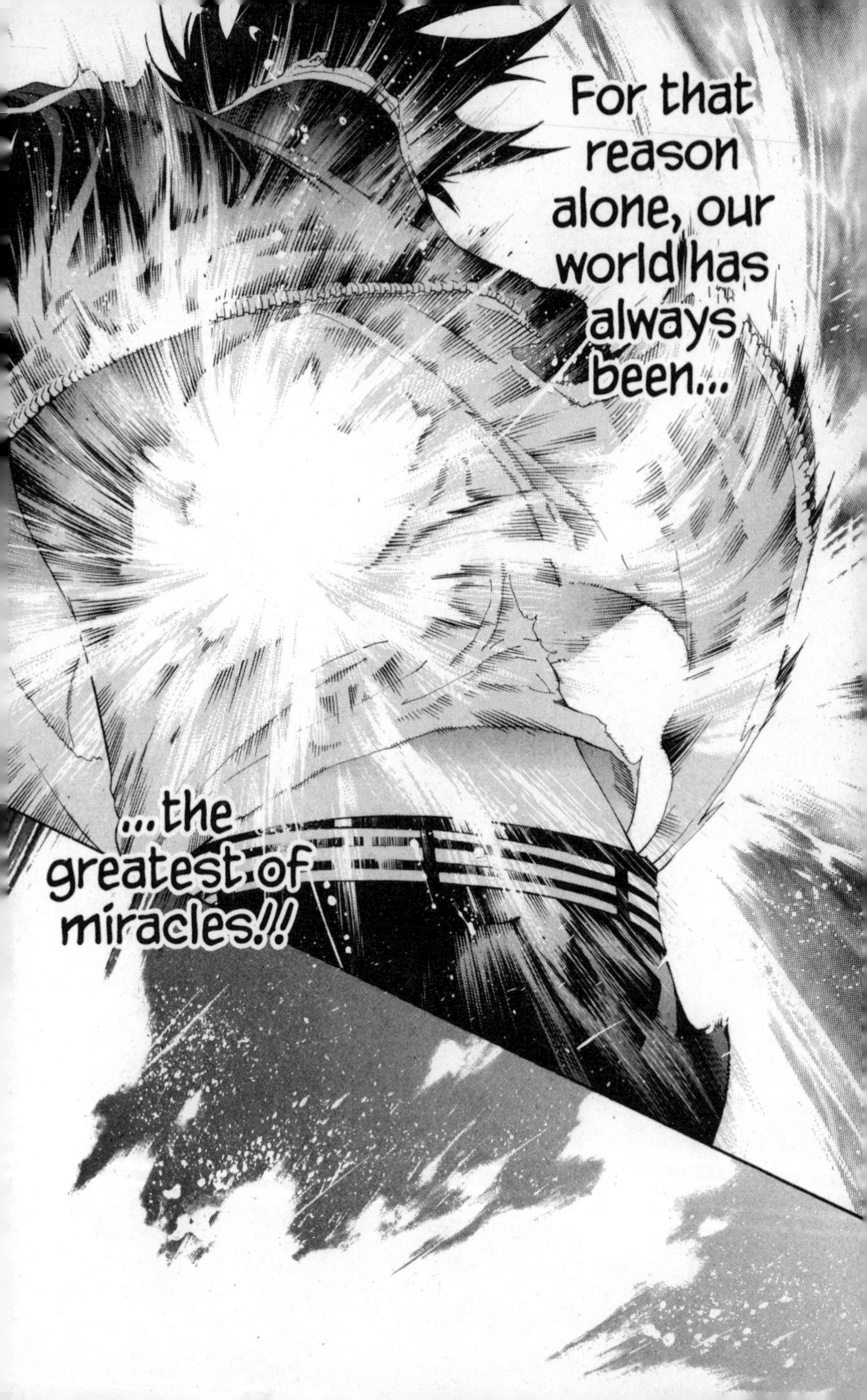
For that reason alone, our world has always been...
...the greatest of miracles!!

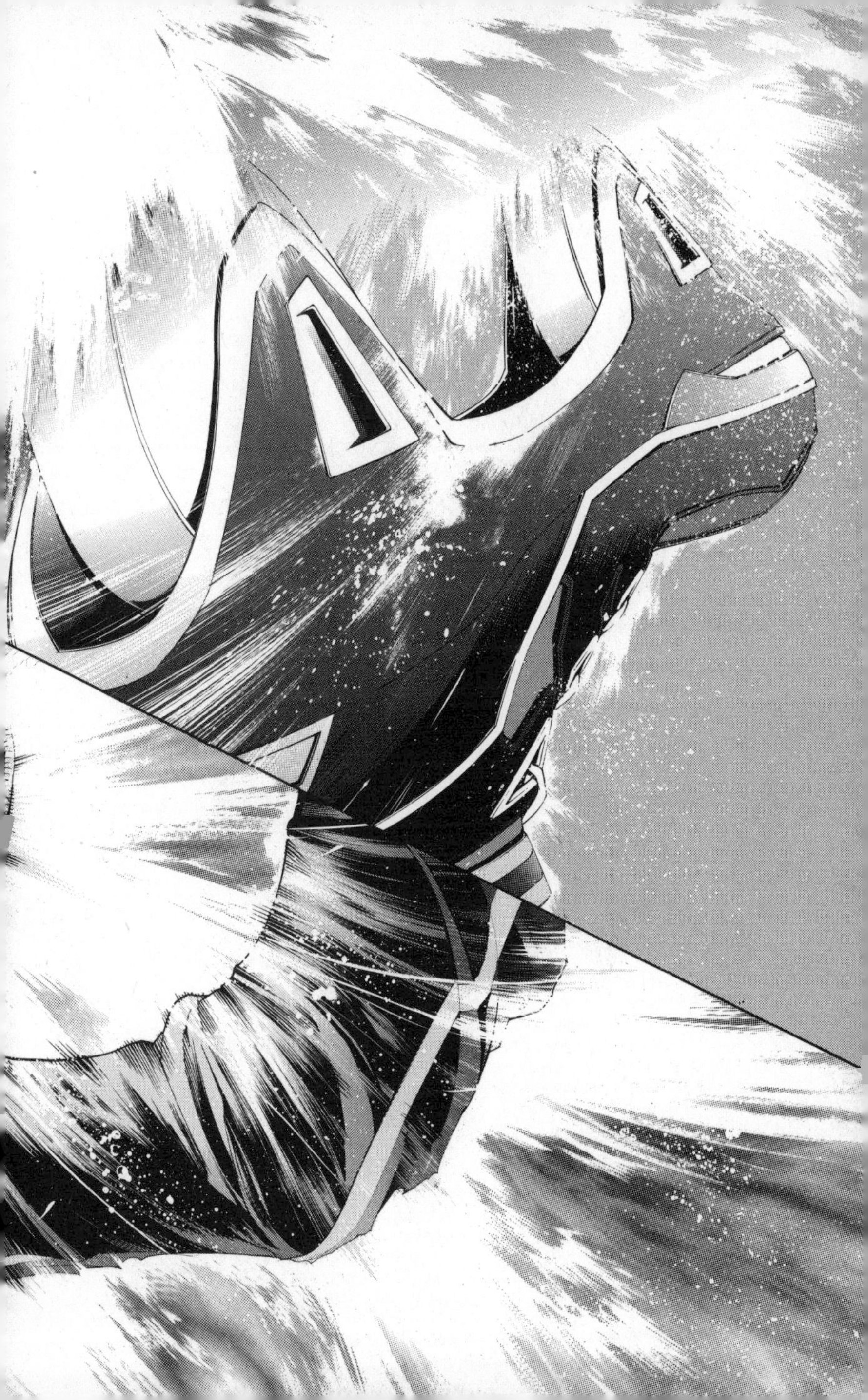

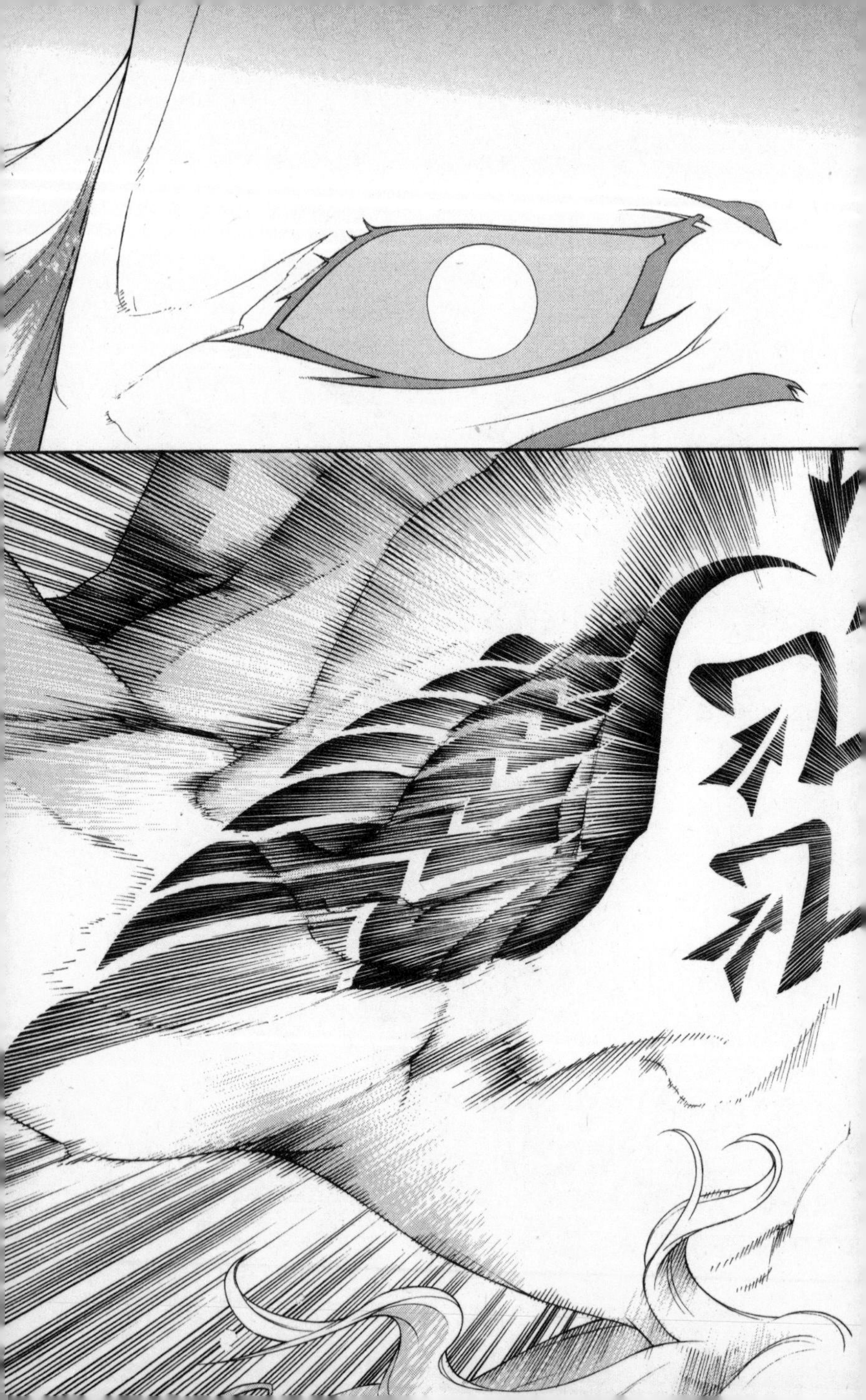

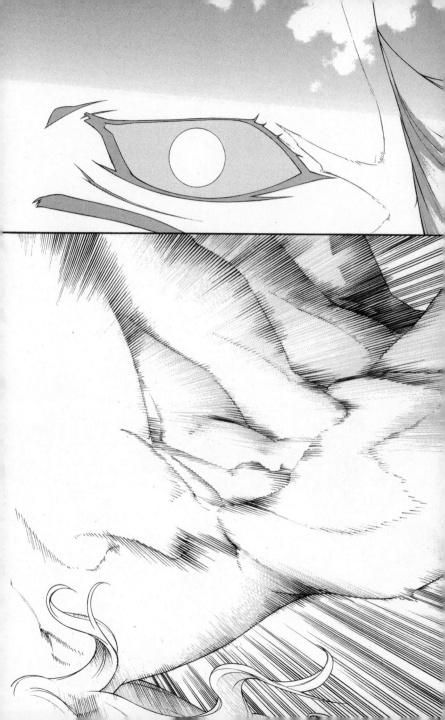

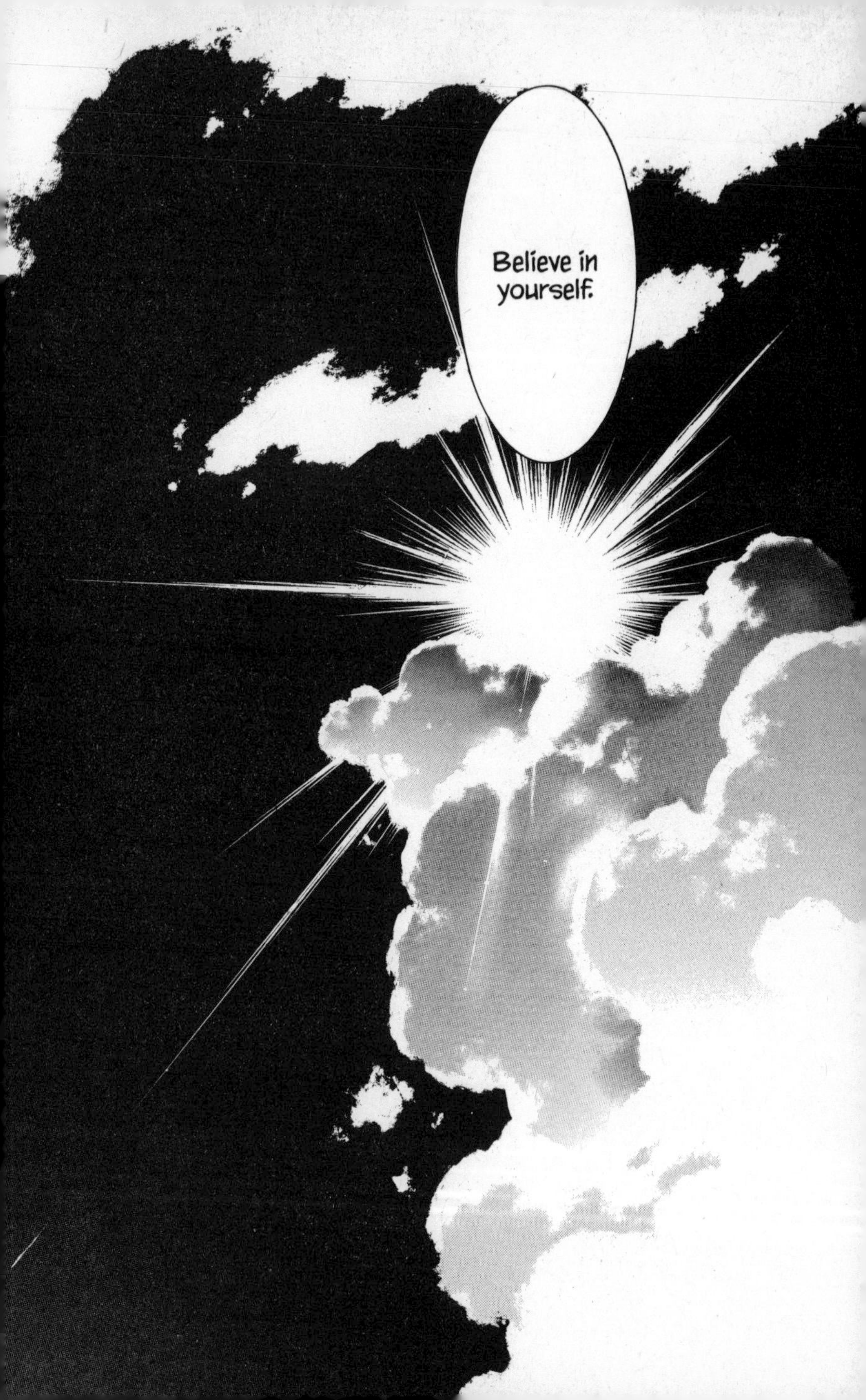
Believe in yourself.

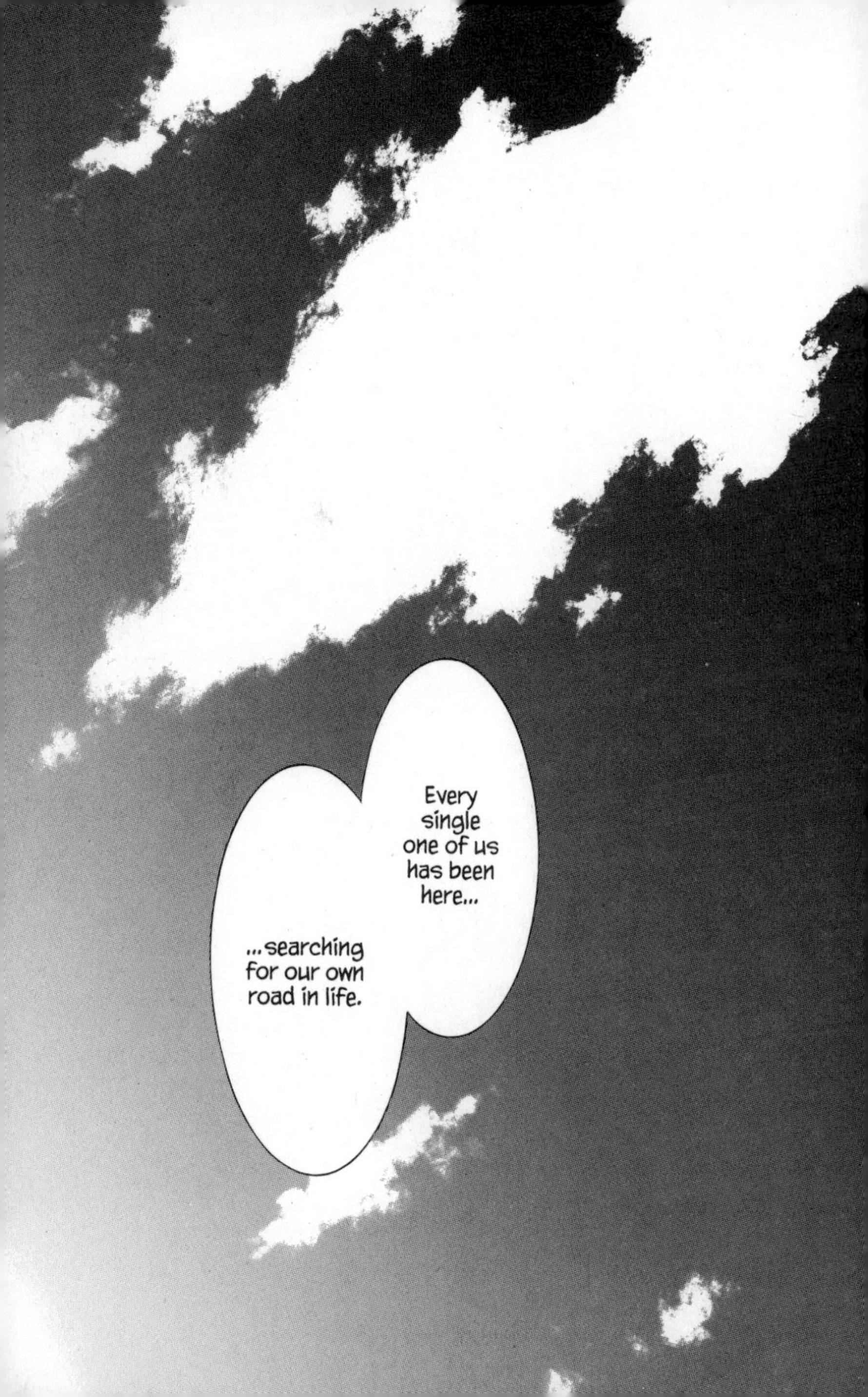
Every single one of us has been here...
...searching for our own road in life.

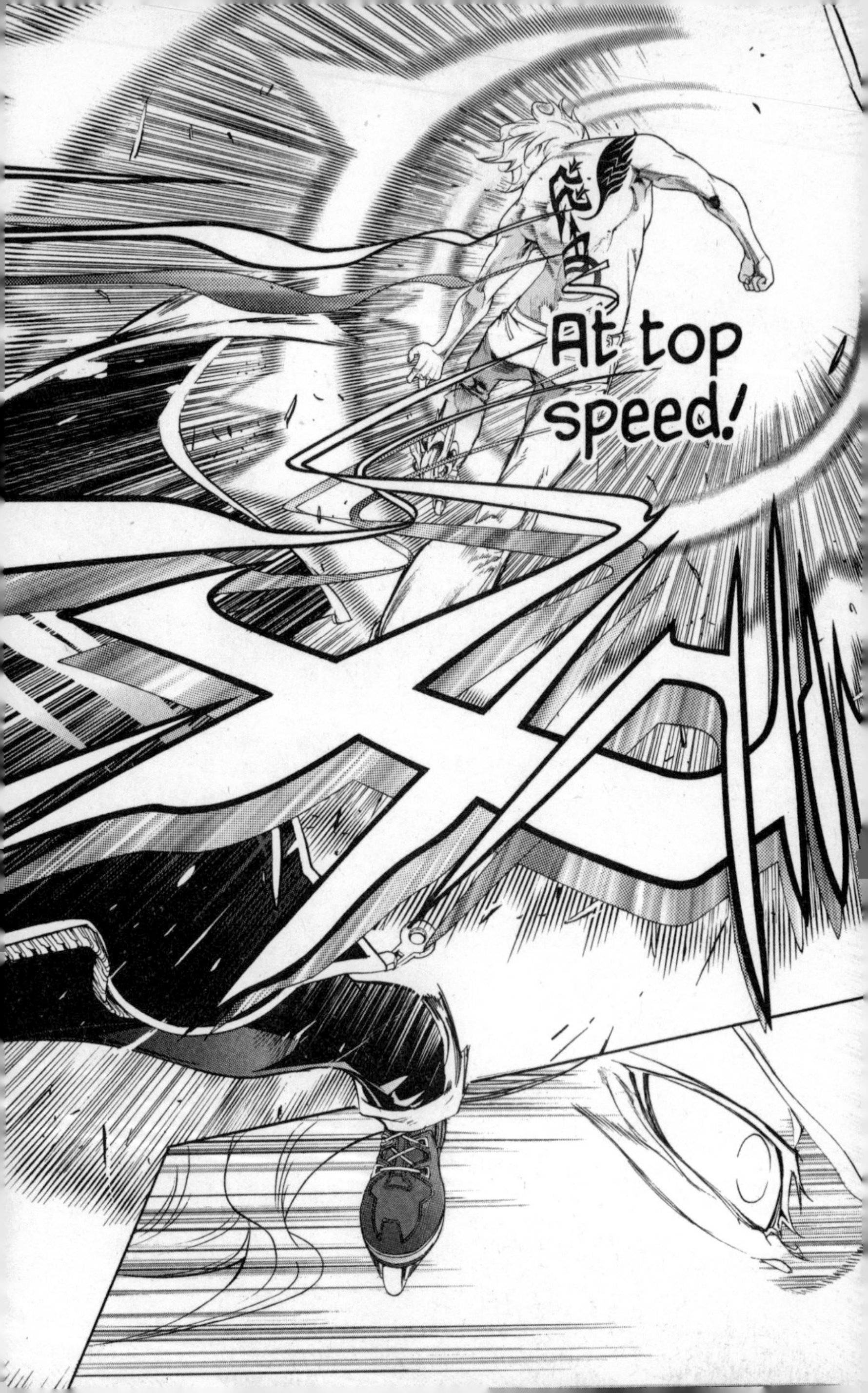
At top speed!

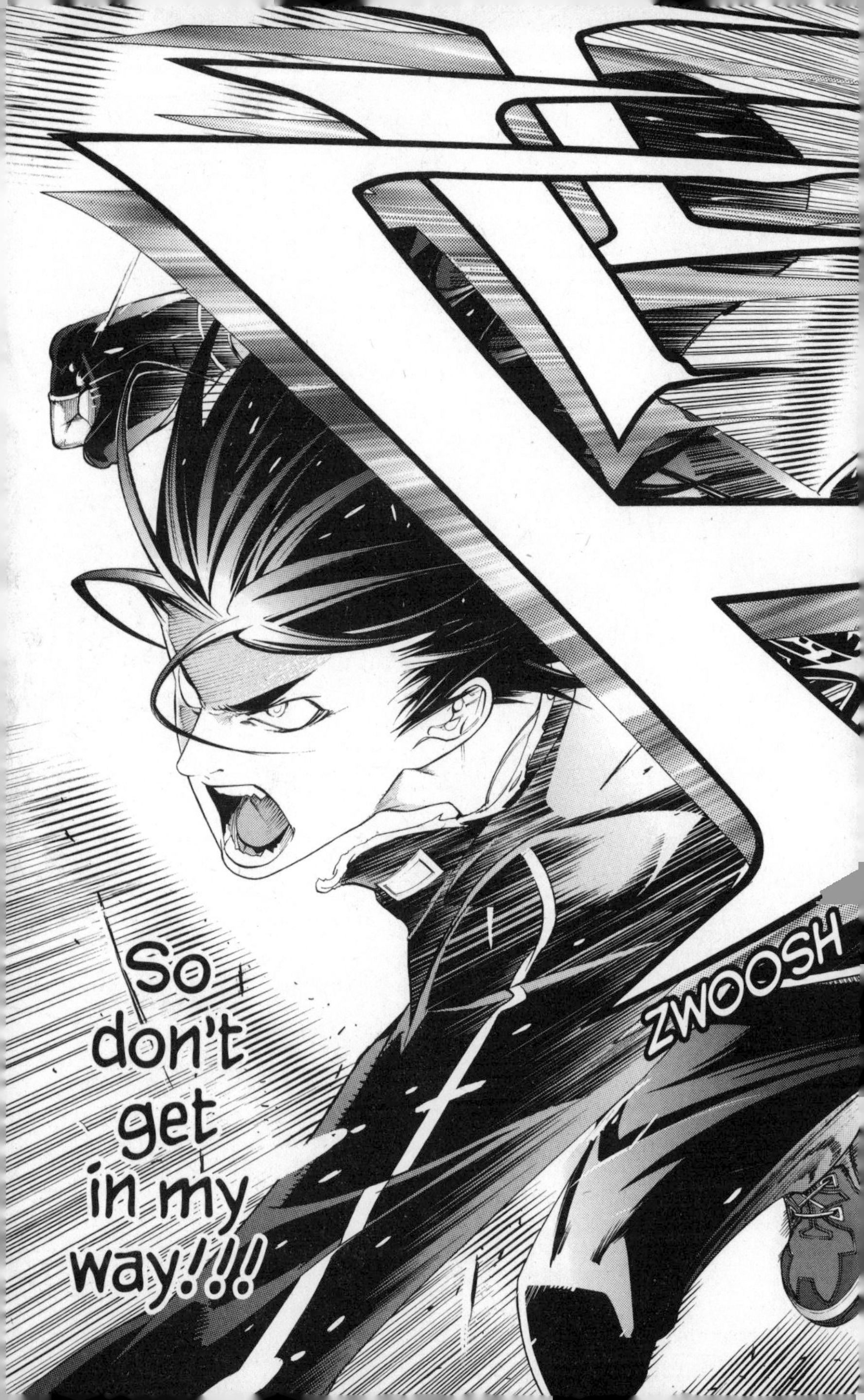
ZWOOSH
So don't get in my way!!!

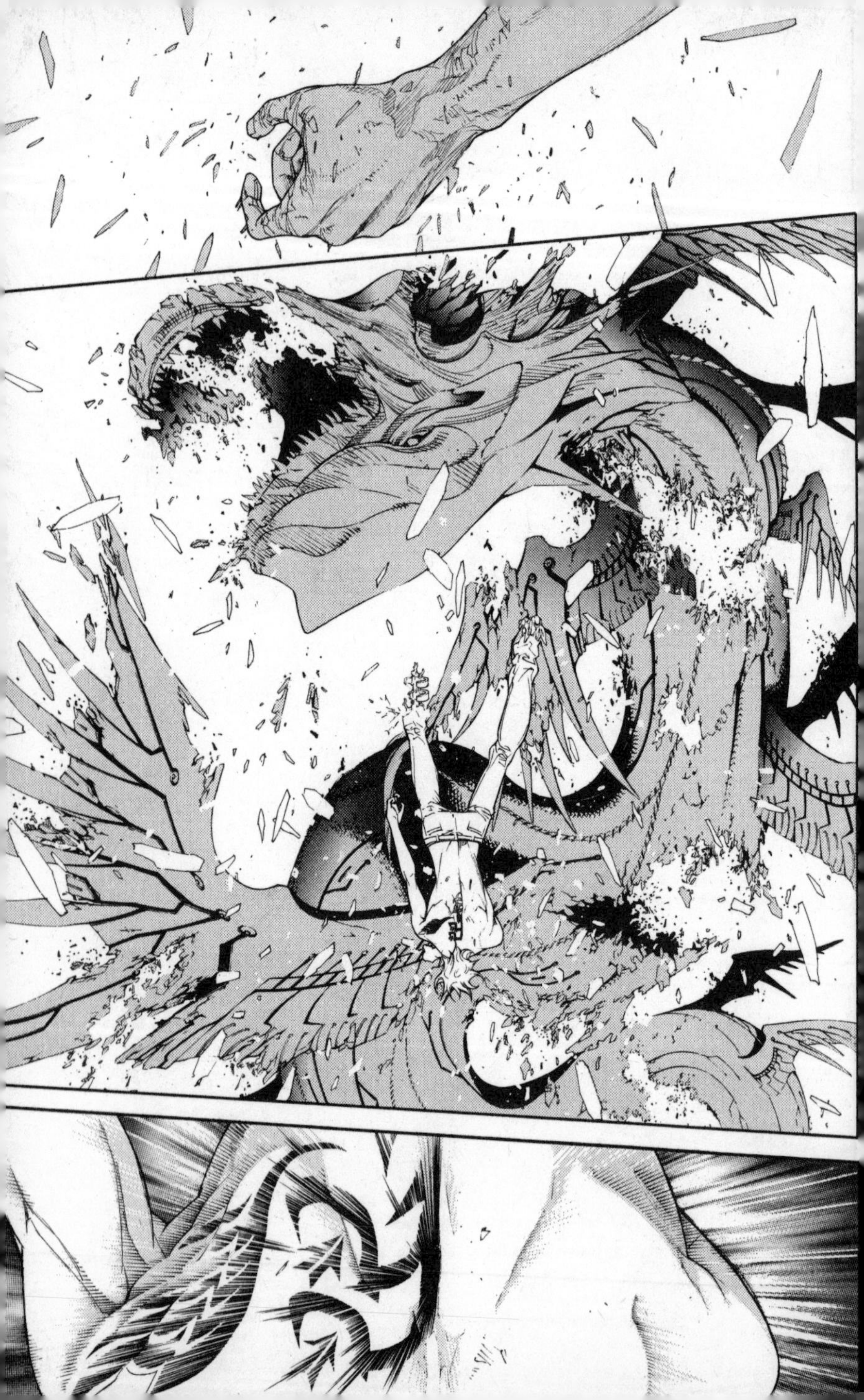

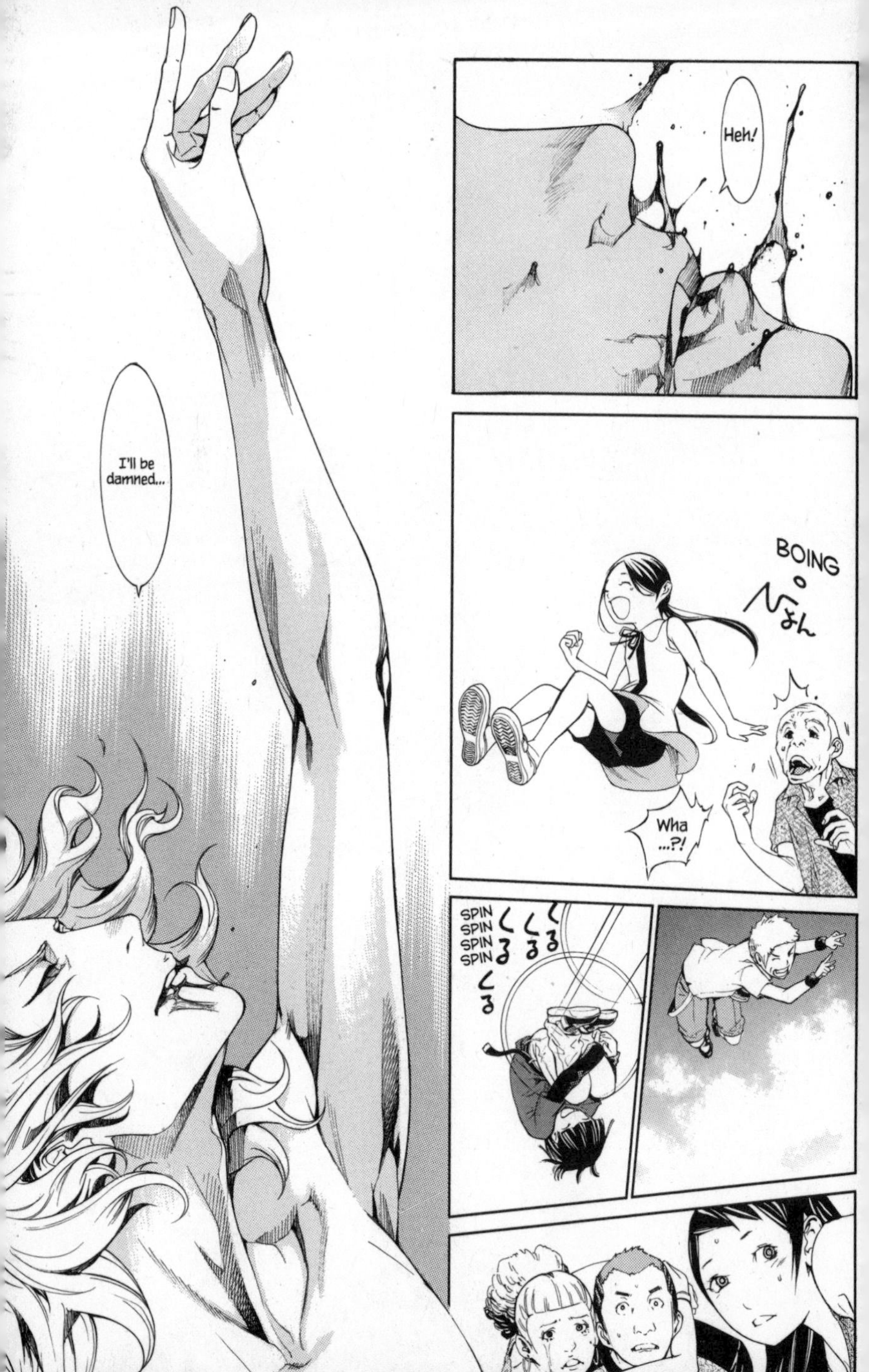
Heh!
BOING
ぴょん
Wha ...?!
SPIN SPIN SPIN SPIN
くるくるくるくる
I'll be damned...

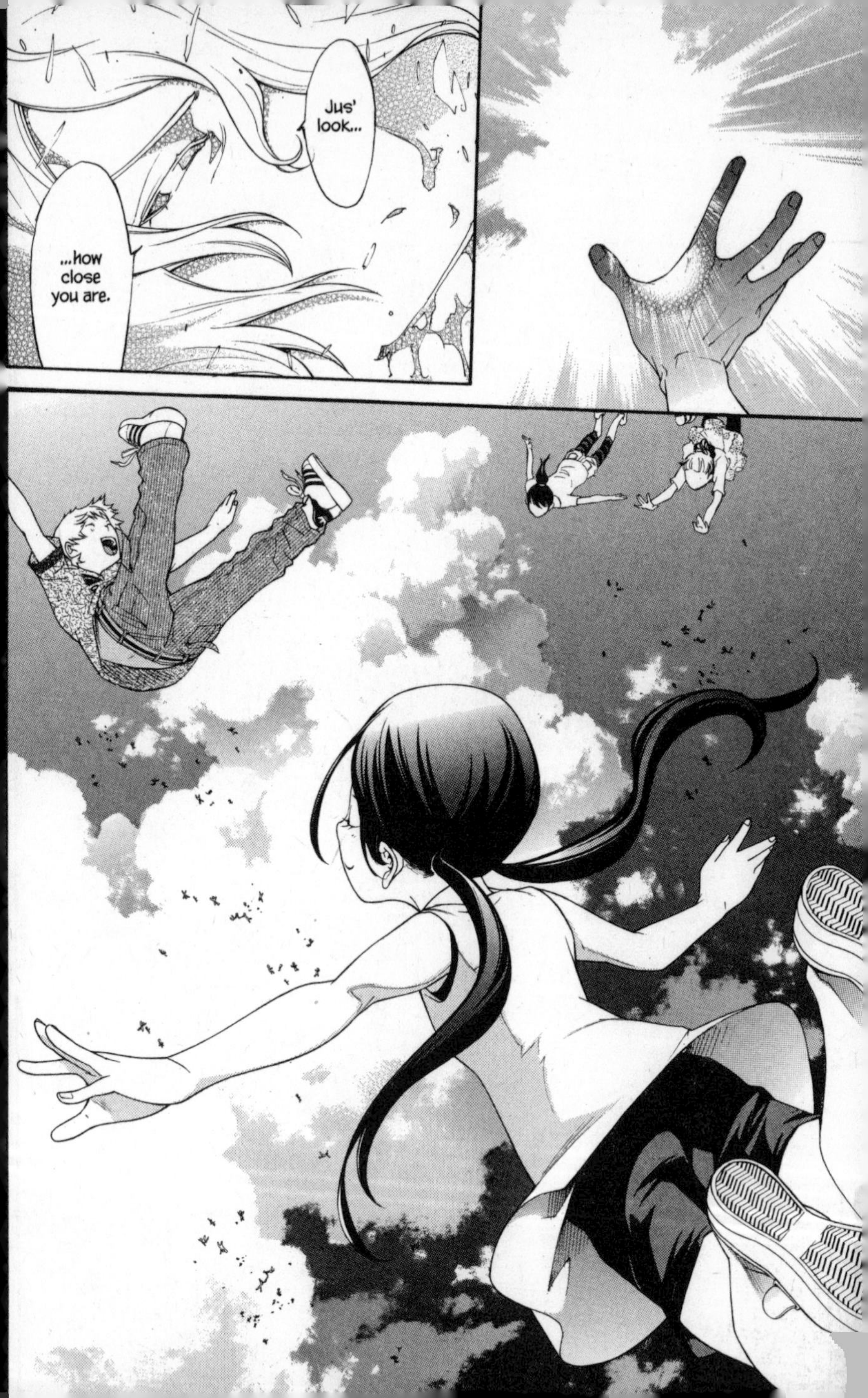
Jus' look...
...how close you are.

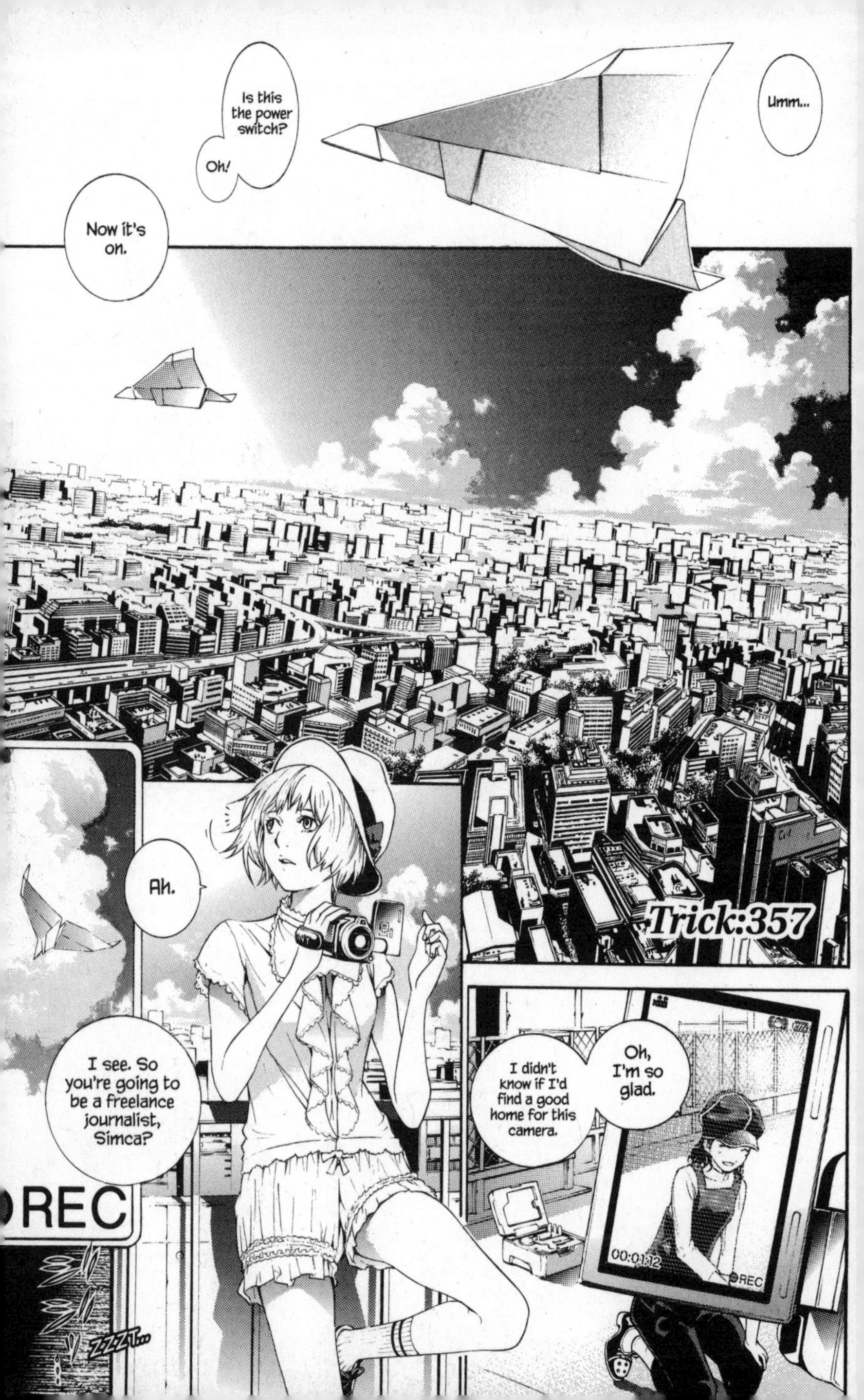
Umm...
Is this the power switch?
Oh!
Now it's on.
Trick:357
Oh, I'm so glad.
I didn't know if I'd find a good home for this camera.
00:01:12
REC
Ah.
I see. So you're going to be a freelance journalist, Simca?
REC

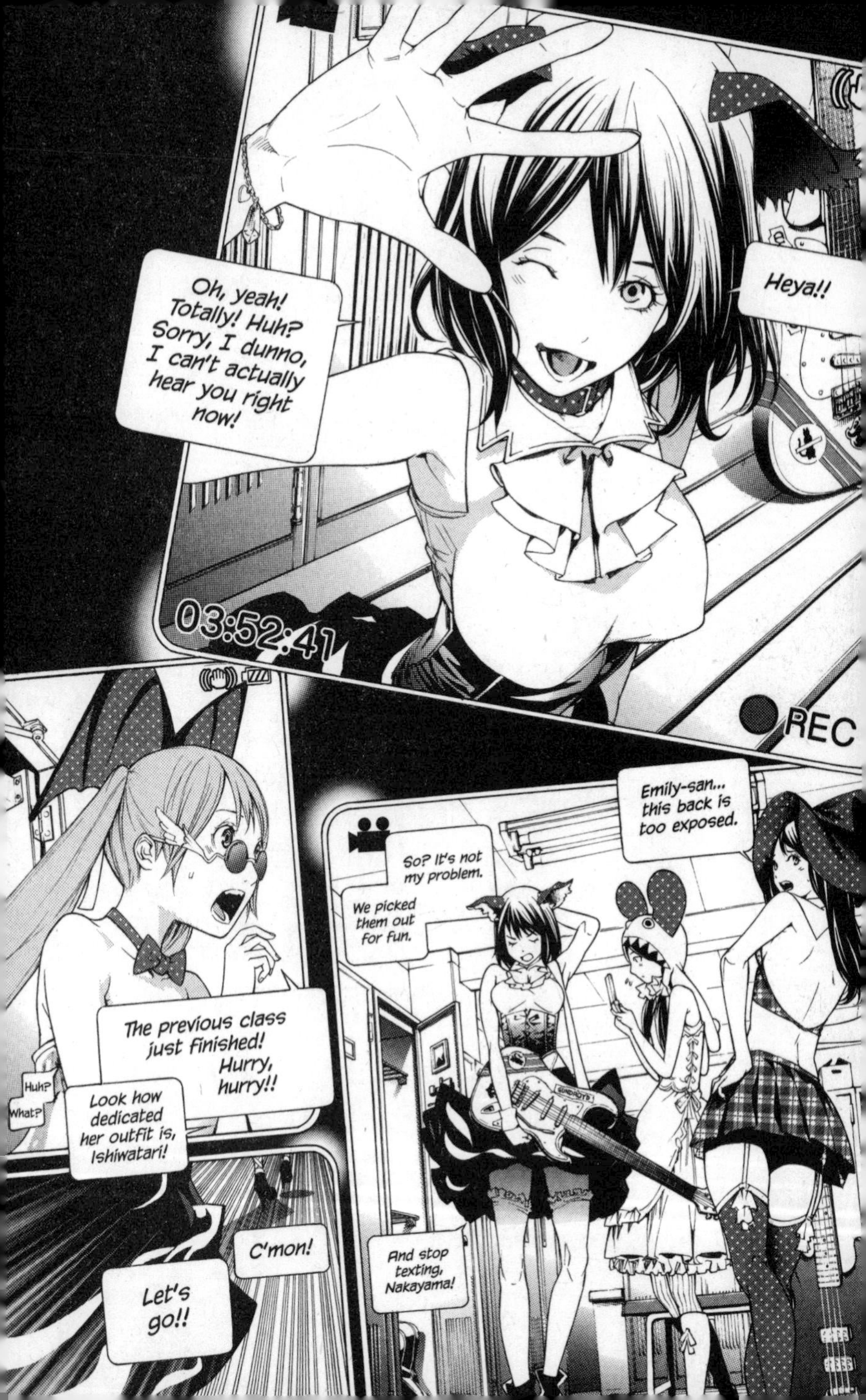
Heya!!
Oh, yeah! Totally! Huh? Sorry, I dunno, I can't actually hear you right now!
03:52:41
REC
Emily-san... this back is too exposed.
So? It's not my problem.
We picked them out for fun.
And stop texting, Nakayama!
The previous class just finished! Hurry, hurry!!
Huh? What?
Look how dedicated her outfit is, Ishiwatari!
C'mon!
Let's go!!

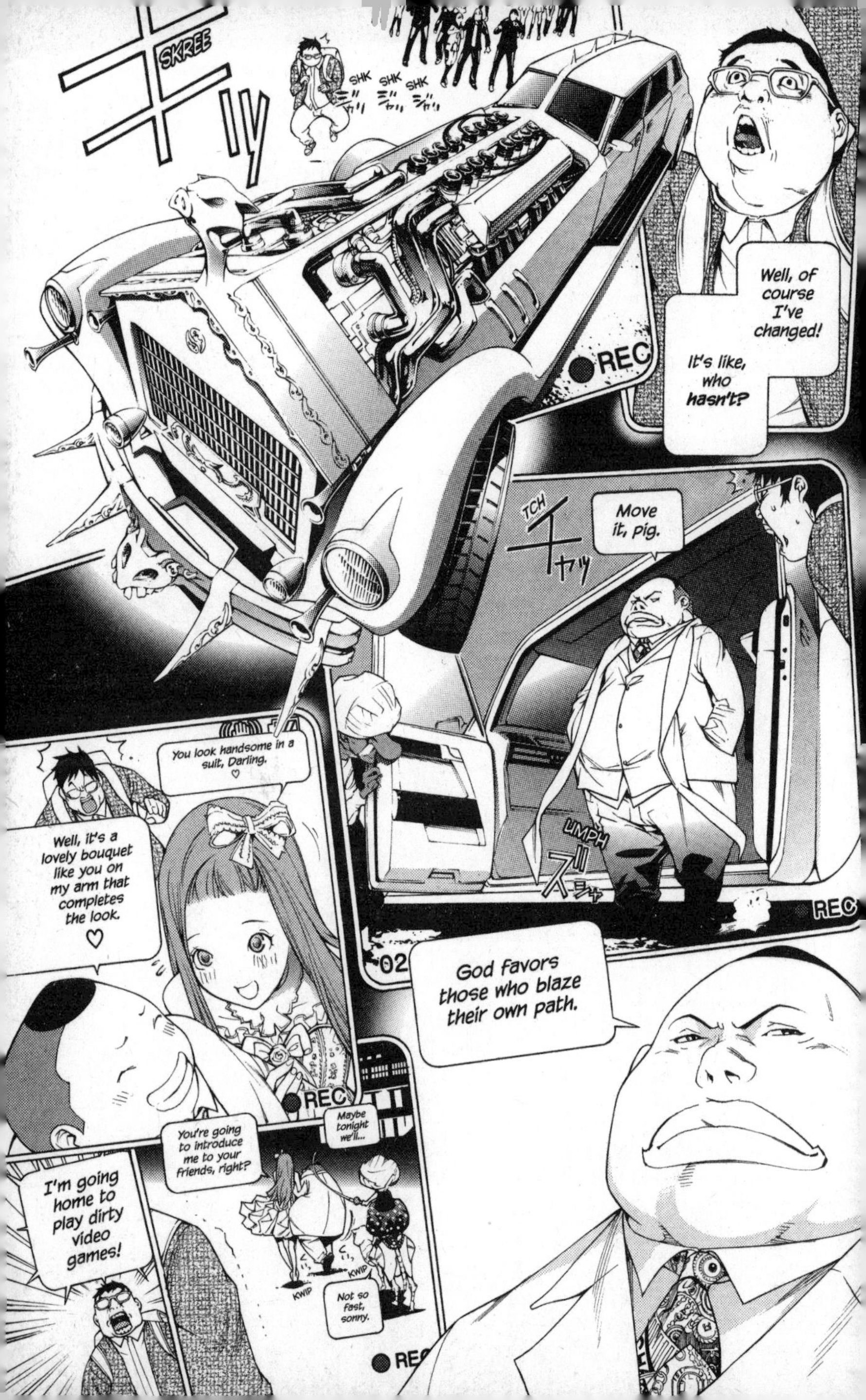
Well, of course I've changed!
It's like, who hasn't?
REC
SKREE
SHK SHK SHK
TCH
Move it, pig.
UMPH
REC
You look handsome in a suit, Darling. ♡
Well, it's a lovely bouquet like you on my arm that completes the look. ♡
REC
02
God favors those who blaze their own path.
Maybe tonight we'll...
You're going to introduce me to your friends, right?
KWIP
KWIP
Not so fast, sonny.
I'm going home to play dirty video games!
REC

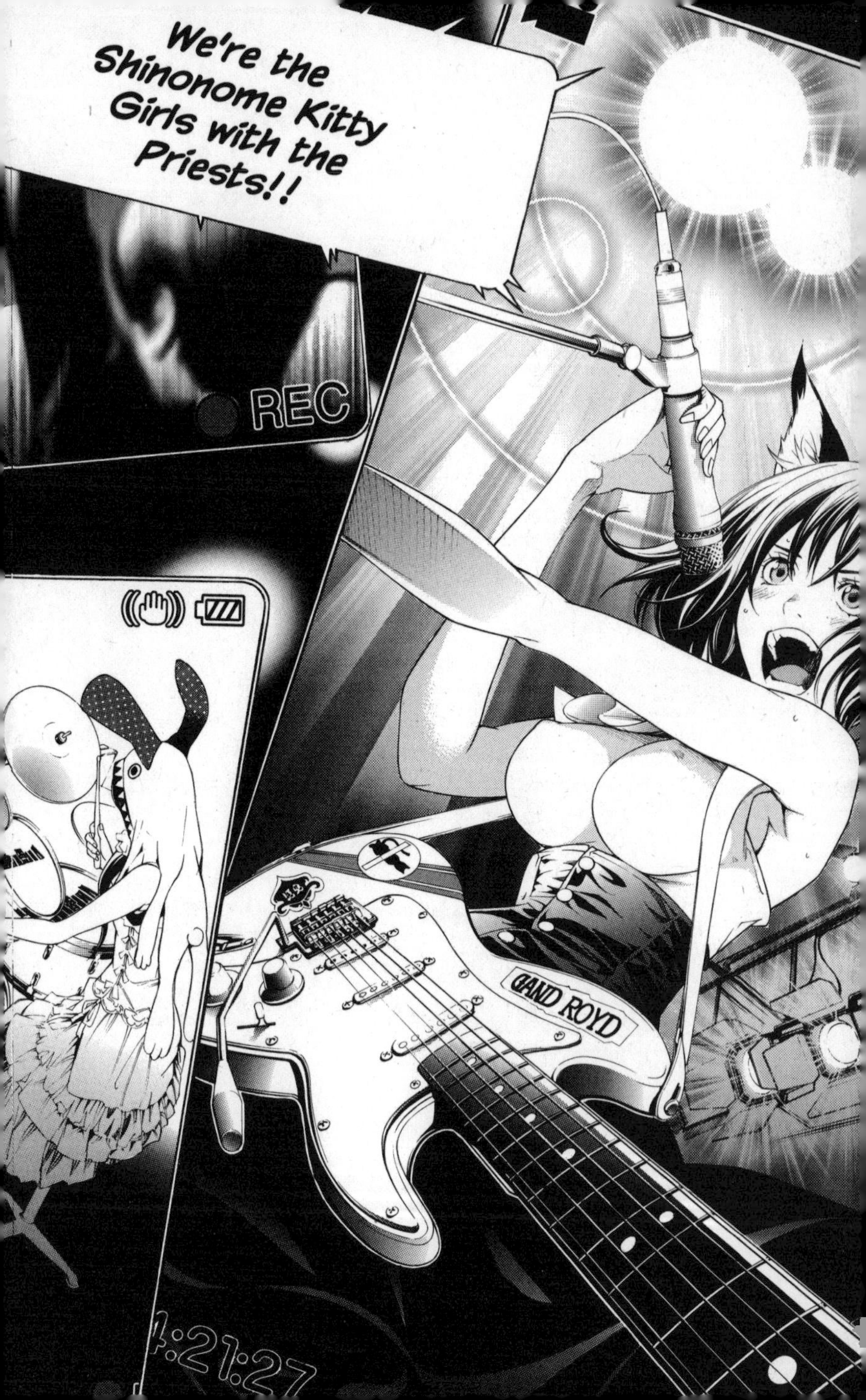
We're the Shinonome Kitty Girls with the Priests!!
REC
GAND ROYD
4:21:27

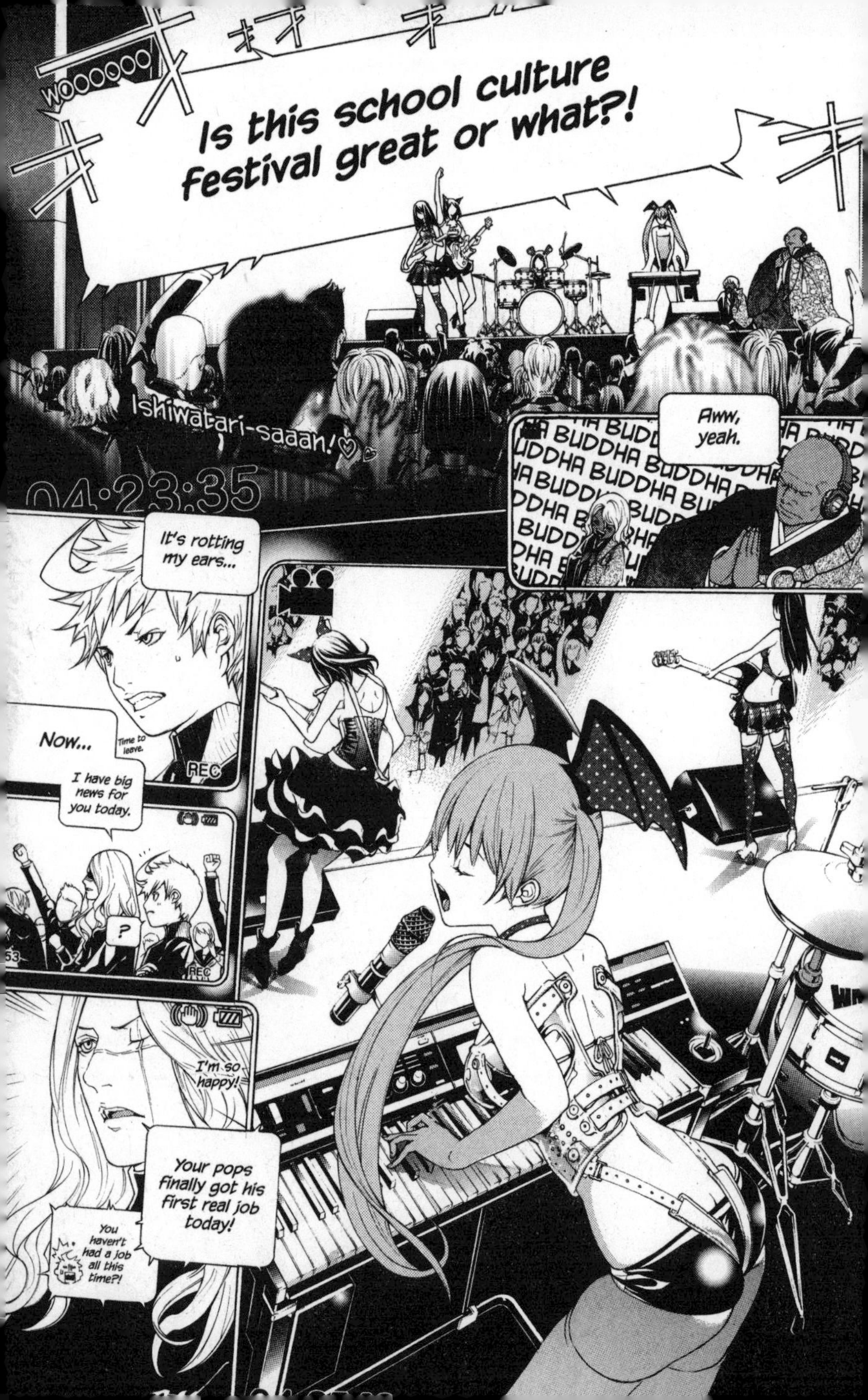
WOOOOOO
Is this school culture festival great or what?!
Ishiwatari-saaan!♡
04:23:35
Aww, yeah.
BUDDHA BUDDHA BUDDHA BUDDHA
It's rotting my ears...
Now...
Time to leave.
REC
I have big news for you today.
?
REC
I'm so happy!
Your pops finally got his first real job today!
You haven't had a job all this time?!

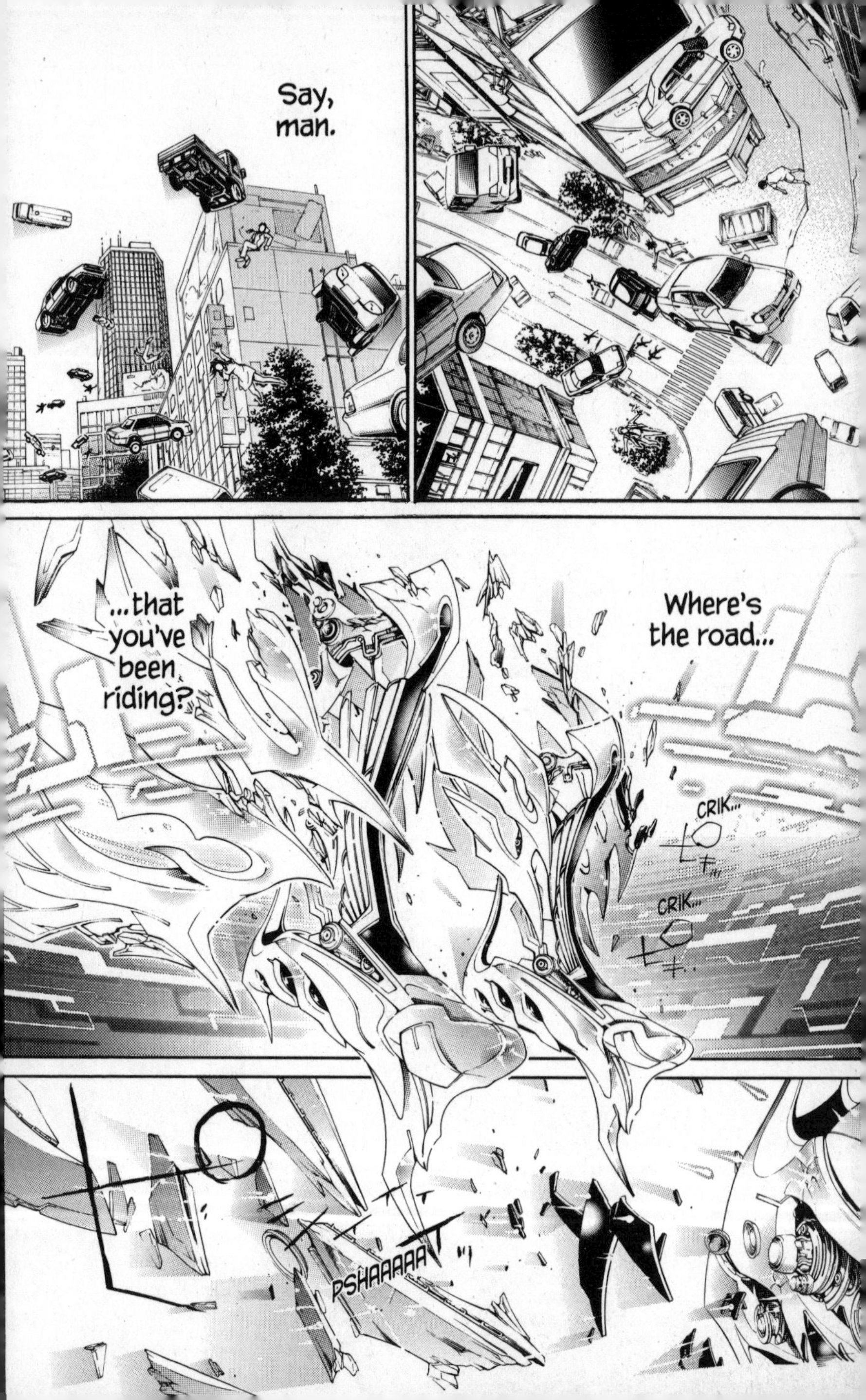
Say, man.
Where's the road...
...that you've been riding?
CRIK...
CRIK...
PSHAAAAA

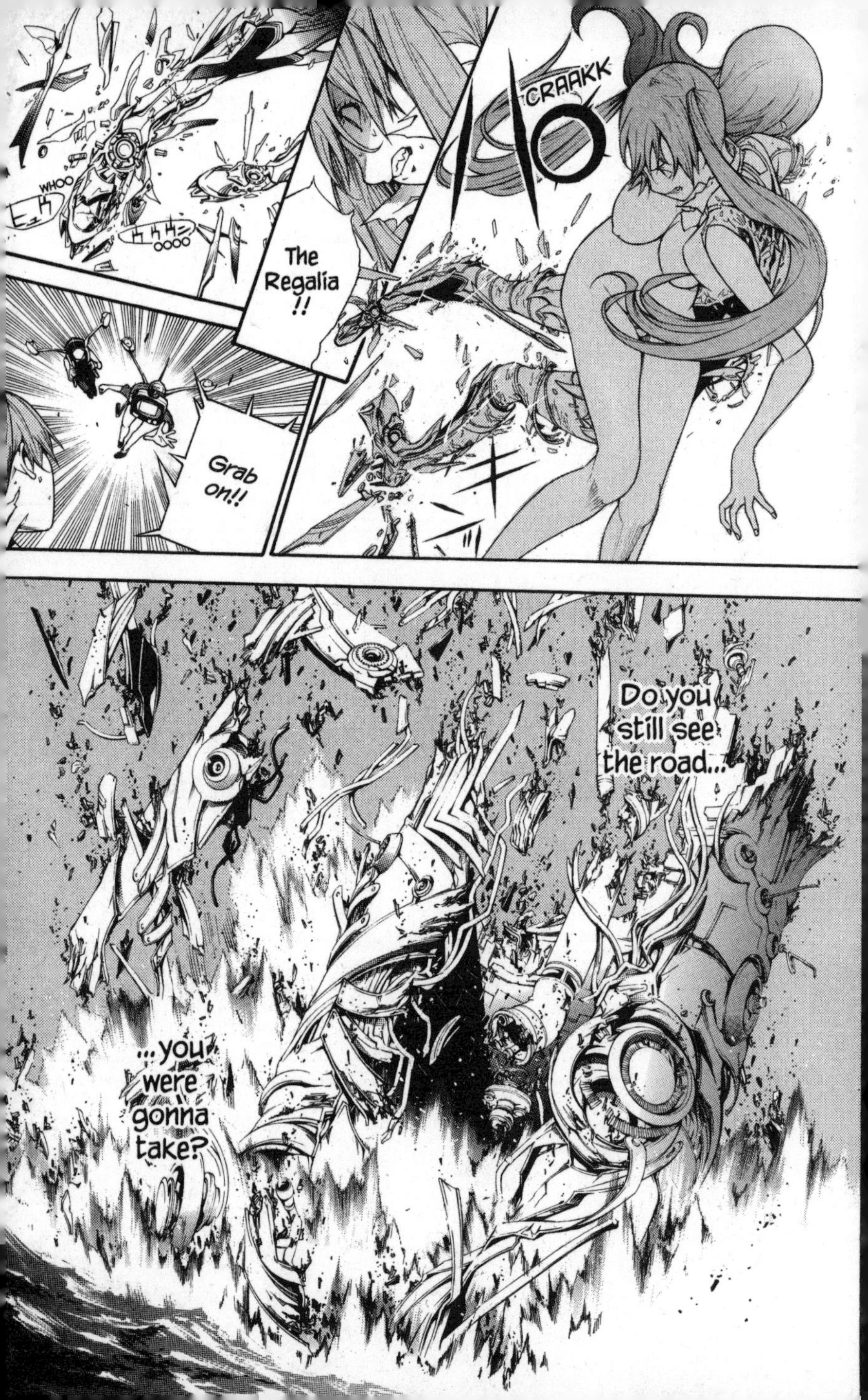
CRAAKK
The Regalia !!
WHOO
oooo
Grab on!!
Do you still see the road...
...you were gonna take?

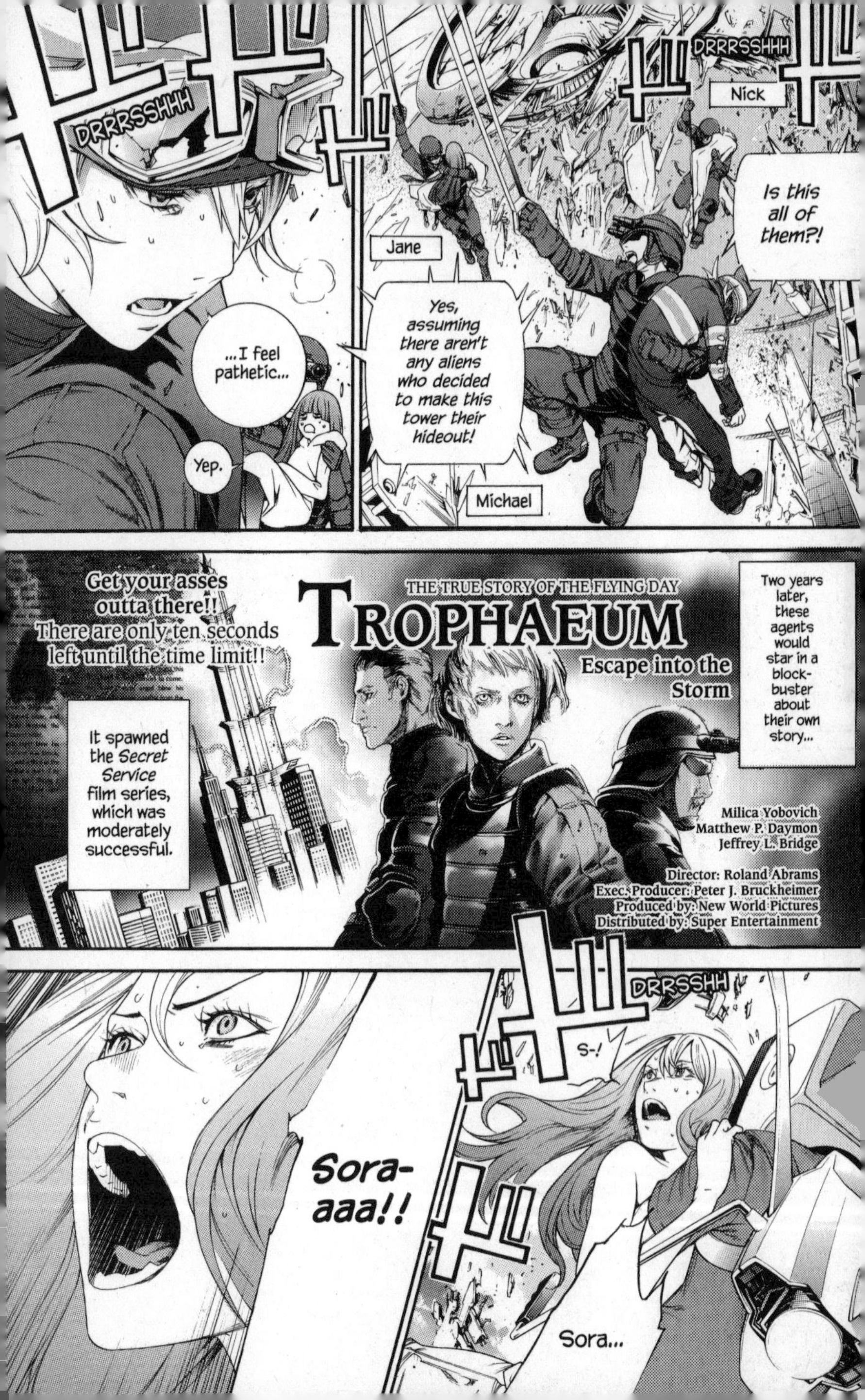
DRRRSSHHH
Nick
Is this all of them?!
Jane
Michael
Yes, assuming there aren't any aliens who decided to make this tower their hideout!
DRRRSSHHH
...I feel pathetic...
Yep.
Two years later, these agents would star in a block-buster about their own story...
THE TRUE STORY OF THE FLYING DAY
TROPHAEUM
Escape into the Storm
Milica Yobovich
Matthew P. Daymon
Jeffrey L. Bridge
Director: Roland Abrams
Exec. Producer: Peter J. Bruckheimer
Produced by: New World Pictures
Distributed by: Super Entertainment
Get your asses outta there!! There are only ten seconds left until the time limit!!
It spawned the Secret Service film series, which was moderately successful.
DRRSSHH
S-!
Sora...
Sora-aaa!!

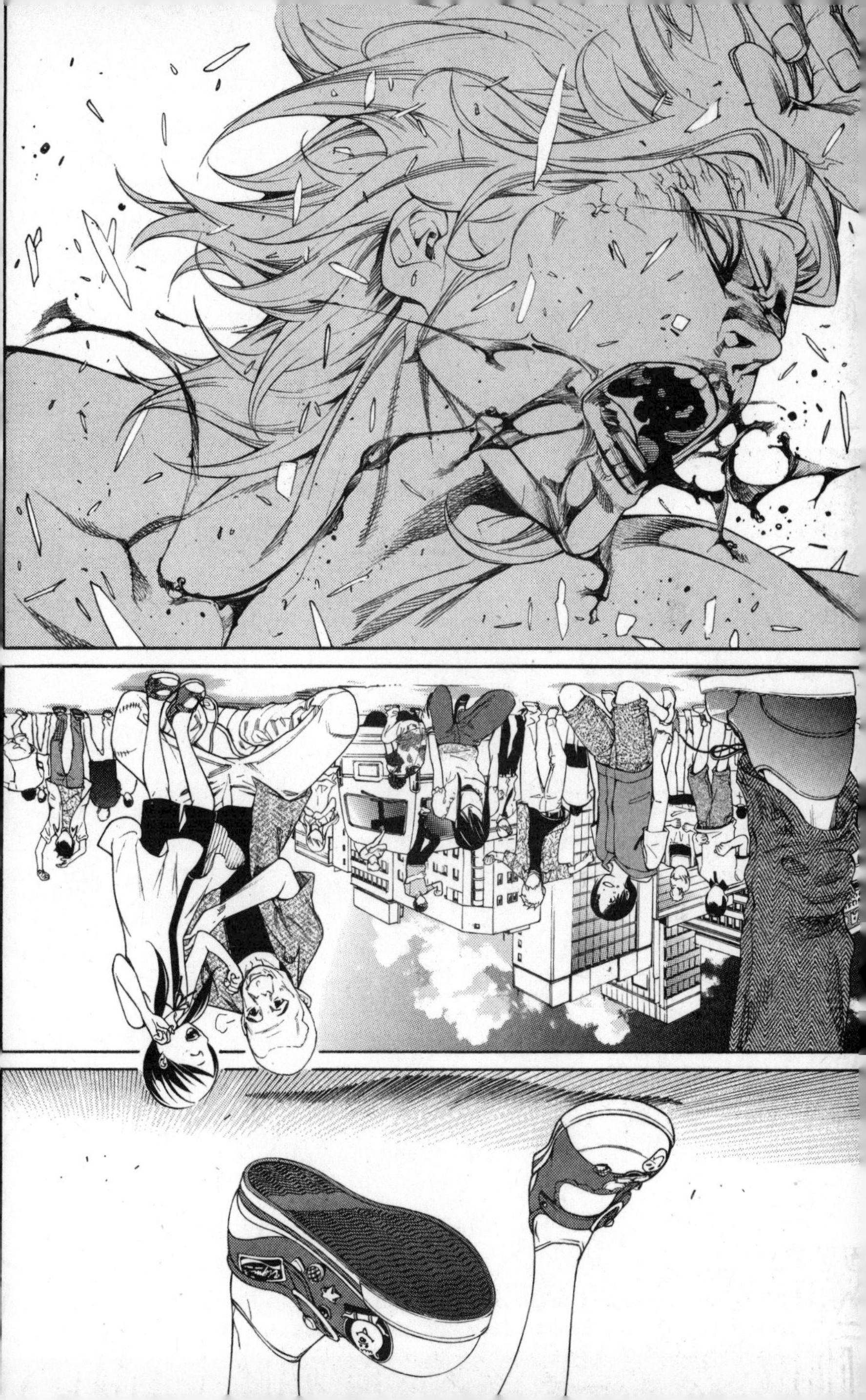

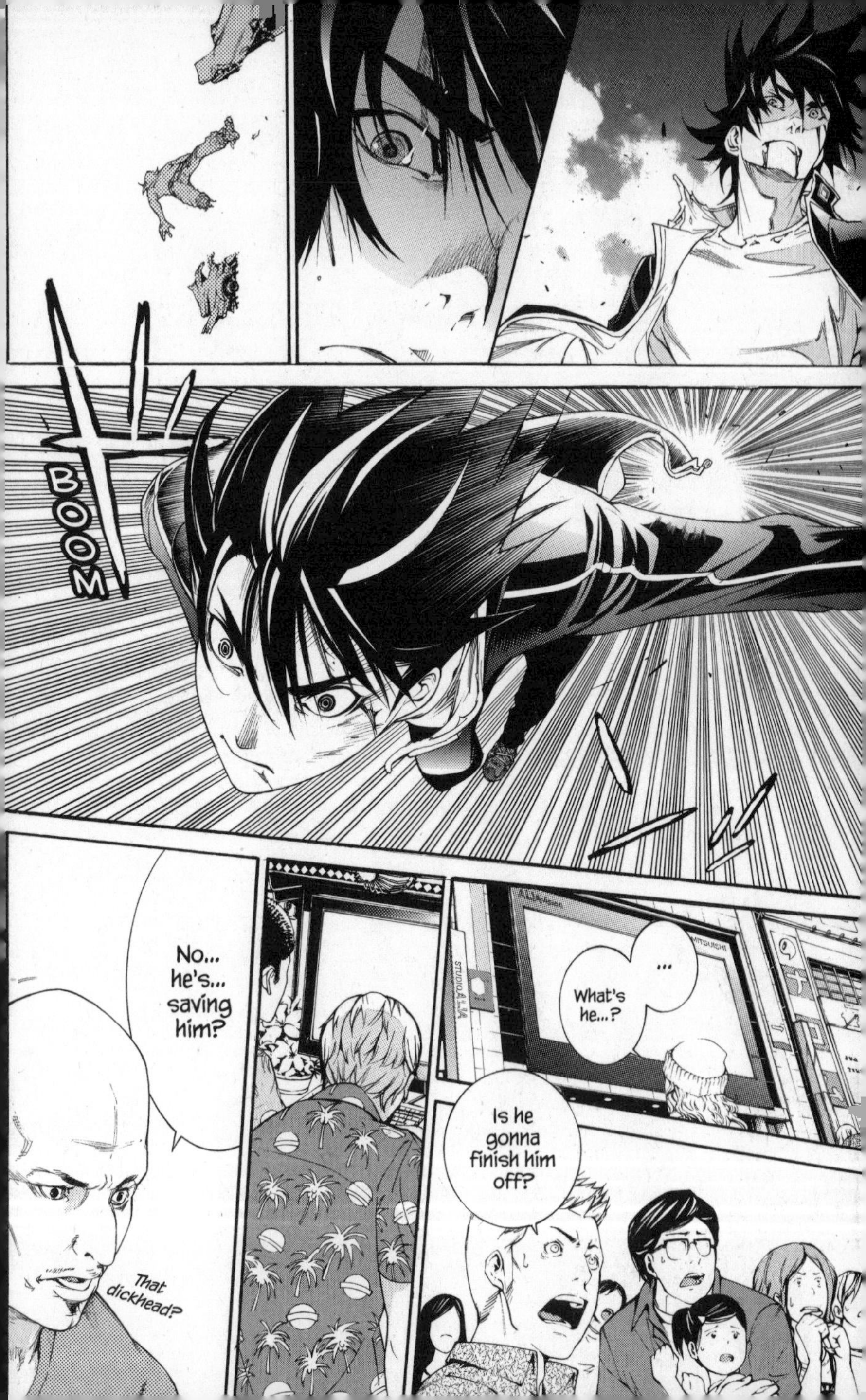
BOOM
...
What's he...?
Is he gonna finish him off?
STUDIO ALTA
No... he's... saving him?
That dickhead?

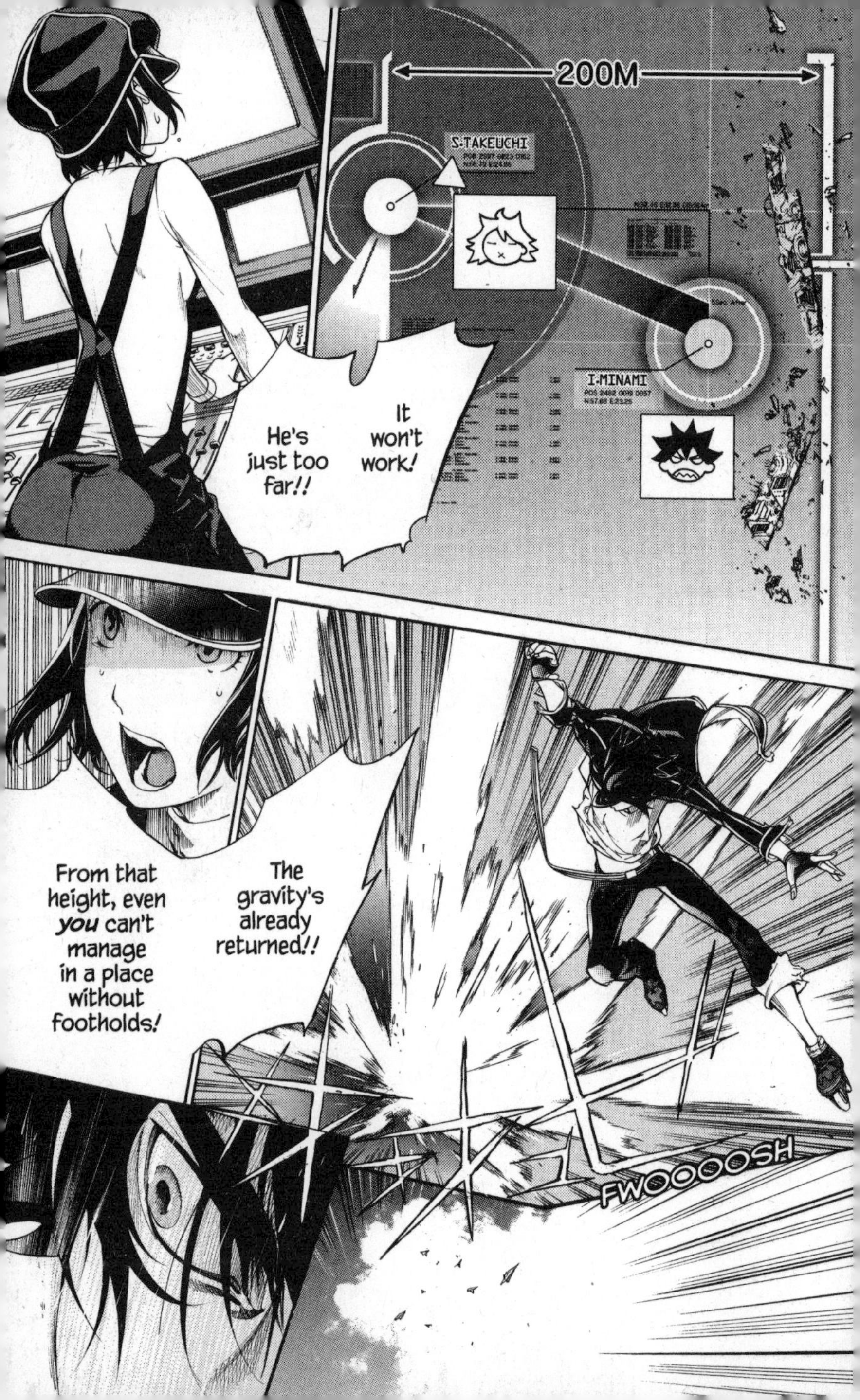
200M
S.TAKEUCHI
I.MINAMI
It won't work!
He's just too far!!
The gravity's already returned!!
From that height, even *you* can't manage in a place without footholds!
FWOOOOSH

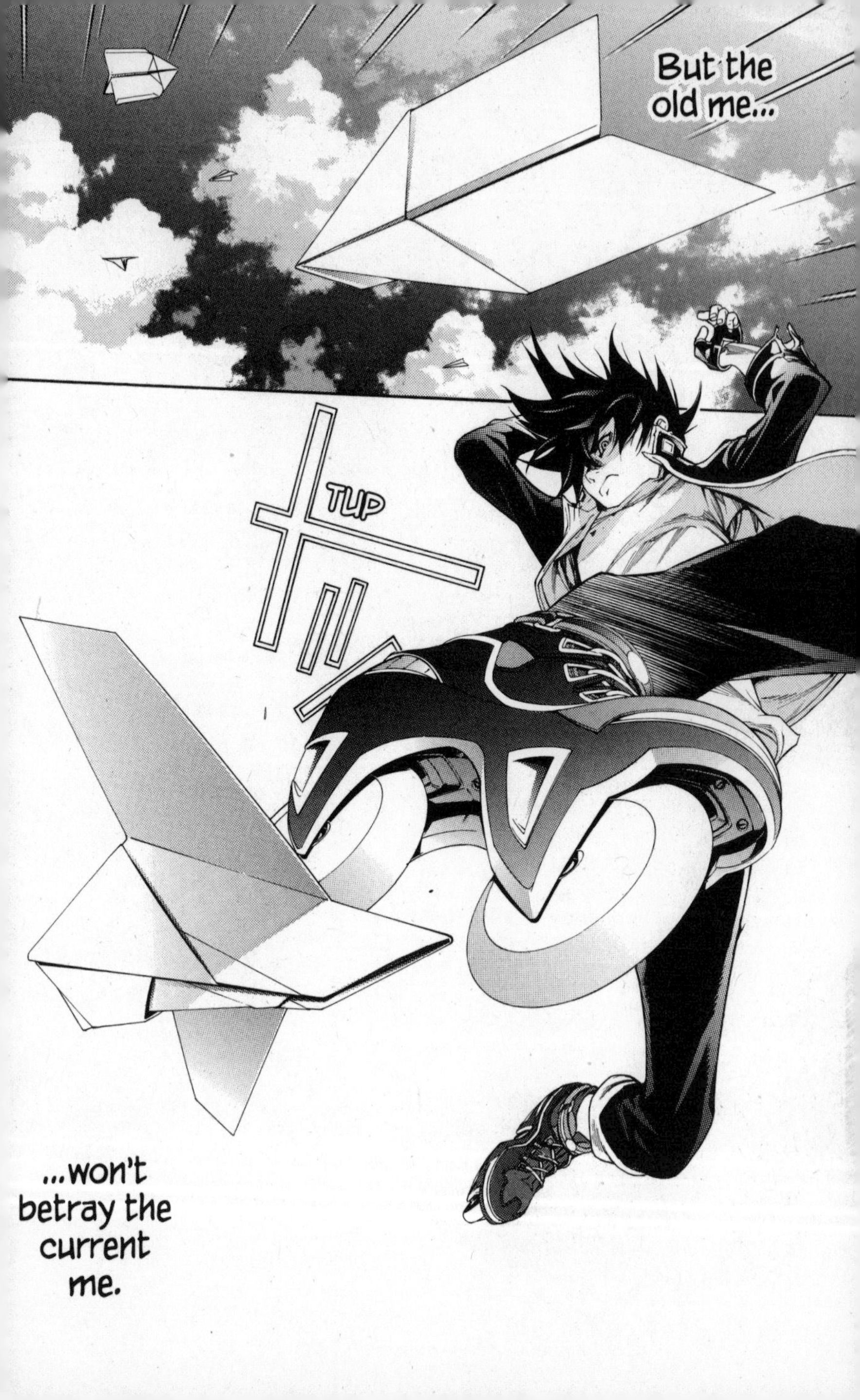
But the old me...
TUP
...won't betray the current me.

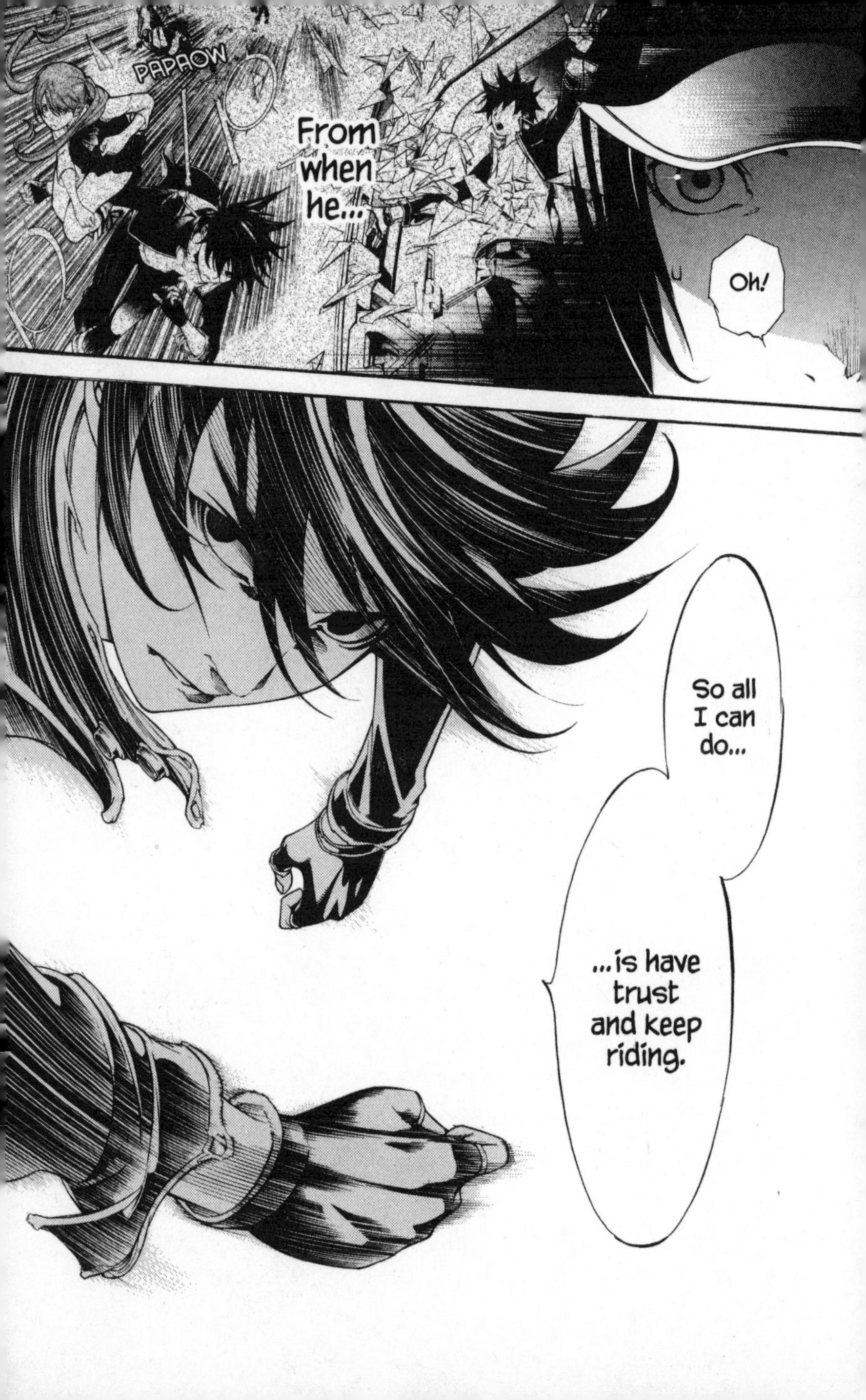
Oh!
From when he...
PAPAOW
So all I can do...
...is have trust and keep riding.

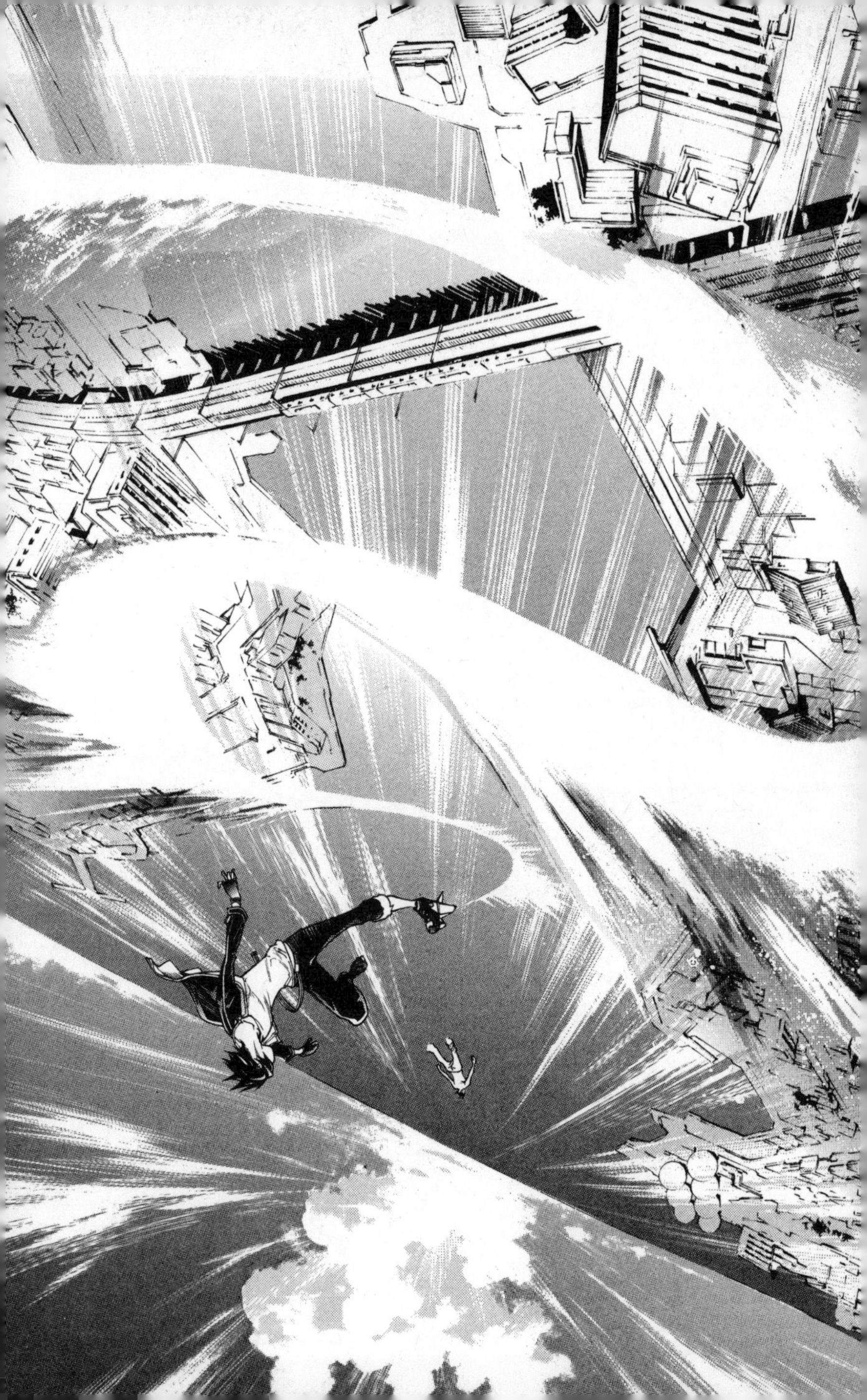

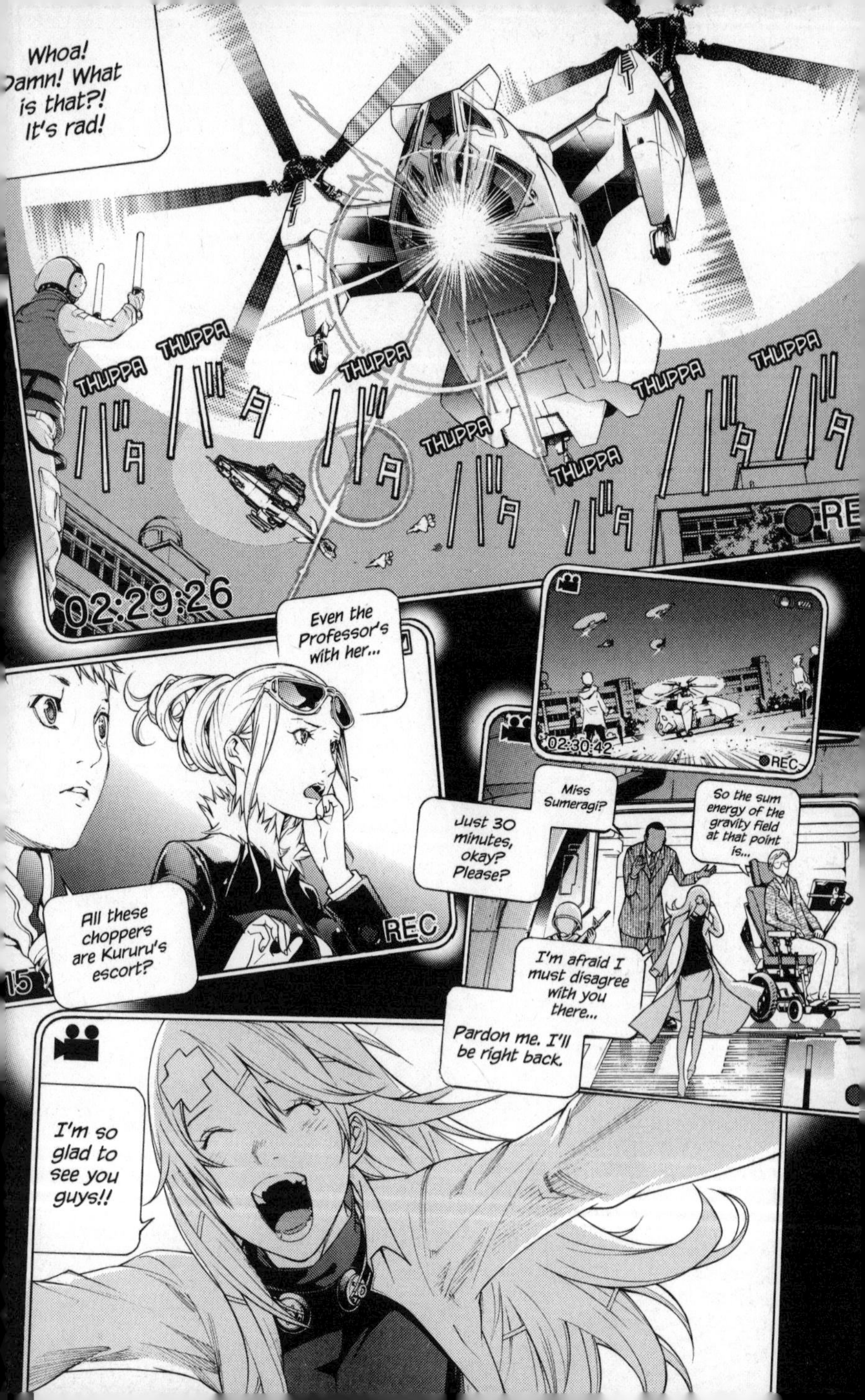
Whoa! Damn! What is that?! It's rad!
THUPPA
THUPPA
THUPPA
THUPPA
THUPPA
THUPPA
THUPPA
REC
02:29:26
02:30:42
REC
So the sum energy of the gravity field at that point is...
Miss Sumeragi?
Just 30 minutes, okay? Please?
I'm afraid I must disagree with you there...
Pardon me. I'll be right back.
Even the Professor's with her...
All these choppers are Kururu's escort?
REC
I'm so glad to see you guys!!

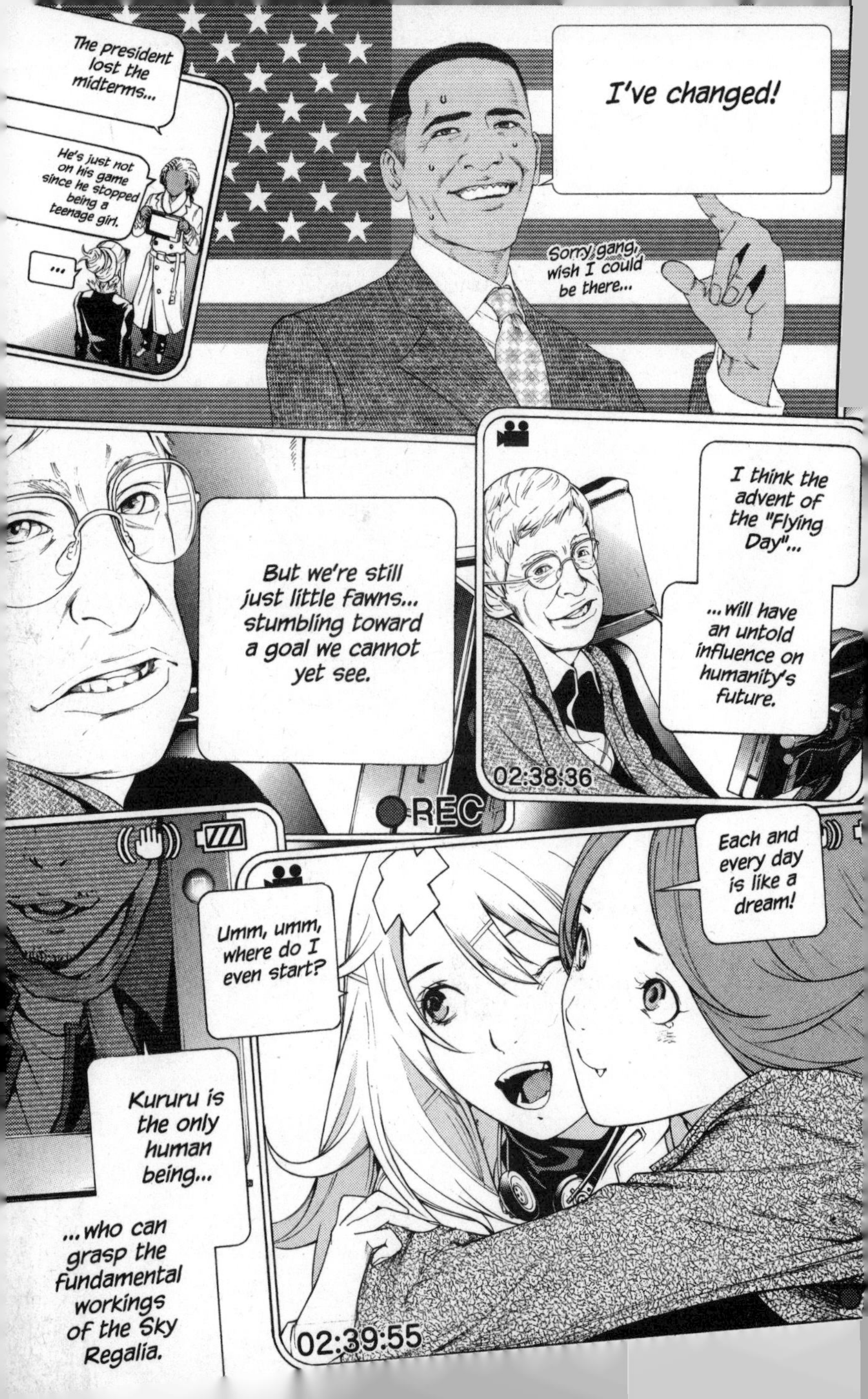
I've changed!
Sorry gang, wish I could be there...
The president lost the midterms...
He's just not on his game since he stopped being a teenage girl.
...
I think the advent of the "Flying Day"...
...will have an untold influence on humanity's future.
02:38:36
But we're still just little fawns... stumbling toward a goal we cannot yet see.
REC
Each and every day is like a dream!
Umm, umm, where do I even start?
02:39:55
Kururu is the only human being...
...who can grasp the fundamental workings of the Sky Regalia.

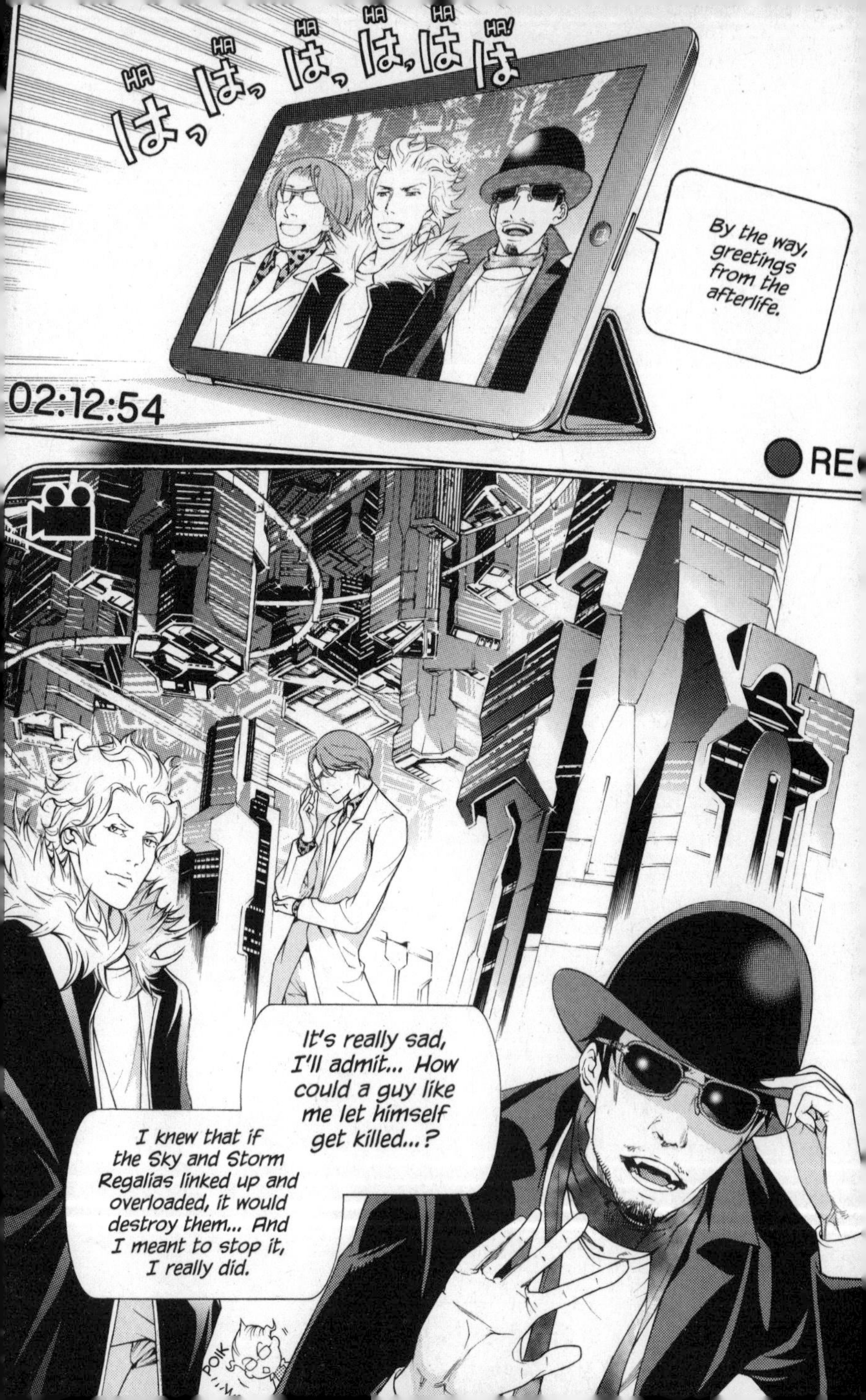
HA HA HA HA HA!
はっはっはっはは
By the way, greetings from the afterlife.
02:12:54
RE
It's really sad, I'll admit... How could a guy like me let himself get killed...?
I knew that if the Sky and Storm Regalias linked up and overloaded, it would destroy them... And I meant to stop it, I really did.
POIK

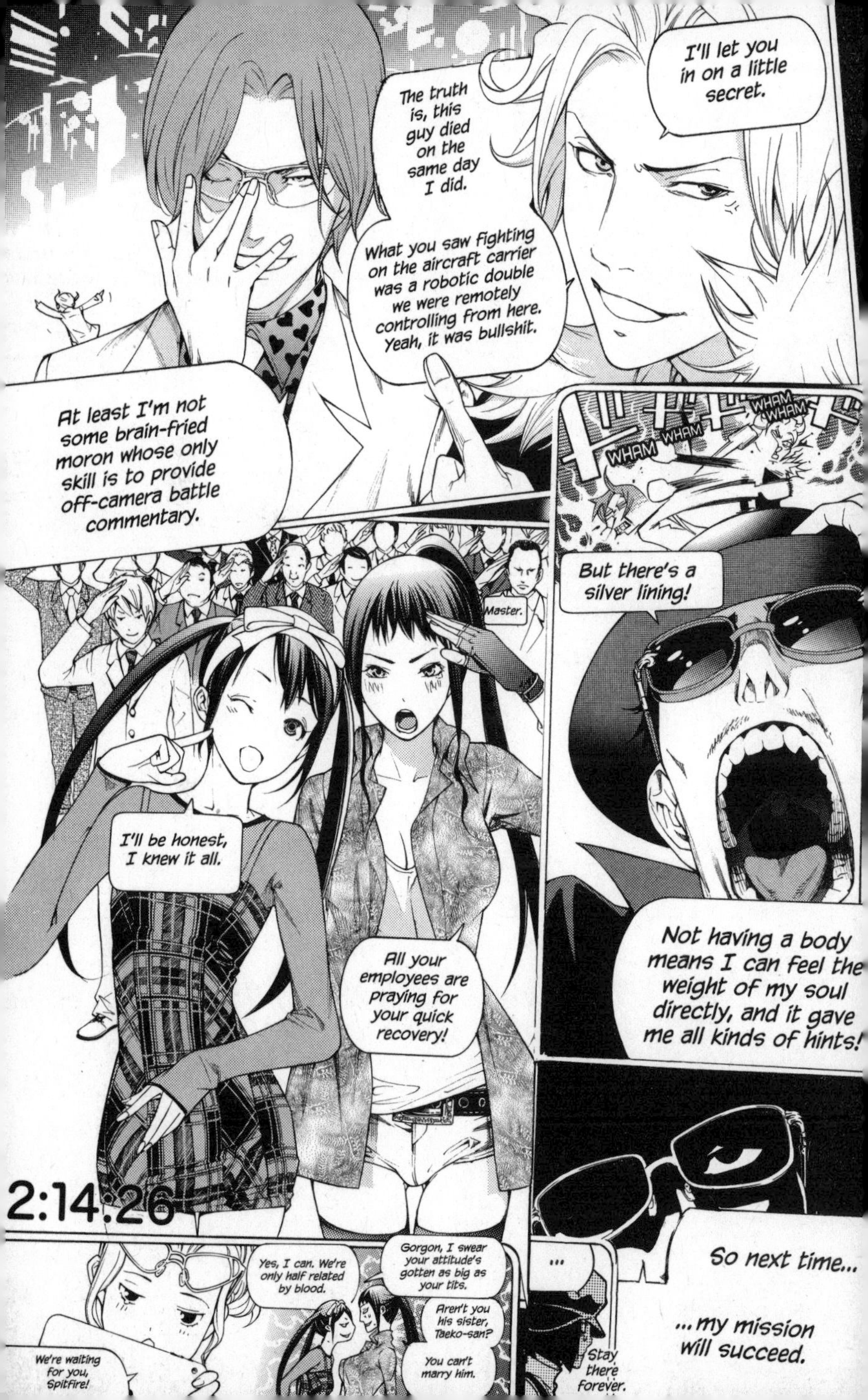
I'll let you in on a little secret.
The truth is, this guy died on the same day I did.
What you saw fighting on the aircraft carrier was a robotic double we were remotely controlling from here. Yeah, it was bullshit.
At least I'm not some brain-fried moron whose only skill is to provide off-camera battle commentary.
WHAM WHAM
WHAM
WHAM
But there's a silver lining!
Not having a body means I can feel the weight of my soul directly, and it gave me all kinds of hints!
So next time...
...my mission will succeed.
Master.
I'll be honest, I knew it all.
All your employees are praying for your quick recovery!
2:14:26
...
Stay there forever.
Gorgon, I swear your attitude's gotten as big as your tits.
Aren't you his sister, Taeko-san?
You can't marry him.
Yes, I can. We're only half related by blood.
We're waiting for you, Spitfire!

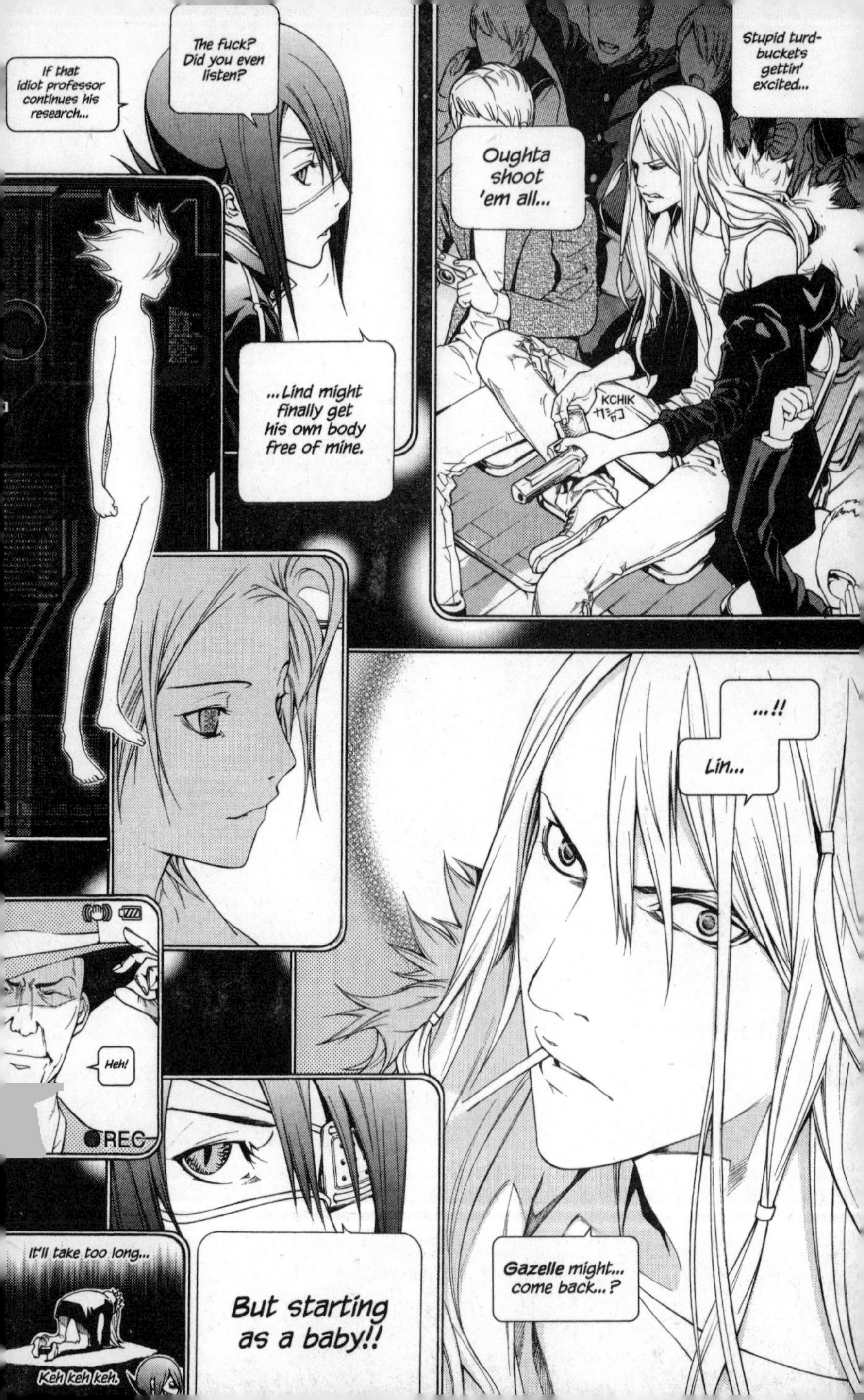
Stupid turd-buckets gettin' excited...
Oughta shoot 'em all...
KCHIK
If that idiot professor continues his research...
The fuck? Did you even listen?
...Lind might finally get his own body free of mine.
...!!
Lin...
Gazelle might... come back...?
Heh!
REC
But starting as a baby!!
It'll take too long...
Keh keh keh.

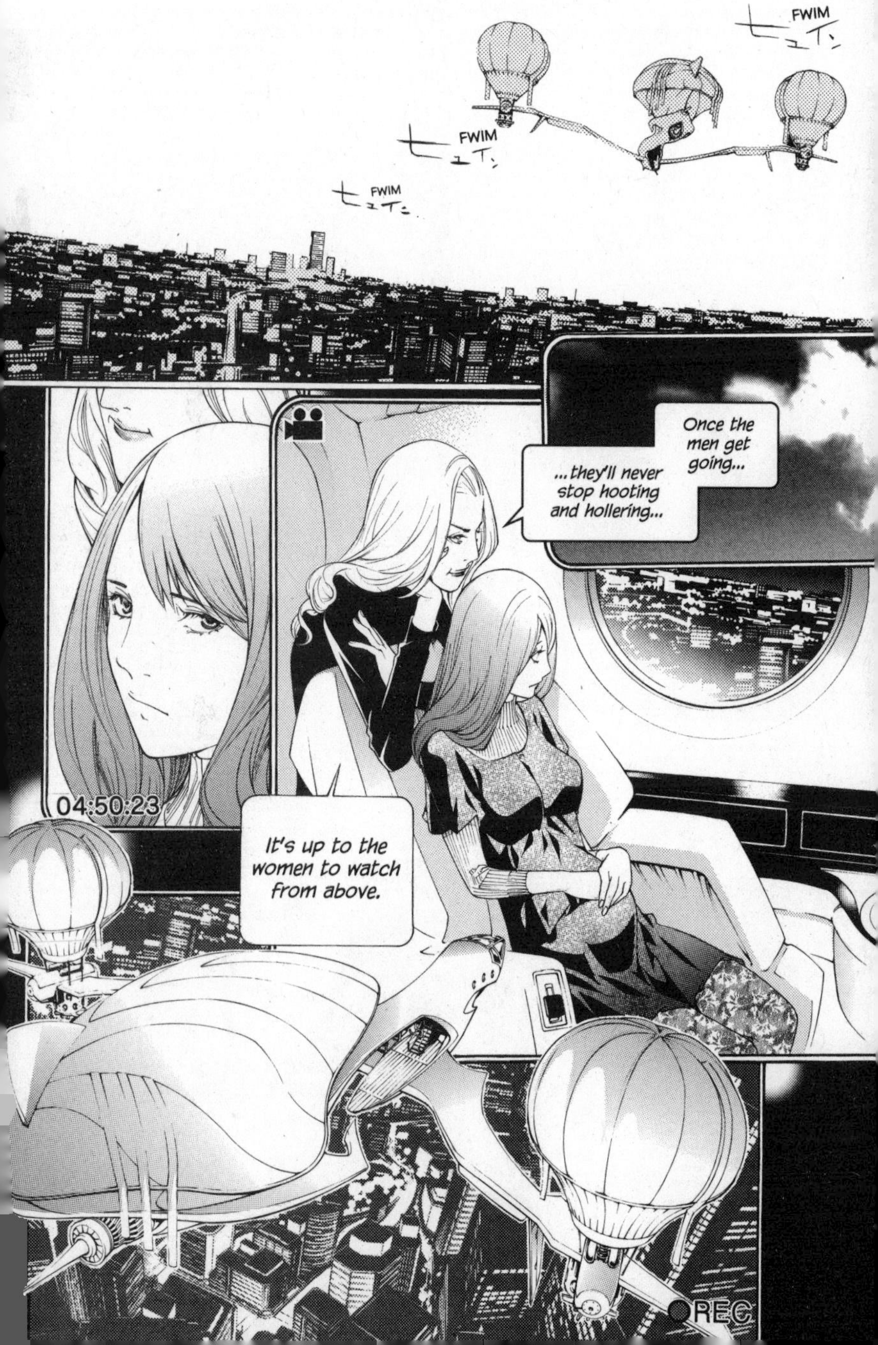
FWIM
FWIM
FWIM
Once the men get going...
...they'll never stop hooting and hollering...
04:50:23
It's up to the women to watch from above.
REC

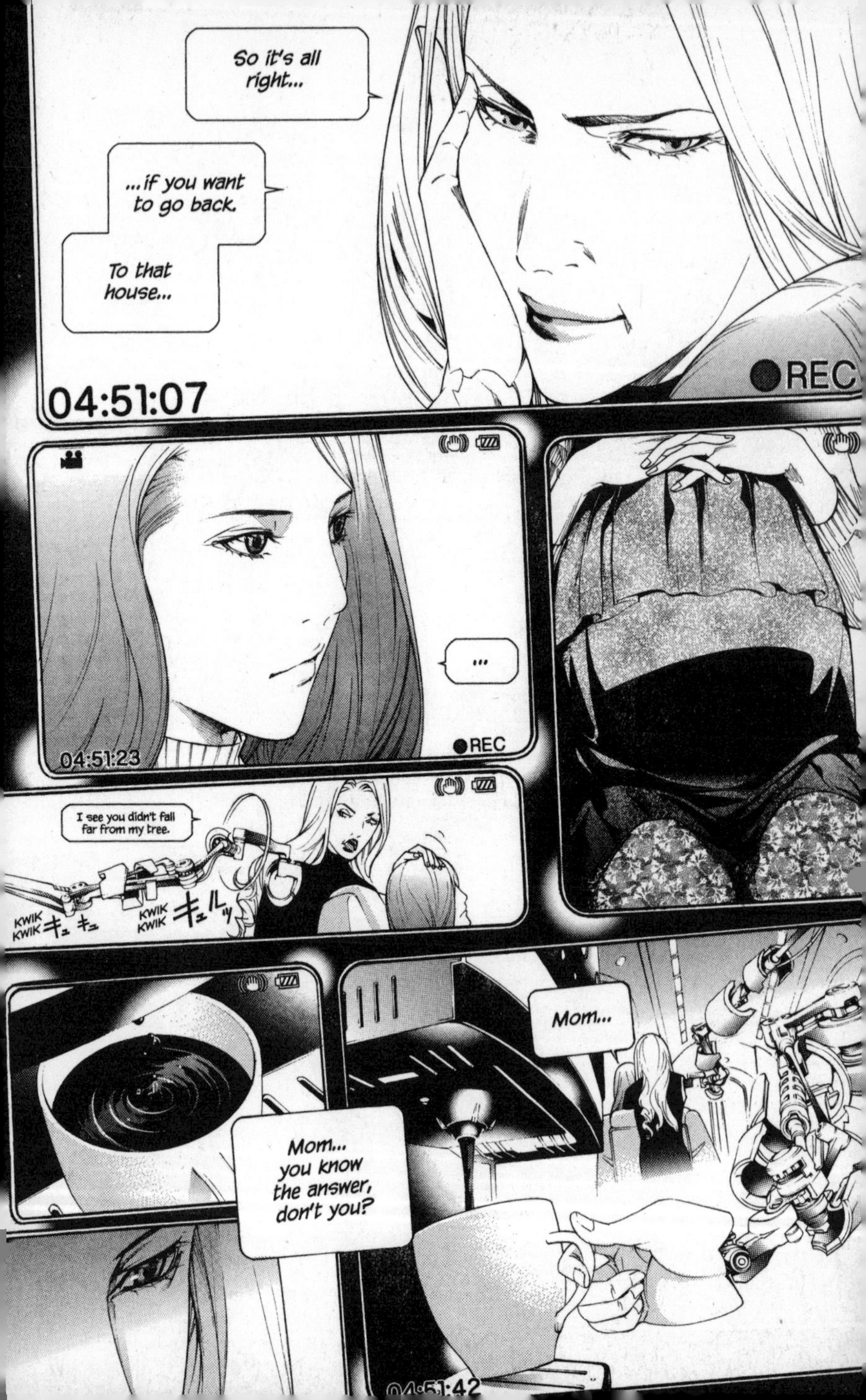
So it's all right...
...if you want to go back.
To that house...
●REC
04:51:07
...
●REC
04:51:23
I see you didn't fall far from my tree.
KWIK KWIK キュルッ
KWIK KWIK キュ キュ
Mom...
Mom... you know the answer, don't you?
04:51:42

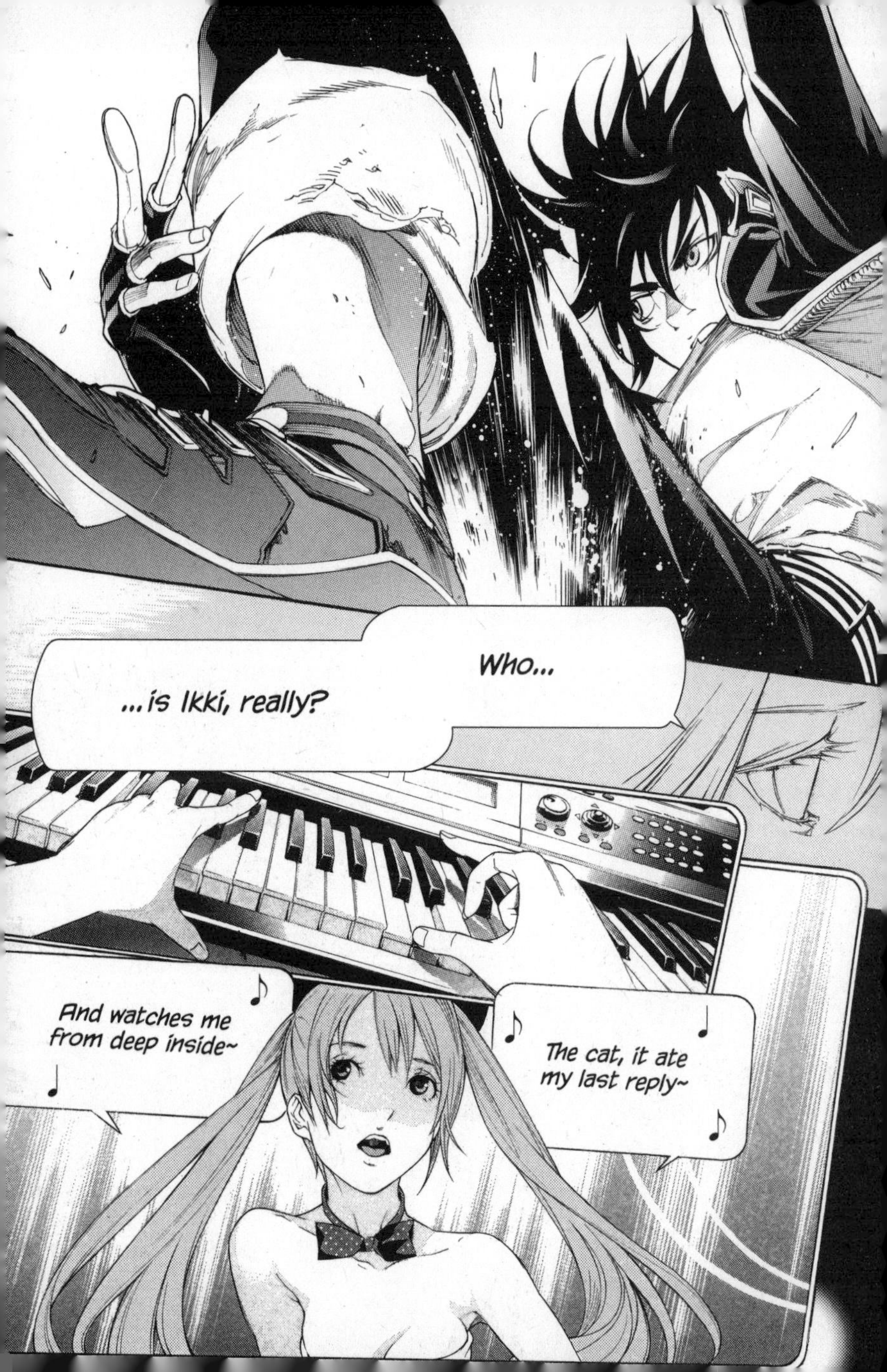
Who...
...is Ikki, really?
The cat, it ate my last reply~
And watches me from deep inside~

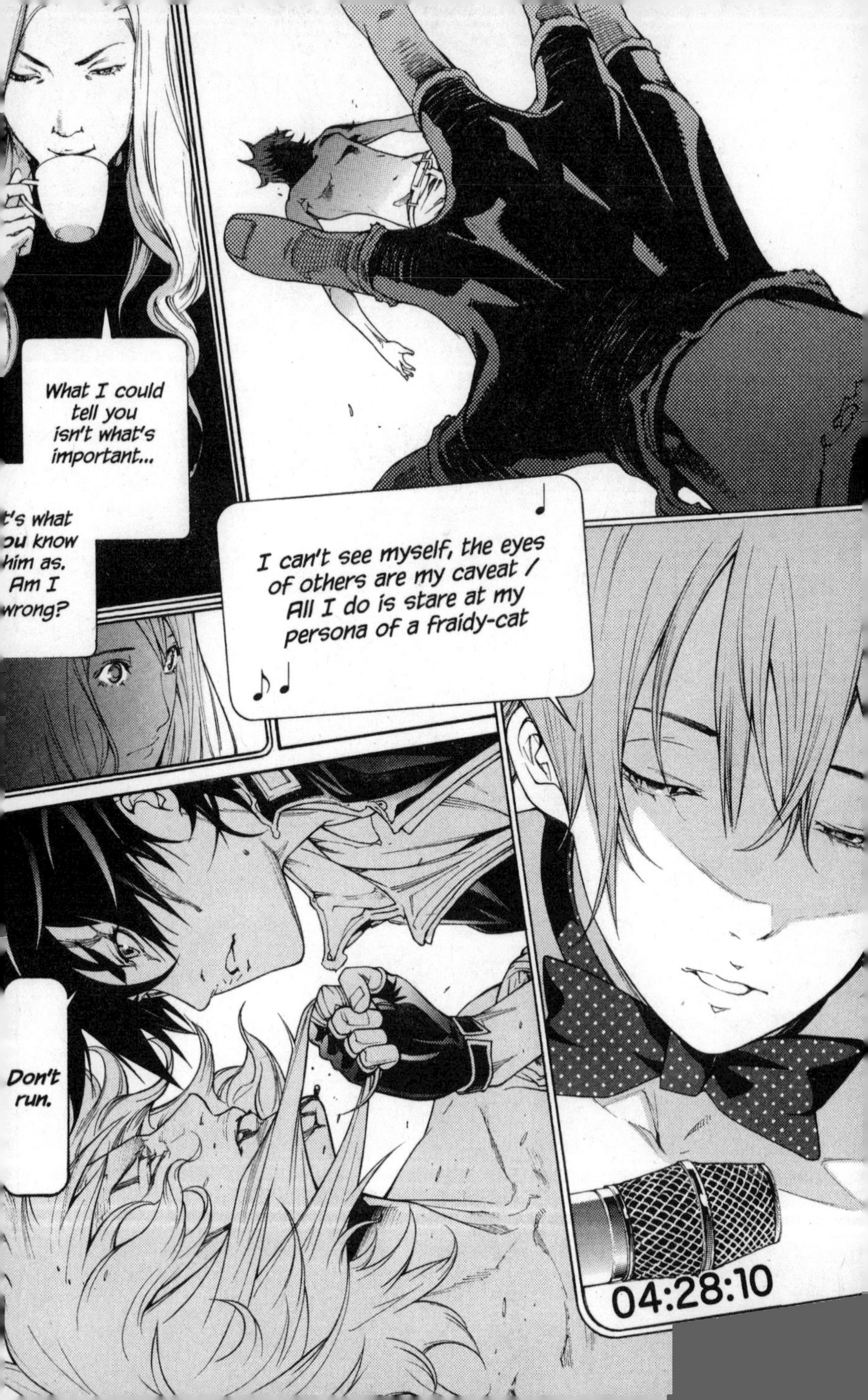
What I could tell you isn't what's important...
t's what ou know him as. Am I wrong?
I can't see myself, the eyes of others are my caveat / All I do is stare at my persona of a fraidy-cat
04:28:10
Don't run.

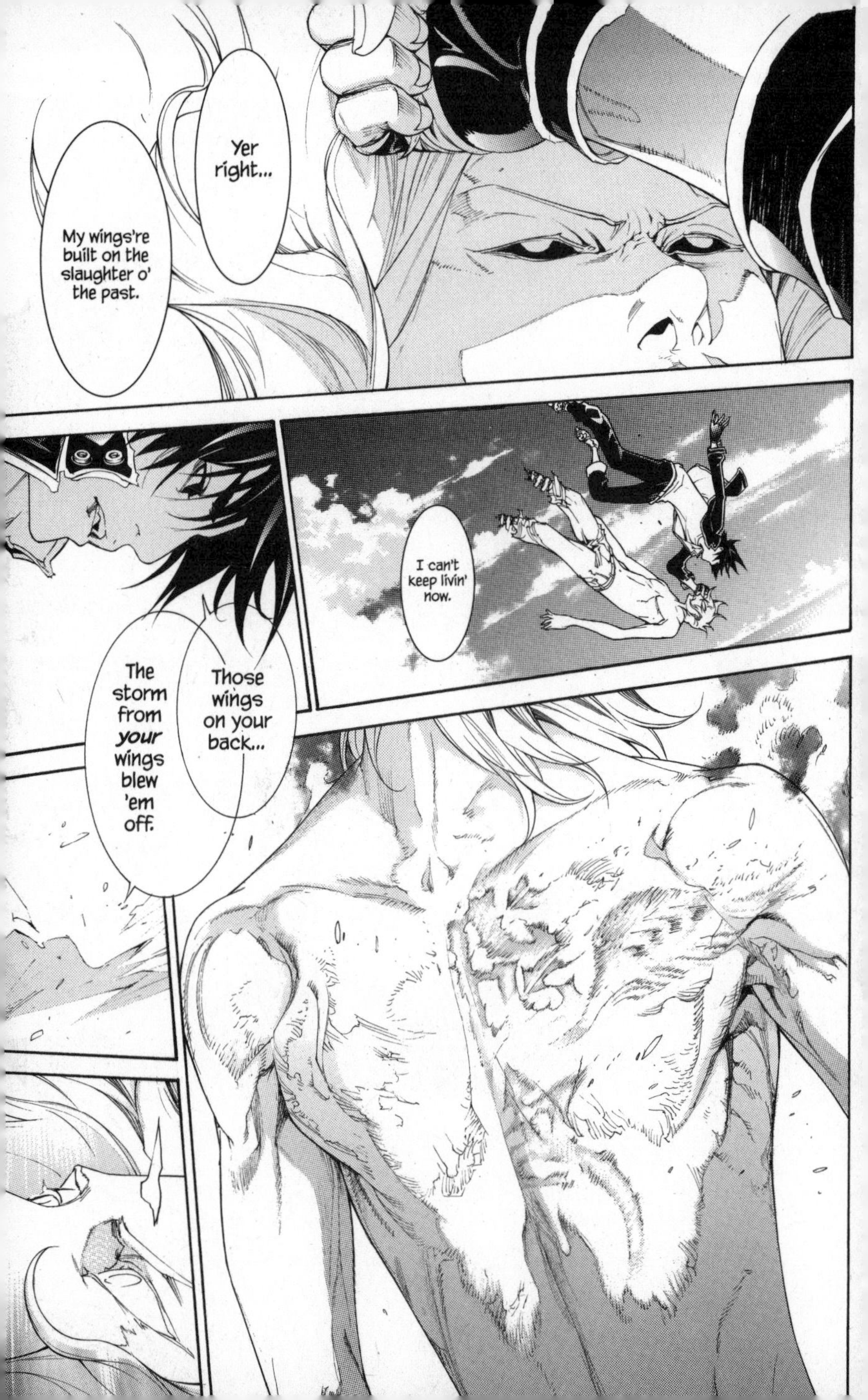
Yer right...
My wings're built on the slaughter o' the past.
I can't keep livin' now.
Those wings on your back...
The storm from *your* wings blew 'em off.

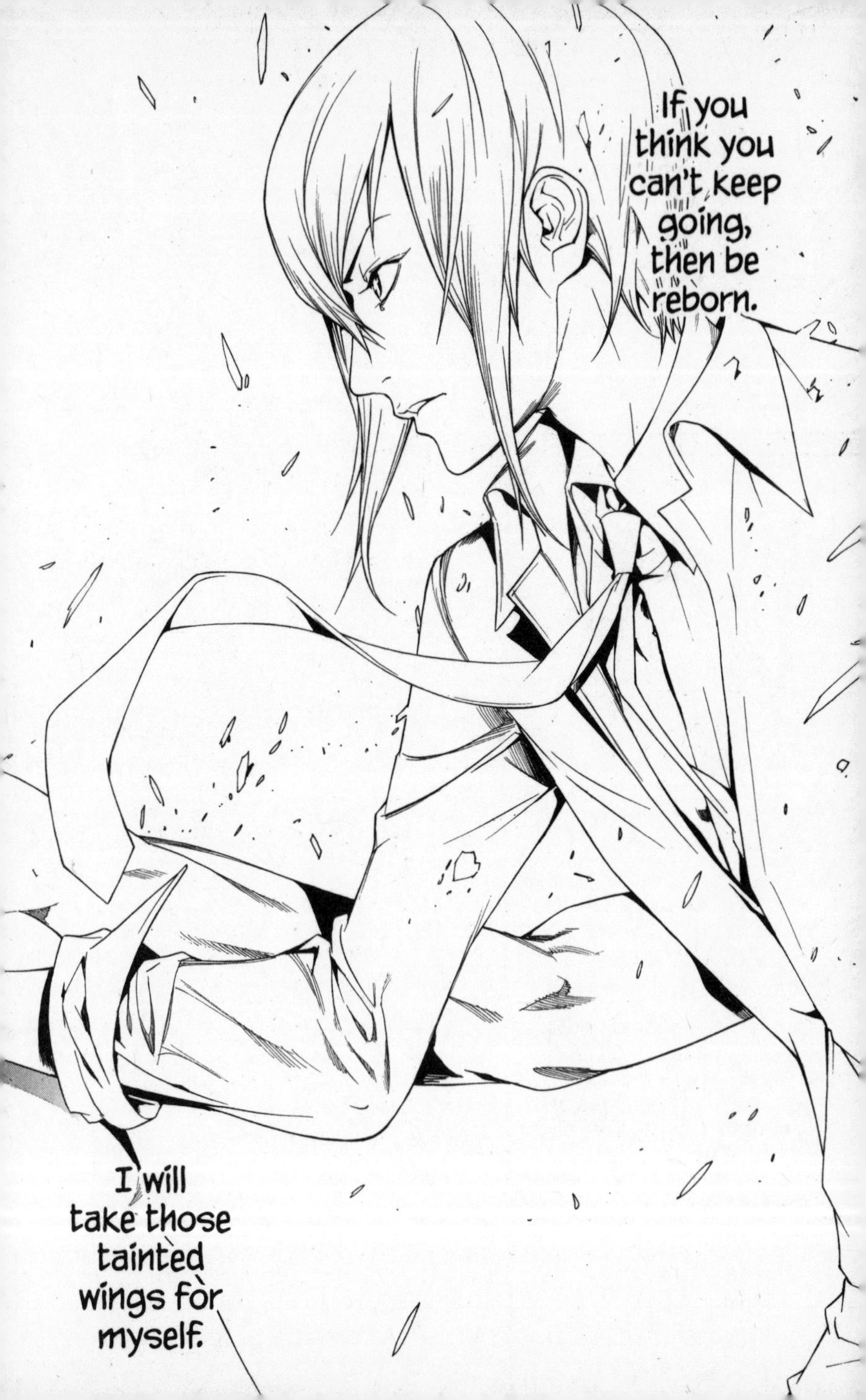
If you think you can't keep going, then be reborn.
I will take those tainted wings for myself.

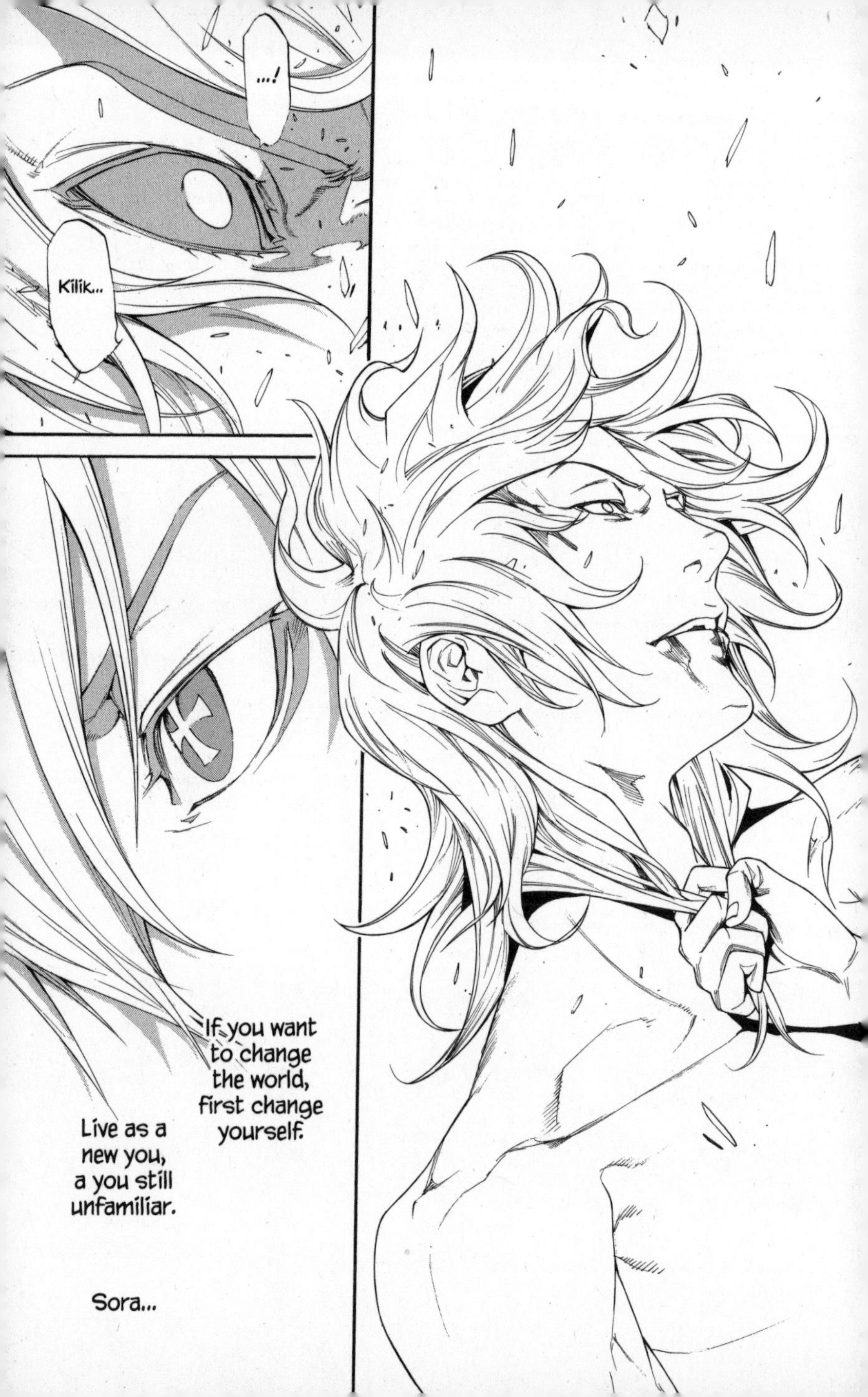
...!
Kilik...
If you want to change the world, first change yourself.
Live as a new you, a you still unfamiliar.
Sora...

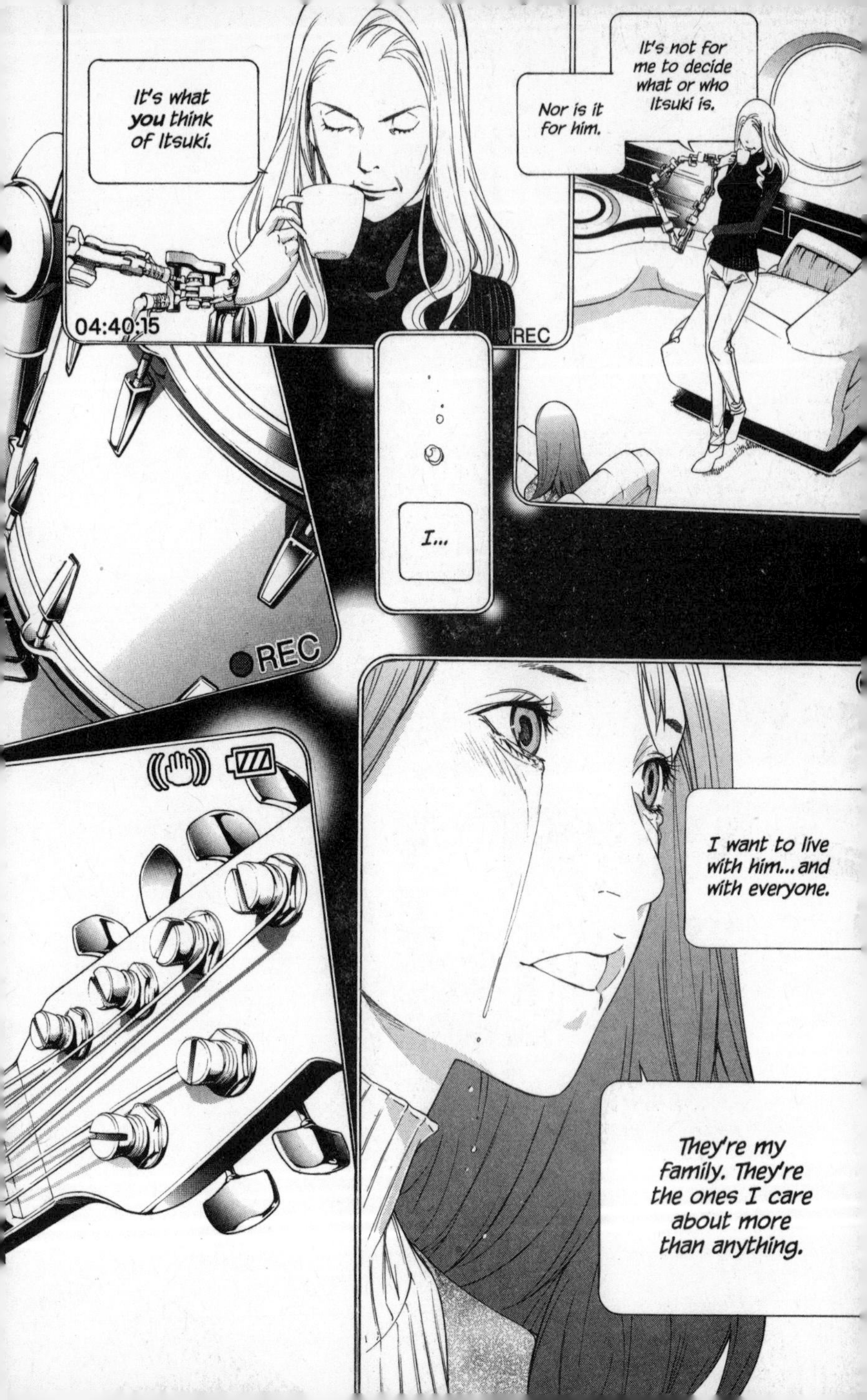
It's not for me to decide what or who Itsuki is.
Nor is it for him.
It's what you think of Itsuki.
04:40:15
REC
I...
REC
I want to live with him...and with everyone.
They're my family. They're the ones I care about more than anything.

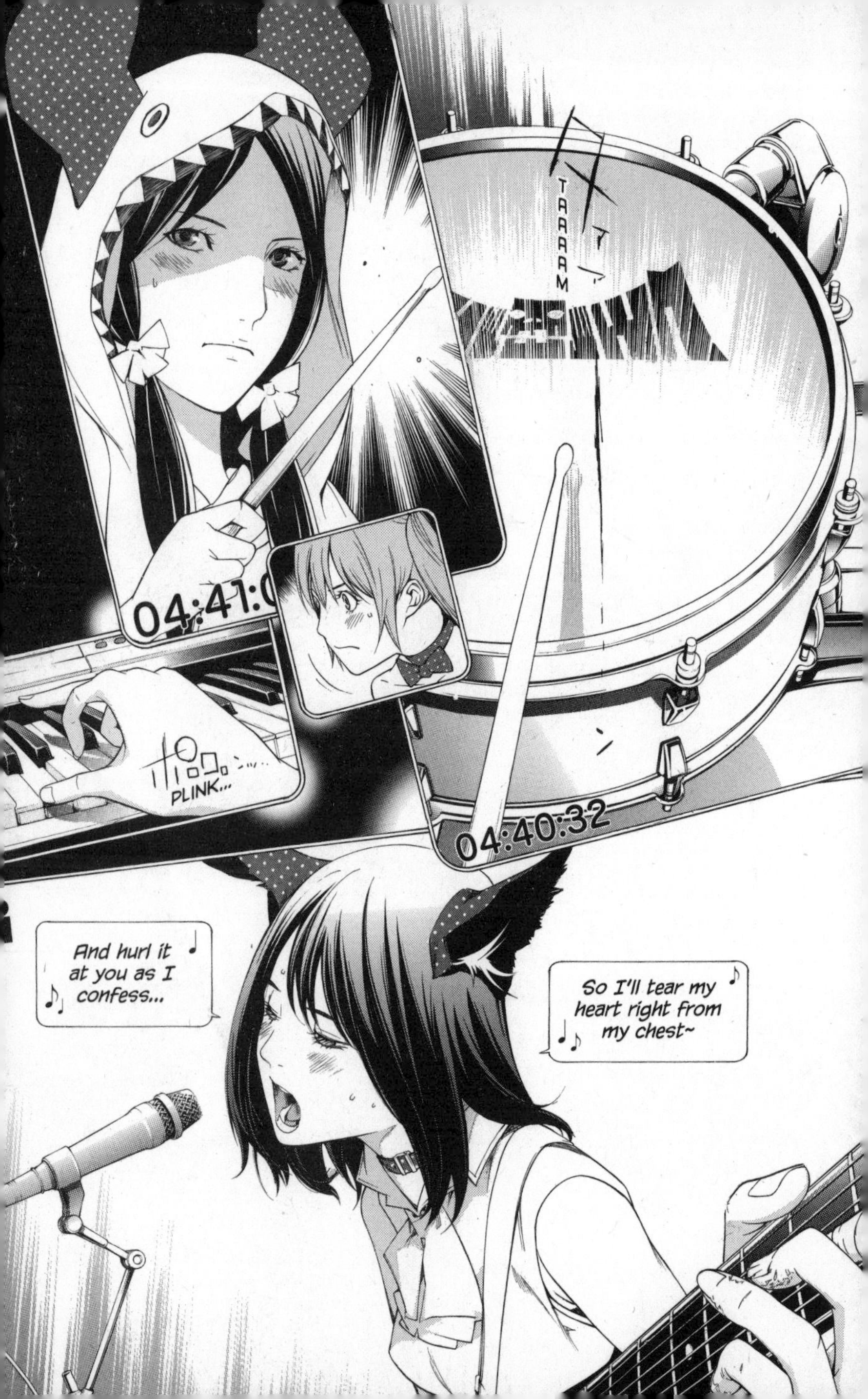
TAAAAM
04:40:32
04:41:0
PLINK...
So I'll tear my heart right from my chest~
And hurl it at you as I confess...

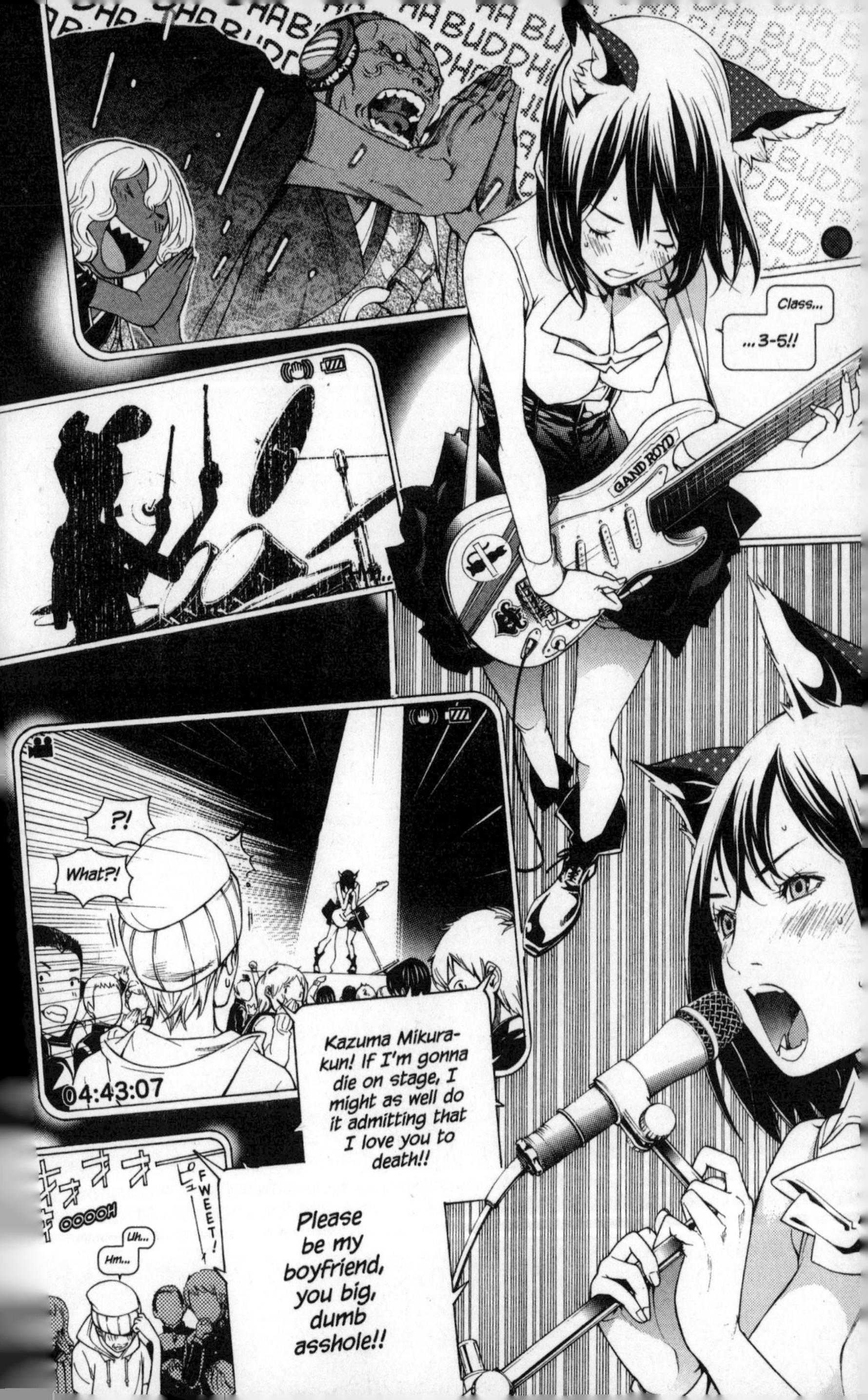
Class...
...3-5!!
GAND ROYD
?!
What?!
04:43:07
Kazuma Mikura-kun! If I'm gonna die on stage, I might as well do it admitting that I love you to death!!
Please be my boyfriend, you big, dumb asshole!!
FWEET!
OOOOH
Uh...
Hm...

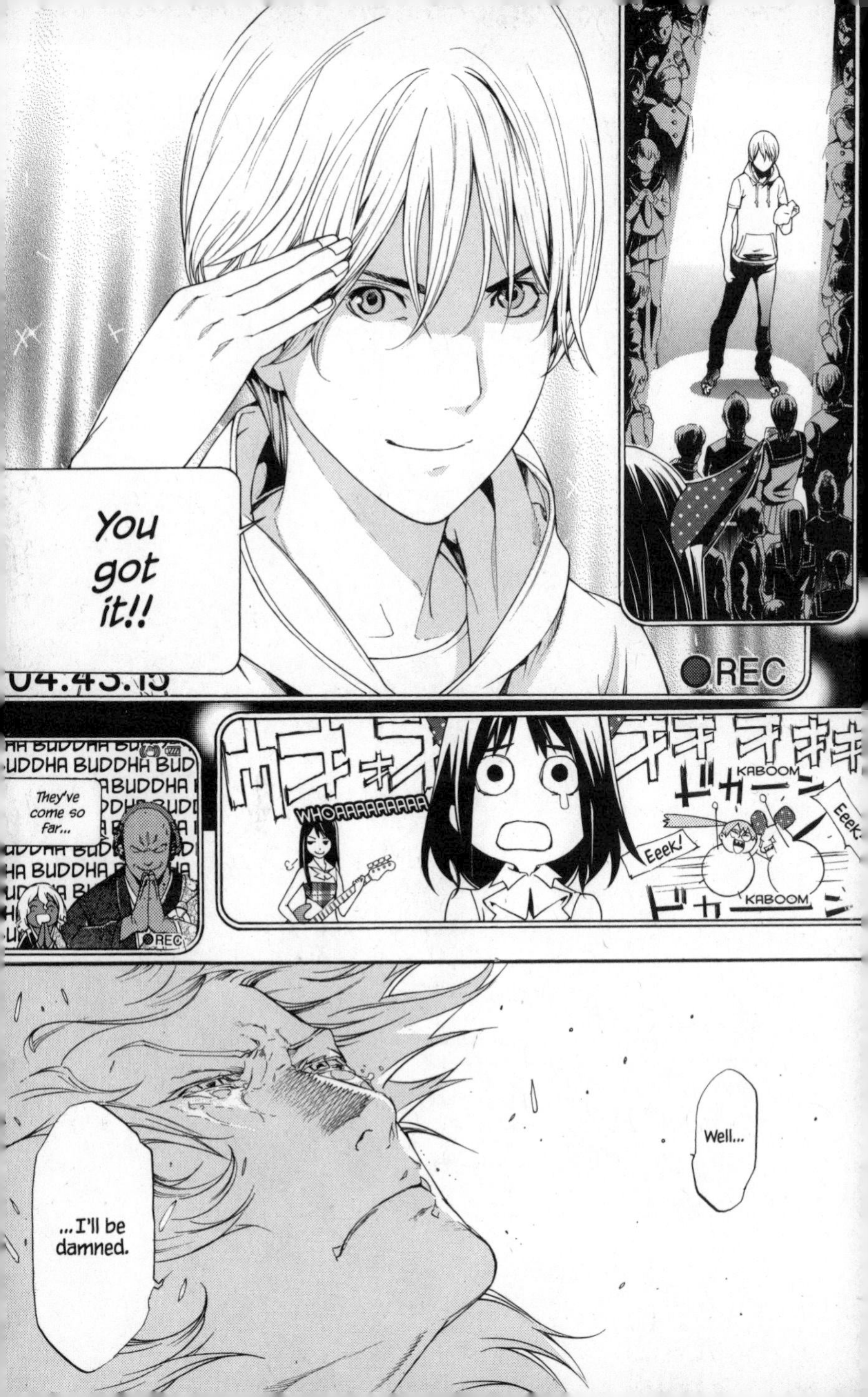
REC
You got it!!
04.43.15
ギャオオオオオ
KABOOM
ドカーン
Eeek!
Eeek!
KABOOM
ドカーン
WHOAAAAAAAAAA
ギャオオ
BUDDHA BUDDHA BUDDHA
They've come so far...
REC
Well...
...I'll be damned.

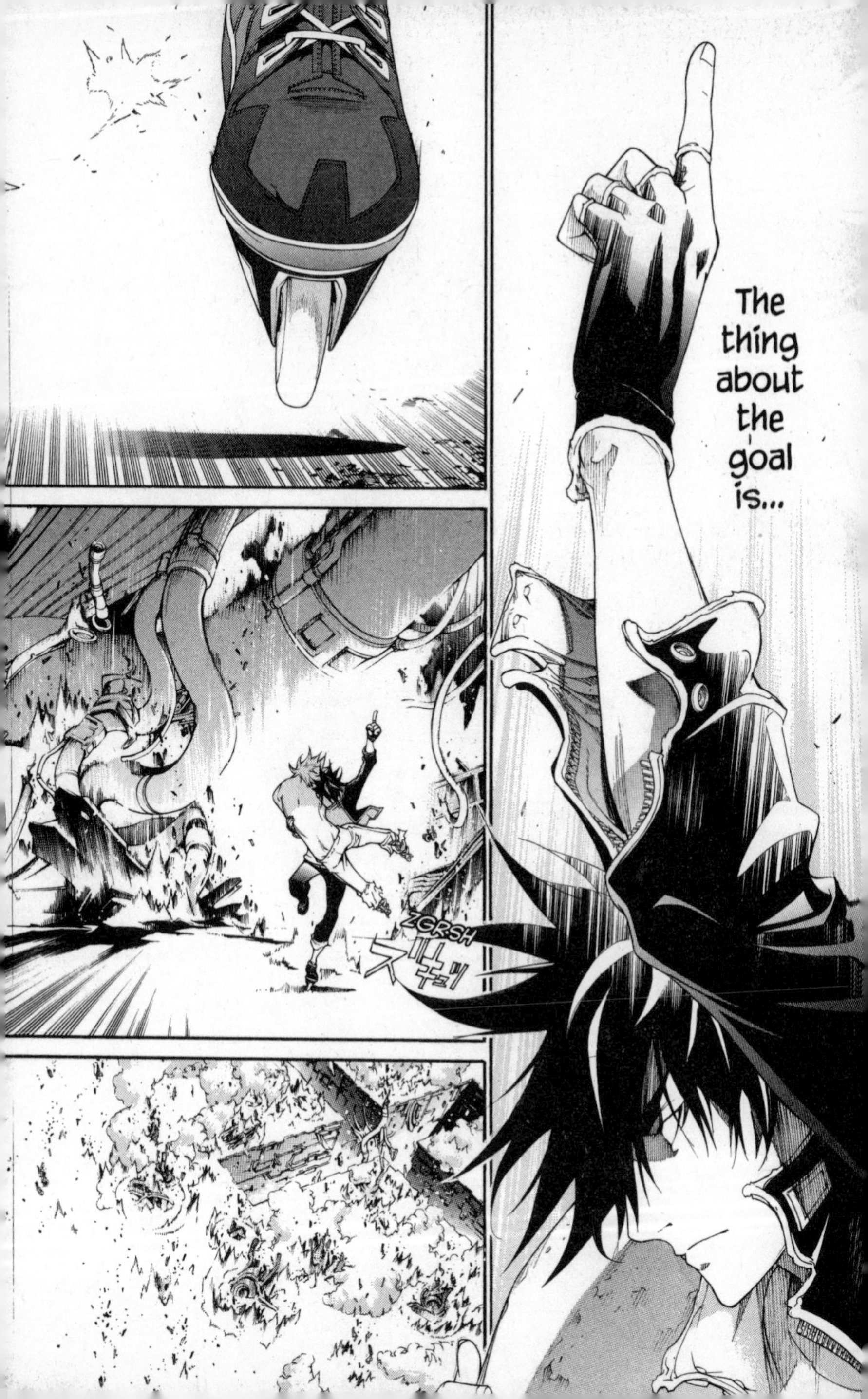
The thing about the goal is...
ZGRSH
スギュッ

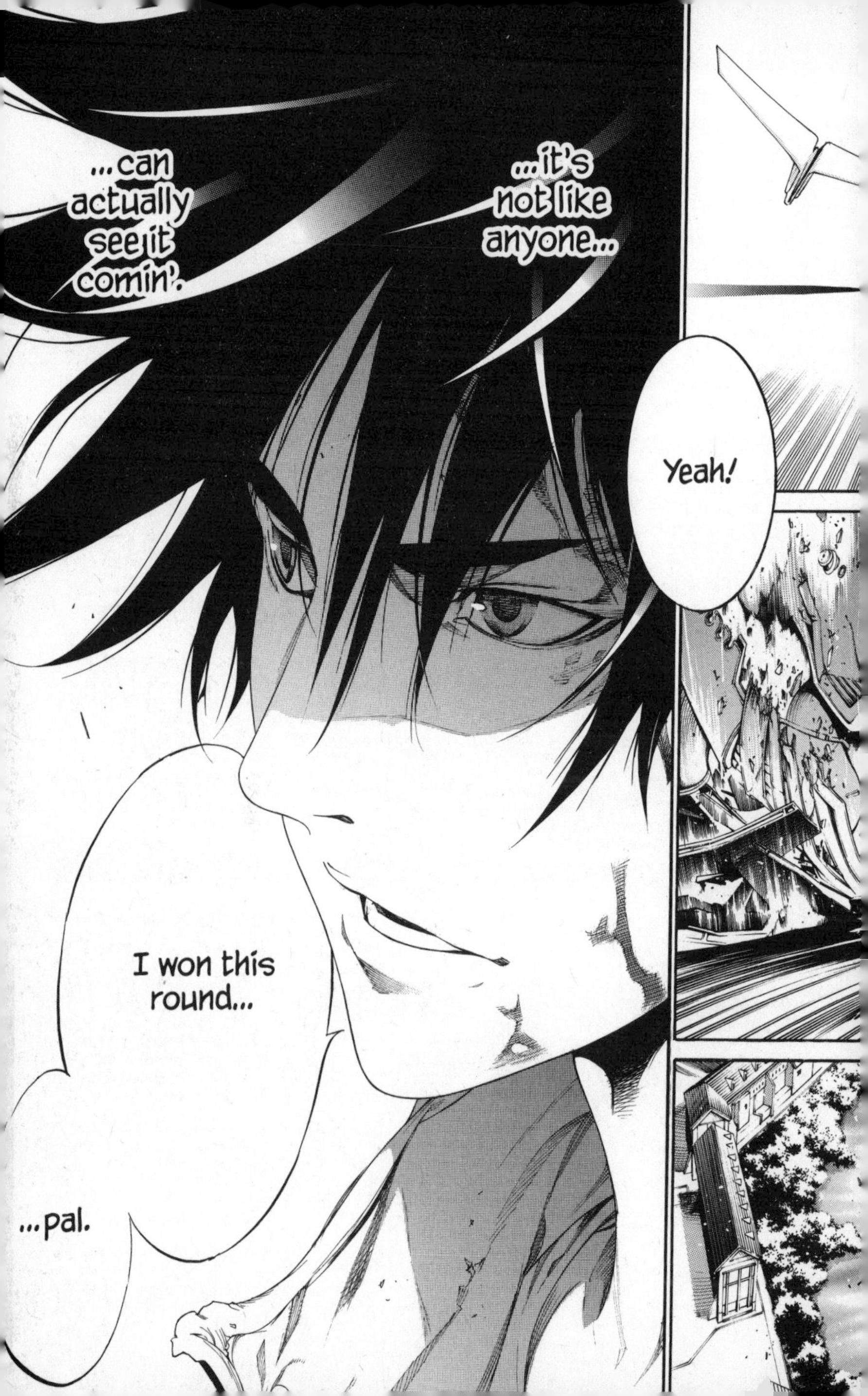
Yeah!
...it's not like anyone...
...can actually see it comin'.
I won this round...
...pal.

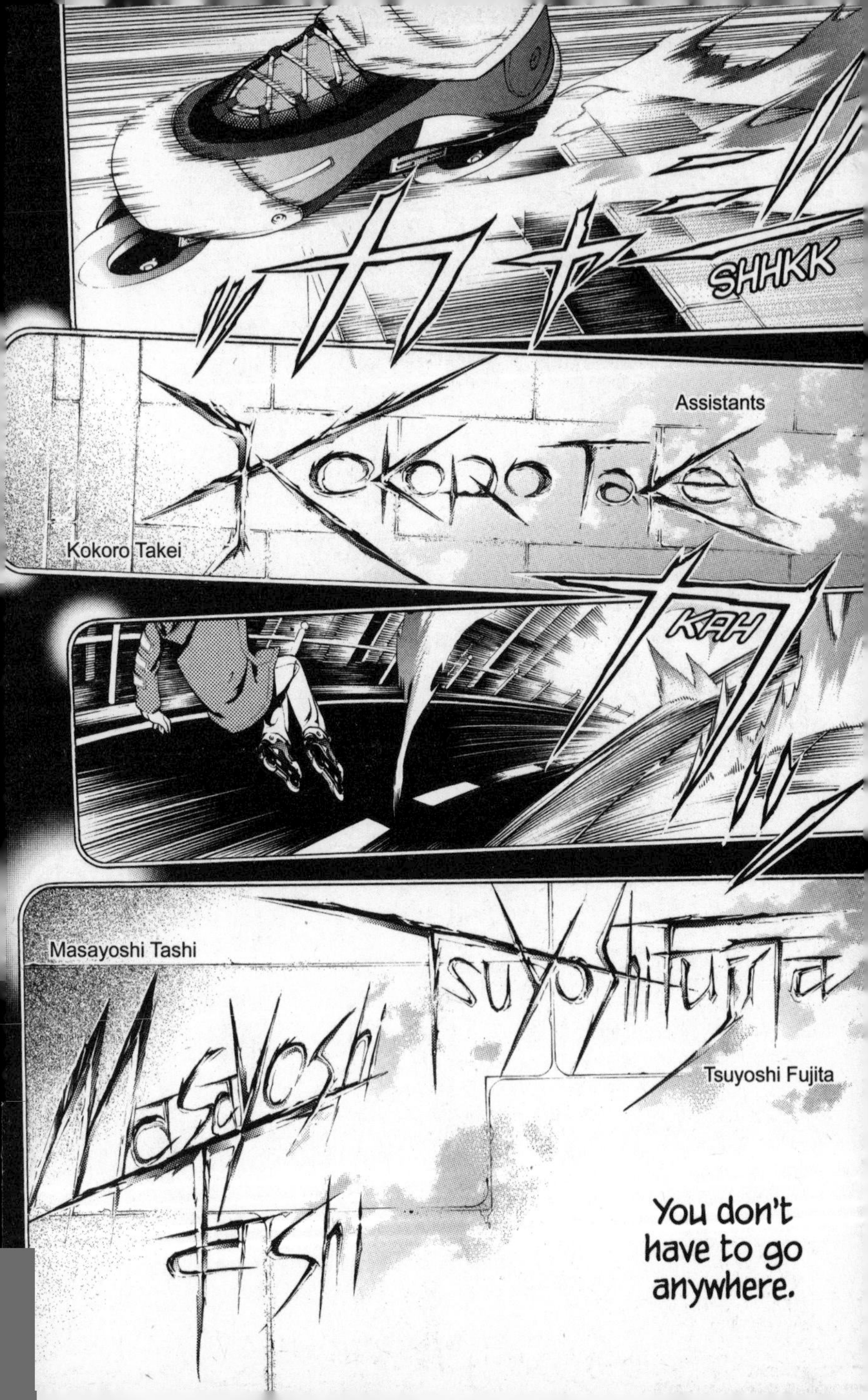
SHHKK
Assistants
Kokoro Takei
KAH
Tsuyoshi Fujita
Masayoshi Tashi
You don't have to go anywhere.

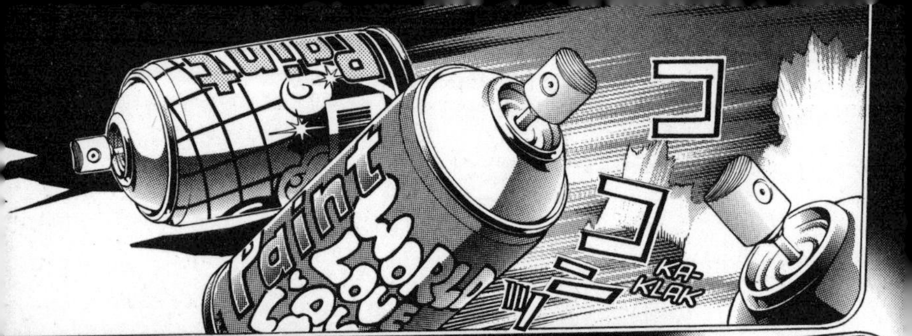
KA-KLAK

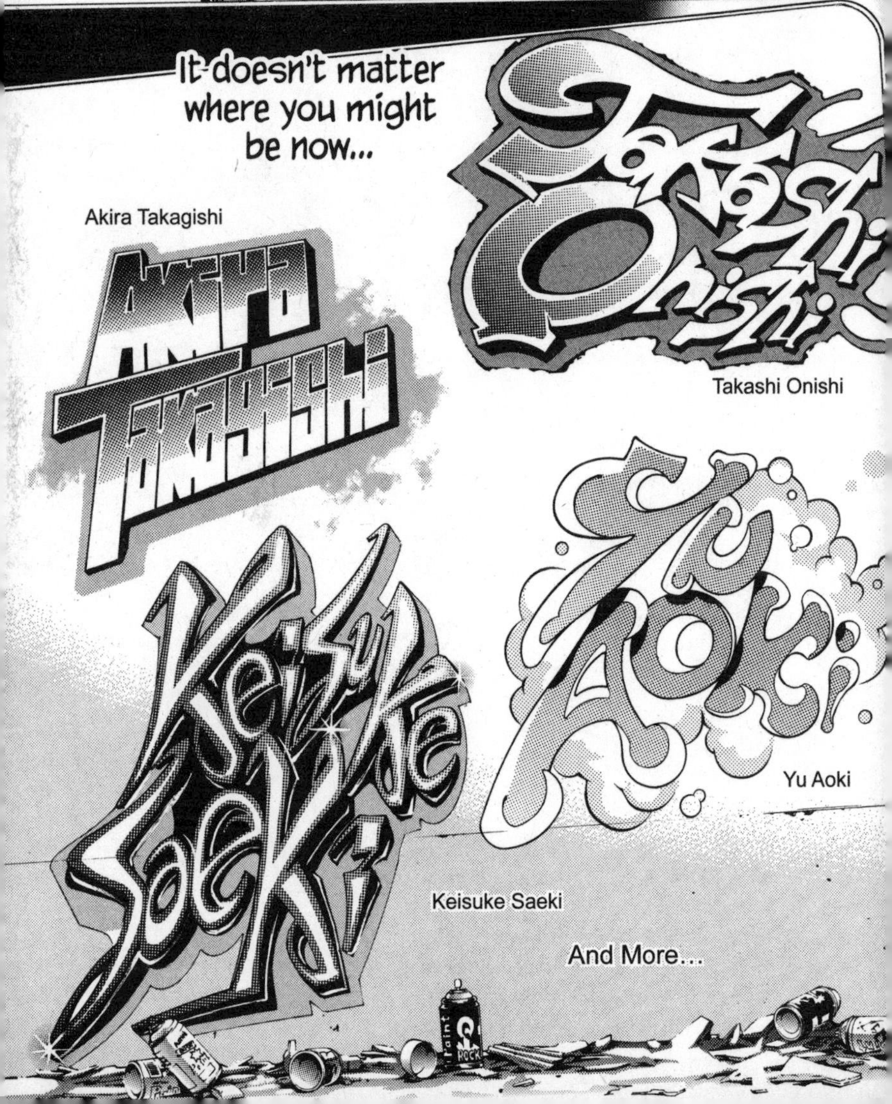
It doesn't matter where you might be now...
Takashi Onishi
Takashi Onishi
Akira Takagishi
Akira Takagishi
Yu Aoki
Yu Aoki
Keisuke Saeki
Keisuke Saeki
And More...

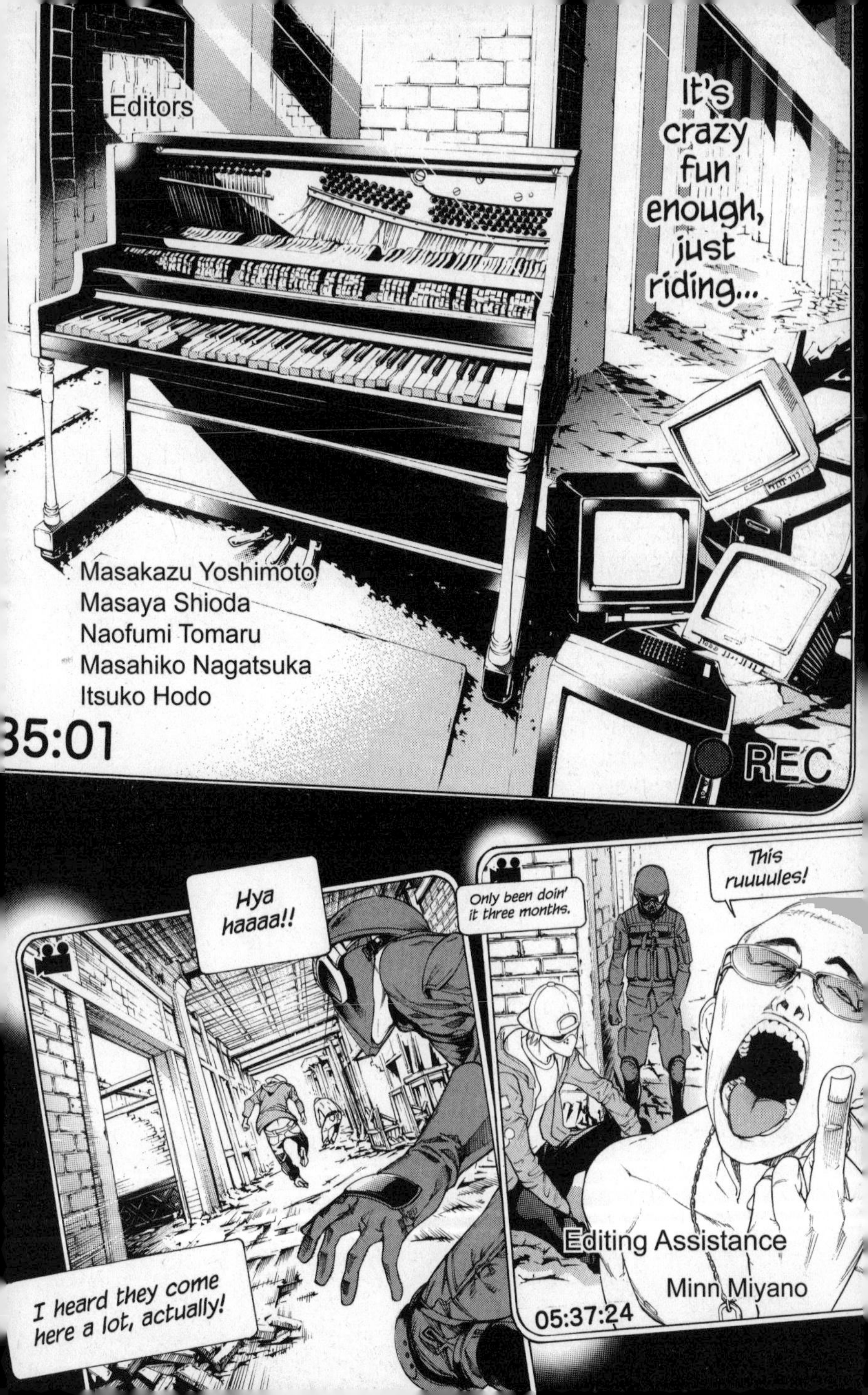
It's crazy fun enough, just riding...
Editors
Masakazu Yoshimoto
Masaya Shioda
Naofumi Tomaru
Masahiko Nagatsuka
Itsuko Hodo
35:01
REC
This ruuuules!
Only been doin' it three months.
Editing Assistance
Minn Miyano
05:37:24
Hya haaaa!!
I heard they come here a lot, actually!

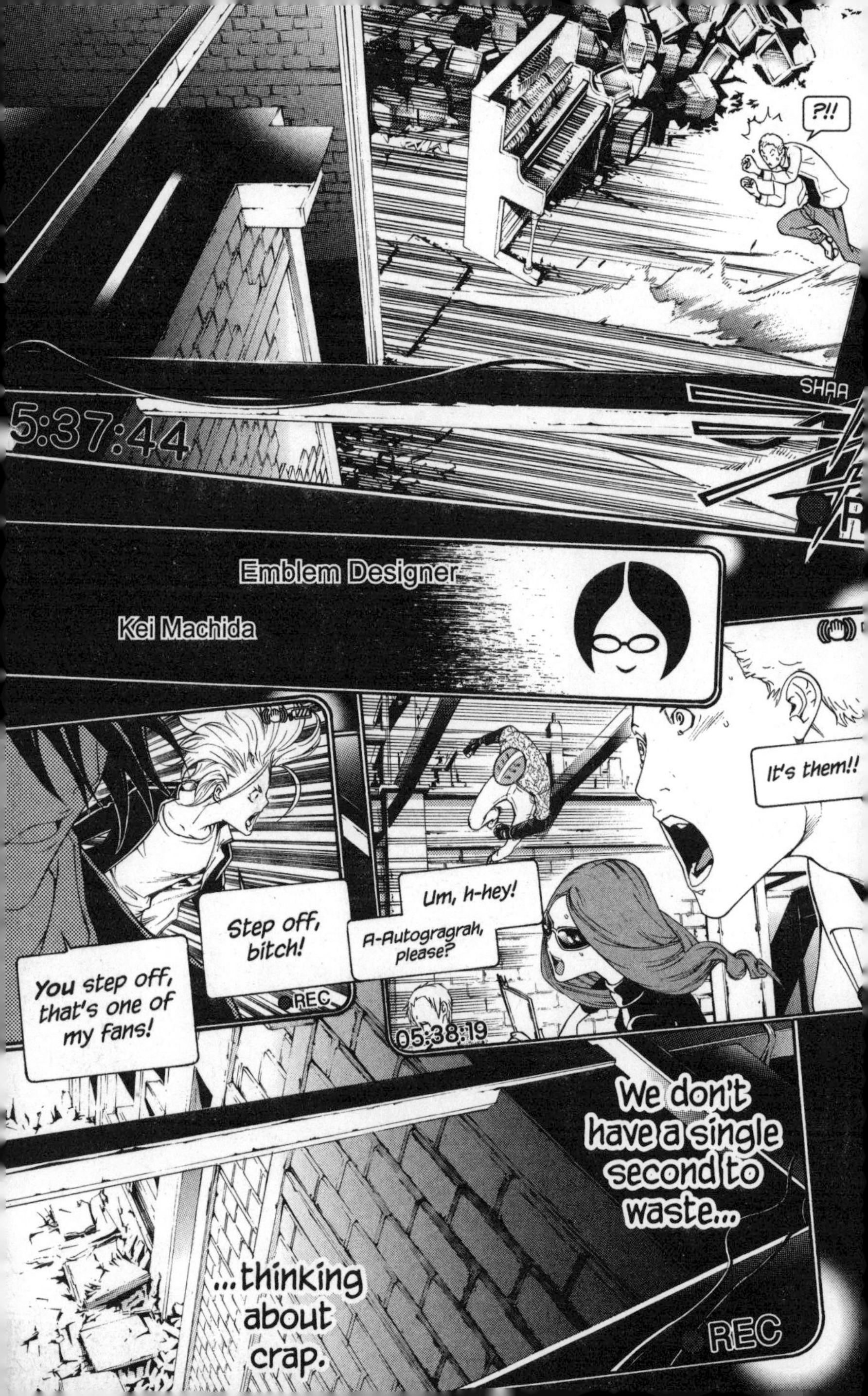
?!!
SHAA
5:37:44
Emblem Designer
Kei Machida
It's them!!
Um, h-hey!
A-Autogragrah, please?
Step off, bitch!
You step off, that's one of my fans!
REC
05:38:19
We don't have a single second to waste...
...thinking about crap.
REC

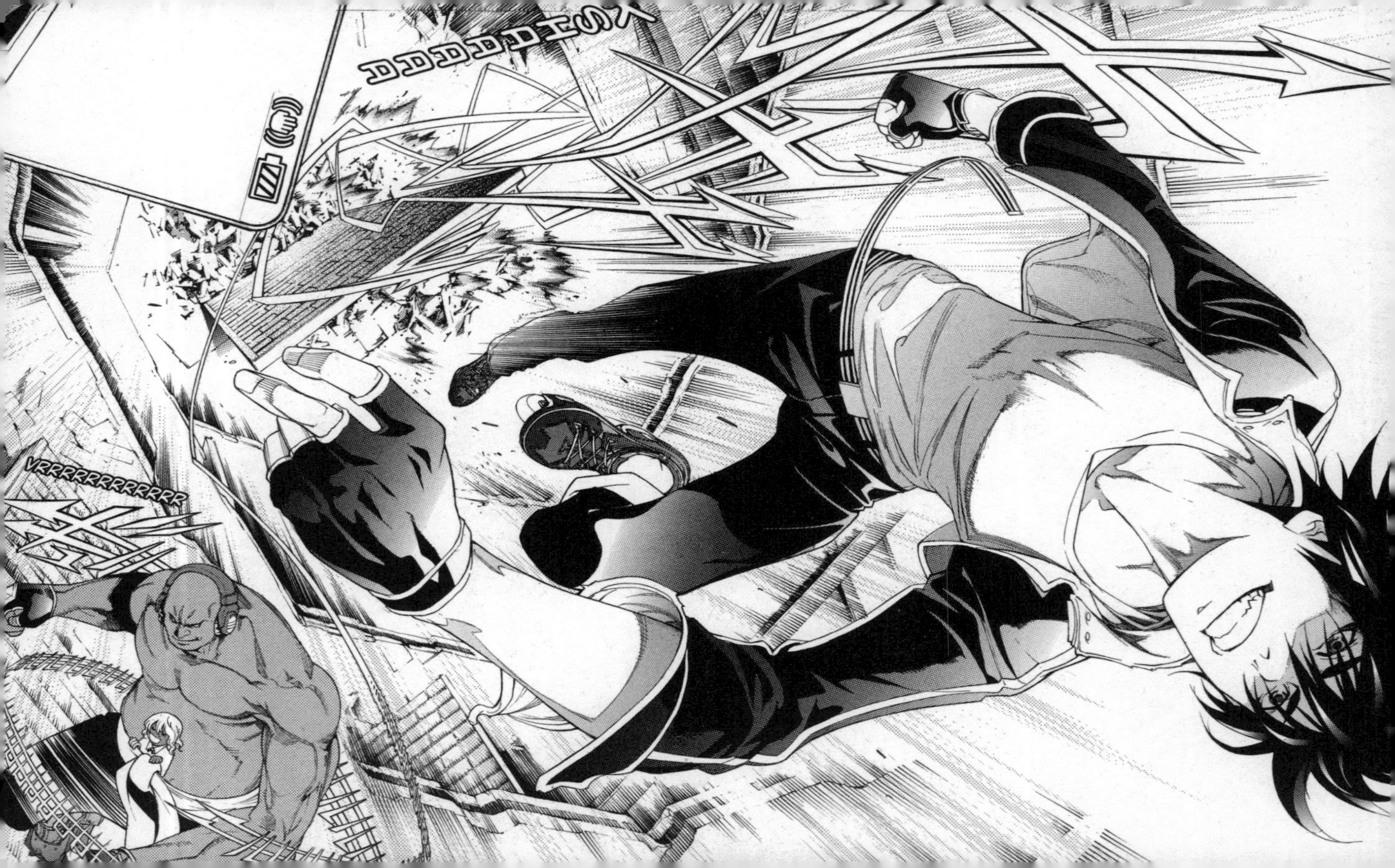
SHDDDDDD
VRRRRRRRRRRRRR

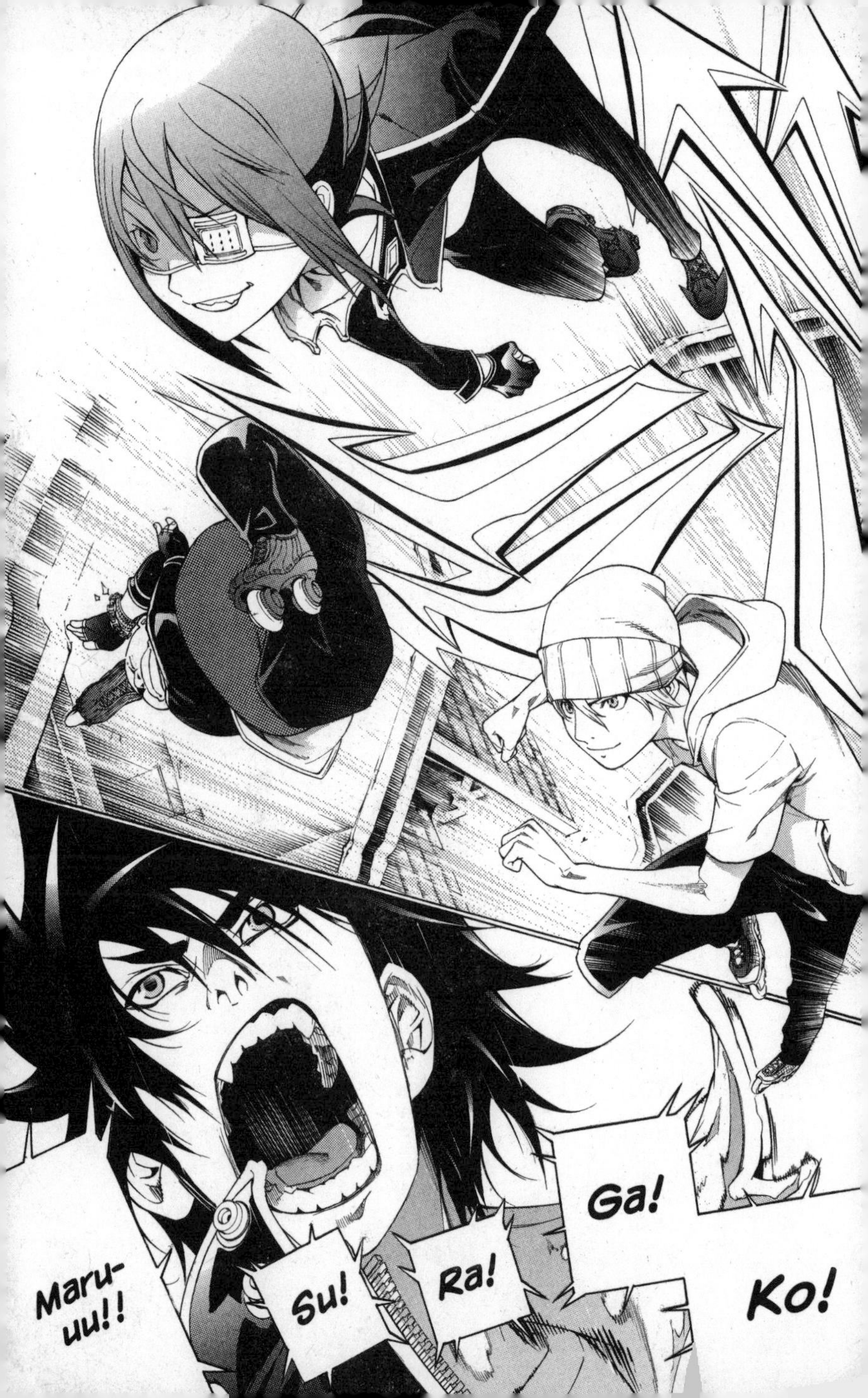
Ko!
Ga!
Ra!
Su!
Maru-uu!!

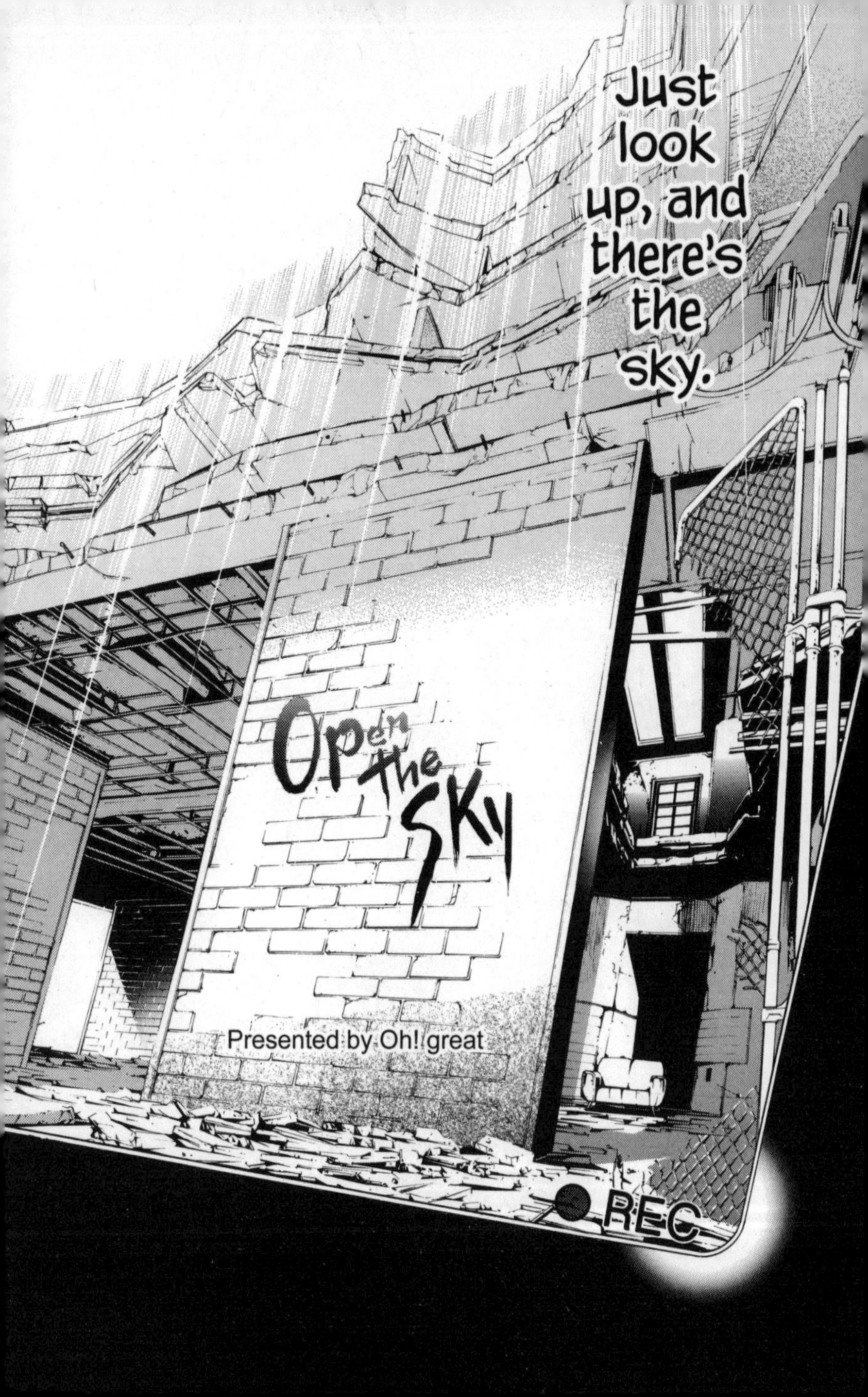
Just look up, and there's the sky.
Open the Sky
Presented by Oh! great
REC

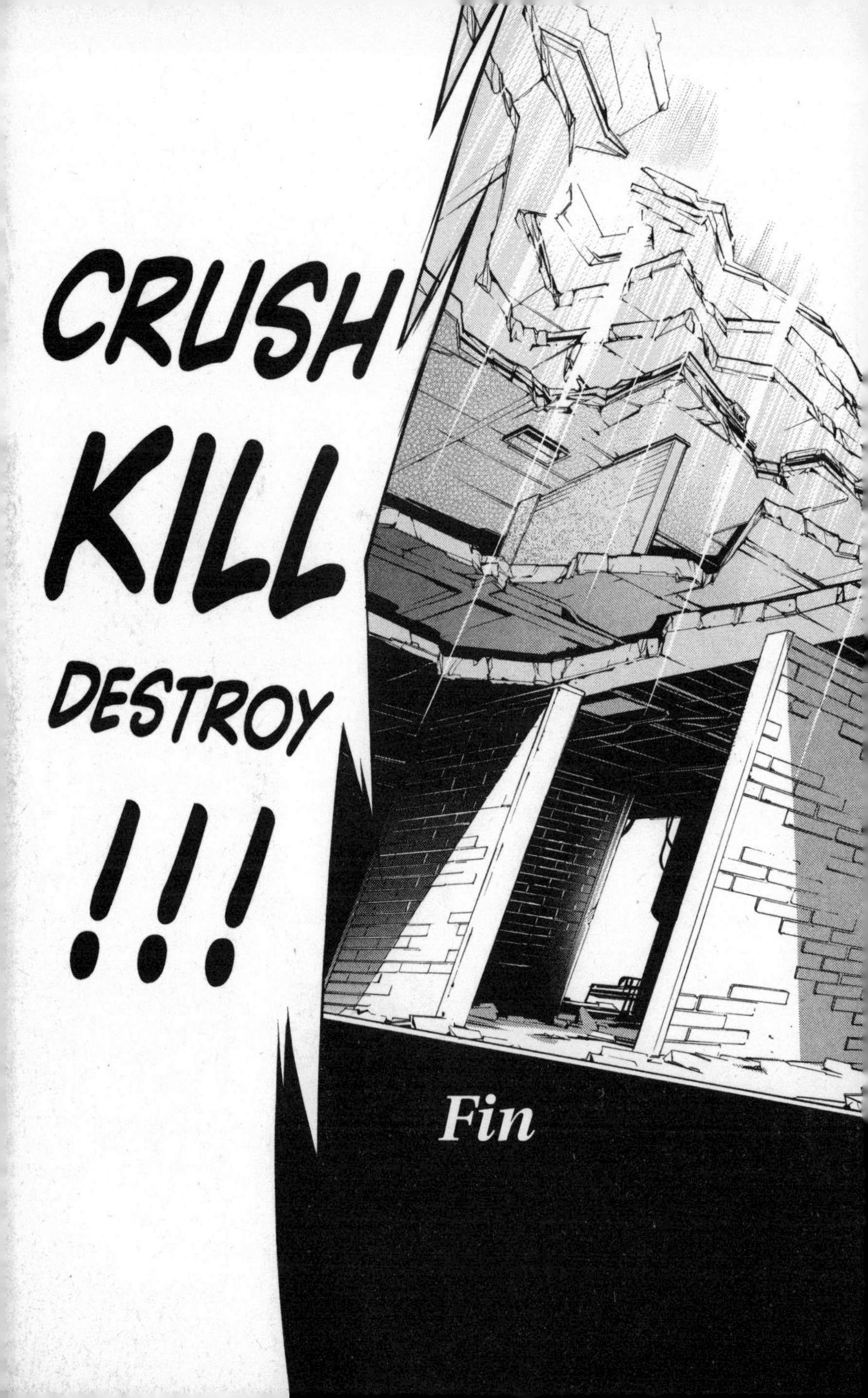
CRUSH
KILL
DESTROY
!!!
Fin

Translation Notes

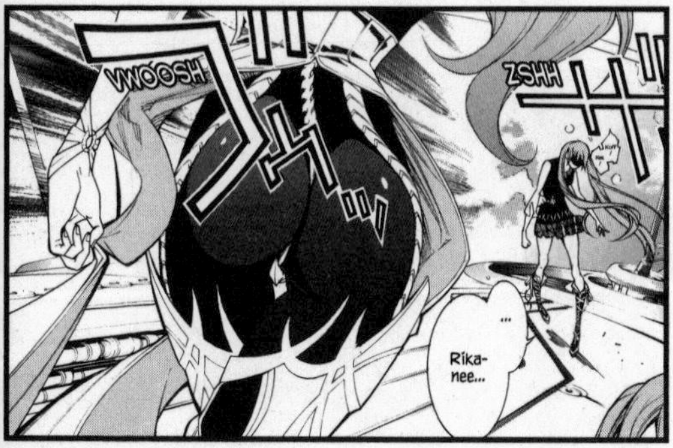
WOOSH
ZSHH
...
Rika-nee...

-Nee, page 41

When talking to Rika, Ringo uses the honorific -nee, from the Japanese word, *nee-chan*, meaning "big sister." Nee or *nee-chan* is often used with respect and affection when addressing girls or young women to whom one looks up to. In the original Japanese, Ikki uses a similar term of endearment, *an-chan*, meaning "big brother" with Sora. For Ikki's dialogue, this word has been translated into English throughout the series as "man" or "pal" to reflect the particular dynamic between them.

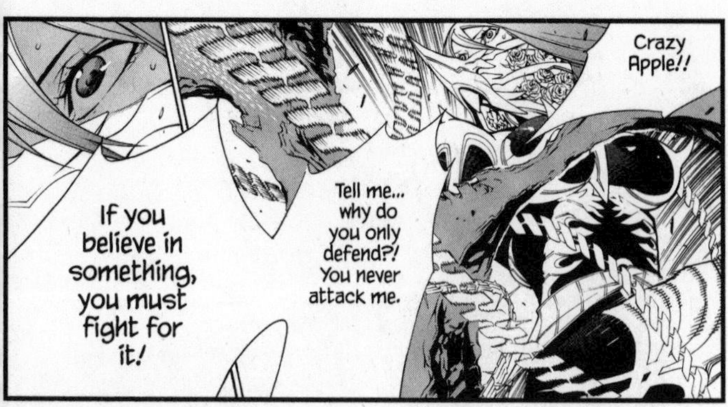
Crazy Apple!!
Tell me... why do you only defend?! You never attack me.
If you believe in something, you must fight for it!

"Crazy Apple," page 43

This is addressed to Ringo, whose name in Japanese means "apple".

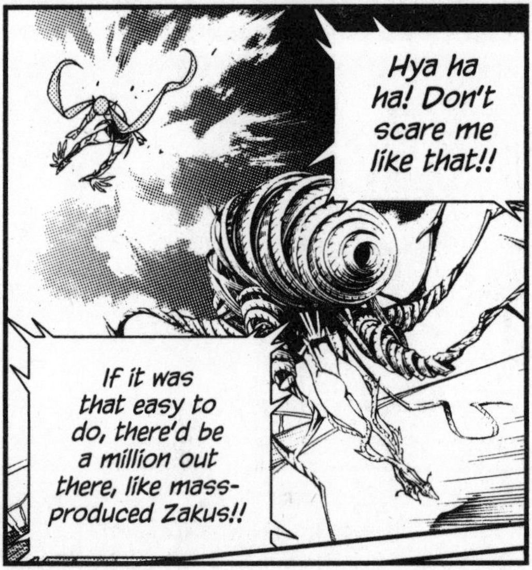
Hya ha ha! Don't scare me like that!!
If it was that easy to do, there'd be a million out there, like mass-produced Zakus!!

Zaku, page 126

One of the staple mass-produced mecha units from the Mobile Suit Gundam franchise (specifically, the Zaku II). The Zaku is the ultimate grunt unit for the Principality of Zeon, and serves the purpose of being cannon fodder for the Gundam mecha to destroy in impressive fashion. Much like the TIE Fighter from Star Wars, the Zaku is one of the iconic designs/concepts from Gundam and is almost always referenced or redesigned for each new series in the same continuity.

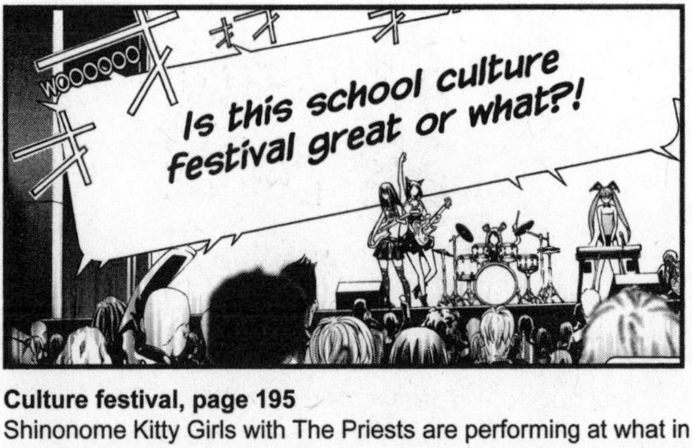
WOOOOOO
Is this school culture festival great or what?!

Culture festival, page 195

Shinonome Kitty Girls with The Priests are performing at what in Japanese is called *bunkasai*. Most Japanese schools hold this annual event featuring the artistic and creative achievements of the students. These festivals are typically open to the public and provide opportunity for prospective students to observe the general atmosphere of the school.

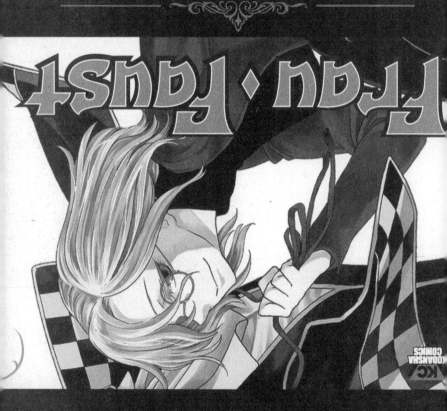

Frau · Faust

From the creator of *The Ancient Magus' Bride* comes a supernatural action manga in the vein of *Fullmetal Alchemist!*

More than a century after an eccentric scholar made an infamous deal with a devil, the story of Faust has passed into legend. However, the true Faust is not the stuffy, professorial man known in fairy tales, but a charismatic, bespectacled woman named Johanna Faust, who happens to still be alive. Searching for pieces of her long-lost demon, Johanna passes through a provincial town, where she saves a young boy named Marion from a criminal's fate. In exchange, she asks a simple favor of Marion, but Marion soon finds himself intrigued by the peculiar Doctor Faust and joins her on her journey. Thus begins the strange and wonderful adventures of *Frau Faust!*

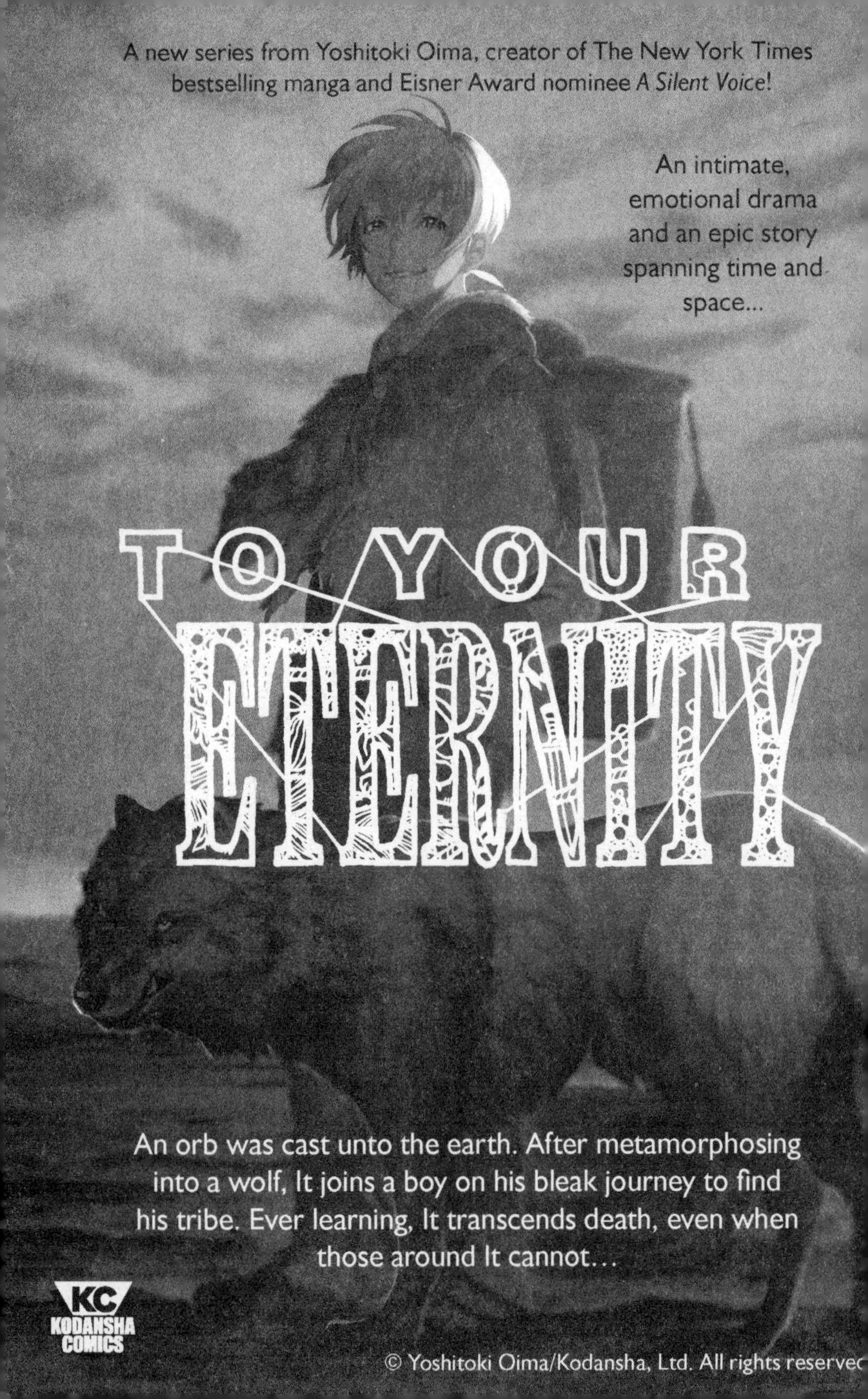
A new series from Yoshitoki Oima, creator of The New York Times bestselling manga and Eisner Award nominee A Silent Voice!
An intimate, emotional drama and an epic story spanning time and space...
TO YOUR ETERNITY
An orb was cast unto the earth. After metamorphosing into a wolf, It joins a boy on his bleak journey to find his tribe. Ever learning, It transcends death, even when those around It cannot...
KC KODANSHA COMICS
© Yoshitoki Oima/Kodansha, Ltd. All rights reserved

Cardcaptor Sakura

✿ CLEAR CARD ✿

KC KODANSHA COMICS

17 years after the original *Cardcaptor Sakura* manga ended, CLAMP returns with more magical adventures from a beloved manga classic!

Sakura Kinomoto's about to start middle school, and everything's coming up cherry blossoms. Not only has she managed to recapture the scattered Clow Cards and make them her own Sakura Cards, but her sweetheart Syaoran Li has moved from Hong Kong to Tokyo and is going to be in her class! But her joy is interrupted by a troubling dream in which the cards turn transparent, and when Sakura awakens to discover her dream has become reality, it's clear that her magical adventures are far from over...

Aho-Girl

\\'ahô͵g rl\\ *Japanese, noun.*
A clueless girl.

**Anime now
available on
Crunchyroll!**

**Fans of anarchic slice-of-life gag
manga like *Azumanga Daioh* –
these are the new laughs you've
been waiting for!**

Yoshiko Hanabatake is just your average teenage girl. She
hangs out. She goes to school. She doesn't like studying. She's
got the usual ambitions - win the lottery, play around all day,
and never have any responsibilities. And she likes bananas. She
really, really likes bananas. Okay, maybe she's not average.
Maybe she's below average. Way below average. Fortunately,
Yoshiko can rely on her old friend Akkun to keep her in line.
Assuming he doesn't strangle her first.

  **AHO-
GIRL**

CE4A

Air Gear volume 37 is a work of fiction. Names, characters, places, and incidents are the products of the author's imagination or are used fictitiously. Any resemblance to actual events, locales, or persons, living or dead, is entirely coincidental.

A Kodansha Comics Trade Paperback Original.

Published in the United States by Kodansha Comics, an imprint of Kodansha USA Publishing, LLC, New York.

Publication rights for this English edition arranged through Kodansha Ltd., Tokyo.

First published in Japan in 2012 by Kodansha Ltd., Tokyo.

ISBN 978-1-61262-107-4

Printed in the United States of America.

www.kodanshacomics.com

9 8 7 6 5 4 3 2 1

Translator: Stephen Paul
Lettering: Paige Pumphrey
Editing: Tomoko Nagano
Kodansha Comics edition cover design: Phil Balsman